The
ARTICULATED
PEASANT

GOSE
Deathly Waters and Hungry Mountains
Water and Power in Highland Peru
ANDEAN LIVES
Peasants on Plantations
JUNE NASH
WE EAT THE MINES and THE MINES EAT US
and Power
Indigenous Mestizos

The
ARTICULATED
PEASANT

Household Economies
in the Andes

ENRIQUE MAYER

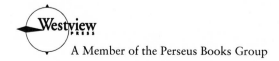

A Member of the Perseus Books Group

Westview Press books are available at special discounts for bulk purchases in the United States by corporations, institutions, and other organizations. For more information, please contact the Special Markets Department at The Perseus Books Group, 11 Cambridge Center, Cambridge MA 02142, or call (617) 252-5298.

Published in 2002 in the United States of America by Westview Press, 5500 Central Avenue, Boulder, Colorado 80301–2877, and in the United Kingdom by Westview Press, 12 Hid's Copse Road, Cumnor Hill, Oxford OX2 9JJ

Find us on the World Wide Web at www.westviewpress.com

Library of Congress Cataloging-in-Publication Data
Mayer, Enrique, 1944-
    The articulated peasant : household economies in the Andes / Enrique Mayer.
    p. cm.
    Includes bibliographical references and index.
    ISBN 0-8133-3716-X (pbk.)
    1. Indians of South America—Peru—Economic conditions. 2. Indians of South America—Land tenure—Peru. 3. Indians of South America—Agriculture—Peru. 4. Peasantry—Economic aspects—Peru. 5. Home economics—Peru—History. 6. Land use, Rural—Peru—History. 7. Encomiendas (Latin America)—History. 8. Agriculture—Economic aspects—Peru. 9. Peru—Economic conditions. I. Title.

F3429.3.E2 M38 2001
330.985'63—dc21

                                                                 2001024874

This book was set in 10-point Sabon by the Perseus Publishing Services

The paper used in this publication meets the requirements of the American National Standard for Permanence of Paper for Printed Library Materials Z39.48–1984.

10   9   8   7   6   5   4   3   2   1

For Lidia

Contents

Tables and Illustrations

Preface

The house shelters daydreaming, the house protects the dreamer, the house allows one to dream in peace.

—Gaston Bachelard, from The Poetics of Space, translated by Maria Jolas, The Orion Press, 1964

This book represents thirty years of consistent research into aspects of Andean peasant economies based on long-term fieldwork. It examines the relationship between the household and the external forces that impinge on it, focusing in both substantive and formalist ways on culturally constructed economic relationships including tribute extraction, reciprocal forms of labor exchange, and barter and cash transactions among households and between households and commodity markets. It also examines the effects of a diverse mountain environment on determining land-use and land-tenure patterns and analyzes how Andean households collectively manage their commons. The last chapter considers all of this research in the light of changing relationships brought about by neoliberalism, currently the dominant but contested model of economic organization.

The focus here is on the household as an economic unit, and the main argument is that although the household is the foundation of the system, it does not stand alone, unaided in a vacuum. Indeed, an understanding of the household economy requires attention both to relationships between households and to those that bind them into a community. The household is also affected by the kinds of links it establishes to commodity markets and to the money introduced to the Andes during the period of Spanish colonial domination—money that increased in importance as the markets expanded and became more inclusive. Hence the household members are articulated peasants, in the sense that they are interrelated ("articulated") with other households, their communities, and the commodity markets.

Small-scale peasant household–based units are ubiquitous in the Andes. This fact indicates the resilience of their technology, which is closely linked to the household's kinship organization of production. Indeed, the household has a strong and fascinating relationship to communal village–based institutions. Concomitantly, this system is associated with the relentless impoverishment of its peoples and with environmental degradation. I have approached the problem of environmental degradation through the social sciences, combining methods and insights from anthropology that stress aspects of organization and a strong dose of economics, but without neglecting an understanding of the biological dimensions that underlie agriculture and herding practices. The causes are difficult to understand, and the possible solutions under contemporary conditions are even harder to envision. The aim of this book is thus to explain how the Andean case of small-scale peasant agriculture persists as a mode of livelihood among other such systems in Third World societies.

For four thousand years the household, though not unchanged, has remained the basic institution in Andean economies. By emphasizing the inherent differences between the institutional arrangements of households and those of firms, I hope to contribute to the continuing discussion of how agricultural producers, though linked to and affected by world capitalism, in some ways remain outside of its main transformative thrust.

This book is composed of two new chapters plus eight revised ones that I had previously published in Spanish or in English. The latter have had limited circulation and never before appeared in a collection that moves smoothly from one theme to the next. Originally, each paper was written for a particular audience over a period covering almost three decades—in most cases, for my Peruvian colleagues and students who urgently and intensely debated issues on economic and social issues of peasants. Vivid ethnography and persuasive writing were my goals. I emulated those writers who, rather than explicitly enunciating their theories, subtly buried them in the text so that they became part of the story being told.

I now have rewritten the entire book. The introductory Chapter 1, on the household, and the concluding one, Chapter 10, on neo-liberalism, are written expressly for this book. They provide the explicit theoretical background for an overview of how to approach households as an economic institution. In revising the previously published chapters I put a lot of thought into each sentence in terms of whether I should let it stand or modify it. The revisions are in dialogue with my older self, and with an enormous amount of fruitful scholarship in the Andes and elsewhere, concurrent with or subsequent to their original publication. I engage in issues that the scholarly work of my colleagues has expanded on or critiqued. Postscripts in most chapters describe the context of the original publication and some afterthoughts.

I start with the Incas in Chapter 2, because a book on the Andes cannot do without them; but I focus on trade and commerce as a commentary on the important interpretation that John V. Murra (one of the founders of Andean studies and my mentor at Cornell) advanced on how reciprocity and redistribution organized what to him appeared to be a marketless society. Chapter 3 is a historical reconstruction of an important period in early colonial society—the sixteenth century—describing the operation of *encomiendas* and how the payment of tribute affected the households. It shows in a holistic way what a household is and therefore completes what is said theoretically about households in the first chapter. Chapter 4— which focuses on reciprocity, a key institution in the economy of the contemporary Andes—is taken from my dissertation.

Chapters 5, 6, and 7 deal with forms of trade and the circulation of commodities, picking up the theme I started with in the Inca chapter. The sequence is representative of people's progressive incorporation into ever-widening spheres of interaction outward from the household; it moves from "things" to "commodities," whereas the mechanisms of exchange of goods move from barter to ever-increasing degrees of market-dominated purchase and sale. Members of the household are currently articulated through trade, wage work, and migration with the larger national society and the international economy. The chapter on coca is especially interesting because, unlike another well-studied drug—namely, coffee—coca enters the world market through different channels and has other consequences, thus meriting my unorthodox treatment.

Chapters 8 and 9 deal with how Andean communities are organized and how they manage their "commons" (a term I was not familiar with when I first wrote those articles). The unorthodox logic of placing these chapters at the end is justified by the fact that the community is ultimately the home base of Andean peasant social and economic organization. But the conflicts, contradictions, and process of change in the home base can be better understood if, in the light of real and relative individual household autonomy and its wide network of connections within and across communities and in the labor and commodity markets of the nation, they are treated as antecedents to an understanding of social life inside the contemporary *comunidad campesina* ("peasant community"). Seen this way, the strength of communal organization is better comprehended, because neither the supposed disruptions of market-driven interests and emigration nor the inequalities among members of the community seem to weaken it at all—despite the numerous difficulties associated with such organization. The concluding chapter looks to the future. It describes the impact of structural readjustment programs of the 1980s and 1990s while also taking a harsh look at neo-liberal policies and their devastating effects on family income. It takes issue with the new obsession with the term *poor*, discusses property, and ends with a somewhat resigned environmentalist recipe for containment of the damage that the free-market dogma is inflicting on the lives of families in rural villages and shantytowns as the new century gets under way.

My fieldwork was initially conducted in 1969 in Tangor, a community in the Central Andes that was situated within the sphere of influence of the Inca administrative center of Huánuco Pampa and today is on the bound-

ary line between the Department of Pasco and Huánuco. After my doctor-
ate, in 1974, I studied the ecological, organizational, and economic determinants of Andean traditional agriculture in the Cañete Valley in the Department of Lima, with Laraos as the base community—a joint project
undertaken with César Fonseca. A report on land use in the Mantaro Valley, my home territory, was completed for the International Potato Center
in Lima, in 1976. In 1984–1986 I participated along with Stephen Brush,
César Fonseca, and Karl Zimmerer in a study of genetic erosion in the Tulumayo and Paucartambo valleys of the eastern slopes of the Andes in the
Central and Southern Andes, respectively. Descriptions of the local geography and history of these places can be found in individual chapters where
the context requires it. For easy reference, these and other places mentioned throughout are shown on a map at the front of the book.

Enrique Mayer
New Haven, Connecticut

Acknowledgments

Since this is a book that takes reciprocity, counting, and accounting seriously, my debts have to be acknowledged. Andean people sometimes stress this process of counting and acknowledging debts, as in the *morocho* ceremony I observed in Tangor in 1970. There, persons who have passed their year in community service are publicly counted, each man and his wife represented by two little stones placed on a poncho for each *cargo* performed. If I were to do this, I would run out of stones. And I would lose count if I were to acknowledge the scores of professors, friends, colleagues, and students who have actively participated in shaping the thinking that has found its way into a retrospective book such as this. All I can say is that I have lived in interesting times and was entangled as an anthropologist in several dimensions. The support, human touch, and personal relationships that came with the exercise of my profession in two countries and two cultures have made me what I am, and my debts keep growing all the time! When I think back to the people in the institutions I passed through, I am inundated by waves of grateful affection. I recall a long procession of faces: those in the Instituto de Estudios Peruanos, the Catholic and San Marcos universities in Lima, ONERN (the natural resources office), The Instituto Indigenista Interamericano in Mexico, the University of Texas at Austin, the University of Illinois at Urbana-Champaign, and Yale University—along with so many others I have met in so many parts of the world.

Nonetheless, a few little stones must be placed here to gratefully acknowledge the help I received on the present manuscript. Financial support for completing this book was provided by Yale's Institution for Social and Policy Studies. Karl Yambert, Paul Gootenberg, Susan Ramirez, Benjamin Orlove, Richard and Lucy Burger, Rolena Adorno and Vladimir Gil read drafts and provided comments, encouragement, and advice. Students in my Andean ethnology class at Yale reacted to early drafts. Juan Fernando Núñez and Tae Kwak helped with the bibliography and the figures. The maps and sketches are by Vladimir and Sally Gil. I am most grateful to Barbara Greer and Christine Arden for their accomplished editing work at Westview Press. And, finally, Lidia Santos persuaded me to chuck the sentimental gushing that came as an unwanted byproduct of revision. Thank you, Lidia, for being the most delightful companion when, in this business of writing, I became ornery and withdrawn.

E.M.

Map 0.1 *Location of selected places mentioned in the text*

1

The Household in Perspective

This chapter focuses on the household as an economic unit and makes the argument that although the household is the foundation of the economic system, it does not stand alone and unaided. The theoretical review herein relates the home, family, gender, and age with the circulation of goods and services in order to clarify the inner workings of the home and the ways in which it links up with wider spheres. Toward this end, four theoretical models are presented along with descriptions taken from ethnographic works on the Andes.

House, Field, and Money

It is difficult to penetrate the privacy of people's homes, to understand the economic processes that occur within it, or even to apprehend the magical transformations that take place among family members in the intimacy that surrounds their hearth, much less the events that bring them either fortune or penury. In economic anthropology, the concept of "household" turns out to be an elusive one. Although this concept appeals to common sense, the working definition—which specifies the functions of a household as the basic unit that organizes production, distribution, and consumption and ensures its own reproduction—is not a good place to start. Instead, I single out three elements—house, field, and money—to provide a picture of its dynamics. The house is the place for shelter, storage, individual growth, identity, and autonomy. The field, also part of the household, is the place where seed turns into crop. And money comprises the tokens that members of the household incessantly struggle to obtain and love to spend on consumer goods as well as drink, music, and fancy costumes. Field and house integrate nicely, but money is the disturbing element.

There is a sense of dealing with the concrete and tangible when one starts looking at houses, their layouts, and the activity patterns that take place within them. This fact was vividly brought home to me in Tangor in 1979 when I participated in a private ceremony connected with the process of providing a new construction with a thatched roof. Members of the family whose house was being built had gathered after supper in the new house and made themselves comfortable among the piles of straw. They spent most of the night chewing coca, conversing, and drinking. The atmosphere was solemn; participants were there to divine whether the new residents of this house would be happy and successful. Late in the night, the wife's brother-in-law appeared for the *terrado yupay* (the counting of the rafters). He was to crawl and jump from one ceiling joist to another, counting them as he touched them with his feet and hands. The more rafters, the bigger the house—and the greater the ostentation.

Later, the brother-in-law took some straw, braided it into a thin rope that he wound around the necks of the owners of the house, and, candle in hand, guided them around as if they were unseeing. He pointed to the places where they should sleep, where ears of corn should be hung, and where the woman should suspend her balls of spun wool. He took them to the attic to show them where they should store their potatoes. He populated the house with future guinea pigs, and he placed imaginary tools in their correct places. To inaugurate the dwelling, he took the candle to the attic to blacken the rafters with candle smoke. (When a house is actually inhabited, its rafters become black from the rising smoke of the kitchen fire.) Aptly, this little ceremony is called *wasi pichuy,* a phrase that, in Quechua, means "the where-at ceremony," for it converts inanimate adobes, wood, and straw into a living thing—a house that creaks, groans, and may even become haunted.

I also found out that it was easier to peer into the private lives of people when I visited them in their fields—partly because we were free from prying ears out there, but also because, in their own fields, farmers were involved in a project they were eager to share. A field in the Andes is a *chacra*, a powerful object and symbol that conveys states of being and feeling. Julio Valladolid (1998: 51), a Peruvian agronomist, says that words are a difficult medium in which to convey the nurturing feeling that a *chacra* evokes. How can words express, he asks, "the profound feeling of affection and respect that the peasant feels for the Mother Earth, or the joy and gratitude towards the mountain protectors the peasant experiences on the birth of an alpaca that is treated like a new daughter?" He goes on to say: "The nurturing of the *chacra* is the heart of Andean culture which, if not the only activity carried out by the peasants, is the one around which all aspects of life revolve." Julio Valladolid belongs to a group of professionals who, as members of an organization called Proyecto Andino de Tecnologías Campesinas (PRATEC), strongly argue for the regeneration of Andean life through a "back to the earth" movement, on the one hand, and a rejection of Western values, particularly development programs, on the other. To make *chacra*, PRATEC members affirm, is to cultivate Andean cultural values.

As for the third element, money, I refer to my conversations with my *compadre* Don Victor in Tangor in 1970. Money certainly has mysterious sources and more uses than just exchange. The two of us reminisced about how people go treasure hunting on the 24th of June because buried treasure on that night emits a strong bluish flame revealing its whereabouts— a flame, known as *antimonio*, wielding so strong a force that it can knock over a man who gets too near it. Don Victor supposed that *gringos* like me were immune. We commented on the elaborate costumes required for the dance of the "Ancestor Old Man" and his "Inca princess," whose handbag shimmers with polished antique silver coins sewn on the outside. *Qolque* is the Quechua term for both "silver" and "money," as is the Spanish word *plata*. Don Victor's musings found their way into my dissertation (Mayer 1974a: 310):

> My grandmother told me when I was small. She said that the time will come when everyone will be rich, even the most insignificant man will know money in thousands, in millions. Now even a nobody handles a thousand, two thousand *soles*. But all that money is no good, things have become expensive. For example, in those times five *soles* for a sack of maize, potatoes were two fifty, really cheap, really cheap. Now it is more, one hundred up to two hundred. When I was small, I earned five *centavos*, later, they paid me ten cents, and when I was bigger I went to the sugar cane *hacienda* and they paid me thirty cents. My grandmother said that when everybody would have lots of money, then the end of the world will come, and when the world ends then we shall all die, there will be nobody.

Anyone traveling in the Andes today cannot fail to notice the importance of markets, fairs, peddlers, traders, and shops in the livelihoods of Andean peoples. Most migrants have experience as street vendors in the informal sector in cities. There is even a popular god that ensures luck in trading. Known as the *ekeko*, it is a small plaster figurine depicting a rounded jolly man loaded down with merchandise. People keep the *ekeko* in a niche in their house where they also place miniatures of the consumer goods they most ardently desire: perfect small models of houses, trucks, tools for carpentry or mechanical trades, and canned or bottled supermarket goods; tiny university degrees suggesting the status of doctor, lawyer, or architect; minute passports, airline tickets, and credit cards. These items are available at special fairs called *alasitas* (the word is derived from the Aymara language and means "buy from me"), which have become very popular in Bolivia and Southern Peru. During *alasitas*, people engage in a playful game of acquiring tokens of their most coveted wishes. Stalls are set up where the miniatures are exhibited and sold. Young and old alike move from stall to stall, choosing among the perfect reproductions of diminutive cans of Carnation milk, boxes of soda crackers, bottles of rum, and bags of flour and sugar—all those things that fulfill their ardent desires (*wanlla* in Quechua). The *ekeko* has an open mouth so he can smoke cigarettes given to him by the family members. It is believed that if he is properly propitiated, during the year, the simulacra on his altar will bring in the real things. To be effective, however, one's *ekeko* figurine has to have been stolen or given as a gift. A bought one is useless, and the good fortune it is capable of bringing is likely to abandon a person as easily as it came (Arnillas 1996: 133).

Most conspicuous during *alasitas* is the presence of play money. Perfect imitations of bills in various denominations of national currency are tied to the *ekeko*'s belt. People use the play money to simulate buying and selling urban and rural properties, obtaining miniature land titles, and paying fees to lawyers and notaries. The only item not miniaturized is the one hundred dollar bill—an enlarged version of the American bill, but with the image of the Bolivian Virgin of Urcupiña printed in the middle. Even more gross is the fetishized, poster-sized "one thousand dollar" bill, which features the *ekeko* image in the center, loaded down with flour, sugar, car, chalet, television, guitar, and Sony-brand sound equipment.

The Household in the Andes

In a publication on kinship and marriage in the Andes (Mayer 1977b: 64), I stated:

> In Tangor, the basic units of production, distribution, and consumption are households. Each household produces enough food from agriculture to feed itself but not much more. Most agricultural labor inputs come directly from the household. Surplus labor available to the household is dedicated to cash pursuits which, except for a few cattle breeding families, implies migration out of the village. Insofar as it is possible, each family divides itself into two sections, one staying in the village to take care of the agricultural front, the other migrating to obtain cash.

While still basically true, this statement needs to be updated in the light of recent research on households in general and in the Andes specifically. In a volume on the household economy (see Wilk 1980), Peggy Barlett (1987: 4) discusses households in terms of four basic categories: (1) personnel and household composition, (2) production activities and the division of labor, (3) consumption activities and inter- and intra-household exchange, and (4) patterns of power and authority. In addition to providing an overview of these categories, I intertwine my description of Andean households with a discussion of four models of the household as an economic unit.

The first model posits the household as a "black box" within a larger system. Decisions that are made inside the box have observable effects in terms of what flows in and out of the house. The black box approach asks us to focus on the inflows and outflows and to be less concerned with what happens inside, but it also stresses the overall internal unity of the household and lays great emphasis on its boundaries. The second model focuses on personnel and patterns of authority within the household, reducing economics to kinship in order to explain decisions and outcomes in terms of kinship norms and gender relations. I call this the "kinship model." The third model focuses on the production process, rather than on people, in order to pinpoint the ecological and economic processes that take place within the household. Following Stephen Gudeman and Alberto Rivera (1990), this model will be called the "house model," although the house I am thinking of is the smallholder/householder family farm (Netting 1993). The fourth model is called the "rational choice model," for it bypasses the household as a unit in order to focus directly on the individuals within it—individuals who make cost-benefit choices, within the context of the household's means and needs, between rewards and punishments and between investments and payoffs. The household in this model is a miniature marketplace where rational actors trade in everything—food, affection, authority, leisure, pleasure—and compete with each other.

Models in economics, says Gudeman in *Economics As Culture* (1986: 38), are "... a way of searching, coping, adjusting and making sense of things. ... [T]hey represent an exercise in human control and a form of public communication." Because models draw attention to certain features while ignoring other possibilities, they are partial constructions that nevertheless represent a totality. Models often employ primal or axiomatic metaphors that warrant validation because they are based on personal experience. Each of the four models mentioned above highlights some important features about the household while suppressing others. Therefore, these models must be judged in terms of what they contribute to our understanding; but we also need to realize that this understanding often depends on the angle of approach.

The Black Box

No scholar really wants to subscribe to a "black box" model, as this approach has been widely criticized.[1] Yet, there are defensible appeals to such a label, the least of which is the lure to peer into the black box in an attempt to unravel its mysteries. The aim of such a model is to stress that what goes on inside the box is different from what goes on outside the box, and what goes into or comes out of the box is transformed into something else in the process. For example, noodles and sugar may be bought in the market as commodities, but once they enter the household they become food. Labor within the household is domestic but becomes something else once it crosses the boundary. Another benefit of the black box approach is that it conveys a sense that the inside constitutes a unit that is more than the sum of its parts. As a unit, it must have boundaries, and where there are boundaries, there are gateways, mechanisms that control inflow and outflow, customs agents and smugglers. Thus the black box model helps us to emphasize efforts at boundary maintenance, along with such interesting features as privacy, autonomy, identity, and the uniqueness that is magically generated within the sanctity of a home.

A moment's thought about how words such as *family, women's work, privacy of the home,* and *private property* have become politicized reveals that even so neutral a term as *black box*, if it is to be useful at all, underscores the fact that the features that create this concept are cultural constructs and sustained by ideologies. In the social sciences, black boxes are associated with systems theory. They are derived from the way electrical circuits are drawn on paper to represent the interrelatedness of parts to a larger grid; indeed, this is a useful image to keep in mind, because grids represent electrical flows that are dynamic. Unlike circuits, however, social science systems are capable of transforming themselves. Finally, by substituting the term *black box* for others commonly used in the literature such as *home, family*, and even *household* itself, we can use the black box construct to avoid the tendency to "naturalize" the household, as if it were universal, irreducible, and constant throughout human societies and incapable of changing historical content (Harris 1981)—which it decidedly is not.

The word *householding*, coined by of Karl Polanyi (1997: 41), can be associated with an interesting formulation of one version of a black box theory associated with the household: "In ancient Greek as well as in Germanic, *householding* is the term used to denote catering for one's own group. *Oikonomia* in Greek is the etymon of the word economy; *Haushaltung* in German corresponds strictly to this. The principle of 'provisioning one's self' remains the same whether the 'self' thus catered for is a family, a city or a manor." In householding the flow of material goods and services is circular and circumscribed, the boundaries are important to contain the flow within it, and the mode of integration (provisioning, pooling, and sharing) is different within the household from other forms that Polanyi identified—namely, reciprocity, redistribution, and market exchange.[2] In Marxism, *natural economy* has similar connotations. Barbara Bradby (1975: 127) cites Rosa Luxemburg's definition of the term as based on the "production for personal needs," and William Roseberry (1989: 205) states that "economic organization is essentially in response to internal demand." This latter definition, however, goes beyond the household to include the economy that contains it."[3]

Insofar as my main research interest in Tangor focused on inter-household exchanges, as described in Chapters 2, 5, 6, and 7, my treatment of households in this book focuses on what goes on outside or across the boundaries of the household, and I thus find some of the features of the black box approach useful because it helps me stress differences between inter- and intra-household activities. A comparison between sixteenth-century Tangor households and those of Tangor in 1969 shows that household composition did not differ substantially between such separate times.[4] The predominant household composition in Tangor during my census (Mayer 1972, 1974a) was the nuclear family (61 percent). Nonnuclear families were of two kinds: Incomplete households were due either to the death or separation of one of the spouses (6 percent) or to the temporary absence of a migrating member (14 percent). All incomplete households were managed by women, a fact that is related to the division of labor whereby men are in charge of productive tasks while women administer the resources. In Tangor terms, a man cannot live alone because he has no one to cook for him, whereas a lone woman can obtain male help for productive tasks. Extended families (18 percent) included portions of either spouse's parental family or incomplete children's families (i.e., with a spouse missing).

In terms of the development cycle of households (Goody 1966), the tendency to establish nuclear families when children marry implied that the household's corporate agricultural enterprise did not persist over time. Rather, households were established at marriage with resources contributed by both spouses and grew as the family developed and children began to contribute, until they, in turn, married. Then the resources of the group began to be split up among the newly constituted families. For this reason it is better to consider transmission of landholdings through partition rather than inheritance. By the time the parents died, fields had usually been turned over to the children, and those not actually turned over were designated among them. The child who stayed with aged parents inherited the house and movable possessions. Billie Jean Isbell (1978) and Jane Collins (1986: 658) report parallel transmission of lands, men from men and women from women, which, though pooled during the household's existence, were maintained as separate legacies.

Households were "independent" in the sense that each household held independent rights to decide how to allocate labor and land resources and each acted as a unit of account in inter-household exchanges. A man could discharge a day's labor debt by sending his son; contributions to other families were acknowledged as household contributions by providing a feast not only to the member who contributed but also to the adult members of the contributing household. The community assessed labor obligations by the household and not by the individual.

Mary Weismantel (1989: 56), however, cautions us not to assume that Andean households possessed any degree of permanence. Her study in

Zumbagua, Ecuador, stresses their ephemeral nature in two important ways. First, the household is not so much a static social unit as "a set of ongoing economic activities." Second, and even more important, the process of division of households into new ones "is a constant and intrinsic aspect of household formation itself." Here the emphasis is on the fuzziness of the boundaries between households, on the one hand, and the social and cultural *work* that is required to affirm its existence, on the other. The independent household needs to be constructed and asserted in every moment, at every step, and with every activity, against the tendencies and forces that want to slow or impede its formation or speed up its dissolution. As one household is growing out of the hearth of two others, the boundaries between them form only gradually, the transitions between the old and the new take place extremely slowly, and the very processes of separation stress the act of becoming rather than being.

Weismantel realized how entangled the process of division is when she recognized the need to separate sleeping from eating. Once married, couples can begin to sleep together, often under a separate roof, but for a very long time they continue eating all their meals in their parents' kitchen. In the same gradual way, consumption and productive activities are slowly diverted from the household of origin to the new one with the step-by-step establishment of a fully functioning separate hearth. Children "are born and nurtured in the kitchen of the mother-in-law [and] are subject to the senior woman's authority at all times, just as she [the mother] is (Weismantel 1989: 62)." The cluster of interdependent households, with complex relations between them holding back forces that pull them apart, implies that household boundaries are ultimately unimportant.

In Zumbagua it is the individual who owns the assets, not the household; most of the provisioning is not done independently by each household, nor is this unit the single consumption unit. Thus it seems that our black box would vanish under close scrutiny; or, as Weismantel puts it (1989: 62), "Analysis of the separate processes making up the domestic sphere has led us first to dismantle the household completely, but now to reinstate it as one of the most significant of a series of concentric social and economic groupings." That it does not vanish, Weismantel argues, can be explained by the centrality of women's control of cooking the food and those who share it—an attribute considered to be essential to a constituted household.

The Kinship Model

Like cells that continuously grow, subdivide, and then die but form enduring tissue, the process of household formation and division is an aspect of constitutive kinship systems in the Andes. A kinship model of household analysis subordinates economic transactions to an analysis of kinship structures, behaviors, and norms. This change of focus permits an understanding of the strictures on the behavior of individuals within groups. But, first, an important caveat introduced by Silvia Yanagisako (1979), who warned researchers not to assume that family group and household automatically overlap. Indeed, the household may also contain other co-resident persons, as well as animals (dogs, cats, mice, and lice), and family members may for various reasons be residing in other houses and places.

Kinship systems, as cultures, create roles, define behaviors, and enforce them through the logic of the kinship norms. Kinship systems also arbitrarily assign power to some individuals and subordinate status to others by age, birth order, degree of relatedness, and gender. A household in this view becomes a *family* as well as a constitutive element of a larger kinship system in which economic behavior is embedded and subordinated to the norms of family life. And in the Andes, the defining characteristic of the family is the married couple.

Partially following James C. Scott (1976), David Cheal (1989: 14) delineates one possible analysis of economic behavior among members of the household. Specifically, he follows Scott in his choice of the term *moral economy*, which was brought into social science discourse by the British historian E. P. Thompson. Cheal does not necessarily subscribe to this model, but he states that one could analyze relationships within a household "as if" the actors themselves take such a model for granted. An excellent example is Edward Banfield's (1958) study of a village in Italy in which he described Hobbesean competitive, uncooperative, selfish behavior outside the household as serving the purpose of saving and protecting those inside it, where behavior is decidedly different—a phenomenon he termed "a-moral familism." According to Cheal, the norms of a moral economy inside the household imply that members of the household are motivated to produce socially preferred (i.e., moral) relationships between incumbents whose roles are defined by the kinship system and the division of labor. Conflict (which may arise out of self-interest) is avoided or minimized. The framework of established relationships is maintained by the individual, for whom such roles and role attributes define the structure, the direction, and the quantities of the resource flow. This moral economy hangs together because, as Cheal (1989: 14) explains,

> [i]n order to ensure participation of others in such transactions, household heads engage in verbal and non-verbal discourses that construct the meaning of the household as the natural center of economic life. Within the relational culture of the household economy, the pattern of resource flows is accepted as taken-for-granted reality.

Social relationships are "naturalized" within the household, and behavior is judged as moral when it conforms and as immoral when it deviates.

The household must therefore be examined within the culturally constructed kinship system of which it is a part. A kinship-based household model would strongly question the basic tenet of formal economics: that the individual is free to act on his or her own or in a depersonalized manner. He or she can, however, strategize and manipulate affective and normative role patterns ascribed to her- or himself and others only within certain limited bounds and "negotiate" for improvements. Such negotiating is not bargaining but, rather, a political negotiation that, using differential power attributes, may succeed in adjusting the attributes of role ascription and its contents in terms of material advantage.

For example, one way for a young woman to get relief from work, more attention, and special food would be to malinger, thus temporarily adding the culturally constructed prerogatives of "sick" to one's role as daughter. The acceptance or rejection of the claim to being sick and the seriousness of such a claim are subject to "negotiation." A young woman in the Andes may have little room to negotiate with her mother-in-law the precise contents and attributes of her role, but she certainly cannot bargain with her as a free agent would.[5] The point is that these struggles take place within a framework of culturally prescribed normative roles, which a person should conform to and sometimes may even radically challenge, but at the risk of being labeled deviant.

The features of the kinship system in the Andes privilege the autonomy of the household in several ways. In the Central Andes, kinship is mostly bilateral (Lambert 1977),[6] such that a person traces descent from both parents and transmits membership to male and female children. Such a system creates overlapping memberships and for this reason, unless some other criterion such as residence is added, members of a bilateral descent group (a kindred) cannot form corporate groups that persist over time. Therefore, bilateral relationships can be activated only sporadically, focusing on one individual or couple at a time. Action sets composed of consanguineal kinsmen (by blood) and affines (by marriage) may be assembled for specific purposes. Lambert (1977: 3) stresses that new solidary groups must be created in each generation from the debris of dissolved families. Thus there are losses in the relationships between siblings and parents for the sake of the new conjugal couple. That the process is gradual has already been mentioned; even the establishment of a conjugal relationship between husband and wife is underlined both by the dramatized reluctance of the parents and their kinsmen to allow a new household to come into being and by the drawn-out process of the marriage process itself, which takes may years to complete (Bolton 1977; Carter 1977).

The married couple as heads of household in the Andes are surrounded by kinsmen of various kinds with diminishing degrees of relatedness. Consequently, obligations and counterclaims, which need to be activated from time to time as the need arises, are governed by established norms of reciprocity and degree of relatedness, as I demonstrate in Chapter 4 of this book. Kinship ties "beyond the nuclear family" can be activated or let go through exchange (see my article by the same title in Mayer 1977b). Lambert (1977: 22) notes, too, that it is easy to create kinship with nonrelatives by establishing fictive kin or co-parenthood (*compadre*) relationships. Beyond the nuclear family and the household, then, the Andean kinship system places fewer constraints, creates fewer predetermined roles, and allows more flexibility than other kinship systems. Consider, for example, the African or Chinese lineage systems. The latter case is well presented by Margery Wolf (1968) in her study of the break-up of the House of Lim in a village in Taiwan.

However, when one looks at the fixed roles, attributions of authority, and distribution of power inside the household/nuclear family, a different picture emerges. The following is a description of the division of labor within the household in Tangor in 1969. Men were in charge of the fields. They did the plowing, cultivating, weeding, and other work connected with the actual processes of production in the fields. Women, on the other hand, were generally not involved in these activities. Although they helped out at harvest time, they rarely worked at tasks connected with digging the soil or using implements. Men built houses and repaired them, manufactured tools and ropes, and were responsible for procuring the cash with which to buy grocery and market-bought items. Women, in turn, were responsible for the care of animals. The daily trek after breakfast to take the animals out to pasture was largely the task of women, unmarried girls, or young boys. Men sometimes tended the animals when the women were too busy, but it was clear that, in doing so, they were essentially performing a women's task.

Women managed the household supplies. They were in charge of the disposition of the crops and other foods stored in the attics of their houses and pantries near their stoves. Once the harvest was out of the ground, it passed into the control of women. If some of this should be sold, it was the women who made the ultimate decision. Women also managed the day-to-day purchases of food, with money given to them by their husbands. They were responsible for establishing credit with storeowners and for making weekly lists of items to be purchased in the market town, and it was the women who bartered in the marketplace with other women or with male highlanders when they came to the village. Spinning and accumulating wealth in wool and clothing were also the women's prerogative, whereas the men wove the ponchos and the cloth out of which shirts and pants were made. Much clothing was bought for cash in fairs. An important part of this management was the cooking and distribution of food—again, the prerogative and fiercely defended domain of women (Weismantel 1988).

In short, male heads of household were seen as the producers and female heads of household as the allocators or managers. Getting money was a man's concern; spending it, a woman's. The handing over of money by men to women was a recurring problem (Bourque and Warren 1981: 125; Mc-Kee 1997).

Additional members of the household contributed to the tasks according to their gender and age, but even the development of gender roles in children was a gradual process. The dress, hairstyles, games, and activities of little boys and girls remained undifferentiated until a certain age—at which point play abruptly turned into work. The separation started earlier for girls, as they initially played at, and later helped in, female activities; boys, by contrast, tended to play games that did not necessarily mimic male work roles. Isbell (1997) notes the reverse trend in old age, a life stage when gender differences between men and women became less obvious.

As a unit, the Andean husband-wife team receives much ideological attention in ceremonial and ritual contexts. Olivia Harris (1978: 22), in a widely discussed article on gender relations among the Laymi in Bolivia, argues for a view that complementarity between husband and wife characterized gender relations in the household. She notes that in the Aymara language of the Laymi, the term for man or husband, *chacha*, and the term for woman or wife, *warmi*, can be combined as a single substantive, the conjugal unit known as *chachawarmi*. As a model, husband-wife represents a powerful symbolic relationship, identified by Tristan Platt (1986: 245) as *yanantin*—which is translatable as "pair" and "man and woman," but a pair that is made up of unequal parts such as "left and right" or the two halves of a mirror image.[7] Isbell (1976), following this approach, aptly designated each member of the pair as the "essential other half." Basic to Platt's understanding is the assumption that the male ranks higher than the female, whereas Harris (1978: 30), in her discussion of *chachawarmi,* stresses the role of husband-wife in running the household as complementary and egalitarian, at least on the ideological plane. Inside the household the concept and the practice coincide nicely. Harris concludes that Laymi relationships within the household do not fit the classic outlines of the *patriarchal* peasant family, despite the fact that the *chachawarmi* ideology does not recognize the double shift in the allocation of labor for women and the fact that women have a whole series of domestic duties not shared by males.

But Harris also argues that it is a mistake to treat the household as an isolate: Within the conceptual domain of the private house, men and women are in complementary equality, but they are decidedly not so in the wider social sphere. In inter-household exchanges, women play an unequal part. Politically, Laymi women experience no real participation in community affairs or within the wider context of the Bolivian society. In the market, men are supposed to handle the money and they get into arguments with their women about it (Harris 1987). Moreover, the world of ritual, both Catholic and Andean, is marked by women's subordinate roles or absence. The point is that the complementarity of the couple may operate in the private sphere, but in the public sphere, where *chachawarmi* is frequently invoked as a symbol, it does not (see Chapter 4). Nor is the *chachawarmi* concept useful in portraying or representing the Laymi to themselves, given the frequency of domestic conflict and violence—including wife-beating, which often occurs when men come home after drinking with other males (Bolton and Bolton 1975; McKee 1992).

In recent decades, efforts at improving gender equality and the empowerment of women have become mandated in rural and urban development programs. A host of studies, participatory methodologies, grants, and serious as well as token efforts to promote an improvement in the situation of women have spread around the world, including the Andes. The poor-quality research that often accompanies these programs is reviewed by Allison Spedding (1997a) for the Bolivian case; it is treated with a healthy dose of skepticism along with a questioning attitude about strict dual (*chachawarmi*-type) gender division of labor and women's subordination in her own study of coca-growing farmers in the Yungas of Bolivia (1997b). Pointedly showing that even though a division between tasks may be posited, if a person is not present, capable, or willing, the task is easily performed by persons of the wrong age and gender without too much fanfare.

Many scholars also note that the independence of women as traders in urban settings, where they acquire a generic designation as *cholas,* is difficult to reconcile with the subordination of women by men or the idea that only men handle money (De la Cadena 2000; Seligmann 1989; Ann Miles and Hans Buechler 1997; Judith Maria Buechler 1997; Buechler and Buechler 1996; Babb 1998; Collins 1986). Class and ethnicity considerations affect gender relationships, as Marisol De la Cadena (1997) shows in her study of marriage in Chitapampa, Cusco. Marriage there is a token of alliances, and strategic unions between families seeking power and economic advantage use women as pawns in complex ways to enlarge land holdings, to control labor, and to gain prestige along the *indio* (low) to *mestizo* (high) status ladder, with the consequence that women are relegated to Indian status in order to control their labor, exclude them from land rights, and treat them as subordinates.

Now that we have reviewed how these assessments differ from the moral economy that is said to prevail inside the household, as summed up by Cheal above, it is appropriate to present Cheal's (1989: 16) second model, the "political economy" model. In this model, individuals within the household seek their own advantage rather than harmony, and competition for resources is subject to "implicit negotiation of advantage, explicit bargaining or open struggle." These agonistic[8] behaviors determine outcomes as a result of differences in manipulative skills, differences in the possession of resources, and inequalities of power. Jane Collins (1986: 667) reminds us that within Aymara households, as everywhere else, "economic decisions of individuals are not always made with regard to the well-being of the household, and its members do not always have common interests and goals." Cheal (1989) suggests that elements of both models make up the real world of householding, in parallel ways—sometimes emphasizing harmony and unity and the "moral" economy, and at other times being driven by competition and strife generated by politics and coercion in the "political" economy of the household. The moral model may be invoked by those in power to hegemonize.

A manifestation of these contrary ways has its correlate in behavior. The internal solidarity of the household is said to exist inasmuch as no one should count and account for exchanges and transactions that occur within the house; this is the essence of pooling and sharing. When no one counts and everyone gives freely but takes modestly, then it is said that the home is in harmony. On the other hand, when counting and accounting for begin to hold sway inside the home, it is said that the home has problems. Whether an aspect of ideology or of real behavior, one interesting indicator of boundary maintenance and boundary crossings is therefore marked by where counting and accounting for explicitly and/or implicitly cease in transactions. Marshall Sahlins (1972) called not counting "generalized reciprocity," and he, too, drew an inner-sanctum concentric social circle within which such generalized reciprocity is circumscribed by the injunction that exchanges should not count—although he supposed that in the long run exchanges might tend to balance out. I would instead argue that, when characterized by generalized reciprocity, social situations work because monitoring of flows is no longer relevant or is considered to be inappropriate. Obsessive (Western) searching for gender and other equalities may also entail intrusive efforts to count, to measure, and to weigh that which one should not.

The House Model

In a book with an especially apt title, *Smallholders, Householders,* Robert McC. Netting specifies precisely those components of the house model that I want to discuss in this section. The subtitle also says it all: *Farm Families and the Ecology of Intensive, Sustainable Agriculture.* The Andean households I have studied fit Netting's descriptive definition of the smallholder, a type of food producer found in many parts of the world. Indeed, Andean households practice "intensive, permanent, diversified agriculture on relatively small farms in areas of dense population" (1993: 2). Harmoniously or conflict ridden, the Andean *chachawarmi* pair and its children constitute "the major corporate social unit for mobilizing agricultural labor, managing productive resources, and organizing consumption" (1993: 2).

For the Peruvian highlands three decades ago, José María Caballero (1981: 176) calculated that predominantly small-scale family agriculture produced 48.8 percent of the gross value of agricultural food crops and 53.1 percent of animal products. Self-consumption of agricultural products fluctuated between a maximum of 77 percent of home production and a minimum of 48 percent and between 20 and 30 percent of animal products (Caballero 1981: 228), corroborating Netting's (1993: 2) description that "[t]he household produces a significant part of its own subsistence, and it generally participates in the market, where it sells some agricultural goods as well as carrying on cottage industry or other off-farm employment." Countering the negative images of development professionals who see irrationalities that they hope to correct, Netting (1993: 2) insists that "[c]hoices in allocating time and effort, tools and land and capital to specific uses in the context of changing climate, resource availability and markets must be made daily, and these choices are intelligible in rational utilitarian terms"—a statement with which the Peruvian scholar Adolfo Figueroa (1984) would probably agree. As we will see in Chapters 8 and 9, Andean farmers also have, as Netting (1993: 2) observes, "ownership or other well-defined tenure rights that are long term and often heritable," and Andean households ". . . are also members of communities with common property and accompanying institutions for sharing, monitoring and protecting such resources."

Turning to the house model, we note that the emphasis shifts to measurement and quantification; but here we need to ask what it is that we want to measure, and why. In this section we will examine the Andean household in terms of *material flows*, defined as the pathways created by the physical movement of matter needed to produce the goods that provide humans with sustenance and livelihood. Energy flow, nutrition, and crop yields will be specifically discussed as aspects of ecological dimensions of farming in the context of the Andean bio-geographical environment.

The Household as an Oiko-System

"The word ecology is derived from the Greek *oikos* meaning "house" or "place to live" (Odum 1971: 3). The house model with an ecological bent stresses the way material flows are directed and organized. The peasant house, its animals, and fields constitute small ecosystems in which humans are the dominant species who divert energy flows and modify the cycling of materials through the environment toward their own needs (Bayliss-Smith 1982). The Andes as a tropical high-mountain system are characterized by sharp environmental gradients. Every 100-meter difference in altitude is equivalent to a shift in 10 degrees of latitude. A variety of climates can be found here; condensed in small areas, they form a veritable mosaic of specialized areas or edaphic ecotypes capable of supporting varied ecological life forms that range from tropical to Mediterranean to alpine to desert (Troll 1968; Winterhalder and Thomas 1978; Dollfus 1981; Ellenberg 1955). These conditions have made the Andes an area of nearly unrivaled biodiversity and domestication of crops and animals (Gade 1967; National Research Council 1989; Brush 1989; Zimmerer 1996; Brack 2000). The Andes are comparable to the Himalayas and the Alps; indeed, interesting similarities between household composition and activity patterns have been noted by Robert Rhoades and Stephen Thompson (1975), David Guillet (1983), and Benjamin Orlove (Orlove and Guillet 1985).

Andean households are the agents who carry out the permanent activity of domestication. They manage the biology of food crops and animal races, creating spectacular landscapes through the construction of terraces and irrigation systems (Donkin 1979; De la Torre and Burga 1987). Human ecologists working in the Andes have speculated on the degree to which Andean social organization and the features of the household are adaptations to the environmental conditions of their homelands. Because of the diverse natural vegetation, agriculture and animal husbandry are also very varied (although I make an argument for a process of simplification in Chapter 8). The characteristic peasant adaptations to mountain environments include diversification in time and space as well as in crops and animals. The most practical technology is basically labor intensive: It uses local materials and is locally adapted. The wheel is impractical on steep slopes, and the potential for animal traction is limited. The shared wisdom underlying daily practices reflects considerable "indigenous" or "local" technical knowledge. Above all, the household, because it is small, permits quick, flexible responses to environmental disturbances.

Based on historical documents, John V. Murra (1975) has proposed that a fundamental strategy of the Andean peoples was multiple exploitation of the diversified ecological zones in the Andes. Simultaneous agropastoral exploitation by individual households along a vertical gradient is important in contemporary villages (Brush 1977a; Mayer and Fonseca 1979; Mayer 1979; Yamamoto 1981; Zimmerer 1996), but it is different in form and smaller in scale than the cases Murra demonstrated for pre-Hispanic times. Working many small fields scattered over the landscape at different times is well known and often justified as a risk-reducing strategy against climatic disasters (Camino, Recharte, et al. 1981; Goland 1992).[9]

Smallholders everywhere in the world, because they rely on manual labor and animal traction, are efficient in their energy budgets, producing from five to fifty calories for every calorie expended (Pimentel and Pimentel 1987). A landmark study of energy flow (Thomas 1976), together with an analysis of the biological aspects of a Peruvian highland population in the extremely cold and unyielding *puna* of the Department of Puno (Baker and Little 1976), reveals many aspects of Andean ecosystem management. The annual flow of energy through a typical household with four children is depicted in Figure 1.1. Here a "black box" indicates the place where humans have to make strategic decisions; bin-shaped symbols indicate the places where

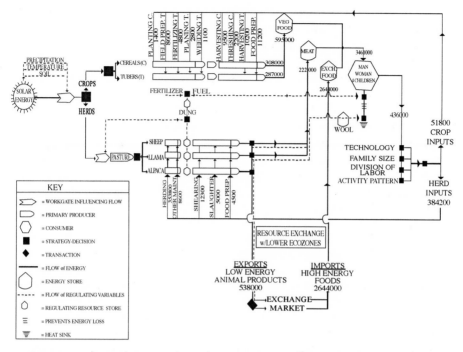

Figure 1.1   Annual Energy Flow Through a Typical Ñuñoan Family. Values are presented in kilocalories produced, expended, and consumed in the course of a normal year by a couple with four children, two to seventeen years of age. (From Thomas 1976: 390.)

energy is capable of being stored; hexagons represent consumption; inverted cone shapes represent heat sinks, where energy is dissipated; and oblongs represent workgates, where biological transformations concentrate energy in usable form as cellulose builds up in plant maturation or herd growth.

An illustration of a strategic choice is how to expend energy in herding or agriculture (addressed on the left side of the figure). Herding requires five times more energy than agriculture but produces only about half the total calorie output of the system; nevertheless it is the predominant activity. This is contrary to common-sense expectations, because agricultural work requires concentrated labor inputs at certain times, whereas herding, though low in labor input per day, is constant throughout the year. It also is surplus labor from the standpoint of agriculture since, despite peak labor inputs at planting and harvesting, both activities can be carried out simultaneously. Agricultural returns per calorie expended are 1 to 11. But agriculture is very risky at these altitudes, and suitable agricultural land may be hard to find. Herding yields a low but reliable return of 1 to 2 kilocalories (kcal). Animal products, however, can be exchanged for high-calorie foods. The Ñuñoan household exports 538,000 kcal in animal products, which convert to an importation of 2,664,000 kcal in high-energy foods, raising the return of 1 to 2 on the energy expended in herding to 1 to 7 through the exchange.

Brooke Thomas (1976: 395) characterizes this system as one of low energy flow, making sole reliance on more efficient agriculture a risky business. He describes several behavioral responses to low energy capture that include a spatially dispersed, multiple-resource base of energetically efficient crops and domestic animals. The exchange network that multiplies animal protein back into calories is crucial to the whole enterprise. Thomas also points to micro-energy saving strategies in daily behavior; for example, sending children out to pasture the animals reduces family energy expenditures, since an adult achieving the same result consumes more energy than a child. Adults also spend more time in sedentary activities, thus conserving energy expenditure.[10] One omission in the figure, though not in the text (Thomas 1976: 403), is the fact that at that time the villagers were still under the *hacienda* regime and as peasants owed the landlord 1,000,000 kcal annually (equivalent to about a 30 percent income tax), which cost the family over 40,000 kcal to produce (equivalent to a 10 percent tax on their physical energy efforts). A second omission in the figure is the outflow/inflow of energy from the one house to other houses. It would be interesting to investigate whether these flows produce a positive or negative balance in energetic terms. Judging from my own research in Chapter 4, the expectation would be that such an external exchange would not always generate balances since unequal exchange is as much a feature of these exchanges as of those that are balanced, and it would depend on the phase in the domestic cycle of the family.

The nutritional study of Ñuñoa people emphasized a bland but adequate diet with high starchy calorie intake, mostly vegetable protein, and, despite their pastoral economy, low animal-fat intake (Picón Reátegui 1976). There were seasonal fluctuations with periods of high intake and months of low food availability. A deficiency in vitamin A was the only one that the researchers considered serious. Benjamin Orlove (1987), generalizing beyond the high-altitude conditions and summarizing the work of Marco Ferroni (1980) involving a Peruvian national nutritional survey on food intake (ENCA 1972–1973), corroborated that the traditional rural household's nutrition standards are not as discouraging as those in some other parts of the world. A common pattern is to increase the proportion of purchased food beyond home production; the nutritional standards, however, decrease with this shift. With rising incomes, overall nutritional standards rise as additional food with more animal sources and greater quantities are purchased. Ferroni shows that this pattern is caused by an urban bias in food policy that favors the national importation of grains and the subsidy of consumption. Rural households also take advantage of cheaper foods available in the market; but when fluctuations in price, inflation, and lowering of wages occur, households can switch back to eating self-produced food. Maintaining their own source of food is a safeguard, and it ensures consumer preferences for genetically diverse varieties (Brush, Carney, et al. 1981; Zimmerer 1998a, 1991, 1996).

A feature of house economies, already noted by Sahlins (1972: 69–74), is that there is a fairly constant percentage of "household failure" (i.e., households incapable of adequately provisioning themselves), and this fact is reflected in nutritional studies. As summarized by Orlove (1987: 489), Ferroni's account shows that at the national level 37 percent of the households were considered to be at risk in terms of nutritional status (i.e., their consumption fell between the minimum recommended and the ideal levels as established by the Food and Agriculture Organization and the World Health Organization) and 16 percent were below minimum standards (i.e., in severe risk situations).

Nonetheless, differential access to food within the household—and child malnutrition in particular—is an issue that merits closer attention. Ulrike Eigner (1997) draws a far grimmer picture than Ferroni, based on more reliable measures of weight/height ratios. Although acute malnutrition is not a serious issue in the highlands, she found on the basis of two studies (1984, 1996) that more than a third of Peruvian children suffer from chronic malnutrition—especially from the medical condition called stunting (i.e., slow growth rates, and short stature when they stop growing). The Cajamarca region in northern Peru had the highest percentage of malnourished children (nearly two-thirds of the total were malnourished), and in the highland departments of Ayacucho, Ancash Cuzo, and Puno about half of all children showed these symptoms. Surprisingly, boys exhibit slightly higher indices of malnutrition than girls. Eigner (1997: 305) also disputes as "sarcastic" Thomas's discussion that slow growth rates and shorter bodies overall are adaptive to low-energy metabolisms in the Andes. Her list of intake deficiencies is longer than those reported previously, and she describes the longitudinal declining childhood nutrition standards in Bolivia and Peru during the past twenty years as "frightening." In short, these studies, as well as the ones on rural poverty discussed in Chapter 10, do not give the Andean house high marks in achieving reasonable standards of well-being for its members.

The Farm House.   Another measure of food production concerns yields in Andean agriculture. The standard litany is that yields are very low, due to geography, climate, small farm size, low technology, and poor management. For example, with data for 1972, Caballero's (1984: 185) compilation shows that for the highlands of Peru, Bolivia, and Ecuador, wheat, barley, maize, and potato yields are at approximately half the level of the world average. Aside from critiquing these figures for errors and mistakes in measurement, a deconstruction of yields at the farm and household levels proves to be an interesting entry into an ecological understanding of production issues.

For the discussion that follows, I rely on an extraordinary book, *Comprender la agricultura campesina en los Andes Centrales Perú Bolivia,* edited by Pierre Morlon (1996). This book reveals the impressive variety of ways in which agriculture and stock raising take place in the highlands, belying the stereotype that peasants in the Andes are technologically backward. Yields are an agronomic/economic simplification of biological measures of productivity, and the gist of Morlon's (1996: Chapter 5) argument about yields is that the further away from official national or regional average figures and the closer to the farm one gets, yields go up but variability increases. In one example, maize yields measured by the ministry were roughly 1 ton per hectare in Cusco, whereas a local study revealed *maxima* of up to 4 ton per hectare. Smaller samples and more careful but expensive data collection methodologies reduce underreporting.

Moreover, there is not one but many measures of yields. One proper way to do it is to count on the positive yield side all the contributions the plant makes to the ecosystem. In the case of maize, one should therefore include the amount of fodder that stray animals eat from the growing field as a positive portion of the yield and not as a loss. So, too, with the cobs that are stolen,[11] and those that are picked from the field by their owners as they mature that go straight into the pot before harvesting. The productivity of the plant also includes the maize the owners give to workers, the amount used as payment for transport of the harvest, and what is exchanged. Official statistics do not consider the plant's subproducts, but householders do; indeed, much maize in the Andes is grown with double purpose, because its stalks are excellent fodder. In addition, yields per surface area should take into account the contribution that associated crops and weeds (also fodder) make to the total biomass net productivity of the field as an ecosystem, not just that portion of the main crop that ends up in the household's storage.

Morlon (1996) also critiques different methods of measuring yields in terms of the inaccurate picture they paint. The larger issue is that household decisions are based on measures that people themselves create and are comfortable with, and as Gudeman (1978) notes, they are often incommensurable with each other. These are not mere quibbles about the appropriateness of various measuring methods, because different procedures lead to different behaviors. In a very influential book titled *Conversations in Colombia,* Stephen Gudeman and Alberto Rivera (1990) argue that householders' economies need to be conceptualized in terms very different from those pertaining to corporations or firms. Gudeman and Rivera's study offers an analysis of householders' thinking about strategies that keep the "house" going. The authors are concerned with eliciting from participants the concepts they use, the semantic fields they cover, and the practical behavior they undertake. Having spent many years listening to them, I find that their words and the authors' explanations ring true to me.

Gudeman (1986) further argues in *Economics as Culture* that everyone is an intuitive economist (as well as an economic actor). This intuition comes not from instinct or rational deduction but from cultural practices that are learned, thought about, and discussed in everyday life. They are derived from *habitus* and *doxa,* as Pierre Bourdieu (1977) tells us. It is the elaboration of practices into intellectual constructs that Gudeman terms "models of livelihood," and these models rely strongly on the use of metaphor and analogy drawn from quotidian practice—that is, from aphorisms, admonitions, and popular sayings. One contribution of Gudeman's work is the insight that fathers of economic thinking such as Adam Smith and John Stuart Mill also used folk models, metaphors, and aphorisms from the cultural milieu of their times, building them into their theories. The Colombian peasantry participates in theory building, too. Further discussion of Gudeman's ideas appears in Mayer (1987), and my own uses of Gudeman and Rivera's approach are explored at length in Chapter 7.

Here I should point out that aspects of the house model resemble the ecological model we have been exploring, but they also differ substantively, and the tension between the *oiko*-system and the farm house is interesting. Gudeman and Rivera (1990) present the house as made up of a *base*, buildings, land, and animal resources. Flows out of the house in terms of labor in the fields return back to the house in the form of crops; as such, they are *base-base* flows. In a schematic way, one can superimpose the *base* model on Thomas's flow diagram (Figure 1.1) by imagining how prudent energy management in one year can increase the herd, build an extension to the house, incorporate a daughter-in-law, and so on. A bad year may require a decrease of the herds or emigration. When ecological climax is reached, the *base* processes all available energy and maintains the largest and most diverse assemblage of species, including the human population. The house model grows through diversification; the corporation grows through specialization.

This is so not only because farmers often rely on biological metaphors to explain their business to themselves, or to anthropologists, but also because farmers have an inherent understanding of the fundamental principles of biological processes; after all, they are in the business of managing it. A farm is a modified ecosystem within its environmental setting; its producers are plants and animals, not machines; and its sustainability relies on recycling of materials. Minding such a process requires skills, sensibilities, and intuitions different from those involved in running a textile mill or a bank. However, one should take Gudeman and Rivera's work not as a kind of ecological reductionism but as a model of and a departure from processes that have ecosystemic properties underlying them. According to ecological reductionism, human behaviors are always adaptive to ecosystems—a concept that is teleological, as exemplified by the writings of Marvin Harris and strongly critiqued by many. The latter are cited in a summary by Roy Ellen (1982: ch. 10).

Gudeman and Rivera's focus on the behavioral and linguistic manifestations of prudent house management is instructive. Take as an example their discussion of remainders and thrift. People's use of the Spanish word

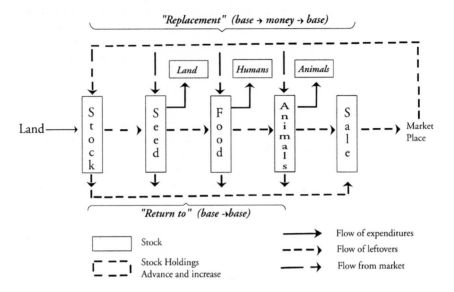

Figure 1.2   *The House Schema. (From Gudeman and Rivera 1990.)*
Source: Gudeman (1990: 119)

sobra is transformed by the authors into a managerial schema that the authors translate as "leftover" or "remainder." The latter is a venerable concept in economics, sometimes convertible to profit (Gudeman and Rivera 1990: 116), but not in the house economy:

> *La sobra,* we came to understand, has several applications, although it almost always refers to the flow of crops within the house. Its opposite expression is *el gasto de la casa,* [meaning] "house expenditure." Together expenditures and remainders make up a processing schema that is applied to agricultural flows. The "expended" and the "unexpended" are paired terms covering a sequence of house uses.

Morlon's discussion of maize yields can be used to illustrate this process, because it is not that different. What is left over after the cornfield has yielded contributions of its product in terms of portions of its leaves for cattle, kernels for household consumption, gifts to workers, and so on, is in each instance a "remainder." Inside the house, the crop is again subjected to a series of iterations. From the remainder of the crop that comes into the house, the first expenditure is for seed, the second is for food, the third is for animals, and the fourth is for sale (as illustrated in Figure 1.2).

In the exercise of each iteration, thrift should always be applied, given that thrift is understood as careful allotment, as prudent estimation of needs of all kinds and how they can be minimally satisfied. "Thrift is the art of turning leftovers to uses, transforming remainders to expenditures, and wasting nothing" (Gudeman and Rivera 1990:117).

The way the remainder is conceptualized in a firm is different:

> The corporate, written schema of accounting has a "bottom line" and this provides the ultimate measure of its success or failure, its competitive position in the market world. The house model has no goal or end, it is a mode of life, a set of practices. The remainder designates not a final state but a momentary leftover within a larger series of house activities. (Gudeman and Rivera 1990: 116)

The house grows, knows no surplus,[12] wastes nothing, recycles everything. By contrast, the firm seeks to accumulate remainders at the end of each cycle and convert them to profit. It exercises a different "thrift" by reducing costs, some of which it externalizes outside its boundaries.

The Rational Choice Model

The rational choice model has as its principal feature the calculating "individual" economic actor who makes rational optimizing or maximizing choices between means and ends, and therefore tends to fall more on the formalist end of the substantivist/formalist continuum in economic anthropology. That the model of rational choice is different from the house model is expressed in a famous debate between Samuel Popkin (1979), who espoused this model, and James C. Scott (1976: 4), who wrote about outraged "moral" peasants defending their subsistence base against the extractions of landlords and tax collectors.

The difference can also be seen in the shift from anthropology to economics. An interesting example of the transition between the house model as ecosystem and the rational choice model is the now practically defunct school of *Farming Systems* in agricultural economics (Shaner et. al. 1981; Chambers 1983; Gladwyn 1989), whose adherents like to model in great detail farm inputs and outputs and measure their efficiencies, identify constraints, and offer suggestions on how yields can be improved, costs lowered, and marketing decisions made more efficient. For example, one practitioner, Robert Hart (1980), presented a flow diagram of a Honduran farm very similar to Thomas's, but the quantities in that diagram are in currency units rather than in calories.

A comparison between energy and money flow through a household would be very interesting. In his study conducted in Lamay, Cusco, Volkmar Blum (1995) analyzed production and consumption in calories and proteins, paying close attention to how much and what was eaten and what was sold by each of the households. Often production does not cover subsistence needs, even though households in Lamay do sell food crops. In addition, a few studies seek to track monetary income and expenditure through the household—most notably, Figueroa (1984) (discussed in detail in Chapter 7) and Beatriz Montoya et al. (1996: 360). The latter study tracked five families for one year. All vegetable food was self-consumed, cattle and labor were sold, and a sizable percentage of monetary income was expended on food in which sugar, oil, rice, and bread predominated. Though instructive, this study is not as well done as Rosemary Firth's (1966) budgetary studies of cash expenditure among Malay housekeepers.

Ecological economist Joan Martínez Alier (1987), who has worked in Peru, distinguishes between what to him is the false calculus of economics (which, following Aristotle, he labels as *crematistic*) and the calculus of energy flows as the real measurement that is used in ecology. *Crematistic* reasoning for Martínez stands for the rational calculus of profit or loss that actors pursue in the market; but according to him, it is a false calculus for it does not adequately count on the cost side all the physical processes implicated in the extraction of biological materials from the environment. The unaccounted-for parts of the process often appear as negative externalities that can manifest themselves in environmental degradation. Many of the measurements one sees in farming system studies involve *crematistic* calculations that undervalue subsistence production.[13]

As the focus shifts from the household to the individual, the rational choice model has to specify a spokesperson for the house, and this is usually modeled for the male head of household, who makes all the decisions for the household; as Frank Ellis (1988: 14) disarmingly puts it: "Taking the household as a single unit of economic analysis poses problems for [integrating women], since it subsumes the distinct position of women and men to the joint economic behavior of the household." Collins (1986: 666) and Harris (1981: 56–61) cite the role of the state in creating the male bias; since colonial times, they say, the state made the male head of the household responsible for tribute payments and assuming legal responsibility for its members.

Shifting the focus of the household to the rational choice model also introduces the larger context in which these households operate: the region and national society, the persistence of extractive markets, exploitation of peasants, and their role within ever-expanding global capitalism. The term *peasants* is associated with this approach and will be used from here on more frequently, although I strenuously argue that the concept of "household" and the term *peasant* are not synonyms. They frequently overlap, but the condition of peasantry may be shed whereas the household persists. A concern with the rational decisionmaking peasant also stays within the question of whether peasant households (rational as they may be) are, or are not, a distinct type of enterprise requiring special theories to understand them. Eric Wolf (1955) posited two types for Latin America: open cash cropping enterprises and closed corporate enterprises. A more frequent discussion is whether the ever-awaited transition of peasants becoming business farmers is finally taking place.

Against all expectations and desires, farm household systems seem to persist in world history. Thus news of their imminent demise is premature, especially every time a study of the *"disappearing peasantries?"* is published—an example being Bryceson, Kay, and Mooij (2000), where the question mark after the title is revealing. But no one denies that peasantries are always changing, flexibly adjusting to extreme conditions of resource insufficiency, unfavorable markets, and the insensitive state. The literature on peasants in the Andes and throughout the world is vast and impossible to review here. Instead, I have selected a few specific issues for which Andean research has generated interesting insights. My discussion here is also oriented toward themes that are more thoroughly treated in subsequent chapters.

The Overworked Peasant Household.   The influential but much-critiqued work of Russian economist V. A. Chayanov (1966) written in the 1920s opened up an interesting perspective on the differences between household economies and firms. He argued that the household's main endowment is its labor power, which is rationally invested in agricultural activities in order to achieve the goal of satisfying the household's consumption needs. Because farm work is, as he says, associated with unpleasant drudgery, and because labor invested in land is subject to diminishing returns, the Chayanovian peasant works grudgingly only until he has met his family's consumption needs, and then he rests. He makes rational choices between work and leisure against his assessment of needs. The immediate appeal we have here is the landlord's stereotypical image of the "lazy peasant." An interesting twist to the argument, Chayanov added, is that because the needs of the household can never be met, the moral peasant overworks himself trying to be a responsible provider. The idea that peasants stop work when drudgery levels become intolerable is difficult to reconcile with the fact that farmers have to milk the cows twice every day, no matter what. Paradoxically, then, the self-exploiting peasant is as much part of the Chayanovian approach as the low-labor-input hunter-gatherer that Sahlins (1972) described as being a member of the original affluent society (in his book he gleefully shows readers that hunter gatherers work very little compared to peasants or contemporary Americans). Esther Boserup's (1965) position is also derived from this idea; she makes the point that intensification of labor inputs (which bring down labor productivity) in order to raise output per surface area is implemented only when pressures (such as population or land degradation) build up. Whether these theoreticians are correct or not, on a practical level we may note that every development scheme, hygiene improvement, local participation scheme, and community improvement project demands increased labor inputs from the people for whose benefit the programs are implemented.

In my opinion, a useful application of Chayanovian theory is to posit that returns to labor inputs are important considerations in Andean household economies. Household members seek to optimize returns to labor as best they can, deploying labor between different tasks within the farm, between different environmental zones up and down the vertical environmental gradient of the Andes, and between on- and off-farm work. Important, too, is the concern that certain needs have to be met first, such as subsistence; so completely smooth labor allocation between farming and off-farm work may not always be possible. Jürgen Golte (1980) explained Murra's verticality by showing how labor inputs in only one zone did not absorb much of family's labor. Verticality, in Golte's analysis, becomes an important aspect of scheduling that coordinates seasonal activities so that working the potato crops integrates nicely with those in maize production, and so on. The aim is to optimally employ the family's labor over a longer period of time in the agricultural calendar, rather than bunching all the labor in one zone at one time beyond the household's capacity to provide it. Moving up and down the mountain slope smoothes out labor input requirements for the household and increases returns to labor because they are more fully employed in productive activities.

My study in Tangor (Mayer 1974a: 74) also showed how people shifted labor between the village and subsistence activities to off-farm labor and trading. A family with a larger labor pool exported surplus labor to the cash economy rather than enlarging their farm enterprise. My stratified sample of rich, middle, and poor families showed few differences in household composition; but more husbands in the richer households were away from the village than husbands in the poorer households, as the latter could not so easily split their activities between home and off-farm. Although the average size of households in Tangor remained constant regardless of wealth, the average size of families (counting those in the village together with the migrating portion) showed a steady increase from 4.9 persons at the poor end of the wealth scale to 6.83 persons at the rich end. Tangor peasants were part-time peasants; they sold labor to the national cash economy, not agricultural commodities.

One question that is interesting to explore with a Chayanovian approach is why Andean peasants so often allow their environment to degrade. A concern with returns to labor, and the choice between returns from work in the fields versus other forms of employment, neglects necessary long-term maintenance work on the farm (Brush 1977b). Scholars tend to calculate labor inputs in terms of days required for plowing, tilling, and harvesting a particular crop, but they do not count the "overhead" labor needed to keep the fields from eroding and fertile. Low returns on work effort compared to off-farm returns lead to abandonment of less productive lands (Denevan 1987) in a country where agricultural land is scarce. Overextended households in the Altiplano of Puno that opened up coffee plantations in the tropical foothills led to farming practices that eroded the soils and caused nutrient loss in both highland and tropical areas (Collins 1988). The demand for outside money obtained from wages probably has a long-term negative impact on the ecosystem stability of Andean farm landscapes, because they increasingly neglect maintenance work—a trend PRATEC would like to reverse, arguing that the countryside should increase in population density and intensify production on the *chacra* (Rengifo 1991). Note that the pattern is ancient: Inca tribute was off-farm work, as was the colonial *mita* labor draft that forced households to contribute labor for colonial mines.

The absence of male workers due to migration shifts the workload onto women, whose work schedules are already full, leading to a reduction in farm work, a shrinking subsistence base, and other negative consequences. The issues relating to the feminization of agriculture, including the fact that female-headed households often are at a severe disadvantage compared to households with the male complement present on the farm, are many and complex (Deere and León 1982). Weismantel's (1998) study, cited above, is concerned with the implications for women and for men of having semi-proletarian husbands trying to find compatibility with their farm-based wives. Moreover, Collins (1986) and Painter (1986: 235) argue that the household's participation in the capitalist sector as coffee producers, wage laborers, and traders so drains the subsistence activities of the household that it becomes practically nonviable. The result is a case of "progressively pauperizing the peasantry."

In a study by Carmen Diana Deere and Alain de Janvry (1981) conducted in the Department of Cajamarca in northern Peru, where land is extremely scarce, the authors found that Chayanovian explanations of family labor composition and land size were insufficient to explain class relations in the rural population. According to Chayanov, family size was the independent variable and amount of land worked was the dependent variable that adjusted "like clay" to consumption needs and workforce availability. Chayanov therefore posited a steady-state situation for the peasantry, with households expanding during the growth period of the domestic cycle and then declining as they lose labor. Lenin (1974) found Chayanov to be in populist error, for he placed greater emphasis on permanent stratification among the peasantry through differential ownership of land. Deere and de Janvry (1981: 346) suggest that the Lenin approach holds better than the Chayanov position for the Cajamarca situation because "access to additional land is limited." They also point out, however, that within each class—near landless peasants (who average 6.64 members per household), smallholders (5.31), middle peasant households (5.68), and rich peasant households (6.25)—the phase in the domestic cycle that determines household labor strength influences household choice of activity, particularly when other income-generating activities are important sources of household net income. Chayanovian explanations hold within each class: Households with greater labor power are better off than their peers within their class than households with lower labor power, and since this is a cyclical phenomenon, variation in family size plays a role in maintaining a steady-state class structure. The poverty studies discussed in Note 1 of Chapter 10 do not support this conclusion.

Even more depressing results are reported by William Mitchell in his study of Quinua, a large peasant community in the Department of Ayacucho and the scene of much Shining Path army and police violence in 1987–1992.[14] In Quinua, Mitchell (1991) reported, population growth on a fixed resource base with limited possibilities of expansion were the basic forces of change. Population growth rates increased from 1.2 percent in the 1960s to 2.8 percent in 1980. Such an expansion created a largely young population with an overrepresentation of adult women compared to men in the village. "Excess" people migrated, leaving an insufficient number of workers to work the fields. In 1987 more than 50 percent of the people born in Quinua lived elsewhere, and remittances in both directions (money one way and locally produced food the other) attempted to sustain those in Quinua and the migrants to varying degrees.

Quinua's lands are arid and infertile. The agricultural land base is very limited. In 1972, a total of 4,000 hectares (12 percent of the district's surface area) divided among the farm units yielded a range of one-quarter to one-half a hectare of farmland and a mean of three cattle, eight sheep, and/or eight goats per household. Agricultural production was low. The wide range of crops grown in different cycles and at different altitudes was insufficient to cover the basic household food needs. One *yugada* (0.124 of a hectare) produced a median net consumable yield of 1,150 kilos of potatoes and 490 kilos of maize. Consumption data gathered by Mitchell suggested an intake of 182 kilograms of potatoes and maize per person per year. Converted to land, a person required 0.5 *yugadas* of combined potato and maize land to feed her- or himself. Adding in the other crops and food-intake requirements, Mitchell concluded that one *yugada* per person was a minimum land requirement. The average household had 4.4 occupants. The mean number of *yugadas* per household was 2 to 4 *yugadas*. There was not enough land to feed all the members of the family.

No significant expansion of agricultural land has taken place in the interim; nor has the considerable investment needed to expand the irrigation system been implemented. Instead, Quinueños, like most household members in the Andes, have massively turned toward seeking nonfarm sources of income. In particular, they have decided, individually and collectively, to invest in education to provide the next generation with the social tools and skills necessary to seek nonagricultural occupations. They have also left the countryside in large numbers.

These measures did not bring in much more. The cash flow of one family for thirty-eight days in 1974 in the postharvest dry season showed a weekly income of US$12.00 and a weekly expenditure of US$17.00, of which nearly half was spent on food and a third was needed for productive purposes. Were this study to be updated today, the imbalances would be even higher. The cost of nonlocal foods and materials have increased enormously since the days of cheap gasoline, when Mitchell collected the data. Since the 1960s and 1970s wages and salaries have plummeted, employment opportunities have shrunk, and sources of income in the informal sector have become difficult to secure. Studying these numbers leaves one wondering how people manage to survive and yet maintain a basic level of dignity. Mitchell is correct in pointing out that the trends causing such concern are not unique to this village; nor are they unique to the Ayacucho region, as Carmen Diana Deere's (1990) study of the Cajamarca region shows. Indeed, they represent what is happening in many places throughout the Third World.

The Informal Household. Since the peasant system can be conceived of as both a firm and a household, a shift in focus to how well a peasant household performs—in its role as a firm—provides another avenue for understanding household economies. Such an approach tends to deny the fundamental differences between firm and house that Gudeman and Rivera insist are important, because their house model is on the margins of the market, whereas the informal household in this model, if not squarely within it, makes strenuous efforts to penetrate it. Being rational, efficient, and optimizing, these households—so this argument goes—should be treated as if they were enterprises; and neo-classical equilibrium theory developed for the firm in micro-economics (and its variants in agricultural economics for small-scale agriculture [Ellis 1988]) should hold for the peasant as much as it does for the small firm. In this view, differences between the firm and the peasant enterprise are differences of degree, not of kind. House businesses are extreme cases, not separate types—although the Marxists I discuss below do contend that petty commodity producers are a type.

As a model the family business would have the following features. The moral father-figure/head of the household operates his business from his home. He becomes the shrewd businessman as well as the *patrón* ("boss") who runs his firm with an iron fist and imposes strict business ethics on his wife and children employees. He is in something of a bind: He can't fire them because they are his family, but he certainly can make them work harder, and they can't unionize. The family business may have two faces, one depicting the head as exploitative and grasping, the other presenting itself as virtuous entrepreneurship. Many households are also run by women, but these two images remain. Both emphasize extremely hard work and low consumption levels for the sake of saving money for business reinvestment. This is done as a family effort; by pulling itself up by its bootstraps, the household provides the next generation with a better base.

The first sweatshops in the world were in people's homes, and the piece-rate system still exploits home-based labor. This firm may have an inflexible labor supply, but it can lower the wage rate, lengthen the shift, and use women, children, and poor attached relatives. Orlove (1977b) observed cloth manufacturing families in the town of Sicuani Cusco that take in children of poor relations from the countryside to spin and weave in exchange for nothing more than food.

Some writers suggest that a qualitative change in orientation takes place within the "black box" of household ethics and solidarity. Almost as if Max Weber had been hired as a consultant to develop Latin America, a massive conversion to Protestantism is often associated with this shift. Sheldon Annis (1987), working in a village in Guatemala, found that conversion to Evangelical Protestant sects is associated with a change in economic orientation. Protestant households outperformed traditional Catholic households in agricultural productivity and commercial handicraft weaving, and they eagerly branched out into other ventures. They extolled entrepreneurship and embraced modernity with gusto.

Such an embrace of modernity is also associated with a rejection of the popular Catholicism that is practiced in villages with saint worship and *fiesta* sponsorship. Mitchell (1991) reported that the Protestants in Quinua reputedly comprised over half of the population. To the new converts the change of religion is seen as a progressive and enlightening step away from obscurantism and ignorance. To Mitchell, the high expenditures in *fiesta* sponsorship are impossible to marshal in the face of impoverishment, and these are what really account for such a momentous changes in ideology. The convenient excuse of having converted allowed people to refuse the pressures of accepting sponsorship. Material expenditures aside, though, it is important to note what is in fact being repudiated. There is a rejection of collective commitment to the locality that used to govern itself and run its affairs in a fairly autonomous way. Instead, individual strategies of family enhancement are emphasized. Money that would have been spent on a *fiesta* is now invested in education or in capital development or even personal validation. Lavishly funded family feasts that celebrate a birthday or marriage have become much more prominent today. The closed corporate community is being forced to open up to wider economic, political, and ideological influences.

David Lehmann (1982) describes a system of successful cash-cropping potato farmers in Carchi, Ecuador. He calls it the "capitalized family farm," and it relies on profit sharing, share cropping, and pooling money for joint ventures. It takes out loans from relatives and banks, and its members are keen and skillful users of the instruments of the monetized market economies. They employ modern technology and seek value-added strategies in their firms. These house firms also mercantilize kinship relations and exploit the mechanisms of reciprocity for the sake of the business. All this to keep costs down and to sell agricultural products in a competitive money market based on *crematistic* accounting and profit calculations. To overcome problems of small scale, several households related to each other join forces to extend land availability: They reorganize the division of labor in terms of the needs of the enterprise rather than those of the household. Managerial specialized roles are entrusted to a relative who performs the services for associated households.

Examples of capitalized family farm growth and decline can be found in the work of Jane Collins (1988), concerning people who expand their enterprise by colonizing the tropical lowlands for commercial crops while maintaining their home base in the highland plateau of Puno. See also Robin Shoemaker's (1981) study of coffee growers in Satipo, Junin; Sutti Ortiz's (1973) landmark study of uncertainty in cash-crop farming in Colombia; and the excellent study by Nola Reinhardt (1988) of vegetable and coffee growers in Colombia. Within this group, no doubt, we should also count contemporary coca producers. All of these studies show that initial success is associated with larger boom-and-bust cycles of commodities on the world market, that monetary inflow at the expense of a rising food bill may not necessarily change the level of well-being of families after the prices of their commodities sink to low levels, and that it is very, very hard to transmit the firm's initial success to the next generation. Lehmann, though, insists that this scenario is a transition to capitalism. A real household enterprise, in contrast to the abstract models presented here, has to combine the methods and characteristics of both the house model and the family firm model, contradictory as they may be; and as shown in Chapter 7, the two can also be in a negative-feedback relationship.

I also contend that these strategies are characteristic of the urban informal sector. The informal sector, too, rests on a household *base* that allows individuals to participate in the market. Studies of survival strategies among urban poor in Lima during the prolonged economic crisis reveal patterns not very different from Gudeman and Rivera's pooling, thrift, and recycle procedures together with Lehmann's partnerships, profit-sharing schemes, and nonbank loans (Bustamante et al. 1990; Blondet and Montero 1995; Golte and Adams 1987). Urban informal enterprises rely on commercialization of women's work through selling and processing food and on Chayanovian efforts to maximize utility of available labor resources. The diversification in trades and the support network of kin (Lobo

1982) are aspects of informal life in Lima's squatter settlements, just as they are in the home villages.

The term *petty commodity production* became fashionable during the 1980s within the Marxist tradition of accounting for what, to Marxists, were fundamental differences between capitalists and family firms, whose resemblance to capitalistic firms they said was only *formal*. Petty commodity production was attractive for it seemed to provide a model that helped explain the increasing use of money and market relations without producing any significant changes in household economies or historical transformations (Bernstein 1994). Unlike businesses, petty commodity producers, although they predominantly use money and behave as penny capitalists to seek money income advantages, do not become prosperous businesses; nor do they accumulate.

The model for petty commodity production is the family-owned artisan shop in a bazaar anywhere in the world—or, in the Andes, in a crowded side street next to a market. It could be the family farm, too. The producer owns the means of production, tools, and raw materials, and obtains them freely and individually in a free market where conditions of competition exist and its actions respond to price incentives. Technology is simple; skills are learned, but not very difficult to learn; and there are few restrictions to entering the business. The tools are handworkers' tools and often are partially made in the shop itself. Low output per shop, many shops, and competition between them for the sale of small outputs are typical. No shop can control the market price. There is separation of producers from each other, each one acting as an autonomous and free agent. The organized market is the place where the shop can sell its product and buy tools, raw materials, and the means of subsistence (food, clothing, etc.). The home is often part of the shop.

Money is involved, but the circuit is commodity → money → commodity—unlike the capitalist circuit, which is money → commodity → money. An advance from the customer to buy the raw materials is often required to start the circuit. There is free mobility and many businesses do go under; some grow but seem to succumb sooner or later anyway. (A lucky few become big business corporations and get to keep the family name as a trademark, such as Levy Strauss.) There is no separation between the household and firm. Again, it is household labor that predominantly works in the shop. Casual wage labor is secondary and hired and fired as needed. The tendency is to substitute labor process for capital process in order to remain a market player.

What is the effect of improved small technology, such as electric sewing machines in the clothing trade? Joel Kahn (1980), whose study of the Minankabau iron artisans in Indonesia prompted him to relaunch the term *petty commodity production* for academic interest, cogently argued that there are benefits to technological improvements, but not to the particular firm. Under capitalism, such improvements feed back to the firm with increased profits, allowing it to plow back the profits and continue expanding. In petty commodity production, technological improvements may reduce the number of firms that supply a given line of commodities, but low sales prices keep profits at the subsistence level. Those firms that were displaced by the new technology go into another branch of trade. So in the long run there is a greater diversity of products and more firms in a larger petty commodity production sector; but the overall standard of living is basically at the same low level, a culturally tolerated subsistence level across all participants in all trades. All that has changed is that there are more firms involved in producing a wider range of products, and more choices between cheap products for those who buy them. There is a horizontal expansion of more firms, rather than a differentiation and concentration of business through profits. Studies of handicrafts in the Andes and Latin America include those of Mirko Lauer (1989) and June Nash (1993), whose insights corroborate these views.

In the Andes, Gavin A. Smith (1989) applied this approach in his study of how rural petty commodity producers resisted and eventually invaded *hacienda* lands that they rightfully claimed as theirs in Huasicancha, Junín. In contrast to the model of atomistic competitive households outlined above, Smith argued that petty commodity producers do band together into some form of association, whether as a guild for artisans or a community for farmers, in order to provide themselves with minimal protection, sociability, and the setting of rules under which they will compete with each other. Unable to expand herding, the Huasicancha migrants ganged up in Lima, where most of them migrated to create a special niche in the marketing of fresh strawberries in the food markets and house-to-house sales in the elegant suburbs. Solidary bonds of kinship and community membership were actively maintained both in Lima and in the highlands. Migrants financed the lawyers that led the fight against the *hacienda* back home, and they reserved spaces for their fellow villagers and kinsmen in strawberry peddling. A theoretical summary of this argument in complex Marxistese can be found in Smith (1985).

Peru's influential economist Hernando de Soto (1989), on the other side of the political spectrum, comes to the same conclusion but adds an important dimension to the understanding of the process. It is, he says, not only collective but very political. Individual families in the informal sector band together in ways similar to those of rural households in order to carve out a market niche for their trade and a place where they can create their neighborhood. A key concept for me is de Soto's emphasis on squatting.

With massive migration from the countryside, Lima has experienced an unprecedented increase in squatting. (Squatting here refers to the illegal occupation not only of a piece of land but also of street corners, and rights of way on public roads, and to the infringement of registered trademarks and manufacturing processes.) The image of a defiant squatter is a good one through which to understand informal behavior. *Informality* is a process that implies individual and collective defiance to existing legal regulations. Openly illegal, squatters assert their right to break the law by appealing to higher moral principles such as need and the right to work. Informality in Peru has become a pervasive and persistent challenge to existing institutions, comparable to a civil disobedience movement. It is confrontational in attitude and behavior. Like other similar social movements, informality is a process whereby discriminated groups seek, through a set of tactical maneuvers, to wrench from existing institutions recognition and legitimacy to their claims. Informal squatting is characterized by energy and creativeness at the individual enterprise level and by effective political leadership at the collective level.

Distinguishable stages in the process can be identified. First is invasion. Second is expansion in numbers to achieve a critical mass of members with which it is possible to defend the invaded street corner or bus route, not only from eviction but also from competing informals. Third is a process of growing and expanding internal organization while wrangling concessions and permits from the authorities. Fourth is the political co-optation of these organizations, because as they negotiate for their special interests, they deliver votes and demonstrators to support whichever political party or candidate makes them the better promise. With gradual official recognition they acquire a degree of formality (never complete formality)—and with it, as de Soto hopes, comes security, increased investment, economic growth, expansion, and legitimacy.

Micro-enterprises, small credit programs, and gender-specific credit programs are all based on the notion that a little push, a little bit of credit, and some support to renegotiate gender and kinship roles within the household and among the associated kinsfolk will produce desired results through existing and expanding markets. But studies also focus on the extremely high failure rate of micro-enterprises and how quickly they succumb in competitive globalized markets. They show how structural readjustments wipe away any margin they could have had, and how very often a small change in the fickle market forces the firms back onto a renewed reliance on subsistence survival or wage work in both city and countryside (Chávez and Chacaltana 1994; Portocarrero 1999).

The magnitude and uses of the profits that are sought in rural or urban family businesses are important to consider as well. If the profits these businesses make do no more than cover the food bill of the household, the emphasis on the category of "profits" seems misplaced since such households are not profitable because they don't accumulate; rather, they have, in Polanyi's terms, only provisioned themselves through the market. They may embrace the spirit of capitalism, but they do not reap any of its benefits.

The situation described above is one in which the economic notion of competition applies in full force. Textbook economics has it that competition is a desirable state since it pushes firms to greater levels of efficiency. This would hold as long as certain social rules, those that define the lines along which firms compete, are established. I would add that small firms in the informal sector work under conditions of cut-throat competition among many firms, fighting for limited share and ruthlessly carving extremely small niches for themselves with whatever weapons they may have. Gavin Smith (1985: 104) says that community culture and the "moral tone" with which informals defend their associations becomes an "oppositional expression essential for survival within the cut-throat competition of dominant capitalist relations." The rules of the game are hardly the civilized ones practiced by Wall Street, and limited liability is never present. One is more likely to find cut-throat competition in bazaar situations among shoe repair stalls, street-side mechanics, and food vendors than in the competitive conditions of telephone, soft drink, or beer companies. Between thousands of small-scale competitors fighting for a limited market share who undercut each other, normal profits to be made in this situation are extremely low. At the same time, petty trade faces competition from organized industry and supermarkets, and the playing field certainly is not level between the formal and informal sectors.

The Household in the Community

The capacity to act collectively is the most outstanding characteristic of Andean households. It was one of the first topics that Peruvian writers addressed when ethnographic writing became acceptable. The most famous was Hildebrando Castro Pozo's (1924) *Nuestra Comunidad Indígena,* in which the author affirmed his project to convert Indigenous communities into socialist cooperatives. Castro Pozo is probably responsible for perpetrating the myth that Andean communities today are direct descendants of the communalistic Incaic *ayllu.* Scholars since then have convincingly demonstrated a more direct link between the contemporary community and the sixteenth-century colonial *reducción,* the brutal reform that concentrated dispersed households into villages where they could be controlled, evangelized, and taxed (Fuenzalida 1971; Spalding 1984; Gade 1991). The policy was most vigorously enforced in the Mexican and Peruvian viceroyalties and gave origin to the closed corporate community that Eric Wolf (1995) described for American anthropologists in the 1960s and Gonzalo Aguirre Beltrán (1979) described for Latin Americans.

Reducciones created the conditions for discrete territorial units, for land-tenure patterns that persist until today, and for collective responsibility and autonomy of the village community. Catholicism nuclearized their families, and the state made men responsible for delivering tribute. The tribute system was responsible for inserting into the peasant household a cash-market economy that intertwined with subsistence production and other methods of surplus extraction. The labor tax *mita* (which had pre-colonial antecedents) institutionalized the patterns of migration away from the home village to centers of production important to the colonial economy, without the migrants' loss of identity or foothold in the village. Undoubtedly, the Spaniards and the Indians constructed the *reducción* on the basis of certain pre-Hispanic traditions and practices, but the break was radical.

Following the colonial pattern, each new community today is born through an act of *fundación* or creation. This provides a charter of legitimacy, an identity for the group, and a place on the map. The *fundación* implies a process of recognition by officialdom, a name, and a dedication to a saint and sacred places that give it identity. Land is adjudicated to it as a collectivity, a place where the central village and settlements are located. Authorities within communities are locally chosen; they exercise authority by collective agreement on what competencies are necessary for each one of the many positions they create, and they decide on the limits and limitations of how much power and pressure can be brought to bear on individual households concerning matters of social, political, religious, and cultural life. The community, supervised by the state, establishes the criteria that determine who is to be a member of the community and what rights and obligations accrue from such membership. Communities are associations of householders with varying and changing legally recognized juridical rights in the laws of Andean and Mesoamerican republics. The resurgence of community organization dates from the 1920s in Peru, with similar and yet distinct processes in Ecuador, Bolivia, and Colombia.[15]

The numbers for Peru are instructive: According to the 1994 Agricultural Census, as reported by Guillermo Valera Moreno (1998) and Carolina Trivelli (1992), the number of recognized highland communities in Peru reached an all-time high of 5,680 in that year.[16] The rate of official recognition of communities grew unevenly depending on each government's willingness to recognize groups of petitioning peasants as communities. As a result of the collapse of the rural cooperatives created by the 1969 Agrarian Reform, most cooperatives became communities in the 1980s, so the large expansion of their numbers in the last twenty years is a reflection of land distribution and choice of land-tenure regime by the recipients, who opted for the community regime over individual private property in their resistance to agricultural cooperatives.

The communities harbor 711,571 rural families as members, since communities recognize the household, not the individual, as the basic membership unit. On average, each community has 125 member families. In the highland departments of Puno, Cusco, Apurimac, Junin, and Huancavel-

ica, the average is around 100 families. The population reaches an estimated 3 million people, which is about 43 percent of the total rural population in the country. In the departments mentioned above, the proportion
exceeds 50 percent. The 1994 Agricultural Census also indicates that territory assigned to communities adds up to 18 million hectares—one-third of
the total land in agricultural territory of the whole country and half the total land in production. In the departments listed above, the proportion of
land in community assignation exceeds 60 percent; in Apurimac, it is 98
percent. In addition, more than three-quarters of natural pasture lands in
the high *puna* areas are controlled by communities. These numbers reveal
that communities are an important and growing component of rural settlement patterns and tenure arrangements, and not, as is often expressed, a
declining left-over of traditional backward rural systems or an empty shell
of colonialism that should be abolished.

An economic understanding as to why households band together thus
requires analysis of the relationships between independent households, the
basis for cooperation, and the conflicts that may be generated through this
process. Households in communities, of course, comprise the main topic of
this book, and the subsequent chapters give ample detail. An excellent
summary is given by Marisol de la Cadena (1989: 80–89). Households, she
tells us, cooperate because they have to. No household is capable of performing all agricultural tasks by itself. Second, they cooperate because
tasks have to be scheduled to permit the careful inter-digitation of all these
tasks without damaging either themselves or third parties. Third, because
these forms of cooperation become organized, institutionalized, and ritual-
ized, the cooperation becomes an issue of membership in groups of various
kinds. In short, relations of cooperation become socialized and subject to
rules, sanctions, and social pressures. Within this framework, the main
thrust of my own argument is that these social relations of cooperation
need to be analyzed as transactions or exchange relationships wherein the
individual actor has room to maneuver and exercise choice in the context
of the institution that creates the norms and sanctions them. The socialized
institution sets the stage as to how the rules of the game are to be played,
by giving the mode of transaction a cultural content, whether it is a reciprocal labor exchange, or a barter partnership, or a sale; but it leaves room
for the pursuit of personal interest in each case.

An ethnographic delineation of these groups is therefore a necessary
step. De la Cadena (1989: 83) suggests that we pay attention to three different levels: (1) the basic household; (2) a group of closely cooperating
households organized along kinship lines, which she calls *grupos de cooperación;* and (3) a series of formalized groups such as subdivisions of the
community, voluntary associations, and so on, all of which coalesce with
the formal organization of the community as a whole. John Earls (1992:
164) also highlights the importance of these extended families, even

though they are less formally recognized in most communities. In Chapters 9 and 10 I call these coalitions of households *interest groups*.

De la Cadena (1989: 101–111) has delineated the forms that conflicts about cooperation can take inside peasant communities. Her first observation is that conflicts occur between groups rather than at the individual level. She proposes a typology to analyze such conflicts. Some conflicts of interest, she says, surface among groups and are resolved inside the community through rule making and rule breaking as well as through internal courts that adjudicate contested interpretations. Other conflicts arise when the situation is not resolvable, leading to permanent divisions and fissures inside the institutional frame of the community; these manifest themselves in the politics of community governance through power struggles. Still other conflicts take place when the exacerbated factionalism leads to secession movements, separating the factions and their interests into independent communities. The final stage involves secularization and dissolution of the institution as such. Frequently the nonformalized extended families that De la Cadena and Earls describe coalesce into powerful cliques and elite groups that wrest control of the formal offices of the community and from there rule it in ways that further their own interests and control excluded people through political manipulation.

This leads to the question of stratifications within communities, and whether these can be described as antagonistic class relations. César Fonseca (1988), for example, distinguishes wealth from class in communities. Wealth ranking in communities can be pictured as a diamond rather than as a pyramid. Communities harbor a large group of middle peasants with mid-level access to lands and heavy reliance on agriculture, but also important commercial links for cash crops and wages. They form the bulk of the support network of the community institutions but seldom control power within it. Below them are households with little or no land, and those I described above as broken households due to adverse family tragedies. The latter are incapable of sustaining the independence of their domestic units and become dependent through clientship to wealthier households. They are generally described by other community members as "the poor." Because of existing kinship and other safety networks, there are fewer of these households than the middle-level ones; hence the inverted pyramid shape at the poor end of the social stratification pyramid.

The top part of the pyramid comprises the wealthy households, and they do form a dominant class. These households derive their wealth through unequal control of land and other resources, disproportionate access to more productive lands, and greater success in agricultural production and commercial links with the outside. In all cases, the kind of link with the outside—whether market, better paid off-farm jobs, or more productive social networks and political connections—is crucial in solidifying the class and power base of the elite groups. The cooperation groups and extended families mentioned by De la Cadena and Earls, when combined with wealth, create within each community family coalitions whom Fonseca (1988: 168) aptly describes as "power elites." But that label does not distance them from active interest and participation in community affairs; on the contrary, they benefit directly from it:

> In rural Peru, the powerful peasants extract surplus from the poorer sectors. Thus, while the poor peasants use the civil religious hierarchy, the barter systems, and the *minka,* etc., to operate their family subsistence sphere, for the rich and powerful these same systems serve to accumulate wealth, to validate their power and personal prestige within the boundaries of the community.

There are class relations inside communities. Many of these are marked by ethnic divisions between so-called mestizos and indios or other variants that express social difference, and their modes of livelihood are linked and marked by cooperation as well as conflict. Therefore, the symbolic manifestations of institutionalized interaction between them, such as public ceremonies, also reveal themselves to be expressions of class conflict, as vividly demonstrated in Peter Gose's 1994 study of the tense relationships between the notables and commoners of Huaquirca in Andahuaylas. Even more interesting is Karl Yambert's (1989) analysis of Peru's oldest and largest community—Catacaos—located on the irrigated coast in the Department of Piura. There the community was a beneficiary in the Agrarian Reform of 1969 as the corporate owner in cooperative. The cooperative was maintained by a power elite inside the community, in alliance with government bureaucrats who benefited from the payoffs from the cooperative. But groups of middle and poor peasants who were getting no benefits dramatically invaded their own cooperative and distributed the land. Indeed, despite differentiation, members of communities do, most of the time, form integrated wholes (an integration based on heterogeneity); and even its richest members identify with the community, because they draw considerable material benefit from the institution.

Andean communities are institutions that manage a commons for the constituent households. Elinor Ostrom's (1990) notable book and Bonnie McCay and James Acheson's (1987) edited volume on the commons provide an understanding of how Garret Hardin's (1968) proposed explanation of the tragedy of the commons is overcome by the creation of rules of use and their enforcement by members who share the common resources in small-scale contexts applicable to the Andes. These communities must be bounded systems clearly defining the rights of members, and they must have mechanisms for enforcing their rules, punishing offenders, and discouraging free-riders. They must be small enough so that management problems do not overwhelm the users. And they must have time to develop, refine, fine-tune, and change the rules they themselves create. A degree of homogeneity or coincidence of interests also helps build consensus, creating the sense that agreements so reached are voluntary and not coerced. The degree to which members internalize these rules, follow them, and police themselves and others reduces the transaction costs of enforcement, litigation, and punishment. High degrees of solidarity among members can create rules that go farther than the minimum common denominator that the veto power of the least compliant household can impose.

Andean rural communities are similarly organized. There is a communal governing body empowered to create rules of land use, to enforce those rules, and to sanction the people who break them. There is also a mechanism, through general assemblies, to change the rules of land use. This mechanism is concerned with scheduling productive activities so that one family's activities do not interfere with or cause damage to another's. Through communal labor it maintains and expands existing infrastructure, such as irrigation systems, roads, and bridges; it also provides access to communal resources by allowing open access to firewood collection and pasture land and by organizing forestation programs and occasionally redistributing unused land to new or needy members. Communities also defend the communal territory from outside encroachment, and confront or cajole the state into supporting public programs such as road building, schooling, and health services. In the Andes, distinct inequalities between wealthy, middle, and poor households within communities nonetheless manage to operate their commons—despite these differences.

An interesting feature of the Andes is that although communal rules intervene fairly directly in the production process, it is the individual family members who unequivocally reap the benefits. Communal processes function to overcome constraints posed by economies of scale for the really small-scale household in terms of factor proportionality, infrastructure, the scheduling of tasks, and the collective expansion and defense of available land. David Guillet (1978) aptly referred to these activities as the "suprahousehold sphere of production" in order to emphasize that the household alone is not capable of providing them but needs the collective action of the group in order to complete a production cycle.

Economist Efraín Gonzáles de Olarte (1994: 236–246) posits a distinct "community effect" in returns to scale for individual households through the generation of positive externalities that underlie communal institutions in Andean communities. Working with input/output matrixes Gonzáles lists the positive returns in work efficiencies and in communal production on top of each household's own production. The provision of large infrastructure such as irrigation canals benefits each household in proportion to the resources they already have and, consequently, tend to perpetuate resource inequalities among households. Alternatively, when communal work is applied to the creation of public goods where the criteria of participation and benefit distribution are defined differently, then the poorer households may benefit proportionately more than the richer households.

Another important feature of commons management in Andean communities, which they share with Alpine (Netting 1976) and Himalayan villages, is the continuum of communal intervention from high to low related to land and labor-intensive ways of working open fields. High up, where biological regeneration is slow and yields are low and unreliable, land is worked extensively and with low labor inputs, and it is in these areas where communal arrangements are most prevalent. Lower down, land can be worked more intensively, and with more labor, and greater yields can be obtained. Under these conditions, there are few communal controls.

Gonzáles' colleague Bruno Kervyn (1989) uses an institutional economy framework to describe the effects of communal provision of infrastructure in reducing negative externalities and risk, but with costs involved in providing the service. Communal organization of production appears when the benefits the individual family can obtain through the community are greater than the costs involved in the maintenance of the institution that provides the service. If risks are low, contributions to communal work low, and yields low, the communal organization provides greater benefit than would be the case if the same service were provided with household resources. On the other hand, if risks are high, yields are also high, and communal organization is expensive (or unreliable), the household expends greater effort and higher costs in reducing these externalities. That is why in a single community one may entrust crop theft protection to communal organization in the high potato fields but must guard the maize fields oneself. The commons in the Andes are fine-grained mixes of high and low degrees of regulation and communal intervention.

Andean communities are also villages—that is, residential centers where social life carries on. The management of land, agriculture, and livestock overlaps with the creation of public goods and services such as streets, parks, schools, public safety, religious and civic ceremonies, health services, and so on, reinforcing one another so as to enhance community solidarity with a sense of purpose and feelings of identity and belonging.

I cite the works of these economists because they are helpful in overcoming the tendency to posit essentialist arguments that Andean households are inherently more cooperative and virtuous than other groups of citizens anywhere in the world. The communal institutions that Andean people create are often less efficacious than they themselves expect, and these institutions frequently break down. But it is instructive to revisit the Andean case in the late twentieth century because the Andean rural community has emerged as a strong, viable and growing institution. During this same period, collective agriculture in the form of cooperatives in Peru and collective farms in the ex-socialist countries was collapsing. Seeking explanations as to why there has been an expansion of collective organizations that respect the autonomy of the household (as in the Andes) and a decline of those systems that sought to destroy it (as in China or the ex–Soviet Union) should provide interesting food for thought to future generations of scholars regarding the importance of the household as a form of social organization.

Notes

1. Critiques of the black box approach in studying households include Netting, Wilk, and Arnould (1984), who complain about too much emphasis on form or morphology and too little emphasis on functions. Elsewhere Wilk (1989: 25) remarks that "the details of what goes on inside households, how they manage and combine their production, exchange, investment, inheritance, sharing, minding, pooling, preparing and consuming, are rarely the central focus." More cogently, Narotzky (1997: 120–137) points to the dangers inherent in using this black box approach. First, she says, it tends to homogenize what is not uniform inside the household. Second, the culture of privacy introduces a deliberate opacity that tends to stop analysis of consumption at household borders, leading to the erroneous assertion that circulation ends at the household door. Narotzky questions the utility of measures such as average family income so often used in national statistics because they do stop at the household level. Instead, she urges scholars to follow the trail of circulation inside the household to observe how they are affected by gender and age differences. Fourth, Chayanov (1966), despite his influential insight into the inner workings of the household, creates a circular argument by erroneously defining consumption in terms of levels rather than needs Narotzky (1997: 126). And fifth, the tendency to merge family and household into a single concept leads to the inclination to "naturalize" the historical construction of family as a given, contributing to a reification of "the household" that contains the "natural" family. Indeed, the cult of privacy leads to a reluctance to closely scrutinize the inner workings of the household. Narotzky (1997: 129) dismisses the contention by economists that values become incommensurable inside the household, urging students to try to "break through the boundaries of the household consumption unit." In another vein, and without mentioning the phrase *black box*, Harris (1981) argues that the tendency to assume that relationships within the household are based on "natural" functions arises because activities that service the immediate physical needs of the human organism tend to occur within the domestic sphere. The locus of these activities is but one aspect of the ideological effort that "naturalizes" some social relationships as a given, with the result that women's roles are confined to the domestic sphere.

2. Polanyi, having enunciated householding as a fourth form of integration, never really developed it (although he wrote two interesting articles on householding in ancient Greece). With respect to householding, Halperin (1994: 148), sifting through Polanyi's unpublished papers, found the following quote: "Householding as a form of integration of economic activity embodies the principle that action is directed by the interest of the group that runs the household. How egalitarian or oligarchic, enlightened or narrow-minded the outlook of the planner is indifferent.

We are stressing the formal characteristic of the method of integration, which is essentially different from that of reciprocity or redistribution."

3. Regarding the term *natural economy* in Marxism, note that although few take the concept seriously, Roseberry (1989: 201) contends that it nonetheless continues to influence scholars, "even ... those who could only use the phrase while grimacing and placing it within quotation marks," because it "plays an important if residual role in most definitions of the self-sustaining self-reproducing family farm." And thus, by extension, our definition of peasants "may be rooted in natural economy assumptions." Basic to Luxemburg (1968), Bradby (1982) and Roseberry's (1994) characterization is the fundamental opposition between production for use and the production of commodities for sale and, derived from this, how commoditization and the expansion of the market destroy or do not destroy the natural economy. Bradby (1982), working in the Andes, tried to show, first (as Luxemburg and Wallerstein [1974] contended), that capitalism in its expansion did not always destroy the "natural economy" but in certain places and at certain times articulated with it, creating peripheries and semi-peripheries. Second, and in this I agree heartily, even if commodities are exchanged and money is used, and goods circulate through the market, capitalist relations of production are not so easily established even if these formal characterizations of exchange relationships can be acknowledged. Romano (1986) also employs the concept of natural economy; see his discussion of the circulation of coca in Chapter 6 of this book. A second Marxist concept, petty commodity production, is discussed in the present chapter to underscore this point. Note, too, that the ecology of household biological production as analyzed in the present chapter is not the same thing as the eighteenth-century concept of "natural" (akin to "natural law") or "primitive"—a concept that Marx, as Roseberry (1989: 205) so nicely demonstrates, readily assimilated because it "was an idea that was very much in the air."

4. In comparing this sixteenth-century Tangor material with my contemporary data I do intend not to stress long-term continuities but, rather, to point to similar historical circumstances. One aspect that did change, however, was the emphasis on monogamy forced on Andean society by Christianizing efforts.

5. I set up this contrast between bargaining and negotiating in order to limit the application of equilibrium theories to economics. In bargaining, economic actors confront each other as equals and dicker along narrowly defined parameters as free agents. Negotiation in a political sense is unequal exchange by definition (although parity between negotiating parties may also occur). There is power, force, obligation, threat, even ideological domination in the negotiation of role attributes. Most of the time, however, the person knows that she is being suckered but cannot do much about it. Hence, resentment, avoidance, unwilling compliance, and resistance may characterize the attitudes of the person at the bottom. The weaker side resorts to "weapons of the weak" (Scott 1985)—tactics that raise the costs of compliance for the more powerful. There is no equilibrium point in a negotiation process, only a sort of tension that can change any minute. Negotiations between husband and wife are concluded when both sides have made concessions; but this circumstance does not set the same kind of equilibrium as that provided by price setting, whereby, theoretically, both sides are satisfied. The negotiating process brings all sorts of "extra-economic" forces to bear on the negotiation, whereas the price-setting mechanism does not. Ultimately, negotiations are a showdown of

power and counterpower that decides the outcome, but it is not some kind of economic equilibrium that maximizes efficiency. Rational choice theory, when applied to negotiation, moves from the department of economics into political science. The end of a conjugal strife is like a peace treaty, with both sides assessing their losses, licking their wounds, and declaring victory. The outcome is so unstable that it most often gets codified as a working arrangement between husband and wife. The dissatisfactions, interpretations, and conflicts regarding the terms of the treaty are subject to litigation, which can start the conflict and the negotiation all over again. But for an opposing view, see Blau (1967) and Becker (1981).

6. Since the publication of the Andean Kinship and Marriage Volume (Bolton and Mayer 1977), several scholars have remarked that the bilateral emphasis of the symposium, particularly Lambert's (1977) summary, overstated the case. Zuidema's (1977) work on Inca kinship stressed parallel descent, and Platt's (1982) ethnography on Machaca in Bolivia clearly shows the existence of patrilineages, as did early ethnography in Vicos, Ancash. A review of the recent issues surrounding patrilineal and parallel descent can be found in Arnold (1997 and 1998).

7. *Yanantin*, Platt (1986: 245) specifies, is made up of the stem *yana* ("help") and the termination *-ntin*, which implies "totality" or the identification of two elements as members of the same category. The parts are unequal, as with eyes or hands. The concept is probably also related to the institution of *yanacona* (see Chapter 3) and to the color black, another translation of *yana*. Urton's (1997) study of ordinal numbers in the Quechua world shows that numbers form pairs, such that odd numbers are complicated: They are "bad" omens in prognostication, and they stand alone as incomplete. Pairs, however, are conjunctions of two opposite but complementary things, intimately bound together as one. A member of a pair that is torn asunder is said to be single, alone, incomplete, and odd. Pairing elements are therefore elements of ordination—an aspect of dual organization that is fundamental to the Andes. The fruit of the *wayruro (abrus precatorius L.)*, a tropical bean with red and black colorings, is carried in people's purses to ensure the bountiful presence of money in them. A seed that is either black or red (i.e., only one color) is termed a *soltero* in Aymara (*chulla* in Quechua). See Mayer (1977b) and Note 9 in Chapter 3 for discussions of other contexts in which *yanantin* may be applicable.

8. *Agonistic* is the term that Marcel Mauss (1954: 5) introduced to describe combative, competitive gift giving.

9. Murra's ideas about verticality, discussed throughout the present book, posit an interesting model of ecological adaptation. It is instructive to contrast this model with Frederick Barth's (1956) discussion of interethnic relationships to environment in another mountain area, the Swat valley in the Pakistani mountains bordering on the Himalayas. Briefly, Barth treats each ethnic group as if it were one species occupying a specific niche along an environmental gradient. The members of each ethnic group have their own mode of specialized exploitation of the environment—some are agriculturalists, others pastoralists—and the way they distribute themselves over the valley is analogous to the way species come to occupy special niches along an environmental gradient. In Pakistan, then, production and ethnicity are associated. Surpluses are traded in markets where ethnic groups meet. Murra's studies show that ethnic groups specialize not in exploiting a particular niche but, rather, in exploiting as many as they can organize themselves; therefore,

in the Andes, technical specialization is not a marker of ethnicity (understood as a *señorío*, as discussed in Chapter 8). In Swat, technological specialization is intraethnic whereas exchange is inter-ethnic. But in Murra's schema, technological specialization is inter-ethnic and exchange is intra-ethnic; hence his suggestion that markets are absent in the ancient Andean economy.

10. Another example of the efficient energy expenditure of Ñuñoan pastoralists concerns animal dung, which they use because fuel for cooking is scarce. They have also made a strategic choice between its use as fertilizer and its use as fuel. Indeed, the Ñuñoans have it all figured out: Llama dung contains more straw and less nutrients and also burns better, whereas sheep dung is moister, contains more fertilizing nutrients, and does not generate as much concentrated heat when burned. Moreover, llamas defecate in one place, making it easy to collect, whereas sheep defecate everywhere, evenly spreading their treasures; thus they are pastured in places where the next season's crops will be planted. To concentrate sheep dung, the Ñuñoans confine the animals nightly in corrals, which later can be transformed into well-fertilized, early-maturing potato fields (Winterhalder et. al. 1974).

11. Crop theft is very common in the Andes. Gade (1970) discusses the social conditions involved and the social organization and efforts that are required to avoid damage from it. Special huts are constructed next to the fields to guard the crop as it matures. Studies of labor inputs rarely quantify this as a labor requirement. Maize production has another interesting aspect: complex animal-plant interactions. Cornick and Kirby's (1981) study in Ecuador shows that as harvest times approaches, women go into the maize fields to rip off leaves of the stalks to feed to guinea pigs, because fodder is extremely scarce at that time. Their timing is biologically correct, since by that time the maize cobs have set, no longer needing the action of the leaves to come to full maturity. Both plants and animals benefit from this optimizing micro-ecological technique.

12. The notion of surplus is important in the discussion of peasant economies. There is a way in which the statement that "there is no surplus" makes inherent sense, as substantivist economists have maintained. Because householding is selfprovisioning, the cycle is complete when all that is needed is produced—or vice versa, when that is produced is consumed (Dalton 1960). Surplus then appears as an "othering" cultural construct, and surplus extraction requires extra-economic agents to force the household to give up some of what it produced to others, subsequently replacing what was taken away by more work. As agricultural producers, peasants throughout history have had to give up part of their production; this is the fund of rent that Wolf (1966) specified. Those who took it were the ones who defined it as "surplus"—that is, as a quantity beyond what others felt were "their" (the peasants') basic needs. Scott (1976) describes how peasants resist this extraction. At the other end of the spectrum, a substantivist view of basic needs is culturally determined and internal to the household. Current concepts of basic necessities used in studies of poverty (examined in Chapter 10) also partake of the same "othering" cultural constructions, but in more complicated ways—as when the World Health Organization decrees basic calorie and protein intake *minima* or certain standards of hygiene.

13. Even if one does not accept Martínez Alier's contention that the *crematistic* calculus is a false calculation, these studies assume that one can use national currency denominations as the common unit of account against which to measure dif-

ferent choices and their outcomes. To do so, however, is to assume that markets exist and that supply and demand conditions operate to establish the right prices. In some cases the market is present; in others it is not. And where it is not, the procedure is to impute a price to items that are not transacted through the market. To impute accurately is complicated (Barlett 1980; Chibnik 1978; Mayer and Glave 1992: 103–113).

14. Regarding conditions in Ayacucho, it is important to note Antonio Díaz Martinez's (1969) book, *Ayacucho, Hambre y Esperanza*— a widely cited description of poverty and hope in the Department of Ayacucho written by an agronomy professor at the University of Ayacucho during the 1960s. Díaz Martinez's observations are very close to Mitchell's. Díaz Martínez was arrested and died in prison for his pro–Shining Path convictions. His writings are extensively reviewed by Starn (1992).

15. Comparative data for Ecuador in 1988 specified 1,581 *comunas* for a population of nearly 3 million, covering about 67 percent of the rural population in the highlands. For Bolivia, however, the data are missing. The closest estimate is a 1985 Food and Agriculture Organization report that argued convincingly that after the Agrarian Reform of 1952, there were about 2,500 communities with an average range of 60 to 80 households controlling 22 percent of the territory and 26 percent of the cultivated area (Mayer 1989b).

16. Peru began recognizing communal titles for Amazonian ethnic groups in the tropical lowlands. Called *comunidades nativas*, these are discussed briefly in Chapter 10.

2

Redistribution and Trade in Inca Society

This chapter focuses on the principle of redistribution as prac-
ticed by the Inca state and the smaller chiefdoms that were part
of the empire. It outlines the ideas of John V. Murra, who, in
discussing the significance of redistribution, argued that mar-
kets were not important in the Inca economy, a society that did
not use money. The presence or absence of trade is an issue that
several scholars continue to debate. Both pro- and anti-market
arguments are reviewed here.

John Murra was my graduate teacher at Cornell University. He was an
inspiring mentor with an enormous influence on scholars interested in
the Andes. Along with John Rowe and R. Tom Zuidema, he changed
the way in which my generation understood pre-Columbian societies.[1]
Murra's contribution was manifold. Because scholarship on the Incas is beset by particular difficulties, given the notorious unreliability of the Spanish chroniclers, he searched out new archival sources and developed ways
of interpreting sixteenth-century bureaucratic records. He published several house-to-house, village-by-village questionnaires, which the Spaniards
termed *visitas,* and sifted them for information that could illuminate the
daily workings of Inca economy. He also encouraged historians working
with old papers to collaborate with archeologists and field ethnographers.
An indefatigable promoter of seminars and other projects, he mentored
scores of scholars, who, in turn, vastly increased our knowledge of this civilization. As an activist in progressive causes, he broke down nationalistic
barriers among scholars from Ecuador, Peru, Bolivia, Chile, and Argentina,
promoting an understanding of Andean history that included a reinterpre-
tation of the pre-Hispanic past and its important influence in current social

arrangements. And, significantly, he popularized the use of the word *Andean* (*lo Andino*) with a clear political content—one that today might be called a "subaltern agenda."[2]

Murra argued that Andean civilization, unlike others, did not rely on trade as a mechanism of growth or of territorial expansion. His dissertation in 1956 made a strong case for characterizing the Inca state economy as one based on reciprocity and redistribution, using concepts that anthropologists and social historians such as Marcel Mauss, Branislaw Malinowski, and Karl Polanyi had introduced as part of the functional revolution in anthropology and economic history. Murra deemed the then-current interpretations of the Incas to be Eurocentric, because they relied too heavily on European concepts and categories. For, example, he dismissed Louis Baudin's (1961) *The Socialist Empire of the Incas,* an account that was popular at the time, written by a French conservative medical doctor who used the case of the Incas as a foil to argue against socialism. Margaret Mead (1972), in her autobiography, describes the excitement she felt when, during her student days, she explored Inca collectivism with Columbia students.[3] In the 1950s Murra reread the chronicler's accounts in the New York City public library and gave the available information a different twist.

Murra had a socialist upbringing in Romania, and although he left the party after participating in the Spanish Civil War, his insistence that a material base underlies social and ideological processes is crucial to an understanding of his work. The Romanian nationalism with which he grew up, as it expressed itself in its anti-Soviet/Russian stance, was paralleled in Murra's political argument that Andean peoples who had once been part of the Inca empire and its civilization resisted Spanish conquerors and Western cultural imperialism not only in remote villages high up in the mountains but also in jungles, coast, and cities since the European invasion, continuing to do so today. Resistance (which for Stern 1987 did include accommodation), however, should be understood as a positive and stubborn effort to continue to do things in the "Andean" way. Andean civilization, he insisted, was still very much alive underneath the dominant Hispanized veneer, although continuities with the past certainly were not "unbroken"—as later critics of Andeanism would characterize this agenda.

The Andes are one of the areas in the world where statecraft developed independently. The Inca state was a late conquering empire that subjugated preexisting smaller groups, which, in turn, had already internally organized economic and political systems. Murra stressed that there was continuity between the local groups and the state that incorporated them. Reciprocity among members of the local ethnic groups, and between them and their leaders, was the key to the economic and political organization; and when the Inca state conquered these groups, the same systems of exchange couched in the polite language of reciprocal obligations extracted energy from the local population to maintain the state and the elite that ran it. The state, in Murra's argument, was indifferent to the potentialities of trade as a source of growth, although barter and trading expeditions did exist and were tolerated by the rulers.

In the 1970s, after Murra directed a field project on an Inca province in the region of Huánuco in central Peru, he further expanded his vision of a civilization that grows without trade and markets as a significant element in its dynamic expansion. He showed that pre-Inca Andean polities tended to control and occupy disparate geographical areas in order to use them as resource bases for direct production. Rather than relying on trade to move the products between remote areas, these polities sent out colonists to produce them and bring them back to their home base. Because the Andes has a very complex broken vertical ecology, direct control tended to move up and down the mountain slopes; Murra therefore used the image of "verticality" to sum up these ideas.[4]

In this chapter, I will first summarize the model that Murra (1956, 1958, 1961, 1964, 1967, 1968, 1995) used to interpret Inca economic and social institutions. Influenced by the ideas of Karl Polanyi regarding the way that ancient states and empires organized economic and political life without the centrality of markets, Murra described locally dispersed self-sufficient or autarchic ethnic groups that controlled direct access to the varied ecological niches that furnished the ethnic group with the natural resources to produce for themselves. According to Murra, the internal organization of these groups was such that free trade was minimized or even absent. Likewise, Murra argued that the economy of the Inca state was organized around labor tribute that did not tax commerce and, therefore, was not inclined toward encouraging trade or conceding rights and freedoms to individual traders.

This chapter examines the evidence for trade in the light of these two models and attempts to determine the extent to which such evidence—if found to be significant—enhances our understanding of that model. I argue that peasant markets in pre-Columbian times were a function of the autarchy of ethnic groups, although they were not central to their economy or that of the Inca state. This conclusion should lead us to modify our understanding of the implications underlying vertical control in the economic history of the Andes, without undermining verticality's original startling significance for cultural ecology and economic anthropology (Salomon 1985: 511–533).

The Ethnic Group

The Inca state was a conquest state. It was made up of a dominant group of Incas and noblemen from Cusco who controlled a multitude of local alien groups. Some of these, such as the Chimu on the north coast, were large kingdoms; others were small ethnic entities occupying intra-montane valleys, coastal fishing communities (Rostworowski 1977; Ramirez 1995a), or highland pastoralists. These groups persisted as integral elements of the Inca state after conquest. Archaeological studies provide clear evidence that the Inca was not the first state. The Cusco polity was representative of the social and cultural complexity of its conquering groups at that time. Innovations introduced by the Inca consisted of an expanded military, administrative capacity, and the ability to enlarge the scale of operations of the incorporated groups. *Pax incaica* ("Inca peace"), although it left a certain degree of economic autonomy to the local groups, also led to increased output.

The ethnic groups whom the Incas subdued were more or less linguistically distinct, and they constituted organized political entities. They were subdivided into large and probably dispersed kinship groups and family households. The ethnic groups had clear forms of political leadership as well as a jurisdictional base that defined an area as their homeland; settlements agglomerating several households can still be identified from archaeological and archival records. Ethnic group autarchy seemed to be the norm. All inhabitants of the village received land by kinship rights and helped each other clear land, plant, and harvest. There was a well-devised formula of reciprocal exchanges (couched in kinship obligations) to help out households in tasks they could not perform themselves. The kinship groups assumed responsibility for the aged, sick, and lame, most likely by working their lands so that these people could continue to cook their own food and maintain separate—albeit dependent—households. The local residents, organized by groups and subgroups, each one with a hierarchy of one or two acknowledged heads, cultivated extra land for religious purposes. The local political leader was also entitled to free work from his people in return—or, more accurately perhaps, as acknowledgment by the subjects of the leader's level of preeminence (Murra 1961: 51).

The higher-level leaders of these ethnic groups were termed *curaca*, but the Spaniards adopted the Caribbean word *cacique* when they reconfirmed their titles in the Spanish indirect-rule system. Before being assimilated into Inca suzerainty, *curacas* were war leaders, administered internal justice, and were responsible for the welfare of the local group. They received special privileges couched in terms of reciprocity. The people performed services for them such as farming, weaving, specialized craft production, herding, transporting, and house building. Colonial documents also reveal that *curacas* were privileged to have retainers (*yana*) working for them. Retainers were exempt from tribute obligations, but as dependent households they were often devoted to full-time specialized work. (Examples of this institution within the Yacha ethnic group are provided in Chapter 3.)

The ethnic group was also a spatial entity—though, strictly speaking, not a territorial unit. Susan Ramirez (1985: 437) adds an important caveat based on her research in the northern coast: "[T]he *curacazgo* was people" rather than a delimited territory. Loyal followers of a *curaca* belonged to it wherever they might have been living. However, largely owing to the environmental conditions of the Andean mountains and deserts, the territory claimed and defended by such a group would attempt to expand in such a way as to gain access to as many as possible of the specialized ecological zones that permitted autarchy. For highlanders, what thus became necessary were potatoes and Andean tubers from temperate and cold areas; maize (which is more sensitive to altitude) from areas lower down; semitropical fruits and spicy peppers from warm and protected valley climates; coca and wood from the tropical foothills on the eastern slopes; cotton and marine products from the hot and dry western slopes; and llamas, who grazed in the higher *puna* plateaus or in fog vegetation (*lomas*) on the coastal foothills. The population of such a polity had to be deployed over an environmentally diverse area to create the appropriate productive conditions to obtain these needed products—even if intermediate areas, lacking productive capacity, were not effectively occupied or actively defended.

Murra (1972) gives examples. For a small highland ethnic group such as the Yacha or Chupachu in the Huánuco area of Central Peru, this meant control of the slopes of an intra-montane valley, where the highlands served as pastures and high-altitude potato grounds, the middle-level slopes were temperate zones for potatoes and other tubers, and the lower parts of the valley accommodated the growth of varieties of maize and beans, all of them accessible from the centrally located settlement situated near the potato- and maize-growing zones.

The Chupachu peoples also grew coca and cotton in the hot lowlands two to three days travel from the core area, and the *visita* indicates that they obtained salt from high *puna* pans in places they named Yanacachi and Caxamalca. Coca and cotton lands were located in the territories of other ethnic groups (such as the Pillao), who nonetheless permitted some members of the Yacha, Yaros, and Chupachu peoples to cultivate coca there. Salt pans and coca fields were exploited by several ethnic groups in the same geographical location (Murra 1967: 384–386). These lowland areas thus seem to have been not the exclusive territorial units of one ethnic group but, rather, sites at some distance from all other ethnic groups' homelands that were exploited in common by co-resident people who remained members of their respective ethnic groups.

Murra's *visita* also reveals that distant resources were exploited by colonizers from each ethnic group who lived permanently or temporarily in these areas. From time to time, people were sent there to harvest, to process, and to transport the products back to the main population centers. A Yacha *curaca* testifies as follows: "[S]alt and wax comes from outside and it takes six days to bring it . . . and they do not give anything in exchange for these things, because they have placed there the ten salt-gathering Indians who have their houses and *chacras* out there" (Murra [ed.] 1972: 29).

Once the salt, wax, and coca arrived in the village, it seems not to have been bartered; but Murra strongly suggests (because no written evidence has yet come forward) that it was redistributed to the consumers along kinship and political lines. Moreover, the colonists did not lose their rights to land in the highland home village, where they kept their houses and produced their own food. Coca had important religious uses and might have been distributed to consumers on the basis of kinship and politically motivated claims or, even more interesting, as customary acts of generosity practiced by headmen in gratitude for having received other kinds of services.

The same inter-ecological colonization pattern was in evidence in the larger Aymara pre-Inca kingdom of the Lupaqa, on the shores of Lake Titicaca. Murra (1968: 123) relies on evidence from the chronicler lawyer Polo de Ondegardo and the *visita* by Garci Diez de San Miguel to describe this situation:

> The Lupaqa kingdom was an archipelago which included beyond the nucleus around Chucuito a series of far-away oases planted to maize and cotton, dotted along the Pacific coast from Arica at least to Moquegua. The neighboring kingdom of the Pakaqa . . . had its oases in the same area, apparently interdigitated with those of the Lupaqa.

Compared to the Chupachu, whose colonies were only a few days away, the pattern of colonization was enlarged in scale to include much larger colonies in very distant areas. Maintaining far-away oases interdigitated with other polities was a function of the political organization of these small states. At the very least they had to have mutual agreements to allow each other's caravans to travel through their territories unmolested: "The control of far-away ecological floors could be done through mutual concessions, through conquest and subordination or through colonists sent out from the center (Murra 1968: 121)." Recent archaeological excavations in the coastal lowlands of Moquegua have identified the presence of highlanders in permanent residences, but they date to the Middle and Late Horizon and Early Colonial periods, throwing into question how ancient the pattern really is (Van Buren 1996).

Economic Organization of the Inca State

John Murra characterizes the Inca state as a redistributive economy based on the ideas of Karl Polanyi, K. M. Arensberg, and their associates (1957) in their work on trade and markets in ancient empires. The uniqueness of the Inca redistributive system was that subservient people provided the

Inca with work energy, and the Inca then returned some of the goods the people had produced.

Based on Murra's published work, the economic system of the Inca state can be summarized as follows:

1. The local community or ethnic group remained self-sufficient (Murra 1956: 66).
2. Certain "revenue-producing" areas were alienated from the local community and "assigned" to the crown or church. On occasion, where possible, more land was opened for cultivation for this purpose (Murra 1956: 66).
3. The common married man owed the state tribute in labor on state or church lands (Murra 1956: 63). Households, not individuals, were liable.
4. Revenue for the state was produced by using tribute labor and local organizing skills on Inca land. No goods in kind were taken from the producers (Murra 1956: 63–64).
5. Corvée,[5] or organized, labor was used for state purposes such as weaving, manning the army, building public works, maintaining roads and buildings, transporting goods, and producing specialized crafts (Murra 1956: 64).
6. When utilizing corvée labor, the state fed and provided for the sustenance and entertainment of the workers (Murra 1956: 188). This "institutionalized generosity" was designed to make the tribute labor appear as if it were part of the mutual obligation of reciprocity.

The state used its revenue to feed the members of the royal family, although "only a fraction of [it] . . . went strictly for court use" (Murra 1956: 204); for military purposes; for Church uses such as making sacrifices, feeding the priests, and supplying provisions to the royal mummies (Murra 1956: 211); for road warehouses (*tambo* and *qollqa*) so that official travelers, the army, and the king and his retinue could be fed as they passed through; as rewards to individuals or ethnic leaders for political loyalty, military accomplishments, and administrative skill (Murra 1956: 204–207); to feed the people doing corvée labor duties (Murra 1956: 222); to supply famine-stricken areas with food, shelter, and other supplies that the local community was incapable of providing out of its own resources (Murra 1956: 222). This last measure, warns Murra, should not be overemphasized as an aspect of a welfare state; rather, it is to be seen as disaster relief.

The economy of the Inca state thus relied on leaving "intact" the capacity of the local people to provide for themselves, while extracting surpluses from the farming population through increased work output. The political machinery created to administer the economy responded to the particular system of surplus extraction. The state organized production of these goods rather than taxing peasant crops (or raiding them), as was common practice in other states and empires.

The Inca economy was also firmly rooted in the political system, inasmuch as the state reserved for itself a monopoly of privileges controlling the distribution of goods and political offices to nobles and deserving people. The organizing of work crews and the redistribution of goods from the *curaca*'s household at the local level was analogous to the actions of the Inca state on a larger scale, and, in all likelihood, the language used to persuade the population to work harder was similar. The degree to which the locals were convinced is another matter, however. As Murra (1958: 34–35) points out, "It is hard to say how many Inca citizens they convinced by 1532, but their effort was at least partially successful: It convinced some European chroniclers and some modern students that the Inca crown controlled the country's whole economic and social life for what were essentially welfare purposes."

To the extent that Murra's model adequately describes this economy, it is apparent that there is no logical function for trade in the Inca state and no place for free trade in the local ethnic community. Hence the "anti-market" thrust in Murra's scholarship, for which he is well known (Murra 1995). Nonetheless, Murra's own research finds that trade and barter did exist. The rest of the chapter describes Murra's findings as reported in the seventh chapter of his dissertation, together with an evaluation of evidence for or against trade culled from the *visitas* that Murra published two decades after that chapter was written. My discussion also includes a restatement of the issues by Murra (1995), ending with an update on the research conducted by others on this issue.

Evidence for Trade

Land, water, grazing territories, and labor were neither bought nor sold in pre-Columbian times, as the following quote by the chronicler Juan Polo de Ondegardo (1940: 194) makes abundantly clear:

> They [Inca citizens] did not have civil courts because they had few personal possessions, and these never changed owners; there were no purchases, no sales, no exchanges, especially in landed real estate, and if some groups litigated against others it was over grazing lands which had been assigned to herd the Inca or the Sun's animals which each group was charged with keeping. [Translation by Mayer.]

When talking about trade in the Inca system, we rule out the movement of goods within the empire that is directed by the political machinery of the state or by the local political system of the ethnic group. Trade would be a movement of goods that is managed by individuals independently as either a full-time mode of livelihood or a part-time activity that complements self-sufficiency. The term *trade* also rules out prestige exchange or prestations[6] of luxuries between people of high status, since these are governed by rules considered morally superior to lowly trading[7] (Mauss 1954; Malinowski 1932; Sahlins 1958). Murra searched for traces that could indicate full-time traders or part-time peasant barters; he also looked for evidence of how the transactions might have taken place, whether through barter or the use of a specific medium of exchange such as money or tokens of value. In addition, he was interested in the magnitude of such trade, whether extensive or minimal, or of crucial as opposed to marginal importance in the livelihoods of people. Finally, he evaluated accounts of marketplaces for evidence of pre-conquest times and attempted to determine whether these places were peripheral or central to the economic system of the Inca empire.

Trade in Luxuries

In most of the Inca empire, there was no trade in luxuries such as precious metals and fine cloth. The chroniclers are in agreement about this, and we can trust their views, given that Spaniards had sharply trained eyes to detect precious metals especially.[8] As chronicler Bernabé Cobo (1979: 41) notes: "These Indians did not have any commerce between one another. . . . Each of these nations was content with the things which were available within its own boundaries, without caring for or seeking anything produced by its neighbors." We need not take the latter part of Cobo's statement literally, since there was considerable movement of goods from one "province" to another, despite each province's apparent self-sufficiency. Contrasting Inca moderation with Spanish greed in the context of gold and silver, Garcilaso de la Vega (1966, I: 253) said: "Nothing was bought or sold for gold or silver. . . . Consequently they were considered to be something superfluous since they were not good to eat nor useful in obtaining food. All this they did not deem to be riches nor treasure. . . . [T]hey did not sell nor buy. . . . [T]hey regarded it as superfluous things."

Luxuries were monopolized by the nobles for political purposes. The state would reward people with luxuries from its own stores for services performed, for political loyalty, and as confirmation of high status. This is particularly true of *cumbi* textiles, which the state produced in large quantities and whose distribution it monopolized and redistributed as tokens of prestige conferred on the receiver (Murra 1962). The political use of cloth and other luxuries was, in this case, closely tied up with status considerations; and in the Inca state, status was used to organize the economy.

Yet in a multiethnic empire there were bound to be differences, and evidence for luxury trade did turn up. Scholars working in today's Ecuador and the north coast of Peru have pointed to evidence that trade in luxuries, along with specialized merchants, played a greater role in that region of recent Inca conquest than was the case further south and in the highlands. An ancient and extensive long-distance trade in pink *spondylus* sea shells (which grow in the warm waters north of Guayaquil), used in jewelery and for ritual sacrifices throughout the Andes, has been documented through both archaeological and archival resources. Indeed, Murra (1956, 1995) has discussed the capture of a sea-going *balsa* raft in 1525 by early explorers of the Pacific in northern Ecuador—a raft loaded with shells and items used to trade for them—and this account has led scholars to look for further evidence of maritime trade in sea shells and other luxuries. For example, María Rostworowski (1977: 97–130) found a copy of a document, whose author, date, and authenticity is still being explored (Ramirez 1995b: 156–157), that describes wealthy full-time traders based in Chincha who traded in *mullu*, the Quechua term for these shells. Part of this document reads as follows:

> The people in Chincha were daring and intelligent and orderly, because we could say only they in this kingdom traded with money, because among themselves they bought and sold with copper, food and clothes, and they had an established value of each unit of copper; and besides this they had valued each gold peso as more than ten times a silver peso and they had weights and scales with which they weighed the gold and silver. . . . (quoted from Ramirez 1995b: 137)

Archeological explorations have not corroborated the merchants' base in Chincha, but Izumu Shimada (1985) has retrieved "copper axe money" in pre-Inca Sican on the north coast of Peru, and this is also known in Ecuadorian archaeological contexts. Anne Marie Hocquenghem (1998: 126–133) suggests that the *spondylus* shells entered northern Peru through an overland route in Tumbes, rather than by sea, because it is difficult to sail south below Piura against the Humboldt current, thus possibly explaining the absence of maritime trade on the south coast.

Even farther north, in today's Ecuadorian highlands, Frank Salomon (1986: 102–105) studied the political economy of the ethnic lords of Quito and their recent incorporation into the Inca empire. Salomon shows that, in the northern Andes, extensive trade linked products from diverse environmental zones and that these products were actively traded in local markets (as previously demonstrated by Hartmann 1971).

Salomon also found that there was a class of privileged independent traders named *mindalaes* who dealt in luxury items and were close allies of the political *curacas* of Quito. *Mindalaes* managed to secure their continued pre-Inca and Inca independence under Spanish rule. They were enumerated separately, not as commoners, servants, or nobles. They paid their tribute to the Spanish in gold, which they accumulated through trading activities, mainly to the north of Quito, linking the highlands with the coast and the tropics to the east. The trade involved exchanges of highland salt for gold, shell beads, peppers, coca, and dried fish. In order to procure these items, *mindalaes* crossed ethnic boundaries into hostile territories. As allies of their *curacas* they handed parts of their inventory to the chiefs as tribute; other parts they kept for themselves and for further trade in the highland marketplaces. Their ability to procure gold attracted European attention. The relative scarcity of *mindalaes* in the southern areas around Quito (which were more Incaized than the north), Salomon (1986: 217) speculates, was due to the gradual transformation of the recently incorporated ethnic economies into the Inca state and economy.

A question of false perceptions continues to cause unease among scholars interested in upper-class merchants in the Andes. There are two views on this. One says that we should trust the early reports; the other, that the Spaniards misunderstood what they saw. The "trust the document argument" goes like this: Without trade in luxuries, an important category of traders, one that would easily have been noticed by gold-hungry Spaniards, seemed to be absent. Merchants who mediated between artisans and their upper-class customers would readily have been detected, since the conquerors were familiar with such people. Since it is this class of merchants that the Spaniards were looking for, the scant mention of commerce and traders in the Spanish records allows us to infer the absence of full-time traders in luxury items. This argument is consistent with the anti-market thrust of Inca studies. At the same time, the "trust the document argument" supports those who argue for the existence of trade in the empire. And when Spanish reports do speak of merchants, so the argument goes, we should accept their limited evidence at face value but with due care to date them to pre-conquest times. Rostworowski (1977), Hartmann (1971), and Salomon (1986) are proponents of this view.

The other side of the argument is represented by Susan Ramirez (1995b: 141): "Given that all the manuscripts were written in Spanish and that the Spanish interpreted what they saw in their own ethnocentric fashion, could not the reports of 'merchants' have described retainers of the lords carrying goods (gifts, or the products of shared resources) from one site to another?" Murra (1995) would favor this view, together with Darryl LaLone (1982), Timothy Earle[9] (1985) and Ramirez (1995b), who strongly support the anti-market side of the debate. Ramirez further argues that the long-distance movement of goods, both luxury and subsistence, was state sponsored, protected, and administered, largely for political ends, and that Europeans mistook their agents for merchants. Households, she adds, also exchanged without state intervention—but, again, not through the mediation of independent merchants. She underlines Salomon's characterization of the *mindalaes* as being "less as entrepreneurs than as political agents" (Ramirez 1995b: 142), and is willing to argue that retainers of the lord acting on their behalf were not merchants but cases of a mistaken identity in the Spanish records (Ramirez 1982). Most documents, she says, refer to genuine merchants who emerged as a result of post-conquest survival strategies.

My perspective on this issue would emphasize that no economic system is as pure as the models that scholars construct for it. Merchants everywhere link themselves to political systems, as attested by the overnight conversion of commissars into entrepreneurs in former socialist countries. I can favor a more complex Inca empire whose northern region gave rise to economic behaviors of greater diversity than those in the south. In the north, merchants in luxuries did, in fact, ply their trade in the context of redistributive *curacazgos* and empire. In Salomon's view, under Inca control, merchants were gradually absorbed by the state. So merchants did not threaten the Inca economic system.

Marketplaces in Cities and Towns

There is unmistakable evidence that local marketplaces existed in towns and cities at the time that the Spaniards wrote, but whether such institutions antedated the Europeans is harder to determine. One such marketplace in Cusco in the plaza of Cucipata was attested by Garcilaso de la Vega (1966, part I: 429): "The plaza of Cucipata is now called Our Lady of Mercies. In my time Indian men and women drove a miserable trade there, bartering various objects one for another. For in those days there was no minted coin, and there was none for another twenty years. It was a sort of fair or market, which the Indians call *ccatu*." Although this is a description of post-conquest times, Garcilaso (1966, II: 702) notes that Hernando de Soto was amazed by the multitude of Indians and the abundance of trades that he saw upon first entering Cusco, "though their wares were poor and scanty."

There is an excellent description by Cobo (1979: 31) regarding the way barter transactions took place between two Indian women in marketplaces organized for new Spanish towns. One woman sat in the marketplace with piles of merchandise ("fruit or something like that") in front of her. The other woman approached her, squatted in front of her, and took out kernels of maize to make her own pile, indicating that she wanted to exchange that pile of maize for the other product. The first woman sat impassive, forcing the purchaser to continue making the maize pile larger until she indicated satisfaction by taking the maize. Not a word was spoken during the whole transaction. Cooked food, fish, raw meat, salt, coca, *ají* peppers, and maize were exchanged. Coca (Las Casas 1967) and maize were used more often as mediums of exchange than other products. As Cobo (1979: 34) points out, "It is true that some things were more common for this use and served as money to buy everything necessary to live on. There were ordinarily the foods they used instead of bread. . . . In this Kingdom of Peru, maize was used for this purpose, and even to this day, the Indians use it to buy other foods." Of note here is the specific mention of women doing the trading—a fact still very much in evidence today (Babb 1998; Buechler 1996), not just in peasant marketing (Mintz 1959, 1961) but in the marketing of food in cities all over the world (Clark 1994).

Mention has also been made of markets in other towns. The chronicler Miguel de Estete saw a large gathering of people in Xauxa (estimated at 100,000). And Pedro Cieza de León generalized that "[i]t is known by those who have traveled in Peru that there were large *tiangues*, which are markets where the natives traded their things" (Cieza 1947: 449). The use of the word *tiangues*, the Aztec word for "market," is troubling in this context, however, because the Quechua word is *ccatu*. Also significant is the fact that these markets coincided with feasts and ceremonies, as Cobo (1979: 34) notes: "On holidays, the women come to make *rescates* in the plazas."

The foregoing are obviously references to local peasant markets, which fit Paul Bohannan and George Dalton's (1965: 5) description of peripheral marketplaces where the "institution of the market-place is present, but the market principle does not determine the acquisition of subsistence or the allocation of land and other resources." Such marketplaces are populated by part-time traders, transactions are on a pin-money level, and buyers and sellers are target buyers who sporadically engage in marketing activities to acquire specific goods that are perhaps temporarily unavailable in a locality. Such markets also serve important noneconomic functions, coinciding with festivals and serving as meeting places and nodes of communication, amusement, and political control. In terms of the Inca political economy, such markets could have been tolerated in keeping with the principle of not taking any goods that peasants produced for themselves and respecting their autonomy regarding the disposition of goods.

We must be careful, though, not to read too much into these accounts, since the markets, especially the better-described ones, were likely postconquest markets held on Catholic feast days and established in cities and towns ruled by Spaniards. David Kaplan (1960, 1965) and John Super (1988) argue that in Mexico and Latin America, respectively, urban markets were created early in the colonial period with the explicit purpose of feeding the nonagricultural urban Spaniards and other town dwellers. Kaplan points to regulations that privileged townsmen with first-quality choice in purchases while Indians had to wait until townsfolk had taken their pick. Similar town ordinances regulating urban markets in Peruvian towns can surely also be found, inasmuch as Salomon (1986) documented rules for the Quito markets.

Deciding on the presence of markets before the arrival of the Europeans is difficult precisely because these urban markets quickly acquired importance during colonial times. Cieza de León (1947: 449) saw a large market in Potosí only two years after the silver deposit was discovered. And Ramirez (1995b: 144–153) describes in detail how Spanish authorities tried to regulate the emerging markets in Jayanca to mitigate conflicts between Indians, forced increasingly to participate in it, and Spaniards who profited from it.

Nonetheless, I think that such places and opportunities for exchange do antecede Spanish impositions. The chroniclers' descriptions point to long-established patterns of ingrained everyday activity rather than to recently learned behaviors. The quaint mode of bargaining described by Cobo seems deeply rooted and is still practiced today. Such markets may have functioned in urban settings, notably in Cusco and near religious shrines, and they may have involved the supply of prepared foods on nonordinary days, serving the needs of people whose temporary presence facilitated the growth of town markets—even though some goods would also have been redistributed by religious and chiefly authorities. Such markets could have been the places where spices, rare ingredients, specialty items, and raw food were exchanged for cooked meals and brewed beer. But then Inca civilization was not notably an urban one; and apart from Cusco, cities and towns were less important than administrative centers such as Huánuco Pampa, where archaeologist Craig Morris (Morris and Thompson 1985) did not conclusively identify any evidence of a marketplace. In Chapter 5, I show how barter relationships frequently bypass marketplaces in contemporary Tangor, since much trading takes place in the houses of producers.

Interecological Trade

Murra's model of the self-sufficiency of the ethnic group through vertical control of various ecological resource areas obviated the necessity of trade between ecological resource zones. This point was restated clearly in his 1995 article:

> . . . [A]ccess to the productivity to contrasting zones becomes indispensable. This could have been achieved by maintaining a series of markets at different altitudes, run by ethnic groups inhabiting each separate ecological niche. However, this was not the Andean solution. They opted for the simultaneous access of a given ethnic group to the productivity of many microclimates (Murra 1995: 60–61).

If clear evidence for inter-ecological trade can be found, we would be forced to modify our view of how inter-ecological control or colonization of these areas worked. Unfortunately, the evidence seems confusing—due in part to the vagrancy of the language and its translations and, as we shall see, in part to the rapid changes that occurred when the political machinery that maintained such a system collapsed during the conquest, when *encomiendas* were set up, and when ethnic leaders' access to distant colonies was lost.

The chroniclers' reports are confusing on this issue: In some pages it is possible to infer colonization of distant lands, whereas in others there is mention of barter, which could be inferred as evidence for trade. A number of chroniclers mention that *mitimaes*[10] were sent out to produce necessary products in the outlying provinces. Polo de Ondegardo (1940: 117), describing the barren *altiplano* of the southern Andes, puts it this way: "When they were settled in the cold lands, [they] distributed lands in the hot areas, even if it was far, and the Inca had Indians from each cold province placed there to harvest from the crops that grow there, and he ordered that the community send out to bring them back on their beasts of burden" [translation by Mayer]. Polo de Ondegardo, the lawyer and astute observer of how the customs of Indigenous groups (*fueros*) should be maintained to benefit themselves and Europeans, described in amazement how the people coming from the lowlands distributed maize in such a way that "not one of them is wronged (1916–1917: 156)." He mentioned that the *Collas* in the lowlands stayed down there for so long that they looked as if they were natives of the lowland regions (1916–1917: 156). And when crops in the highlands failed, most people left the *altiplano* "and stayed in the valleys for four or five months only to eat with their work, and were content to return well fed and with a couple of sacks of maize on the llamas that each one took down (1916–1917: 156)."[11]

Other chroniclers talk of the inter-ecological movement of goods but use such words as *contrataciones, compras, mercadurias,* or *rescate.*[12] There is a significant difference between regular trade between two ecological zones and colonization by one group in another's territory so that every household can obtain the necessary products from all the climatic zones. Since trade and colonization took place in the same geographical areas, we do need to know the mode of transaction that moved these goods. The discussion boils down to whether we can infer barter when the Spanish source uses words such as *rescate* or *contrataciones,* or whether colonization is implied when the word *mitimaes* is used. What are we to infer if these words were used interchangeably? Ramirez (1995b) argues that careless translations were made from native languages. An additional difficulty is that barter was a familiar institution to the Spanish, whereas colonization was not. It required greater sensitivity on the part of the Spanish observer, among whom Polo de Ondegardo (1940, 13: 145) really stands out. He is indeed clear:

Food was not bought with gold or silver; some coastal communities did barter for gold and silver with the foodstuffs they took to the highlands but on this almost all the old men agree that this was before the Inca conquered because afterwards there were few operations of this kind; and what there was, were exchanges like cotton cloth for wool or fish for other food. The first [presumably cloth] was among the chiefs as the common people only bartered food for food, in small quantities. [Translation by Murra.]

The best new sources are really the *visitas* of Garci Diez de San Miguel for Chucuito and Iñigo Ortíz de Zúñiga for Huánuco, published by Murra. They contain actual answers to specific questions. The only problem is that the material refers to the times that these *visitas* actually took place (1567 and 1562 in Chucuito and Huánuco, respectively) unless the respondents were specifically asked to talk about Inca times.

The *curaca*'s answers to a question on trade in Huánuco are fairly uniform, because the scribe wrote them down in formulaic summaries. For example, the text says that on January 3, 1662, Don Francisco Coñapariguana, Cacique of Guarapa, said

that in Inca times there were no large-scale merchants as there are among the Spaniards, but only Indians in the *tianguez* who sold each other only foods. And that clothing was not sold because everyone made those they needed and that the other items were in small quantities and that there were no rich men in merchandise. (Murra [ed.] 1972: 29)

In addition, the *visitas* are full of references that describe barter with people from other ethnic areas. The *curaca*'s testimony continues:

They have the Indians of Chinchacocha and the Yaros and the Yungas as their neighbors. And that they take to Chinchacocha and to the Yaros maize and beans and bring back wool, fish, dried meat, and llamas. And to those who are in the coca [regions] they take dried venison meat, freeze-dried potatoes and guinea pigs. And they bring back coca (*rescatando*) and for this coca they give salt, *ají* and cotton. (Murra [ed.] 1972: 58)

In the Village of Uchec the foreman said that they had enough land to grow their own cotton, but because they were so few, having been relocated back to the highlands after the collapse of the Inca, they no longer planted it; instead, they went to barter it among the people of the Pucaraes, a three-day walk (Murra 1967: 239). By 1562 it was already preferable to barter with other people for cotton than to produce it themselves. The document also gives ample information on colonization, sometimes in the very same areas and for the same products that are bartered (see Figure 2.1).

The *visita* of Chucuito by Garci Diez de San Miguel reveals the same pattern of colonization and barter existing side by side. An example of barter follows:

Figure 2.1 *Indios Ortelano, Pachacacuna. The man says to the woman: "Sister, let's have some coca." She responds: "Give it to me, brother." (From Guaman Poma de Ayala 1980: 811.)*

... [I]n this province the majority of the Indians normally go to Sama and Moquegua and to Capinota and to Cusco and Chuquiabo and other places which are temperate lands which are thirty to forty leagues from here for maize and *ají* and other products which do not grow in this province, and for this they take in *rescate* animals and cloth and wool and dried meat. (Murra [ed.] 1964: 208)

Combing through the *visita* testimonies, Carlos Sempat Assadourian (1995: 106–107) notes extended barter trips by *curacas* and also by commoners with large llama herds that covered the lake region, the long haul to Cusco, coca-growing areas, and areas within the Lupaqa Archipelago on the coast and jungle. By the time the inspection was being made, the people could already quote equivalencies for their barter transactions. They even noted that the equivalencies varied from year to year depending on whether the cropping season had been good or bad: "In times of hunger, one and a half *hanega* of maize for one llama, in times of good harvest, three *hanegas* for the same llama" (Murra [ed.] 1964: 120).

Evidence for colonization is also present in the document that mentions trade; consider, for example, the declaration of the Lupaqa lord, Don Martín Cari: "The principal *caciques* have maize lands in Moquegua and Sama, and in Capinota and Larecaja, and ... some Indians [also] have lands in these same places. In the lowland valley of Chicanoma, sixty leagues from here, they have a little coca that, in his opinion, yields between thirty and forty baskets (Murra [ed.] 1964: 17)." In the next sentence the nobleman says that most other people go to these areas to barter for their grains, taking along their pastoral products of animals, meat, and wool. Mary Van Buren (1996: 346), upon combing through this *visita,* has found forty-five statements on trade by highlanders for maize in the Arequipa lowlands but only a few direct colonization cases organized by "*Curacas* and a few *principales.*" And Assadourian (1995: 108) notes that the wealthy commoners could trade with their surplus wool and meat, whereas poorer highlanders merely went to work in the lowlands in order to get foodstuffs from the lower areas. Animal products were exchanged for maize, *ají* peppers, and "other things they do not have."

Assadourian also distinguishes interethnic trade, such as the exchange of salt between the Yacha, the Yaros, and the Chinchaycocha groups, from exchanges within the same ethnic group carried out between kinsmen. In addition, he notes that the Europeans' biases in formulating their questions, as well as their interests in finding out how commoners supported their leaders, lead to limitations in the available data that would otherwise allow us to understand exchanges among the commoners themselves. Although Assadourian did corroborate the existence of reciprocal labor exchanges between kinsmen, he could not confirm the same for exchanges of goods. In the light of my own contemporary data reported in Chapters 4 and 5, I heartily agree with Assadourian's (1995: 116) assessment of the situation in pre-conquest times: "I believe that reciprocity between related households involved exchange of goods, as well as labor exchange, but am not optimistic about finding data to confirm this." Unlike Assadourian, however, I believe that further diligent searching in other archives will eventually confirm his belief.

Thus there is no clear way to dismiss barter transactions altogether. The only possible conclusion is that, at the time of the *visitas,* peasant barter and colonization existed side by side. Nevertheless, it is possible to provide some tentative hypotheses about the relationship between barter and colonization. We are dealing with basic necessities of life here, not with sumptuous luxuries exclusive to nobles. Wool, meat, spicy peppers, and coca were basic items of consumption, although I am in agreement with Murra's (1960) interpretation that, for highlanders, these items (maize, cotton, salted fish, coca and for lowlanders, camelid wool, meat, and tallow) belonged to a special category of treats: foodstuffs that complemented a daily intake of rather bland starchy foods derived from potatoes and Andean tubers. We could imagine that these treats were consumed in greater proportions during ceremonial occasions and thus constituted the very items that marked hospitality, feasting, sociality, and generosity. The provision of such goods for a household was therefore an important social matter. We can also safely conclude that these consumption patterns endured over a very long time span, from pre-Inca to Inca and immediate post–European conquest times. The mutual dependence between lowlands and highlands, and among pastoralists, agriculturalists, and fishermen, was a factor always present in the history of Andean economies. Complementary products must have moved between the zones for long periods of time and over great distances, so perhaps the question about the modality of the exchange becomes less relevant when looked at through the *longue durée.*

One can envision situations in which people had to be extremely resourceful to satisfy their desires for these goods, even as the political and economic climate of their nations fell into profound crisis and the regular supply of the goods themselves began to falter. In the same vein, an absence of these amenities would have been perceived as a time of want, even if, in terms of calories, enough nutrition was available (an exception being the highland pastoralists, for whom maize was an absolute necessity). Such resourcefulness may explain the rapid rise of barter. Entrepreneurial exploitation of this demand among people through institutionalized generosity is indeed a resourceful invention. Another possible avenue for speculation concerns the quick decline of the Inca and *curaca* capacity to redistribute after conquest became a direct stimulus to venture into direct barter.

Some additional questions to be answered are these: What were the political requirements for interecological barter? Were they different from the political requirements for colonization? Based on available evidence, I cannot say that barter antedated colonization, or vice versa, but the chroniclers' reports and the detailed responses to the viceregal questionnaire suggest that both modes existed side by side—a pattern, I am willing to venture, also endured for a long time in the Andes. Barter transactions required less political centralization and social stratification, whereas colonization implied stronger political centralization than barter. Colonization was a more roundabout way of producing and distributing exotic goods than direct barter, and it provided more opportunities for accumulation and for leakage. Did such a system encourage theft and absconding? And, if so, how were such breaches of conduct punished?

We can also ask questions about who benefited from colonization. That the *curacas* achieved greater prestige and power through the greater availability of exotic products is obvious. How much of this amassed store did they distribute back to their common folks? Is it possible to find evidence that corroborates whether all those under chiefly control benefited equally or, in their eyes, deservedly? Susan Ramirez demonstrates how the *curacas* used such resources to exact more work, more prestations, and greater accumulation (1996: 18–26). But she also emphasizes that the *curacas* redistributed much or most for the benefit of all (1996: 22); indeed, she provides data showing that people tried to shift from a less generous *curaca* to one who provided more (Ramirez 1996: 24).

We can interpret colonization as attempts by the *curacas* to monopolize semi-luxuries in the same way and for the same reason that Incas monopolized luxuries: for greater political control. This explanation is consistent with Murra's argument that the Incas reworked local ethnic schemes on a larger state scale. But it relies on our acceptance of widespread and effective institutionalized generosity. Hawaiian "big men" (archetypes of redistributive chiefs) did run around in rags and lived in skimpy housing, because they gave everything away (Sahlins 1958), whereas Andean *curacas* appreciated finery and enjoyed sumptuous housing. Ramirez (1996: 25) notes, however, that the wealth in their wills was modest by Spanish standards. Has the idealization of the Inca king, so common in past scholarship, now been transferred to the ethnic *curacas*?

For that matter, did the *curacas* suppress peasants' independent bartering, or did they tolerate it? Murra (1956: 229) suggests that the emerging Inca state did suppress trade. Answers to this question hinge on information about the degree of *curaca* capability for monopolizing the redistribution of goods, which available data, at this stage, cannot easily provide. The coexistence of barter and direct colonization raises questions about how effective and extensive redistribution mechanisms were in satisfying every common household's needs. Van Buren's (1996: 346) recent review of the Chucuito material further concludes that "there is no evidence that they [*curacas*] redistributed lowland goods to the poor or for the benefit of the population as a whole." In the next chapter I present the case of Don Francisco Coñapariguana's chiefly household with an enhanced capacity derived from extra work and services it could cajole from commoner subject peoples as well as retainers. But he was not the near-exclusive supplier of appreciated goods such as coca and *ají* peppers to all his subject peoples. More selfish but still institutionalized *curaca largesse* would explain the coexistence of some kind of independent commoner access to these goods, side by side with colonization schemes organized by and for the benefit of *curaca* household enterprises. In such an interpretation, one could still underscore the principles of reciprocity and redistribution that underwrite the political leadership of these ethnic lords, but only by scaling down the coverage of how much they redistributed and how exclusively they controlled alternative means to obtaining these goods. If this is so, our understanding of the ethnic economy under *curaca* leadership achieves a more human and reasonable, albeit stratified, social scale.

A *curaca* household, then, would have been a larger and more diversified unit than a commoner's, able to mobilize some labor to distant zones and with an enhanced capacity to enlarge production within the home territory. Such a unit would have had more resources and higher consumption standards, and the surpluses it generated could have been distributed for more work. But all of this accumulation may have been much more self-serving to *curaca* interests than we would want to read into the data. From the perspective of a commoner household, coca, cotton fiber, dried fruits, and salt could still have been accessed primarily through direct exchange and occasionally through participation in the headman's labor projects and associated ceremonial festivities. Seen this way, a commoner does not willingly go to work for his headman because he expects to receive coca; he goes because he is obligated and punished if he does not.

Conceivably, however, a whole ethnic group could also have benefited from such a headman's colonizing venture. Colonization might have ensured a steadier or even greater supply of enjoyable consumer goods. And the pioneering presence of *curaca* colonization efforts could have encouraged other independent colonizers to settle there and to engage in autonomous exchanges, protected by the ethnic claim to lands negotiated or established by political authorities. Economists would label such an enclave as providing external economies of scale. In this interpretation, colonization might have encouraged an expansive barter that benefited all, rather than pitting the two models against each other.

In conclusion, the evidence is confusing. Small-scale interecological bartering and chiefly enterprises of colonization coexisted side by side, yet did not seem compatible with each other. Tentatively, Murra (1956, 1995) interprets interecological barter as a close alternative to colonization—one that is perhaps more advantageous to the common people. Extending this argument, I, too, could tentatively propose that, as the political and economic power of *curacas* increased, the centralizing and monopolizing flow of goods and services tended to suppress independent inter-household exchanges between ecological zones. When the political support that kept such a scheme in operation collapsed, the common people revived barter relations in the same areas where, before, colonization had been a convenient way to obtain these necessary semi-luxuries. According to the counterargument, which I favor, the *curacas* would have established colonies where barter networks had already established the possibility that such ventures would be successful.

The Growth of Trading in Colonial Times

The same argument accounts for the rapid, almost overnight appearance of traders, markets, and commerce from the earliest years of Spanish rule. Barter that coexisted at the margin of the Inca state and the ethnic economic system grew in importance precisely because the redistributive system had collapsed and alternative modes of behavior were readily available. The common people may have gained easier access to goods previously controlled and restricted through the political organization of the state and the ethnic group. Very often, Spaniards themselves filled this vacuum and become traders in Indian commodities, as Murra (1956: 232ff) astutely notes: "In fact, in post-Columbian times, the Europeans discovered this opportunity and went into the heathen seashell business on a large scale. . . . The same applies to cloth; by 1580 Lima was a center in the Indian cloth trade carried out by Europeans. . . ."

More cogently, Europeans traded extensively in coca (Gagliano 1994; Romano 1996). They also introduced wine and distilled alcohol as additional consumption items that became, together with the others, luxury items extensively used in what Eric Wolf (1966) has termed the ceremonial fund of every peasant household's consumption patterns. In the *visita* of Chucuito, the curacas' constant demand for the expulsion of the Spanish traders in their midst is very interesting. The Spanish traders should be expelled because they sold the people coca, wine, cloth, and other things on credit, which, the *curacas* allegedly insisted, the Indians did not need. They went on to denounce what to Indians appeared to be unethical European trading practices. Having sold items on credit, the traders then requisitioned llamas when the Indians were unable to pay, or sent them to jail. To people accustomed to the polite niceties of reciprocal exchange, the crude European notions of debt and default on payment as punishable crimes must have seemed very unfair.

Omitted from Don Martín Cari's statement is the fact that in colonial times, *curacas* also become active and interested traders in these commodities, and therefore came to regard the Europeans as vile competitors. Karen Spalding (1970, 1973) provides ample evidence of *curacas* acting as merchants, using resources and people based on their relationships with their subject people to engage in entrepreneurial activities. And when Roberto Choque (1987) delved into the dealings of his ancestor *curacas* in the Aymara territories, he found that they owned large herds, ceramic wine containers, coca baskets, warehouses, fisheries, *haciendas,* and fine town houses. Indeed, the rapid growth of the Potosí mines generated an enormous internal market that provided *curacas* with opportunities to become wholesalers of coca and wine.

Peasants, as well, quickly became involved in markets. By 1562, people in the Huánuco area were selling surplus maize in the mines (Murra [ed.] 1967: 104), hiring themselves out to work in those mines (Murra [ed.] 1967: 63), and acting as independent providers of services and labor in the city of Huánuco for money (Murra [ed.] 1967: 57; Assadourian 1995: 109–114). Their *curacas* found it more convenient to pay for items in the tribute list with cash than in kind (Murra [ed.] 1967: 57). The inspectors in that *visita* argued that the monetary part of the contribution owed as tribute should continue because this would discourage Indians from spending the money they earned in the city by forcing them to contribute it toward tribute (Murra [ed.] 1972: 266). The Spanish administrators, however, ruled in that case against this conversion, arguing that it was inconvenient because the city needed food. The Spanish administrators placed in the provinces to oversee the tribute system also became active entrepreneurs, selling goods to Indians whose welfare they were supposed to ensure.

The transition to a colonial economy involved the introduction of markets, the introduction of gold and silver as a medium of exchange and a standard of value, the creation of urban marketplaces as well as rural fairs, and the close regulation of market activities by the Spanish colonial administration. Historians, however, underscore the fact that, in the Spanish colonial economy, markets were subordinate to tribute, to the *encomienda* system, to the mines worked with tributary labor, and to the haciendas that grew crops with servile and slave labor. The economy relied on legal forms of coercion, rather than on market-derived incentives, to accumulate wealth for the colonists. These institutions required the market to convert the products into money wealth, but the markets were not the driving force behind the colonial economy. Merchants played a secondary role in the colony inasmuch as commerce was hampered by Spanish laws that reserved trading within its colonies to itself; nor were they an important social class, given their limited political clout and low status in society.

Olivia Harris (1995b) shows that market participation in the Andes has had a distinctive ethnic twist to it, restricting the Indian's participation in the market and distinguishing it from that of mestizos and Spaniards. Colonial regulations played an important role in this scenario, given that a tribute-owing vassal of the crown (so defined if a person's name was on a list of tribute-paying Indians) was different from a mestizo or Spaniard who was exempt from this tribute but paid taxes on the goods he transported each time he passed a customs house. Thus, although Indians participated as buyers and sellers of products in markets and fairs on a petty scale, the profession of merchant became associated with a mestizo ethnic status. Harris (1995b: 375) shows that, among other ironies, successful Indian merchants had to become mestizos in order to overcome the barriers to market participation. Despite important changes in colonial economies that, after independence, brought about a limited market expansion, ethnic divides characterize the Andean market and marketplaces even today. The historical legacy in the contemporary Andes of a market that is restricted, mercantilist, state controlled, nonexpansive, and ethnically differentiated is the crucial context in which subsequent chapters, especially 5, 6, and 7, develop themes that relate to market activities in relation to the articulated household.

The historical evolution of colonial market relations, however, falls beyond the scope of the present chapter. Recent studies have demonstrated that Indians did actively participate in colonial markets at all levels, as elites, commoners, and laborers. Land, labor, and products were bartered and bought and sold. These studies seek to demolish the commonly held myth that Indians were and are resistant to market participation, as Brooke Larson and Harris emphasize, respectively, in the introduction and conclusion of an excellent book on this topic (see Larson 1995). My chapter here contributes to the demolition of the anti-market myth by underscoring the fact that, before the European invasion, people knew how to trade and exchange goods, and that such exchange enlarged the capacities of the autonomous (not "self-sufficient," as we used to think) commoner ethnic economy that the Incas incorporated into their system.

Postscript

In 1972, even before I had defended my dissertation, I was hired by the *Pontificia Universidad Católica del Perú* in Lima to teach in the recently created M.A. program in anthropology. Faced with a dearth of reading material for our graduate students, the faculty created an editorial committee whose members were to publish select articles suitable for seminar use. Ignacio Prado Pastor offered his editorial skills to the creation of affordable manuals containing translations of articles by leading scholars such as Clifford Geertz and Victor Turner. I remember sitting in the patriarchal colonial house in downtown Lima of the illustrious Prado family under the dining room chandelier endlessly correcting page proofs. Although students in Peruvian universities used the manuals for classroom work, the intellectual impact of the series was negligible. For the course in economic anthropology that I taught, I selected two works by G. W. Skinner (1964, 1968) on market systems in China as well as Sydney Mintz's (1959) article on internal markets in the Caribbean. I also included a contribution of my own (Mayer 1974c), a term paper I had written in John Murra's seminar at Cornell in 1969.

Murra had suggested that I reevaluate the trade issue he raised in his dissertation in the light of new data available in the two *visitas*. But my term paper contained a defect: It presented an either/or option between verticality or barter, which the present chapter avoids. Only the barest skeleton of the original version remains in this chapter. It has been completely rewritten, and the interesting new research that has been accomplished since then has been incorporated.

Accordingly, this chapter serves as an introduction and guide to research into pre-Hispanic topics, as a summary of Murra's important work, and as background to Chapters 3, 4 and 5, which explore the contemporary uses of reciprocity, redistribution, and barter in the peasant economy. Without Murra's stimulus, I would not have studied reciprocity, nor would I have landed in Tangor, a village inspected in the Huánuco *visita* of 1562 and briefly visited in 1965 by John Murra, César Fonseca, Craig Morris, and Ramiro Matos. This rewrite illuminates the influence Murra had on my intellectual development. It also gives autonomous exchanges of goods in pre-colonial societies a little more prominence than they normally get in assessments of Murra's work. In this way, I am able to contribute to an understanding of the Inca economy by focusing on the less visible, less public economic exchanges in pre-Columbian economies.

Notes

1. Rowe (1946) wrote a historical account of the Incas at the time of the Spanish conquest for the *Handbook of South American Indians*, and Zuidema (1990) contributed with a structuralist interpretation of Inca kinship, mythology, cosmology, ritual, ceremony of the royal lineages, religious cults, and organization of the city of Cusco, the capital of the empire.

2. For Murra, the term *lo Andino* emphasizes the study of those structural and organizational ways in which Indigenous peoples' continuous resistance to maintain their own culture is constantly reelaborated and, even with obvious syncretism, does not lose its unity and coherence. Not all situations of Andean resistance were successful in the light of crushing colonial destructuring. Critics in Latin America from both sides of the political spectrum accused Andeanists of promoting a false archaization or, worse, finding reasons for the modern world not to intervene in changing the abject conditions of poverty and domination of contemporary Indians. Archaeologist Van Buren (1996) is critical of Murra's use of *lo Andino* since, she points out, it is derived from another European source—namely, Polanyism—thus again incurring a Eurocentric interpretation of Andean institutions. While it is true that some Polanyism creeps into Murra's work, Van Buren's reading of Murra's Andeanism tries much too hard to shoehorn a political platform

72 REDISTRIBUTION AND TRADE IN INCA SOCIETY

into easily operationalizable intellectual concepts. Andeanism has also been criticized by Starn (1992a, 1992b), but he ignored the political intent that Murra gave the term; nor does he cite Murra. Instead Starn focused exclusively on a U.S. version of exotic cultures, ignoring the fact that the debate within the Andean republics had predated his critiques and had taken a turn decidedly different from his own. Reactions to Starn's argument have been sharp (see Mayer 1992 and Roseberry 1995), and many scholars have commented on both the Spanish-language version of Starn's (1992b) article in the Peruvian journal *Allpanchis* and the English-language one in *Current Anthropology* (1994). Recently, Starn (1999: 19–25) recapitulated his position, acknowledging his excesses but also reaffirming himself where he considers his position to be correct.

3. Comparing Incas to communists in the 1920s did not necessarily follow a Marxist analysis; but the Inca case also interested later European Marxist scholars—notably Godelier (1977), who, in summarizing Murra's work, used the case to illuminate the relationship between mode of production and economic and social formations, two important Marxist concepts.

4. A combination of Murra's ideas expressed in his dissertation, in articles he subsequently published, and in his "verticality hypothesis," which came out in 1972—together with the injunction to search for an Andean civilization different and un-European—form a coherent paradigm that stimulated a generation of scholars. A brief guide to Murra's bibliography follows: His 1956 University of Chicago dissertation, "The Economic Organization of the Inca State," was translated into Spanish in 1978. A collection in Spanish, *Formaciones económicas y políticas del mundo andino* (1975), includes twelve articles originally written in English, Spanish, or both, after the dissertation including the one on "verticality." Important papers after the 1975 collection include those published in 1981 (on demography and politics), 1982 (on *mita*), 1984 (summary and bibliographical essay), 1985 (on the limits of verticality), 1986b (on armies, wars, and rebellions), and 1995 (on markets). Murra edited three *visitas* (1964, 1967/1972, 1991), each of which contains interpretative articles by Murra and his colleagues. The clearest discussion of Karl Polanyi's influence on Murra's work, with presentations, discussants, and comments by Murra, is Dalton (1981: 38–69). With Rolena Adorno, Murra published an authoritative version titled *El Primer Nueva Corónica y Buen Gobierno por Felipe Guaman Poma de Ayala* (Guaman Poma de Ayala 1980). Murra and Barralt (1996) is an edition of Murra's correspondence with José María Arguedas. Autobiographical interviews with Murra can be found in Rowe (1984) and Castro (2000); the latter contains a curriculum. And, finally, Henderson and Netherly (1993) published a *Festschrift*.

5. *Corvée*, a French word derived from Latin, denotes the requisitioning of unpaid labor.

6. *Prestation*, a term derived from French, is used by Mauss (1954: 3) to describe an exchange. Mauss linked it to another concept as well: that of total phenomena, whereby each social phenomenon contains all the threads of which the social fabric is composed. According to him, total prestations form systems in which groups and not individuals carry on the exchange. The persons represented in the contracts are moral persons; they exchange not only goods and wealth but also courtesies, entertainment, ritual, military assistance, women, children, dances, and feasts. And

finally, although prestations take place under voluntary guise, they are in essence strictly obligatory, and their sanction is private or open warfare.

7. I refer here to the lowly *gim wali,* not to the high-status *kula* of the Trobrianders (Malinowski 1932: 189–190).

8. One manifestation of the hunger for gold involved digging for treasure in temples and graves under license from the crown. Ramirez (1996: 121–151) tells a fascinating adventure story of Alonso Zarco, a poor urban outcast Spaniard who befriended Indians and got them drunk, whereupon they revealed where their ancestors were buried. Ultimately, Zarco lost his treasure to other covetous Spaniards.

9. Archaeologist Timothy Earle (1985: 389) attempted to ask questions about changes in trade over a longer time span than archival sources permit. He worked in the Mantaro Valley in Central Peru. In chronologically separate Huanca II (Late Intermediate A.D. 1250–1460) and Huanca III (Late Horizon 1460–1532 Inca) phases, he notes, there "is a clear lack of evidence for increasing regional and long-distance exchange following Inca Conquest."

10. *Mitimaes* were people removed from their home bases by the Incas and placed in foreign territories, notably to act as stabilizing elements in the conquest process. Murra (1972) argues that the local ethnic practice of placing colonists is the antecedent of the state version.

11. See Assadourian (1995) on stratification and trade in the *altiplano* of Polo's and *visita* times.

12. Ramirez (1982: 132) provides the most careful analysis of how to translate the following words from colonial Spanish. *Contrataciones* (contracts as well as commerce of movable goods), *compras* (purchases), *mercadurias* (merchandise), *rescate* (to ransom, redeem, recover, extricate, barter, exchange, commute—and, in Spanish American, to buy ore in the mines).

3

A Tribute to the Household:
Domestic Economy and the
Encomienda in Colonial Peru

*This chapter tells the story of how a household paid tribute in
the sixteenth century. It describes both the continuities and the
sharp disjunctions in the transition from the Inca to the colonial
tributary system. Analysis of tribute obligations and what
households have to do to comply with them is the point of departure here for understanding the household in a holistic way.*

In this chapter I attempt to provide an ethnographic reconstruction of a
group of households in rural sixteenth-century Peru—the reverse of
"model building." Toward this end I have used John V. Murra's superb
work on Andean political and socioeconomic structures (summarized in
Chapter 2) as a model for gaining an understanding of the daily events and
concerns of those people who were the participants and routine practitioners from whose actions and behavior the model was originally abstracted.

In the first part of the chapter the viewpoint of a common peasant, Don
Agostín Luna Capcha (who did exist and whose testimony is known), is
expressed as he thinks about the testimony he is about to give during a
visita. The administration and organization of his time and efforts (and
those of his wife), along with the resources that he will need in order to
produce or acquire the many items he is forced to give in tribute, concern
him. His domain is his home, and in order to administer it, he thinks about
work. Because the economy is embedded in society and household matters,
his thoughts about work lead him to consider domestic affairs, family and
kinship matters, and village as well as regional affairs that affect him.

Having provided a "substantive" (Karl Polanyi's term) and meaningful
insight into the operation of one such household, the chapter moves on to

analyze variations in types of households at the time and place in question, differences in household composition, and the processes that account for these differences. I rely on ethnographic analogy here, because I conducted an ethnographic study of the village of Tangor (spelled "Tancor" in the sixteenth century) in the Chaupiwaranga region, the headwaters of the Huallaga River in the Huánuco region. Tancor was the residence of Agostín Luna Capcha (Mayer 1974a). I have tried to flesh out and fill in where the historical data are skimpy. My purpose is to illustrate, give meaning to, and allow the reader to understand a group of people who were struggling to survive in a remote period of time and in a distant land.

There is a second purpose to this chapter. The events related here took place in 1562, only thirty years after the European invasion. It was a period of flux and change. By reversing the process of generalization—that is, by particularizing situations—I was able to focus on social change and the meaning of that change to these people. The Spanish institution of the *encomienda* (a group of Indians given by royal grant to a Spaniard) provides the chapter's context. The *encomienda* in this case is that of Juan Sánchez Falcón, of Huánuco, who was given the privilege of collecting tribute from the Indians who were granted to him. His *encomienda* included about four hundred households of Yacha (a small ethnic group) and *mitimae* (a group of Cusco people brought by the Incas to man fortresses in conquered territory).[1]

In order to collect the tribute, Sánchez Falcón was bound to the application of the old Andean institutionalized processes and mechanisms that the Inca and the local ethnic lords had been using to extract revenues from the agricultural peasant population. Despite the total crisis that the European presence wrought among these people, conditions were such that past economic institutions continued to exist. At the same time, the old procedures—when applied to benefit the new masters, whose purposes were very different—transformed these institutions in terms of the way they functioned and were perceived. The aim of this chapter is to describe these transformations and their implications for the peasant household. Because the institutions changed, their meaning altered; because the legitimacy of their operation was questioned, the whole system was challenged. The *curacas* of the area commissioned Hernando Malquiriqui of Chacapampa to travel to Lima and appeal to the viceroy to have the tribute level lowered. And so the legal proceedings were initiated.

The judicial instrument used by the Spaniards in such situations was the *visita*. This involved house-by-house and village-by-village inspections intended to determine the validity of claim and counterclaim, followed by recommendations made to the viceroy, who then would rule on the matter. In 1972 John Murra republished the *visita* under discussion, along with other pertinent documents and essays, as volume 2 of the *Visita de la Provincia de León de Huánuco en 1562* (Murra [ed.] 1967–1972). The rich source material contained in this and other such bureaucratic documents published in the last decades has played an important role in shedding new light on pre-colonial society.[2] Volume 2 of this *visita* constitutes my main data source and analytical focus.

The study of the *encomienda* is one instance in which we can look at the articulation of different but linked economic systems. The *encomendero* used ancient Andean institutions to obtain goods that he then sold through the extensive commercial networks that began to develop to support the mining and urban economy of the Spaniards. With respect to his subjects the *encomendero* was manipulating the strings of a peasant-based, pre-capitalist economy, whereas in his dealings with other Spaniards, he behaved as a profit-seeking merchant trying to sell his goods at the best going price in order to gain the highest monetary return. Historian Rolando Mellafe (1967: 338) expresses this duality as follows:

> These documents are the result of three completely different currents; one derived from the forms and ways in which in pre-Hispanic times the Indians worked and complied with their tribute obligations; another current derived from the needs and exactions of their *encomenderos* and *caciques;* and the third current has to do with the exclusive relationship of the crown with the political economy of its territories and its protectionist efforts toward its Indian populations, expressed primarily in the crown's intervention in matters like fixing the tribute rate that the *encomenderos* were allowed to garner. [Translated by Mayer.]

The historical period that produced the *visita*, about midway between its inception and its deemphasis and eventual liquidation, is also the period in which the crown began more and more to interfere with and direct the fate of *encomiendas*. Martha Anders (1990: 20–21), in a masterful summary of the evolution of the institution of the *visita*, describes how it reflects on aspects of the conflicts among the crown, the *encomenderos,* and the Indians. The crown feared the growing power and independence of the *encomenderos*, worried about the loss of direct income that deviation of services and tribute to *encomenderos* implied, and expressed concern about the irreparable damage they were causing among native populations— partly in response to critiques in Spain, but also because the crown realized that overburdening the Indian subjects was killing the goose that laid the golden eggs. In its attempts to control *encomenderos*, the crown needed to determine the capacity of the Indians to pay tribute and to regulate personal services Indians owed the *encomendero*.

The Toledan reforms that began in 1570 radically altered Andean social institutions, changed tribute to a head tax to be paid to the crown (although for a long time the Indians were paying tribute to both crown and *encomendero*), and, through *reducciones*, drastically reordered the relations of the villagers. After the Toledan reforms many of the institutional continuities that had originated in Inca society were abruptly cut off.

Saturday, February 14, 1562

After an all-night rain, the dawn was cloudy. The residents of Tancor went about their usual tasks, even though they were conscious of new and strange masters who spoke a different tongue, rode horses, and wore armor. War had come, and they had been defeated. The new Spanish city, León de Huánuco, was located in the big valley below. Indeed, many economic, social, and political relationships were now oriented toward the lowlands, whereas only thirty years before, their former Inca masters had dominated them from the highlands.

As the sun began heating the valley, the mists drifted upward past the settlements of Wangrin and Wakan, and the lower parts of the narrow ravine of the Colpas River became visible from Tancor. Then the villagers saw them: A party of horsemen followed by carriers on foot was slowly climbing the hill. It was the feared inspection party of the Spaniards and their own headmen, the *curacas*. By noon they would arrive in the village.

From the moment the inspection party was sighted, all normal activities in the village stopped. After a moment of panic, the rhythm of activities changed drastically. Many youths grabbed warm clothing, food, and coca and fled the village to hide in the mountains and in caves as far from pathways and settlements as possible. Women secreted food and possessions. While lighting the fires to cook the welcome meals, they nervously rehearsed the prayers and gestures that the new priests required them to adopt. Children were distributed among different households and instructed not to betray their parents' location. The old *quipucamayoc* limped into his hut to get his colored knotted strings and started fingering them, remembering, as each knot passed through his fingers, what had been committed to memory for each. At the last moment the Tancor headman, who carefully noted the hurried rearrangements of normal family life into these newly constituted households, and who remembered to "forget" the existence of the youths who had vanished into thin air, realized that no fodder had been prepared for the horses of the Spaniards. He also had neglected to warn the next village that it would be inspected after Tancor. Later he would regret this omission, for his kinsman, Don Antonio Pumachagua, headman of Guacor, was caught unprepared. That is why Don Antonio bumbled his oral account and was publicly whipped and punished because "he had lied in his testimony."[3] Once, long ago, the Tancor headman also had been tied and beaten with a stone on the back, that time by the Inca inspectors, when they caught him covering for youths who were evading the levy of able-bodied men for the *mit'a* tribute (p. 54).

By the time the visiting party—the *visitador* (Iñigo Ortiz de Zúñiga), the *encomendero* (Juan Sánchez Falcón), their legal representatives, the scribe, the Greek translator (Gaspar de Rodas), and their own *curaca* (Don Juan Chuchuyaure) as well as soldiers, priests, and carriers—had arrived, a false appearance of normalcy had been restored to the village (pp. 10–23). While the ceremonial greetings were taking place and the party was settling down, the *encomendero* looked around suspiciously. He was convinced that many of the people he owned by a grant from the king were hiding to escape being counted: Their absence would diminish the tribute he would be able to collect. He would keep his eyes open to catch these shifty Indians, particularly that man he had seen before, the potter Agostín, whom he remembered as a potential troublemaker. Today's inspection would be thorough indeed.

Each additional able-bodied man counted would bolster the *encomendero*'s argument that these Indians could pay the original tribute level that he had been authorized to collect thirteen years ago and that the Indians were appealing as too heavy a burden. He needed to win the suit brought against him, as the tribute these Indians were giving him was necessary to enlarge his already-thriving business. It was, after all, worth the discomfort of traveling so far into the interior to ensure success.

The Testimony

Dijo llamarse Agostín Luna Capcha de treinta y cinco años (p. 82). (He says that he is called Agostín Luna Capcha, thirty-five years old.)

I was born in the time of the Incas, though, since my youth, I have heard and seen aspects of Christian and Spanish ways. Occasionally I have been taught the catechism, I have seen the use of money, escaped being shot when I participated in the big rebellion of Inca Illa Thupa twenty years ago that forced the Spaniards to withdraw from the fortress of Huánuco Pampa (Varallanos 1959: 119–123; Murra 1975: 186), and watched how, with depressing regularity, their armies have looted the storehouses of the Incas, of the sacred *huacas* (p. 57), and of the villages. There have been years of famine.

Y su mujer se llama Inés Quispe de treinta y cinco años (p. 82). (And his wife is called Inés Quispe, thirty-five years old.)

My wife was born and raised in Tancor. So was I, but because my forefathers were placed here in the time of the Incas as potters, I am a Caurino (p. 81). Even though I am not one of them, Inés's parents agreed to the marriage because her older and younger brothers had died, so they had a shortage of hands to work the lands. Now we have children.

Tiene dos hijas y un hijo que se llama Catalina Chacara de cinco años, otro que se llama Felipe Guaya de cuatro años, otra que se llama Barbora Vica

de dos años (p. 82). (He has two daughters and one son called Catalina
Chacara, five years old, Felipe Guaya, four years old, and Barbora Vica,
two years old.)

*Dan marido y mujer una pieza de ropa de algodón y para ello les da su en-
comendero el algodón* (p. 82). (Husband and wife give one piece of cotton
cloth, and for this the *encomendero* supplies the cotton.)

Oh, this horrible business of weaving! It never ends. My wife's hands
keep turning the spindle to make all the thread. The cotton that the *encomendero's* henchmen give us is of lousy quality—wild cotton, hard to
take the pips out, difficult to spin, and never enough. I am sure that he
cheats us. Were it not for our neighbor, the tile maker, who has to go to
town to pay his tribute in labor at the *encomendero's* house (p. 80), and
who barters chickens and *chuño* for extra cotton, we could never fulfill our
quota (p. 58). Sometimes I am so tired that I fall asleep at the backstrap
loom. But I have to keep weaving, for it is necessary to have enough clothing for myself and my family, quite apart from the beautiful piece that we
burn as part of our sacrifice at the annual ceremony. I hope that the inspector does not find out that I actually weave more than I said, one for my
own quota, another for my father-in-law (p. 120), and the third for the *curaca*. Weaving never ends. What does the *encomendero* do with so much
cloth? My ancestor once came back from serving the Inca in the army
wearing a beautiful woven piece given him by the Inca (Murra 1975: 158).
Now we all dress in rags and still keep weaving. The Spaniards must eat
the cloth that we all weave.

Dijo que da seis tomines al año (p. 82). (He says that he gives six *tomines*
per year.)

Six *tomines* in cash I am to give! Sometimes I give it and at others I
don't. When I go to León to work as a water carrier or take things to sell,
I have money (p. 63); and when there is no other debt, I give it to Don
Pablo Almerco, my headman, on account of my obligation of the six
tomines (p. 129). Six *tomines*, almost one peso—so hard to gather the
coins. When I cannot complete it, I have to make it up to him in other
ways. When he asks me, I work for him, and when there is a feast, I bring
food, and we help in cooking and serving; but of these and other things we
do not keep account (p. 161). I hear it said that Don Pablo has many dealings and much money. He always says how he pays all our obligations in
silver, so it must be that way. Who knows? I could go to the mines to earn
more *tomines* (p. 120), but the work is too hard, so I will not go. This silver is an amazing thing. If I could only find out how to get more of it.

Y dijo que da una gallina al año (p. 82). (And he says that he gives one
chicken per year.)

Chicken for the *encomendero;* chicken for getting cotton; chicken for food; chickens got killed today to feed the soldiers; chickens get into the maize; chickens make noise in the morning; chickens lay big eggs; chickens don't fly; chickens live in the house instead of in the wild; chickens eat left-overs; chickens shit all over my weavings; chickens scratch in the yard. Damned chickens!

Dijo este indio [que es] con los de Chacapampa (p. 82). (This Indian says that he is with those from Chacapampa.)

I am from the section of Caure people who live in Chacapampa, and that is where my labor tribute, my communal *mit'a*, is accounted for, and it is for my headman, Don Pablo, that I work, not for the one over here. Not that there is no land in Chacapampa (p. 81); with so many people dying off there is plenty of land around all over, but the maize in Tancor tastes so much better and produces more and is less risky. People here make fun of me and call me a *marka masha* (a brother-in-law of the village), because of my marriage, and make me do all the menial things in the ceremonies to drive home the point that I am an outsider. But, then, they trust me, too, because I am a little removed from them. They come individually and ask me favors and entrust me with important missions. By living here, I avoid all those obligations from my own kinsmen, who would have to come here to ask me. I can also avoid the obligations of the Tancorinos, if I find this convenient, because they are not my kin but my wife's. Still, I have to do so much weaving and work for my father-in-law that I often wonder if things would have been easier if I were living with my own people.

Y que con los de Chacapampa hace para el tributo chacaras de maíz y pa-pas en las tierras de Chacapampa (p. 82). (And with those from Chaca-pampa he makes for tribute potato and maize fields in Chacapampa lands.)

Chacapampa is northwest of here, and they get the rains earlier than we do; so they are always a few weeks ahead of Tancor in producing these foods. I have to find out when the headman and the community decide to start the *chacmeo*, the breaking of the ground with our footplows, and when I know the day, I go one or two days in advance to stay with my kinsmen. I bring the food gifts from here, since they like the squashes and *numia* beans that grow so well in this area.

When I arrive in Chacapampa, I visit my *curaca*, who comes down from Caure for the *chacra jitay* ceremony, and I usually have my piece of fine cloth ready for him so that he can use it for ceremony.[4] He wears his new cloth during the ceremony, and he looks so dignified when he sits with the village elders using coca and deliberating over which sector of land should be assigned for this year's potato crop. Each year a new sector as big as half a hillside is opened and left to begin its fallow for several years. Once they decide on which sector to work, Don Pablo and the elders of the community set aside land for the *encomendero*'s tribute, for the church tithes, for themselves, and for the people too old to work it themselves. After that, Pablo Amerco assigns land to all the families in the community for their food. Although I am present, they do not give me land to work, because I have enough in Tancor. Then we make up the teams that will work, and, praying and dancing, we begin to work the lands for tribute, for the church, and for the *curaca*, as well as for the elderly. There is music and drink and food.

The teams of plowmen race each other to see who can finish first their assigned task of breaking the ground of a whole field with their footplows. The women encourage us with songs and drink. When we have finished our section, we get another one assigned. At the end of the day the teams that have worked the most sections are honored and the others taunted. Chacapampa's way of working is different from how they do it in Tancor, because here, once you finish your assigned section, you have completed your task for the day and can rest. It takes more days to get the work done in Tancor. That is why my own kinsmen say that Tancor people are lazy. Usually we complete all the plowing of the higher-lying (*jalka*) and lower-lying (*kichwa*) fields in two days.[5] Starting high, we finish working near the village settlements.

After that I return to Tancor while the people of Chacapampa continue helping each other break the ground of their individually allotted fields. This is, of course, the time I use to work on my wife's assigned fields in Tancor, after the Tancor people have had their own land-distribution ceremony.

When the rainy season stops and the dry season has passed and the new rainy season is about to begin again, it is time for me to go back to Chacapampa to plow the furrows and plant the tubers. And when the people in Chacapampa have finished planting their own fields, I go back, because it is time to start to plant maize for tribute. That feast is even nicer than the *chacra jitay* for potatoes. We eat corn foods, and there is so much *chicha* distributed that we all get drunk. When that is finished, I have to come back to Tancor to plow and sow my father-in-law's field and carry him home after the day's work, because he is so happy that he has had his corn planted.[6]

When I was a young man and unmarried, I had to spend a lot of time keeping the fields clear of birds. All of us still have obligations to fulfill beyond the actual plowing and planting (p. 78). But now that I live in Tancor, I have thus far been exempt from these time-consuming tasks. At least Don Pablo has not yet approached me for any of these tasks, which I'd have to do for a whole year in Chacapampa, and I do not think that he will. In Tancor perhaps I will have to accept one of these tasks, since this is where I live.

So I return to Chacapampa quite often, after planting maize, to hill the potatoes and, after that, to weed and cultivate the corn, and then comes the second hilling of the potatoes, of the *ocas* and *mashuas* and *ollucos* and so on, until harvest time. Chacapampa is where I pay my tribute obligations together with my Chacapampa people.

De [estas tierras de maíz y papas] pagan lo que les cabe de tributo (p. 82). (From these lands they pay what they have to for tribute.)

There are two different groups (*parcialidades*) of people living in Chacapampa: those who pay their tribute to Gonzalo Tapia (pp. 123–128), and those of us who belong to Pablo Almerco, who lives in Caure. We give seven *fanegas* of maize (though four of them he commuted for extra pieces of cloth) and two *fanegas* of potatoes, all out of our communal work (p. 128). What is left over we take to sell at the mines of Corco and the *tambo* of Chuquiguamisca and other places. Some of the surplus also goes for *camarico* of the *encomendero*'s servants (p. 128). (*Camarico* means "something done in favor of he who is absent in *mit'a* obligation, contribution of food for those who could not cultivate, gifts" [Guaman Poma 1980: 1083].)

The tribute has to be delivered in Huánuco at the *encomendero*'s house (p. 129). Because our llamas have been killed in all the wars, every year we have to carry more and more of the loads on our backs. This is the hardest part of our tribute work. Carrying our own food makes the task twice as hard. My parents tell me that when they carried loads for the Inca, along the way to Quito and Cusco (p. 55), they were fed by him. It takes four to five days to get the caravan bearers from here to Huánuco. When we get there we are very tired.

Dijo que se ocupa con los de Chacapampa dos semanas en las chacaras de Pitomama de su encomendero (p. 82). (He says that he occupies himself with the Chacapampa people two weeks in the fields of Pitomama that are his *encomendero*'s.)

These maize fields of the *encomendero* are one league from Huánuco, and all of Don Pablo Almerco's people from Caure and Chacapampa as well as Gonzalo Tapia's people from Chacapampa are responsible for the production of six *fanegas* of maize (here, a *fanega* is a unit of land rather than a measured volume of products). I have to go and plant and harvest with the married adult men and spend two weeks and four days at it (p. 129), and the old men who can still walk, as well as women, boys, and girls from Chacapampa and Caure, go to weed and cultivate the fields, and that takes two weeks (p. 129). The poor people of Gonzalo hate going there because it takes so much time, and they have to weave even more than we do! (p. 124). That man Juan Sánchez Falcón gets maize and potatoes not only from our own communal fields but also from his lands that we have to work.

Dijo que le cabe dos meses al año de servir con los de Chacapampa a su encomendero en Huánuco en traer leña y yerba y aderezar la cequia del molino y algunas paredes cuando se lo manda (p. 82). (He says that he is obligated to serve for two months with the people of Chacapampa at the *encomendero*'s in Huánuco, bringing firewood and fodder and cleaning the canal of the water mill and repairing some walls when he is ordered to do so.)

For two months I have to be his servant in his house! As long as I can plan ahead when it is that I have to go, it is all right. But when I am ordered to go without warning, then problems arise. My fields get neglected, I fall behind in my weaving, and I do not find the time to work as a water carrier. For me it is most convenient to go after the harvests here in Tancor and Chacapampa, but so far I have had to go at all other times and at short notice. When we are in Huánuco we are treated like prisoners. They lock us up at night and feed us little, so that actually we have to bring some of our own food. At least lately, the *encomendero*'s *mayordomo* has started giving us a little bit of coca. His horses, mules, and cows eat so much grass, and we have to carry it on our backs from far away.

Y que no se lo paga el encomendero y que no sabe si es obligado a ello o no (p. 82). (And that his *encomendero* does not pay him and he does not know whether he is obligated to do so according to the tribute assessment or not.)

It is not fair! When I work in Huánuco as a water carrier I get paid, and when I work in his mansion carrying grass I do not get paid! . . . I do as I am told.[7]

Y dijo que se ocupa cinco meses en todo lo que trabaja y hace para el tributo no entendiendo otra cosa (p. 82). (And he says that it takes him five months to do all that he works and makes for tribute without seeing to other things.)

Sure! I spend almost half a year working for the *encomendero*, although it seems to me that it is all the time. Take spinning. My wife and I spin all the time, whenever our hands are free. In this way it takes two months to spin the raw cotton into yarn and another ten days to respin it after it has been dyed. Two days to dye it, if you do not count all the time spent in collecting the firewood necessary to boil the dye. Then one day to make the warp. Ten days to weave, if I have time to do it continuously. Usually I have to do it on three or four separate occasions, because I have to do this and that in the village, or in Chacapampa, or in Huánuco, before finishing it. Time spent on actually weaving and preparing the materials is one thing; the time elapsed from the beginning of the process to the end is another.

Working in Chacapampa, counting the days coming and going, comes to another month to get the tribute crops produced (two days for *chacmeo*, two for hilling and likewise for second hilling, two for harvest, and two for carrying the crops from the fields to the village makes about ten days). Calculate the same time for the maize crop, and that makes twenty days. Then there are eight days of carrying the crops to the *encomendero*'s house and coming back. Two months of *mit'a* at the *encomendero*'s, two weeks at the Pitomama fields. Who calculates the time it takes to earn the *tomines?* Even without this, it comes to more than five months!

But this is really a stupid way to ask the question. I spend about half of my waking time working for the *encomendero*, and he gets much more out of all the work than I myself get when I work the other half for my own things. He can use our different kinds of labor power in different ways. He can disperse us and make us work at home during part of the day at spinning or weaving while we are technically "off duty" to look after our own crops and affairs. He even benefits from our leftover food by making us give him chicken. Alternatively, he can pool all our separate household labor capabilities to work one large field in Chacapampa per year for potatoes and one corn field. He gains even more from us by rotating all of Pablo Almerco's and Gonzalo Tapia's people in Pitomama to get a constant supply of workers for his fields. Though I go to his house only for two months, he has servants all year round. The cotton that his other Indians grow in Huánuco (p. 228) he gives back to us to spin and weave into cloth, and because he gives us the cotton, we have to give more cloth (p. 159). We work the fields of his tile makers, herders, and so on, when they are too busy to do so for themselves. Throughout the year we work in combination on our own subsistence and on the tribute tasks. This way, any task that would take us half the time, because we need less, now fills our days and weeks and tires us out. Every task we do gets intensified through tribute.

Y que lo hace descansadamente cuando no le dan prisa para la ropa, y cuando se la dan, aún no puede hacer su vestido ni el de su mutjer ni de sus hijos (p. 82). (And that he does it at his own restful pace when they do not press him for the cloth, and when they do, he does not have the time even to make his own clothing nor that of his wife or his children.)

It really is a question of timing and how I can distribute my time. If the *encomendero* wants his cloth and wants me to serve in his house in Huánuco during the rainy season, when I am supposed to look after my fields, then it is much harder to comply. But if he lets me assign my own work in such a way that all the tasks get evenly distributed throughout the year, then the tax burden is more manageable for me and my wife.

For instance, when we work our fields, she has to cook for all the people coming to the work party. This means that all the ingredients have to be prepared well in advance, and the firewood collected, and the helpers she needs have to be spoken for; and if there is going to be *chicha*, one really has to calculate weeks ahead. I have to go and collect the firewood; it has to dry; and then the preparations take a week in order for the corn to germinate and the *chicha* to ferment properly. So even if the actual plowing takes only a day or two, if I am not able to be busy those days before my field gets plowed, it is a disaster. To calculate only two days to plow is wrong anyway, even if one disregarded the extra days of preparation. For every helper who comes to work in my field, I have to return the working day in full. And until they ask me, I have to be living in the village, waiting during the whole plowing season, even though I am not actually working the whole extent of the season.

When outsiders begin organizing our lives, it costs us much more to provide the same amount of tribute. This *encomendero* is so demanding that we have to comply, and, out of fear of punishment, we tend to think that his work is more important. What should be more important—our own subsistence—becomes relegated to second priority until we have completed our obligations. By the time we have done so, we are tired, our resources are exhausted, and so we tend to skimp on the work required for the satisfaction of our needs. The drudgery of working for our own needs is thus increased.

Since the coming of the *encomendero*, our resources have changed, but the *tasa* ("rate") has remained the same. The fact that the people are fewer than before and more diseased (p. 86) means that fewer households have to work harder to maintain the same production levels. But it is not only that; other kinds of resources have also changed. For instance, in Caure there is no cotton; the climate is too cold for it to grow. Before the Spaniards came, the Caure people had cotton lands in the lowlands, which they have now lost; so now the *encomendero* supplies the cotton, and because of that, the levy of woven cloth doubles (p. 123). The *mitimaes* of Ananpillao have their own cotton fields, so they give fewer pieces of cloth. If you calculate the work in producing the cotton, it still comes to less than the extra weaving that we have to do (p. 239).

Because our resources are changing, and the *encomendero*'s tastes are different, matters get more complicated. We Caure people have a substantial amount of pasture; therefore, we are supposed to give six sheep per year to the *encomendero* for each of the important Catholic festivals that he and his retinue celebrate. But we have not had much luck in raising the Castilian sheep, and there are too few of them in the pastures. So, instead, Caure people now give eighteen and one-half pieces of cloth, with the *encomendero* supplying the cotton (p. 159). Just imagine the increased amount of work that all that extra weaving implies for us.

Substitutions in the items of our *tasa* can work in our favor, too. For example, in Quiu, the village on the other side of the valley, there is a famous rebellious old man, Alonso Alcachagua, still not a Christian, who spins five extra balls of *cabuya* string in lieu of the two pesos he is supposed to pay (p. 76). Don Juan Chuchuyaure, the head *curaca* of all us Yachas, is asking the *encomendero* to substitute a cash payment for the heavy burden of supplying maize (p. 57). There is internal substitution, too. When I get sick and cannot work for a long time, I talk to my *curaca*, and he may excuse me; but then he has to shift my obligation to other families, since it is clear that the *encomendero* will have no mercy on the *curaca* who is responsible for the delivery of the whole amount (p. 56), and he does not care how the items are collected among ourselves.

There is inequality in the distribution of work, too. My neighbor, the tile maker, is an *indio oficial*, a full-time specialist. He has to make tiles for the *encomendero* all year round, because in the time of the Incas, we were the potters placed here because of the clay. Now the old man has finished working for the *encomendero* and is in Tancor, but he has left his son, who has learned the trade, as his replacement. The old man used to come to Tancor two months out of the year to plant his own fields (p. 81). At times he was too busy even to spare time for that, and Don Pablo had fields worked for him in Chacapampa by all of us. Although the old man has less independence, he has narrower and more specialized tasks to fulfill, at which he spends more time than we do. Juan Perico Quispecoro is completely exempt from tribute. He is the *yanacona* of Antonio Guaynacapcha, the headman of the Yachas (p. 131); yet he too weaves, but the cloth is for his headman and not for tribute.

Don Anton and his wife in Chacapampa are both ancient and have finished with their tribute obligations; they are too old. Nevertheless, their sick daughter spins enough thread for one *anaco*, which other people then weave (p. 130). For me, even if the *tasa* remains the same, the difficulty of producing my share will change over time. In a few years my children will be bigger, and they can then work and help in the fields and house. For my wife the burden will be easier, since she will have more free time once the children stop needing her, although for me it will mean bigger *chacaras* to feed their increased appetites. This extra help, however, has to be counterbalanced with the increased obligations that I will have to meet. My parents-in-law are getting older, and I will have to increase my contributions to them, and there is no guarantee that Pablo Almerco, aware of how my children are growing, will not slap additional obligations on me.

Although our share of the burden is more or less equitably distributed, adjusted by Don Pablo according to our ability to produce, the actual burden of how much it costs us to produce the tribute depends very much on how our own needs vary throughout the year and throughout our lives, and according to our ages and needs and our obligations to our kinsmen. Since the tribute is fixed, it is our own needs that do not get satisfied when the burden of work gets to be too much.[8]

Dijo que no sabe cuanto le cabe al dicho pueblo de Chacapampa en lo del tributo, mas de que hace lo que su principal le reparte y no le da cuenta del repartimiento que entre ellos se hace de lo que le cabe al dicho pueblo (p. 82). (He says that he does not know what Chacapampa's share in the tribute is, that he does only what he is assigned by his headman, who does not tell him of the distribution of work that is done by them or what is due for that village.)

All I hear from Don Pablo and Don Juan is that we have to give more and more. They never cease haranguing us to keep weaving; they nag us for *tomines* and exhort us to work all the time. Whenever I deliver the tribute to Don Pablo, he starts worrying out loud about the many items he has to collect and how slow and unwilling the people are in giving the tribute. He dislikes doing such an unpopular thing. He mumbles to me in confidence that often, when people have not complied and he is pressed by Don Juan, he makes up the difference from his very own stores and supplies. But then the headman and the *curacas* have more and can count on all the help from us. Since the *encomendero* came, there have been so many substitutions, changes, arrangements, and secret agreements between the *curacas* and the *encomenderos* that nobody knows anymore if what the *curacas* collect from us is the amount they are supposed to collect. My neighbor here, he says that the *curacas* are enriching themselves at our expense. This may be so, but on the other hand, Don Pablo has never refused to help me when I needed him. I know nothing!

Y dijo que tiene ciertos andenes en que hace sus chacaras para sus sementeras que le bastan para él y sus hijos (p. 82). (And he says that he has certain terraces on which he makes his own fields, which are enough for him and his children.)

There is land everywhere, because our people are diminishing very quickly, and also because the Inca is gone and does not force us to produce food here in the villages for his *tambos* and storehouses. All those beautiful terraces built by our ancestors are beginning to decay, and nobody makes an effort to maintain them the way they used to. People have lost respect for the land. Who has the time!

Y tiene algunas por sembrar (p. 82). (And he still has some that have to be planted.)

Since I am an outsider in Tancor, my wife's father and his brothers tend to ask me first to help them plow their fields. They will return the work when I plow mine. Thus it is my fields that usually get worked last, for it is not seemly for me to initiate the exchange and get them to work for me first. But once I have worked in their fields, they will come and return the work to me. That is why I have not finished yet. I have to calculate the day that it will be convenient to all of them to plow my field and then go and ask them to return the help they owe me. I hope that the rains hold up for a few more weeks so that my allotted fields will be nice and soft for the day of plowing.

Y que no tiene chacaras en Chacapampa (p. 82). (And that he does not have fields in Chacapampa.)

How can I? As it is, I have to split myself into too many parts and tend to the fields there and here at the same time. If I could, there would be advantages to that, though as that reduces the risks of crop failure, and as they harvest earlier than we do here, I would be able to get fresh food earlier. But it can't be done.

Y que allí hay muchas donde si se pasase tendrá las que el cacique le diere (p. 82). (And that there are many there, and were he to move there, he would have those his headman would allot to him.)

Every year they distribute potato land, and they give maize land for longer periods, because one can repeat that crop for many years without rotation. Should I want it, all I have to do is ask for it, because my *ayllu* is there and it is *ayllu* land, and my *curaca* guarantees that as a member I have the right to it. I also have a right to land in Chacapampa, because I go and work on my tribute quota in their communal fields and I go to Pitomama with all my *allumasi* (*ayllu* mates) to work on the *mit'a*. So, should I ask for land in Chacapampa, they would have to allot me my share.

Y dijo que no tiene ganado alguno (pp. 82–83). (And he says that he has no kinds of domestic animals.)

The land here is too steep and too rough to keep animals. Moreover, I do not have the extra family members at the right age to spend the time herding them. Nor am I sure the Tancorinos would give me grazing rights, seeing that I am but an outsider.

Ni se quejó ninguna cosa de todas las que les fueron preguntadas como a los demás (p. 83). (Nor does he complain about anything that he was asked about.)

Bah!

Household Types

Agostín Luna Capcha's house was number thirty-three on the *visitador*'s list. Thanks to the work of archaeologist Ramiro Matos (1972: 367–382), we can picture a house similar to his in 1562. Matos surveyed the village of Wakan, within the *visita* territory and half an hour's walk from contemporary Tangor. Entrance to such a house was gained through a narrow path that crossed the flat roofs of several higher-lying neighboring houses and led onto a frontal patio where crops were sorted and dried in the sun. These crops were ultimately stored in an underground dug-out place that was carefully lined with stones; what kept it covered and clean was one of the flagstones that made up the patio floor. The patio was where many hours were spent spinning and weaving, as well as completing most of the other daily household tasks, because it was sunny and warm. The structure was shaped like an irregular square on the outside and built of thick, flat fieldstones interspersed with mud; inside, the rooms (ranging in number from two to four) were small and confined, serving not only as storage places for food, implements, clothing, and raw materials but also as sleeping quarters. One of them was the smoke-filled kitchen, where the women cooked while squatting near the stove. They fed the stove with twigs and used clay cooking pots and jars to boil and toast. Guinea pigs scuttled about, feeding on potato peel and other food scraps and nesting in the cracks of the walls. All cooking utensils and ingredients were within easy reach from the sitting position. On the walls of another room were niches—some square, others irregularly shaped—filled with small things like coca bundles and the skulls and bones of Agostín's wife's ancestors, removed long ago from the central burial place to serve as a kind of protective shrine.

The majority of Yacha households consisted of a husband-wife team (who headed the household) and their children. A few households encompassed three generations—a situation that would result when either spouse's widowed father or mother joined the new group. Other such extended units could include a spouse's unmarried brother or sister, even a sister with children of her own. In some households, unrelated children were reared—but these instances were rare (p. 130). In some cases the male head of the household was absent on *mit'a* duty, herding, trading for cotton in Huánuco, or working in the mines (pp. 112, 126, 122, 119).

In contemporary village ideology the marriage bond forms the basis of a new and independent household (Mayer 1977b), and we can assume that this was the case in *visita* times and before (Murra 1956: 169) and that it was an ideal worth striving for but not very easily achieved. The huge number of incomplete nuclear families (in a few cases, even of orphans) is a clear indication of the difficult times the Yacha were having in reaching or sustaining this ideal. The prevalence of incomplete nuclear families must also imply that many of these people from broken homes found it hard to seek refuge with kinsmen and incorporate themselves as part of these other households, and thus had to struggle alone.

Finally, I must mention the infrequent situations (e.g., pp. 92, 140, 203, 204) in which the *visitador* separated joint households into two distinct tribute units. In these cases an elderly couple lived with their growing children, one of whom (usually the son) was married and bringing up his own children in the same household. Yet tribute was assessed separately, counting the new couple as another unit with its own cloth, money, and *mit'a* obligations. One such example (p. 219) was an uxorilocal marriage in which an outsider settled in with a local family and married the daughter.

The cycle of marriage-based domestic groups can account for these variations in household composition, whereby the process of becoming independent households is plainly under way but not complete, and whereby the cycle has run its course and the remnants of the original, older households attach themselves to the households of their offspring (Goody 1966; Lambert 1977).

We can also gain some insight into marriage patterns by examining the records of the *visita*. Many women in these houses are listed variously as *mancebas* (mistresses or concubines), *mujeres de servicio* (servant women), *viudas* (widows), and *solteras* (single women). Murra (1967: 389–390), Hadden (1967), and Mayer (1972: 49) suggest that for at least some of the *mancebas* and *mujeres de servicio*, the existence of polygynous[9] households is indicated.

Regarding the use of these terms in the *visita,* there are two persistent concerns that need clarification. If the couple has not had the Christian marriage sacrament, even the sole wife is called the man's *manceba.* If there is more than one "wife" and neither relationship is sanctified by the sacrament, both are *mancebas.* And if there is more than one wife but one is "properly" married, the others are relegated to the *de servicio* or *manceba* categories. Little is known about the marriage rites of the Yacha at that time; yet one old man insisted, loudly enough for the scribe to record, that one such *amancebado* marriage was *a su ley* ("according to his laws") (p. 88).

The *visitador* was instructed to find out about marriage customs from the *caciques*, but the latter answered evasively, stressing only Inca legitimization of marriage rather than describing the local customs connected to the kinship system. As Don Francisco Coñapariguana explains (p. 31):

> The Inca governor they had would come once a year and in the plaza of each village the young men and women would gather. Then the Inca official would give each man the woman he wanted for a wife. He would tell him to treat her well, and serve her well. To her he would say the same and that she should serve her husband. And so they became husband and wife. And all those born out of that union were held to be legitimate and could inherit. And ... this could only be done by the aforementioned Inca and not by the *caciques* nor anyone else.

Yet the answer is evasive in part, because it is unlikely that the local kinsmen, the parents of bride and groom, and such considerations as status, wealth, and prescriptive or proscriptive marriage rules did not play an important part in the marriage process, as they are known to do in other societies. What Don Francisco's answer implied is that upon marriage a man became a full *tributario*, that the ceremony of giving official blessing to the marriage was probably also part of the census-taking procedure (Mayer

1972), duly recorded in the *quipu*, and that at this time the newly established tribute unit would get its duties assigned: Perhaps the man would be required to join the army or become a member of a carrier team, or perhaps the man's *mit'a* duties—tasks in which he was accompanied by his wife—would be assigned (Murra 1956: 172). The Inca were interested not so much in legitimating marriages as in using such normal social processes to regulate and administer their revenue-gathering system (Murra 1956: 170). Insofar as Inca interests were served by regulating marriages, we can say that the tribute system had a hand in the regulation of household composition and formation.

Many of these procedures remained in force legally in the *visita*, for it was the married Indian who counted as the true *tributario* on whom the *tasa* was assessed (p. 265). Even today, it is customary in Andean marriage processes for the couple to go through several ceremonies spread out over a number of years, each succeeding ceremony being more binding and definitive than the preceding one concerning the rights and obligations of the spouses and their respective kin. One of these steps, usually taken late in the marriage, is the civil and religious wedding, in which state and church legitimize the union long after the community and the kinsmen have done so (Carter 1977; Isbell 1977; Bolton 1977).

The new Christian restrictions on polygamy caused the *curacas* many headaches in 1562. Of the nineteen village headmen and *cacique principal* households, only seven appeared to be monogamous at the time of the *visita*. In his household Don Andrés Auquilliqui declared, in addition to his wife, one *india de servicio* who "is single. And if this woman would want to marry, he would not object. He was given this girl by his *cacique* Don Francisco Coñapariguana and he has no *concierto* [intercourse?] with her" (p. 39). Three other headmen declared that they were *amancebados* with only one wife.

The cases of plural marriages are even more complex. According to the *visita*, there were three headmen with two wives, three with three, one with four, and one with five wives. In addition, one was an accidental case of monogamy, because one of two wives had died (p. 149). *Mitimae* headman of Xigual, Juan Condor Guaya, was under pressure from both Andean and Spanish systems. He said that he had "two *indias de servicio* and that he [was] not married [by church] with either"; one of them was given to him by his *cacique* (Coñapariguana) and the other by the *cacique* Canagua[10] for a wife (*por mujer*) He had not married the second one yet because of the steadfast implacability of the priest! (p. 45). We can surmise that such priestly rancor was due to Condor Guaya's refusal to "get rid of" the first one. We can only guess whether the last part of his statement—"that he will marry her when the priest comes" (p. 45)—indicated that he was capitulating.

The process of "getting rid of" what for the Indians were very legitimate wives has a legal dimension revealed in the document and a practical aspect that remains more obscure. Juan Chuchuyaure had children by his four wives (aged fifty, twenty-five, twenty-four, and thirty-five, respectively). In the house-to-house survey, the first woman is listed as *su mujer*, the second as *india de servicio*, and the third and fourth as *mancebas*. Who decided to list them this way? Were the *curaca*'s words arbitrarily translated? In his previous testimony under oath in Huánuco, Chuchuyaure had said that he "had *three indias de servicio* available for marriage" (p. 61).

Antonio Guaynacapcha was also under pressure. In his house list there appeared one wife, one *manceba*, and one *india de servicio* (p. 168). In Huánuco he had at first listed two *indias de servicio*. Then, when questioned about having children by them, he modified his testimony to say that, in addition to his wife, there were three *indias*, and that one of the *indias de servicio* had borne his children (p. 65). Clearly, European distinctions did not fit the Andean situation.

That some of these women were relegated to a kind of servant status can be gleaned from the case of Cristóbal Contochi. Under priestly pressure he wanted to marry one woman (p. 180). Another *manceba* had borne him two daughters. A third was listed twice, once as his *manceba* and once as the wife of his servant (a young man reared in his household). If this is another example of headman "generosity," by which the headman could "give" wives to people of lower status than himself (as seen in Coñapariguana's case), this document has indeed revealed an interesting new feature of such giving (Murra 1975: 29–30, 175–176).

The person most clearly in a position to utilize fully these marriage customs to his advantage was Don Francisco Coñapariguana himself. He listed one wife and three *indias de servicio*, about whom he said that one was an invalid, that the others were living in his *chacaras* (fields), and that he supplied them with salt, *ají* (spicy peppers), and a house (p. 32). When his house was inspected, however, it turned out that he had children by two of the *indias de servicio*, as well as a son by one who had since "fled." Altogether, then, he had nine children with whom to forge future marriage alliances. In addition, he was an active recruiter of *yanaconas*, some of whom may have been part of his actual household, whereas the rest were separate but attached to households in the locality; the *yanaconas* exploited products in distant, ecologically favorable zones (Murra 1975: 62–74). All of this activity made his residence and his productive activities the largest economic unit in the document; of the thirty-two people declared, eighteen were adult men and women (pp. 199–200). It was no small achievement!

It seems that in a few cases male servants were reared from childhood on in the headman's household. In these situations, the *visita* recorded the name and age and such statements as "This young man is not from here" (p. 33), or noted that they were orphans or reared for the "love of God" (pp. 180, 173). Unattached relatives who could be entrusted with managerial affairs, such as nephews, aunts, and foster mothers, further swelled the productive and administrative capacity of these headman households. That such a household required more physical space and storage capacity is amply demonstrated by Craig Morris's (1967, 1972) archaeological excavations of one such house, in which large *chicha*-making pottery vessels appeared to form the majority of the ceramic remains.

Curaca households, larger and better endowed, had a greater productive capacity and the ability to provide a greater variety of goods for themselves. This capacity allowed headmen to play a crucial role in the local politico-economic structure, as classic "big men." In exchange for "generous" gifts—the distribution of luxuries, feasting, open hospitality, and aid for needy people—a *curaca* household could count on services such as having houses built and roofs thatched or fields worked and harvested when these services were "requested" (pp. 28, 35, 36). The capacity to mobilize resources and to distribute benefactions accounts for differences in leadership and power between such high-ranking *curacas* as Juan Chuchuyeure, lord over 200 households, and Pablo Almerco, village headman of sections of three villages. That many *curacas* used their status to enrich themselves was a common accusation, given the shifts in the economy under the Spaniards (Spalding 1974).

In contrast, commoner houses were smaller, in terms of both number of members and structure. Only 26 of the 436 commoner households—that is, about 5 percent—were polygamous, and the *visita* consistently recorded the women in them as *mancebas*. Missionary pressure produced strange responses, such as the case of the man who discarded his older wife, "who used to be his *manceba* but now is only in his house," in order to keep in official marriage the second, much younger woman (p. 145). As Murra points out, polygamous households—in enough cases to merit further looking into—tended to concentrate among *yanacona* families attached to some *principal* (1975: 238) and were able to evade tribute, Christianization, and other pressures caused by *curaca* protection, protection that worked to the advantage of both parties (Murra 1967: 390). The other households reported the children of their secondary wives without problem; at least the document says nothing to the contrary.

The Burden of Tribute

In Inca times, said Don Juan Chuchuyaure to the *visitador*, the burden of tribute was easier on his people because there were more people than now, because each tribute-paying family was responsible for a fixed amount to be delivered yearly, and because the very old did not work (p. 56). Moreover, the assessment then was made "according to the houses they had, not as it is now, when we have to deliver a fixed quantity per year, divided (*repartido*) amongst those people available" (p. 56). The change from a sliding scale of tribute according to the number of extant households to a fixed quantity divided among a diminishing tax base implied an increasing burden of tribute on every household.

This increased burden fell unequally on the existing households. One-third of the households did not pay tribute, and thus the burden was shifted onto the remaining two-thirds, of which approximately another third were in some way incapacitated or diminished in their ability to contribute fully. There were three categories of exemptions from tribute: status (10 percent of all households), permanent retainership to *curacas* or *encomenderos* (14 percent), and a claim to physical incapacity (22 percent).

Within the category of status exemptions, the headmen obviously came first. If we go over their testimony carefully, however, it becomes clear that there were gradations and hierarchies (see Table 3.1). Don Juan Chuchuyaure (p. 109) and Antonio Guaynacapcha (p. 168), the two dual *caciques principales* of the Yacha, and their colleagues of the *mitimae* groups (pp. 189, 199) were clearly exempt, despite having the largest and best-endowed households. Lower-ranking subdivisional headmen, such as Pablo Almerco (p. 160), said that they contributed a full quota of textiles and money and that they organized the production of the *menudencias* (little items of the list), such as cinches and tablecloths. In addition, they accompanied their people to the *mit'a* fields nearby and to Huánuco in order to "command them" (p. 211).

The second group of exempt households was the *forasteros* (members of other ethnic groups). In the Inca system, the exemption of an outsider from the *quipu* list of one group made sense, because that person would be fully accounted for, together with the reason for his being placed where he was and the kind of contribution that he made, in the *quipu* of his own group; otherwise, such people would be counted twice. In many cases this system was still functioning, as when *forastero* units were on record as contributing with their own group (p. 174). In one house in Quiu, the tribute obligations were split between two *encomenderos* (p. 79). But by 1562 many *forasteros* had become displaced and, until the *visita*, were able to slip through unnoticed.[11] When caught, however, they were enumerated and made to contribute, as the others had to, from then on (p. 96).

Another category comprised the *huidos* and *no visitados*—those who fled or otherwise avoided the impositions of the *encomienda* system. These cases, too, are proof of the desperation of many households. Take as an example the *encomendero*'s shepherd, who, when thirty-two sheep entrusted to his care died, fled in panic and never came back to his wife and children (p. 207).

TABLE 3.1   *Hierarchy of Headmen from Agostín Luna Capcha's Point of View*

Level	Headmen (*parcialidad* 1)	Headmen (*parcialidad* 2)
All Yacha (dual headmanship)	Don Antonio Guaynacapcha (second *curaca* of Yacha with residence in Caure)	Don Juan Chuchuyaure (first *curaca* of Yacha, with residence in Paucar)
pachaca (unit of 100 *tributarios*)	Don Andtonio Guaynacapcha (several villages)	Don Gonzalo Tapia (several villages)
Chacapampa	Don Pablo Almerco (headman of a section of people in Caure, Natin, Tancor, and Chacapampa. He resides in Caure)	Don Hernando Malquiriqui (headman of a section of people in Tuna, Quisicalla, and Chacapampa)
Tancor		Headman unknown
Household Level	Agostín Luna Capcha as part of a contingent of three families from Chacapampa, though he lives in Tancor	Other Tancor residents not recorded in this *visita* or they are not *encomendado* to Juan Sánchez Falcón

Sixty-seven households made up the group of full-time specialists and retainers: Forty-seven worked for the *encomendero*, and twenty were attached to various *curacas* and headmen. Those who worked for the *encomendero* can be enumerated as follows: five house servants, seven field and agricultural workers, nineteen caretakers of animals (cows, sheep, goats, pigs, and horses), eight craftsmen (potters/tile makers, carpenters/lumbermen, millers, and fishermen) and, finally, five unspecified *yanaconas*.

Permanent exemption from tribute obligations, however, was a mixed blessing. Despite the liberation from weaving and attending *mit'a* obligations, many *yanaconas* complained that they were not given enough time to work on their own subsistence activities (p. 220), that they were overworked (pp. 101, 125), or, most frequently, that they did not get paid. To these allegations the *encomendero* replied that the value of their salaries was discounted to the *curacas* by exchanging salary value for specific items in the *tasa* (p. 254). One carpenter, even though he said that his work burden was not excessive, nevertheless would have preferred to pay tribute like all the others (p. 117).

The situation of the *yanaconas* attached to *curacas* was radically different from the situation of those who worked for the *encomendero*. The twenty households listed as such were unevenly distributed among the *principales:* Juan Chuchuyeure had four; Gonzalo Tapia, two; Francisco Coñapariguana, nine; and others, one each. Coñapariguana explained that these people were mostly outsiders from Caxatambo and Condesuyo, obtained by him through his own *industria* [effort?] (p. 200). Perhaps his position as headman of Quechua *mitimaes* placed by the Inca to man fortresses (p. 199) explained his success in obtaining *yanaconas;* but, on the other hand, he may have been in a better position to protect post-conquest refugees. Of the lower-ranking headmen, only Pablo Almerco had one attached *yanacona* household (p. 168)—a fact that shows the limits of the institution of *yanaconaje* within such a small ethnic group as the Yacha.

Murra has cautioned against equating the *yanaconaje* with such European categories as slave, servant, or liegeman. Furthermore, he stresses the ambiguous and complex nature of the *yanaconas'* status, the way they were recruited, and their functions (Murra 1967: 390–391; 1975). In 1562 many of these families were still free from tribute obligations, though increasingly they "helped" (p. 146) by giving chickens, working with others in communal fields, and weaving or spinning a little (p. 168). Their activities in the service of their *curaca* were varied: Some were full-time specialized herders (p. 108), others cultivated fields at a considerable distance from their *curaca's* residence (pp. 79, 127), and all stated that they wove for the *curaca* (e.g., p. 127). Chuchuyaure's trusted Riquira wove and traded for him and presumably helped him administer people and resources (p. 102). These families constituted separate households, cultivated land for their own sustenance, and received reciprocal gifts of clothing, meat, coca, salt, and spices from their *curacas* (pp. 61–65). Furthermore, in some independent households there were unmarried women who were in the *curaca's* service to help make *chicha* (p. 103).

The transition from specialized worker or *yanacona* of the *curaca* to specialized worker or servant of the *encomendero* was a radical break from the past, despite the obvious continuities and willful forcing of this Andean institution into a European mold. It was against this change that the people affected complained most, for the quantity of work was no longer constrained by tacit mutual consent, nor did the *encomendero* have any respect for reciprocal norms (as demonstrated by the fact that so many people complained of not being paid).

Physical impediment, old age, and widowhood were not automatic reasons for exemption. Only 34 percent of the 107 households with these handicaps could be considered in some way exempt. Even so, for practically all of them some sort of minimal contribution involving spinning, if not the weaving of a minor piece, was listed. In addition, a sizable number of households (42 percent) contributed less than their full-paying neighbors. The remaining 24 percent seemed to be able to comply with the full assessment, despite widowhood, old age, or some other impediment listed for the head of household. Sixty-six percent of the households claiming exemption were not even complete nuclear families: Their median composition was between one and two persons per household, whereas the rest of the population had a median between three and four. The average composition of exempt households was barely 2.5 persons per family, compared to 4.23 for all households taken together. When more than three persons were listed in the household, the number of households actually exempt began to drop dramatically in relation to those that paid tribute—complaints of old age, widowhood, and the like notwithstanding. Nor should it surprise us that 33 percent of the people in this category complained that delivering whatever tribute they were assessed was very burdensome; only three households did not protest, partly because their contributions were reduced in comparison to what other families in the same village had given. Six widows in one village were in such straits that the *visitador* ordered their assessments abolished immediately (p. 193).

In Inca times a clear distinction had been made between a certain social age at which a man was freed from the more onerous and energetic tribute requirements (army and *mit'a*)—though he still performed many lighter communal tasks and an occasional administrative or supervisory but honored task—and physically incapacitating old age (which the *visita* records as *viejos muy viejos para el trabajo*) (Rowe 1958; Murra 1956: 172; Guaman Poma 1980: 196–198; Mayer 1972: 345). We find in the *encomienda* a willful distortion of this distinction. There, old age was defined, literally rather than socially, as a stage in life at which the most onerous tribute exactions were to cease. The fine gradations of diminishing obligation and increased responsibility and honor were simply abolished.

The brunt of the tribute base fell on 251 households (52 percent of the total), of which one-third complained about the burden of tribute and another third said that they got by; for the remaining third, unfortunately, no answer was recorded. The reasons people gave for finding the tribute burdensome provide an insight into the workings of the "domestic economy" (Sahlins 1972). I dealt above with the issue of physical incapacity and cases of widower- or widowhood. But of interest here is how this factor combines with other features of the domestic unit. If death, incapacity, or having one's spouse taken away by force (p. 157) beset the household in combination with too many children (p. 221), sick children (pp. 162, 165, 166), or too many members to support (e.g., pp. 162, 165, 182, 191), then it was very difficult to sustain the household, let alone pay tribute. Such difficulties applied equally to incapacitated parents without children (p. 191), children who had left their parents (p. 120), and old people who were alone and without help (p. 123). In describing all of these people we can use the European term *poor*—a term that to Andean people most frequently referred to a person without kinsmen to help out (*waccha*, the contemporary Quechua term for "orphan," is synonymous with *poor*) (Mayer 1972: 358). In short, these were households that had problems maintaining viability, owing to the accidental lack of skilled labor power (Sahlins 1972: 69–74). There was one case of near-blindness that prompted the couple to have their weaving quota done by other people, whom they paid by working on the others' agricultural tasks (p. 120).

Another set of complaints concerned the nature of the tribute itself: "Too much tribute" and "too much work" were the most straightforward replies (seven cases); and the more accurate reply, "it takes too much time" (twelve cases), was explained more fully as "too many occupations in which to expend effort and to hire oneself out" (pp. 242, 121).

The fluctuating nature of the tribute burden is revealed in the observation that "sometimes there is too much work and at others not" (p. 211). And, finally, the interrelationship between subsistence tasks and tribute was explained in terms of "too much work on tribute and his own": "There is no time left to make his *chacaras* nor to clothe himself and his wife and children" (pp. 150. 162).

Specific complaints about tribute ran the whole range: The full-time specialist complained about the distance and time it took to cut wood in the jungle (pp. 230, 231); the sandal maker complained that he had to make all the sandals normally assessed to one *pachaca* (a unit of 100 tributaries) (p. 119; see also Hadden 1967); and all complained about spinning, the onerous services to the *encomendero* (such as carrying food and fodder), the farmwork, the making of adobes and walls, and the *mit'a* in general.

My suspicion that this "loaded" question concerning the burdensome nature of the tribute provoked—as it should have—a political reply is confirmed by the fact that in some places, such as Coquín and Chuchuco (pp. 133–158), strings of like-minded answers to the effect that tribute was burdensome were recorded after a while as *igual que los demás* ("the same as the others") until the suspicious *visitador* demanded a reason. Then followed entries to the effect that "he did not give a reason" (e.g., p. 151); and toward the end of the *visita*, the record of the answers was omitted altogether.

I tried to determine whether there was any difference in terms of household composition between those who said that the tribute was burdensome and those who did not. No differences emerged when the number of household members, the type of family (nuclear, extended, couple, or less than nuclear), or even consumer/worker ratios (Chayanov 1966: 59) were compared in the two groups. Rather, I think that the Yacha peasants answered the question by comparing the new system to that of their Inca masters: The new system was found wanting.

Conclusions

What constituted a household in Yacha territory in 1562? It was a residential unit, with a house, crop storage, and cooking facilities. It was inhabited by a married couple and their children and occasionally augmented by the attachment of relatives of either spouse or of children's spouses. Households considered to be poor were composed of the remnants of a previously existing marriage; wealthier households had more wives and *yanaconas*.

The household was a consumption unit that provided for most of the basic subsistence needs of its members, including the care of infants and aged or infirm residents. In addition, it was a source of labor capabilities, of physical energy and available skills that were deployed in a diversified manner in agriculture, herding, handicrafts, construction, and transportation. As such, it provided itself and the surrounding society with basic goods and services. Because its productive power peaked during a portion of its developmental cycle, at certain stages the household was capable of generating a surplus. At other times its diminished productive skills and power may have required subsidies from the community in which it was embedded. The transition to *encomienda* in colonial times implied that many of the institutional mechanisms that ensured help with work, goods in kind, and exemption from tribute were breaking down and leaving many destitute. Of course, like households everywhere, it was also the place where manpower for armies and unskilled work could be recruited.

In addition, the household was the center of a complex web of reciprocal exchange flowing into and out of it (Alberti and Mayer 1974a; Mayer 1974a). Labor services, goods, gifts, and ceremonial exchanges were the expression of a complex network of kinship and social and political obligations that linked the household to others, to the rest of the community, and to the larger social world. It is quite likely that this web of links to other households, despite the heavy burden of work, was richer, denser, and more complex in the sixteenth century than it is today, even though the *visita* did not tap this dimension (Chapter 4).

Despite its autonomy as a consumption unit, the household was only one component of the overall productive system—though it was the key element and pattern setter as well. It was thoroughly embedded within a hierarchy of larger social units, each one partially intervening in the productive process. The household possessed access rights to land, yet it had to follow the restrictions that bound it to the community. Moreover, given the collective nature of Andean agriculture, it would be erroneous to describe the household as the sole unit of production. Yet the rhythms and cycles of the household affected other productive parts of the system. Allowance had to be made for subsistence production of the household, which, in itself, was diversified in its activities. If labor had to be taken away from subsistence activities, then it had to be diverted at those times when such activities slackened in the activity calendar, or else the time off had to be short enough not to interfere with subsistence production. The full-time specialists and the *yanaconas* had to be supported by other households, or they, too, had to stop their specialist activities to feed themselves from their own crops. When the labor of the household was intensified, it usually did so along all the lines of production already being undertaken. When the opposite strategy was taken, that of allowing the household to specialize, even if it had to be sustained by nonspecialists, the specialized households found the tribute burden heavier than did the rest. Thus there were limits to the number of specialists who could be sustained by the nonspecialists. Under the Inca system, such households, though permanently removed from the community, were fed either by the state or by their masters, or else they were given enough land to feed themselves.

Last but not least, the household was a unit of account in the tribute system. The basic accounting unit was the married man. Murra (1956: 769) translates the chronicler Cobo as follows: "No one paid tribute who lacked a wife or land; . . . it is only from the marriage day on that men became tax payers and took part in public works" (1956: 769). Although, technically, several levels of accounting existed in the *encomienda*—starting with the global amount that the Yacha population was to deliver (the *tasa*) and passing through the several *curacas* and headmen who were responsible for assigning and collecting portions of the *tasa* at lower levels—the assignments stopped at the level of the household. Indirectly, and in a very real sense, this individual assignment implied the economic backing of the household's organizational capacity to produce the tribute. All the spinning and weaving, the other handmade objects, the chickens, and the money assessed could be delivered only if behind every *tributario* there was a viable and functioning household. The great majority of complaints about the difficulties in giving tribute arose precisely when the person in question did not have the support of a viable household. Even communal tasks in the local fields—or in those of the *encomendero*, where the household was a supplier of labor but not the direct producer—could be accomplished effectively only if the tribute payer had his own production to sustain him. The relations not only of production but of reproduction came to rest within the *tributario*'s household. Thus, beyond the problems of accounting, the Yacha household was the crucial node at which the extraction of surplus began.

The tribute obligations and household composition fed into each other, magnifying the problems of those households already in trouble and easing the burden of those better able to produce. Despite attempts at reducing and adjusting the burden of tribute according to composition, the subjective evaluation of basic unfairness came to the fore. Moreover, the changes that the *encomendero* introduced into the system (quite apart from the quantitative increase in tribute that the *encomenderos* demanded) ultimately had a deleterious effect on the level of household welfare. Diminished subsistence production and increased levels of disease and mortality can be shown to have been directly linked to the *encomienda* system. There is also ample evidence of household disruption owing to runaways, work avoidance, and physical punishment. The Yacha were very aware that, despite the apparent institutional continuity with the past, the times had radically changed for the worse.

Postscript

In a work originally published as Mayer 1984, I exploited the dramatic situation that underlies the *visita* to create a narrative out of the driest bureaucratic document. And I was encouraged to do so by the way archaeologists use ethnographic analogy to reconstruct ancient patterns through contemporary observations. Testimonial literature such as Gregorio Condori Mamani's life story (Valderrama et al. 1996) enlivens such ethnographic research; and, indeed, I used Gregorio as a model. I wrote the draft of the original text in two nights, imagining what Agostín Luna Capcha might have said, or kept to himself, because he was under pressure in a very rigorous interrogation. I later went over the *visita* to corroborate the words I had put in his mouth. As the citations in the text show, someone did make similar statements that survived the double compression process of translator and scribe. The only fiction is Agostín's uxorilocal marriage, included in order to provide a link between him and other residents of Tancor who are not on record because the surviving *visita* tracked only Juan Sánchez Falcon's *encomienda*. Agostín is assumed to have been a potter, though ceramic activities do not figure in his testimony. The key point here is that I was motivated to provide a voice to a common person, since archival sources of this period provide few such opportunities. However, I wish to remind readers that any resemblance between Agostín Luna Capcha and Enrique Mayer is not purely coincidental.

Notes

1. These transplanted populations, termed *mitma* by the Incas, came from Canta, Cajatambo, Urcos de Atapillao, and Checras (all located in the present-day Department of Lima). They were directed by the Inca "to guard a house where he [himself] used to sleep when he came to conquer these lands" (p. 239). See Anders (1990) for a detailed analysis of the *mitimaqkuna* described in the *visita*.

2. Critical studies of the *visita* as sources of information and its difficulties are cited in Murra (1967), Pease (1978) and Anders (1990).

3. See Murra ([ed.] 1972: 116). Subsequent references to this source are given as page numbers in parentheses; all translations are mine.

4. The contemporary version of the *chacra jitay* ceremony is described in Mayer (1972); a revised interpretation appears in Chapter 4. For a description of how the sectorial fallow system works today, see Chapter 8 as well as Fonseca and Mayer (1988) and Orlove and Godoy (1986).

5. A description of the ethnoecology of the area and its significance in agricultural activities is provided in Fonseca (1972a: 315–338).

6. For a description of this practice as it occurs in contemporary Andamarca, Ayacucho, where fathers-in-law are carried home after the ceremonial planting of maize, see Ossio (1992: 109).

7. The following is an excerpt from Pablo Almerco's testimony: "He says that he sends people for five months, four Indians in the first four months of the year, and in the fifth month three Indians, and that the *encomendero* pays for this, but he does not know how much, nor how, and he only does what his *cacique*, Don Antonio Guaynacapcha, orders him to do" (p. 160).

8. The following is an excerpt from Ana Guacho's testimony in Chacapampa: "Her *amancebado* (non-Catholic married) husband is gone to trade for cotton, because they are naked, and indeed it was evident to the *visitadores*" (p. 127). And here is an excerpt from Teresa Capia's testimony in Chacapampa: "She says she is sixty years old, widowed, three children. That in giving all that they are required, it is too much work because she is old and poor and they cannot work that much" (p. 131).

9. More on multiple women in the *visita* of Huánuco can be found in Bernard (1998), who used volume 1 (whereas my analysis is based on volume 2 as a source).

10. Canagua, the *curaca* in charge of the *mitimaes* at the time of the conquest, was succeeded by Coñapariguana because Canagua's son was too young to rule (p. 27).

11. As noted by Anders (1990), there were numerous reasons why people were not at their "home base" at any given time. For instance, they might have been taking their turns in labor obligations, working in distant geographical areas, herding, or carrying out assigned tasks. This situation was recognized by the colonial administration in later years. As shown in Wightman's (1990) study of the *forastero* status in Colonial Peru, the colonial administration created its own nightmarish situation of *indios forasteros*. Indians massively evaded the tax burden by fleeing from the village where they were registered. They settled elsewhere and were counted as *forasteros* for which Toledan regulations provided reduced or sometimes even tribute exemptions. Moreover, because the *forastero* status was "inherited," the problem persisted from one generation to the next. Wightman notes, however, that the *forasteros* were probably better off than the *originarios*. This loophole was so effective that 40 to 50 percent of the population of the Cusco region were *forasteros* by the end of the sixteenth century. The percentage was even higher in those provinces more directly liable for the most hated *mit'a* labor contributions to the mines and coca fields.

4

The Rules of the Game
in Andean Reciprocity

This chapter is about reciprocity. Using examples from the community of Tangor, it explains how labor services, goods, gifts, and ceremonial exchanges are the expression of a complex network of kinship, social, and political obligations that link a household to others, to the rest of the community, and to the larger social world. It also demonstrates that these relationships constitute an available resource to be judiciously managed by the household members.

How Reciprocity Works

Reciprocity is the continuous, normative exchange of services and goods between known persons, in which some time must elapse between an initial prestation and its return. The negotiating process between the parties, instead of being an open discussion, is covered up by ceremonial forms of behavior. It is a social relationship that ties an individual to other individuals, an individual to social groups, producers to producers, and producers to consumers.

As an economic institution, reciprocal exchanges imply the flow of services and goods between individuals. The content as well as the manner of what flows from hand to hand are culturally determined. Over centuries, Andean peoples have worked out what was appropriate to be exchanged for what, how much was fair or too little, which variations were acceptable, and which ones were not. Different forms of reciprocal exchanges have been invented and worked out, elaborated, modified, adapted, or abandoned as external and internal conditions have forced the inhabitants of the Andes to retrench, reduce, or cut down their scale of operations. New economic institutions such as buying and selling, as well as contractual obligations introduced by the European conquerors, had to be fitted with the economic organization of the local groups. And market exchange somehow had to be made compatible with reciprocity and redistribution. New obligations and new goods were incorporated into culturally determined preferences, whereas older forms of obtaining goods or services were abandoned or substituted.

This chapter, however, focuses on the present. Based on fieldwork that took place in 1969–1970 in the village of Tangor, Province of Daniel Carrión, Department of Pasco, in Central Peru, it describes the forms of reciprocity I was able to observe and analyze. Toward that end it considers the place of reciprocity in the structure of the village economy, reports on the social context of its practices, explains Andean cultural meanings. As a form of exchange, reciprocity has limitations, and this chapter concludes with a discussion of how other forms of exchange tend to replace it.

A social relationship between people is like an umbilical cord. So much flows between individuals that any attempt to describe it ends up doing violence to it, because description tends to "freeze" the continuous back-and-forth processes. As early as 1929, Marcel Mauss (1954: 1) pointed out that reciprocal exchanges constitute total social phenomena, inasmuch as "[a]ll kinds of institutions find simultaneous expression: religious, legal, moral and economic. In addition, the phenomena have their aesthetic aspect and they reveal morphological types." The closest analogue to reciprocity that Mauss was able to equate with Western institutions was gift exchange. Reciprocal relationships between people in other societies bore similarities to the relationships between people who were exchanging gifts in our society, although reciprocal exchanges in the societies studied by Mauss (and covered in this chapter) meant much more, covered more spheres of social life, and played more important roles in determining behaviors than in ours. Gift giving and reciprocity have one fundamental characteristic in common, which Mauss (1954: 1) took as his starting point. "Exchanges," he said, that "are in theory *voluntary, disinterested and spontaneous*, are in fact obligatory and interested. The form usually taken is that of the gift generously offered; but the accompanying behavior is *formal pretense and social deception*" (emphasis added). In other words, what people tell each other they are doing is not what they are actually doing. They say that they are being generous and concerned with the well-being of others when in fact they are looking after their own interests and acting in a calculating manner, fulfilling the formal requirement that defines economic behavior.[1] In short, a major difference between reciprocity, on the one hand, and buying and selling or barter, on the other, is that calculating behavior is masked or covered up by the etiquette of the supposed voluntary giving and receiving of gifts. The point here is not that the self-interest considerations of reciprocal exchanges are unconscious in any psychological sense but, rather, that they are concealed from public view. We are thus forced to take into consideration several levels of explicitness in the actions of individuals. The fact that they say to each other that they are giving generously, and the fact that in so doing they are pursuing their own rational self-interest, cannot be disregarded. Moreover, we must be aware that no one is deceived by the formal etiquette of politeness. Field observation of such exchanges shows the polite outer mask that people use, but our overall interpretation has to include exposure of the actor's motives. People are able to tell the anthropologist in private what they gave and for what reason, what they expect in return and how.

Another difference is that purchaser and seller openly bargain with each other until they reach a point where both are satisfied with the advantages that can be gained from the exchange, whereas in reciprocal exchanges the evaluation of whether a prestation measures up to the expectation of what one wanted to receive is not allowed to be made explicit at the moment of the exchange. The gift must be received gracefully, whether it is satisfactory or not. The unsatisfied partner can make his or her discontent known indirectly in other ways. Because goods exchanged through reciprocity come wrapped in elaborate etiquette, they have not only value, similar to price in buying and selling, but also *meaning*. The transaction can show intention. For example, Barry Schwartz (1967) has shown that whereas one can insult or praise through gift giving, such intentions are irrelevant in market exchange because the market is premised on the depersonalization of the exchange.

Meaning and intention are manifested in reciprocity in three ways. The first is a function of how one gives, with or without ceremony. The second has to do with the quantity and quality of the goods or services exchanged. These are often culturally specified, and anthropologists use the term *customary* to describe them. Giving more than expected confers prestige to the giver and may, at the same time, belittle the receiver—as when a person overwhelms another with gifts to an insulting degree. Giving the exact amount expected may be an adequate exchange, but with negative social consequences. And giving less than expected can reflect the intention to offend. As Mauss (1954) keenly observed, a streak of rivalry and conflict frequently runs through these exchanges, an understanding of which requires knowledge of the context and a reference to cultural norms. The third way in which meaning and intention manifest themselves is through situations in which there are no cultural specifications regarding the quantities to be given. Here, reciprocity becomes a performance with no script, and evaluations of satisfaction are harder to elicit because imponderables such as considerations of trust, friendliness, attachment, and even love, or hate, enter into the context of the exchange.

Market exchange pretends to be morally neutral, whereas reciprocal exchanges are always evaluated with reference to moral standards in the imputed behavior of self and other. Some forms of reciprocal behavior are judged to be more "generous" and therefore more moral than others. The unsolicited thoughtful and meaningful gift is considered morally superior to the gift that is unimaginative and perfunctorily presented. Social distance also affects reciprocal exchanges, as Marshall Sahlins (1972) has shown. People tend to choose more generous forms of exchange with those they feel or want to be closer to than with those from whom they feel distant. As a relationship develops, the forms of reciprocal exchange tend to become more generous. At the same time, one can use reciprocity to express and enhance existing relationships. Partners placed in social situations involving trustworthy relations usually use generous forms of exchange, whereas those placed in more "distant" positions tend to exchange in less generous terms.

Unequal reciprocity, characterized by unbalanced flows between partners, is indicative of status and power differences. I use the term *asymmetric reciprocity* to express not only the fact that the material flow is unbalanced in favor of the superior partner in these relationships but also the idea that power and status dimensions are inextricably involved in the exchange. For example, a lower-status person may show "respect" to a higher-status person by surrendering services or goods without expecting an equivalent return. Asymmetric reciprocity may also be understood as an obligation that does not apply to the superior person. The return gift by the superior person is readable as an acknowledgment, but it is not necessarily equivalent to what was given. Nonetheless, in asymmetric relationships, the return is inevitably performed as if it were a manifestation of *largesse;* whether the person in the inferior position interprets it as such is not necessarily taken for granted. Reciprocity reaches its limits when one of the two parties decides to unmask the pretense and openly expose the underlying rivalries.

By studying the manner, direction, form, and quality of material exchanges between individuals, I have been able to delineate different kinds of social groupings. In my article on kinship in the Andes (Mayer 1977b), for example, I distinguished different kinds of kin groups through an analysis of how individuals organized reciprocal exchanges between them. Indeed, there is a specificity to the contents and contexts of Andean reciprocal exchanges, as described in the next section.

Forms of Andean Reciprocity

The strongest conclusion of my dissertation (Mayer 1974a) hinged on the clearly marked cultural distinction in Tangor between the exchange of personal services (by far the most prevalent form of reciprocal exchange) and the trade of goods through barter or purchase. (See Chapter 5 for further discussion of the latter.) Just about every social relationship in the village was marked by rules regarding how personal services should be ex-

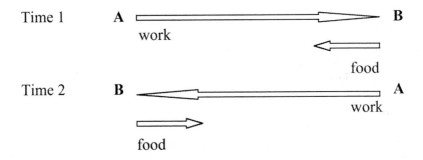

Figure 4.1 *Symmetrical Exchange (Waje-Waje)*

changed, whether in the context of helping to plow a field, preparing feasts, or performing as dancers in ceremonial services.

In general, these rules specified that any service rendered between equals in a symmetrical exchange should be returned at some later time with the same service, resulting in a completed cycle of exchanges that canceled out all debts. What was given had to be returned. A completed symmetrical exchange of services took the form shown in Figure 4.1: B received A's work and A received a meal from B at Time 1; and when the return was made at some future date—namely, Time 2—B returned the work and A offered the meal. What counted here was the work exchange; the exchange of meals remained ancillary. In Tangor terminology, the meal was called a *cumplimiento*, a Spanish word describing an acknowledgment of the service received but not the canceling of the debt. The completed cycle of two work exchanges and two meals is called a *waje-waje*[2] in Tangor; elsewhere in the Andes, where the Cusco and Ayacucho dialects are spoken, it is called an *ayni*.

The formal features of an asymmetric exchange are shown in Figure 4.2. There is no Time 2 in this form, nor a return of work by B to A. Instead, in supposed equivalence to the service that B received from A, B gave to A, in addition to the *cumplimiento* meal, a specified customary payment in goods that canceled out the debt between them. The customary payment was called *derechos* (a Spanish term meaning "a right"). In agreeing to provide a service in a *minka* relationship, A acquired the right to receive the customary payments—known as *derechos*—that were typical of this kind of occasion, but did not have the opportunity to bargain about the amount. César Fonseca (1974: 88), in describing the many modalities of *minka* exchanges in the region where Tangor is located, showed that it was always "superior" B who decided what the appropriate amount to be given to A should be, and A had to receive what B gave him with gratitude, whether

Figure 4.2   *Asymmetrical Exchange (Minka)*

expected or not (rather like waiters expecting a tip in our society). Such status differences were usually aspects of permanent inequality between A and B—as with a *peón* working for a *patrón* or a son-in-law working for his father in law. In certain ceremonial situations, however, the partners in a *minka* relationship could be reversed at another time, with A taking on the superior role of receiver of services and payer of the *derechos*.

Relationships in which one person performed a service for another had a demeaning aspect that no equivalency of goods could fully compensate for. Being fed might have been an expression of generosity that enhanced the giver, but it also diminished the receiver. Peter Gose (1994: 11) has astutely observed that "in the Andes feeding people is an expression of power and proprietorship"; in the same context, Catherine Allen (1988: 151) has discussed the notion of force-feeding someone. Without an opportunity to reverse the situation, a bit of poison[3] creeps into the relationship. In a formal sense, and it may be useful to think of it as such, a *minka* is an incomplete *waje-waje:* In a complete four-way set of exchanges, the role reversal and change of direction in the flow of services and goods at Time 2 canceled out the status imbalances produced at Time 1. In Cusco Quechua, *ayni* is also appropriately translated as "revenge."[4]

Within this framework, Tangorinos distinguished three basic types of exchange:

1. *Voluntad* was an obligation that a person fulfilled because of an underlying relationship—most notably, kinship—that bound two people together. The service had to be provided at times specified by custom by the relative who was in the appropriate kinship category and need. Usually the event itself involved a ritual in the family that was to receive the contribution, such as a baptism, a first hair cutting, a house roofing for a recently married couple, or the death of a relative. The appropriate return was automatically made when the other family celebrated the same ritual. In the meantime the receiving family acknowledged the services rendered by means of a festive meal, the *cumplimiento*.

2. *Waje-waje* was a service performed in exchange for exactly the same service in the context of work, ceremony, even everyday mutual help. In contrast to *voluntad,* the content of *waje-waje* ex-

changes was not specified by custom; rather, it was left to individuals to work out as they wished. Also, although relatives were obligated by kinship to participate in *voluntad* exchanges, a *waje-waje* relationship was initiated by the person who wanted the service by formally asking for it. Anyone could be chosen, and the person asked could refuse without damaging the relationship. Accounts were kept of *waje-wajes* owed, and a person who was owed a *waje-waje* could ask for its return when the help was needed. In general, substitutions of one kind of service returned for another were frowned upon; a proper return was considered to be one in which exactly the same work was provided in return. A day of plowing was not equal to a day of harvesting. Returning a *waje-waje* was a serious obligation that kept the *waje-waje* relationships alive.

3. *Minka* differed from *waje-waje* in that no equivalent return was made for a service received. Instead, a quantity of goods, specified by custom, was given in return for the service that had been performed. People in a *minka* relationship did not necessarily share an underlying kinship bond; nor were *minka* services seen as kinbound obligations. For this reason the incumbent who needed a *minka* service had to find a person willing to do it and to formally ask for it.

As a first approximation we can say that *voluntad* exchanges were based on kinship ties between partners, whereas *waje-waje* and *minka* did not specify that the exchanges necessarily occur between relatives. Each of these three forms of reciprocal exchange could be divided into two subforms: one approaching a more "generalized" reciprocity, the other tending toward the "balanced" point on Sahlins's (1972: ch. 5) continuum. The generalized form of exchange occurred among relatives considered to be close in kinship or partnership; the balanced form was used with more distant relatives or friends.

Kinship obligations could be discharged either by presenting the service unasked or by waiting until the persons who had a right to the service came to claim it. For this reason the first type was called *voluntad,* which in Spanish means "good will." A relative showed good will by spontaneously supplying the service when there was a need. The second type was called *manay* (a Quechua word), understood as a request for a right, a claim, or an obligation that was met only when one called for it.

Waje-waje exchanges were subdivided into *ayuda* and the repeated term *waje-waje.* The former were less formal than the latter. In *ayuda*[5] (which means "help" in Spanish), no accounts of services performed were supposed to be kept, though in actual practice returns were often promptly made. With *waje-waje,* by contrast, accounts were kept. The necessity of keeping a stricter balance between partners was greater in *waje-waje* than in *ayuda.*

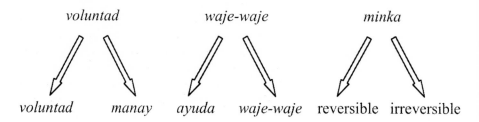

voluntad   *waje-waje*   *minka*

voluntad   *manay*   *ayuda*   *waje-waje*   reversible   irreversible

Figure 4.3 *Six Forms of Reciprocity*

Minka services were also of two kinds: reversible and irreversible. In their reversible form, the partners could change positions at some future date; for example, a *minkador* could become a *minkado*. But in irreversible *minka,* the roles between *patrón* and worker were unchangeable. The distinction is analogous to the two kinds of *compadre* relationships described by Sydney Mintz and Eric Wolf (1967) and Juan Ossio (1984, 1992): those between social equals and those between members of different social strata or classes. The services provided in *minka* tended to be specialized skills, such as the services of a curer, a blacksmith, or an adobe maker; it could also have ceremonial content. Most often, however, it included the provision of unskilled manual labor. *Minka* of this kind tended to shade off into wage labor when, together with food, coca, cigarettes, and alcohol, the *derechos* included a payment in cash. The six forms of exchange discussed thus far are depicted in Figure 4.3.

These six forms, together with the relationships created through barter and cash payments, permitted Tangorinos to organize an extensive web of social relations extending outward from the household into an ever-widening circle of people that formed part of their social world. Such a network included relatives, neighbors, community members, villagers in other communities, mestizo town dwellers, other migrants in the mining centers, and the Tangorinos themselves in Lima and in the colonizing areas of the tropical lowlands. It could change over time, of course, as new people were brought in and other relationships lapsed. A new partnership would begin with cautious balanced forms of exchanging; but as trust grew, it would become more generalized, especially when partners began to eschew the more strict accountings and formalities prescribed in the etiquette of the exchange. Some examples follow.

Plowing and Harvesting

During plowing time in February 1970, César Zamallóa[6] and I visited the field belonging to Antonio, a recently married Tangorino, and asked him how he had recruited the nine men who were assisting him. The atmosphere in which they worked was cordial, almost playful. Six of the men were from the same neighborhood as Antonio, and three were his relatives (one paternal cousin, the brother of his brother-in-law, and a "distant" cousin). A hearty lunch was cooked right in the field by Antonio's wife, helped by some of the wives of the other workers.[7] Antonio was generous in his distribution of coca, cigarettes, and shot glasses of cane alcohol during the work breaks. Eight of the men were working in *waje-waje*, whereas the paternal cousin was there in *ayuda*. Four *waje-wajes* were being initiated by Antonio on that occasion, meaning that he would owe each of four people one day of work. In addition, two *waje-wajes* were being returned that day for work Antonio had previously performed. Four weeks later, when we finished our survey, Antonio still owed four days; but before that, he had already returned the work to his cousin, despite the fact that both he and his cousin insisted that they did not keep accounts with each other.

Plowing the fields with the Andean footplow was probably the hardest and most tedious task in Tangor agriculture.[8] The hardened earth after a long fallow had to be turned over, which could be done only during the middle of the rainy season. The minimum work unit for this task was a group of three persons,[9] two to wield the footplows and one facing them who turned over the sod that was dislodged by the lever action of both footplows acting in coordination. With additional men available, three or even four plowmen could make up a team for one puller. It was rhythmical work. The men with their plows stood in a row facing downhill, while the person who turned the sods faced them with his adz. The plowmen took a leap from about one meter away to drive the steel-tipped points of their plows deep into the ground, pushing hard with their feet on the stirrup. Then they removed their feet and levered the poles toward their chests, sometimes rocking them back and forth so that the action would dislodge the sod and lift its edge above the surface of the ground. At that moment, the man facing them hooked his adz on the edge of sod and pulled it toward him so that it tore free and turned over; he was helped by a final push from the plowmen, who, bending sideways, lowered their plows until they were almost parallel to the ground. When the sod finally turned over, the plowmen prepared to take the next leap a few feet to the right or left of the previous cut, progressing in rows horizontally along the field. Occasionally bushes had to be removed. The plowmen used the sharp tips of their plows to cut through the roots, while the puller, grabbing the stems, pulled hard at the right moment, tearing the bushes out of the ground. The women would come later to collect these for firewood. A well-organized group could usually finish a field in one day, but in our survey (which, on average, involved five men per field) we found families with few workers who took much longer to complete the task.

Eighty-one percent of the workers were recruited from outside the family, whereas household labor provided the remaining 19 percent of the total labor days. *Ayuda* and *waje-waje* accounted for nearly nine-tenths of the exchanges between relatives; only one-tenth of the exchanges between people who claimed some sort of kin relationship to each other involved paid wages. All *ayuda* exchanges were between close relatives, whereas *waje-wajes*, though they occurred between relatives, were also undertaken outside the kinship sphere.

The use of wages in plowing was also interesting, inasmuch as these wages were a relatively unpopular option. The going wage at that time was 12 *soles*,[10] but the remuneration included meals, alcohol, coca, and cigarettes that were distributed to those who were recruited through reciprocity. Significantly, the government at that time was paying a daily wage ten times higher than what Tangorinos paid themselves, but this fact affected neither their own low-wage level nor the supply of laborers available for plowing. Instead, the community signed an agreement stating that the forestry service would not work every day of the week, so that Tangorinos could dedicate themselves to their fields.

Wage labor in this context was the clearest example of an asymmetric *minka* exchange. Those who used this form of exchange cultivated patron-client relationships with dependent people who needed money. For example, a store owner would advance credit and demand that the debt be paid in work during plowing time. In the survey, we categorized Tangorinos as poor, middle-level, and rich.[11] Poor and middle-level peasants recruited extra labor mainly through symmetric reciprocity (93 percent of the poor families and 89 percent of the middle-level families used *waje-waje*). Rich farmers recruited half their needed labor through reciprocity and half through wages. Scarcity of cash was, of course, the main reason for this stratified difference between them, since poor people could ill afford to squander the little cash they obtained on payment of wages. But the rich peasants had reasons other than money-related ones to prefer hiring workers for wages. Reciprocal exchanges had high opportunity costs for them. By using wage work, they would have fewer debt obligations to return the work, allowing them to pursue other activities in or outside the village. Poor and middle-level farmers worked for others two-thirds of the time in reciprocal relationships and one-third of the time for wages (one of the few opportunities they had to obtain cash within the village). The rich farmers did comply with the reciprocal obligations they had committed themselves to return, but these accounted for only 5 percent of all such exchanges in the survey. Not one rich farmer hired himself out for wages.

The context of labor exchanges changed when we looked at the potato harvest, which was more of a family affair. The instrument used was the hook-shaped adz. The laborers straddled the hillocks, working from the bottom to the top in the vertically arranged furrows, because they stooped less when facing uphill. The adz was used to flatten the hillocks with sweeping movements from the sides toward the worker. In the process, the potatoes came to the surface and were then picked up by hand and tossed into troughs dug every three meters on the side of the furrows. The women and auxiliary helpers collected them from time to time, sorted them, put them into sacks, and loaded them onto donkeys to take home, where they were piled up, sorted again, and eventually stored in the attics of their houses.

For this task only one-third of the labor came from outside the household, and the average number of people per field was two. In contrast to plowing, the greatest proportion of exchanges were *ayuda* rather than *waje-waje;* ten out of twenty-six were immediate kin of the harvesting head of the household, another ten were more distant consanguineal kin, five were related by marriage, and one was a *compadre.* In addition, three were *voluntad* exchanges. One young man said that he was harvesting his grandmother's field *de voluntad* because she had no one to help her; he did not expect any remuneration, nor did he expect her to return the help provided.

With potatoes available as a ready form of payment, money wages were a rarity, and people attended others' harvests to gain access to potatoes rather than to accumulate labor obligations. Ten percent of the men and 8 percent of the women were rewarded in kind for their help. Everyone who participated returned home with a small gift and tasted the freshly roasted potatoes that had been prepared right in the field. Working for payment in kind was a special relationship termed *allapakur* (helping each other harvest), a custom widely practiced throughout the region. A rate, such as a carrying cloth full of potatoes per day worked, was informally agreed upon by villagers; it could also be adjusted through discussion between the owner of the field and the worker. In Tangor it was the woman who made decisions about this rate, as she was owner of the harvest. The pay was always more than what could be earned if one worked for wages. As it was a relationship that benefited the workers more than the field owners, those wishing to do so had to develop special ties with the owners to obtain the privilege of participating in the harvest.[12]

Smart management practices among households involved active labor recruitment for plowing, but also judiciously calculated and diplomatically practiced exclusions in harvesting so that villagers could avoid being put in the position of having to part with too great a proportion of their crop. Peter Gose (1994: 11–12), in an extensive study of Andean ritual linked to the agricultural productive cycle and economy in the village of Huaquirca, Andahuaylas, closely links ritual symbolism with reciprocity. He notes two periods in the cycle—one of egalitarian *ayni,* tied to production, and one of hierarchical *minka,* tied to appropriation:[13]

There is one phase of the agricultural cycle in which the crops are an object of production, and a second phase in which they are an object of consumption and appropriation. In Huaquirca relations of *ayni* prevail during the period when crops are growing and are the object of an intensive productive effort. The productivist emphasis in *ayni* is appropriate to the concerns and requirements of the growing season, and its symmetric, egalitarian nature gives this productive effort a collective character. Once the crops begin to reach maturity and consumability after Carnival, however, the *ayni*-based regime of collective production has served its purpose. The order of the day shifts to securing and storing the fruits of this collective labor as private property. Each household harvests its own land, largely in isolation from the rest. What little cooperation that does occur among households at this time of the year takes place through relations of *minka* during the harvest, and stems from the fact that some households have more land than they can harvest with their own labor, whereas others do not have enough land to fully occupy their members.

Although it supports his point, Gose does not make much of the fact that those presenting themselves to help harvest (*yanapa* is his term and *allapakur* is mine, but they mean the same: "to help harvest") are rewarded with more uncooked produce than they would get if they were paid wages in a *minka* or money-wage relationship. We both would agree that this is a special privilege the landowner concedes to someone who has to assume an inferior position in order to get it. Gose's diagram (1994: 10) places *yanapa* right on the ambiguous dividing line between egalitarian *ayni* and hierarchical *minka,* so it can go in either direction. This I expressed by distinguishing a reversible *minka* from an irreversible one.

Exploitation with Reciprocity

Irreversible *minka* was a long-lasting relationship between social unequals. When Doña Juana died, her husband Don Manuel, a man considered to be rich and stingy, recruited three men to dig the grave. Each one received a bottle of alcohol, coca, and cigarettes for this service. That Manuel might someday dig a grave for any one of their relatives was unthinkable, though he might perhaps attend the funeral and supply some alcohol. These three men were known in the village as dirt-poor. They frequently worked Manuel's fields for "wages." They were regularly engaged for house services and given food, and Manuel made them carry loads of merchandise on their backs for his store in the village. In return, he would extend credit to them when they requested provisions from his store, which he marked off in terms of days worked at a specified but difficult to negotiate money (wage) rate. He remained available to them in emergency situations and protected them if they were in judicial trouble within or outside the village. But when he sponsored *fiestas,* he used these people as waiters to enhance his own status in public. They were fed in the kitchen as a clear sign of subservience.

This asymmetric relationship between patron and client has been amply described in the Andean literature, ranging from the *yanacona* servants of local *curacas* in the sixteenth century (noted in Chapter 3) and the services provided to Spaniards during colonial times (Zavala 1978) to the serfdom in *haciendas* of the 1950s (Vásquez 1961; Dobbyns et al. 1971). Giorgio Alberti (1970), Fernando Fuenzalida (1970), and Julio Cotler (1968) use words such as *caste-like* or *semifeudal* to describe *minka* relationships between serfs and their landlords within *haciendas* and between Indigenous people and merchants or town dwellers outside *haciendas*. And Cotler, in particular, describes local contexts of this kind when speaking of a generalized pattern of internal domination in Peru. Indeed, scholars concur that the class relationships so established were characterized by the strong personalized involvement of these unequal partners in each other's lives—an involvement that masked the extreme and abusive exploitation by mestizo or white *patróns* of ethnically marked *indio* peasants or servants. Despite repeated attempts by republican governments to make such relationships illegal, they tended to persist because exploiters found ways to isolate dependents and serfs by foreclosing alternative pathways to survival. Thus the "inferior" persons were entrapped in lifelong systems of personal bondage.

Yet the examples in this chapter demonstrate that *minka* relationships also existed within peasant communities, which, it should be emphasized, are not homogenous but stratified and ranked societies. Fonseca's (1974) seminal article on variations in *minka* relationships indicates the degree to which unequal exchange with associated deferential status behaviors between the partners was integral to daily practice within communities and in personal networks extending outward from the village. *Minka* formed part of a more complex cultural system that served to rank people and groups in superior/inferior relationships—in some cases as a permanent validation of status differences, but in others as a token of complex prestige games. As an expression of difference, *minka* had a built-in inequality, expressed in an aggressive form of generosity that forced food and drink on the hapless victims (Gose 1994).

The issue here is not whether serfdom had its origins in ancient Andean or ancient European feudal cultures. Nor am I discussing a particularity of "Andean" culture per se, for it is clear that the *minka* relationship crossed ethnic boundaries, such that mestizos (or "notables," as Gose calls them) upheld, maintained, elaborated, and benefited from this way of doing things. In addition, it is hard to disentangle the legalities of legislation that upheld landlords in courts for the practice of discounting work obligations provided by the serf on the *hacienda* against the rent owed by the serf for the use of private land, on the one hand, from the peasant and the landlord's perspectives who saw the same relationship as one of reciprocity, on the other. Benjamin Orlove (1977b: 206) described this relationship as follows:

> The relations between the *hacendado* and his herders are also marked by reciprocity. The *hacendado* frequently gives them small presents. On his visits to the *hacienda* he gives them bread. He makes larger gifts at Christmas, such as an old frayed blanket. He gives them rides to the provincial capital and market town in his pickup truck, provides them with food and lodging in town, permitting them to put their blankets on the floor of his kitchen. In some cases, *compadre* ties are established. In return, the *hacendado* receives additional labor. Herders act as household servants in town. The sixteen-year-old daughter of one of the shepherds was sent to Arequipa to be a servant in the house of a cousin of the *hacendado*. The *hacendado* is enlarging his house largely with labor from the *hacienda*.

Rather, one should be able to discern who is benefiting and who is losing from the relationship, what other factors are involved in enforcing such blatant exploitation couched as reciprocity, and how and where the limits of exploitation can be imposed by whom.

Upper classes in the rural Andes used asymmetric reciprocity to impose unequal exchanges and to underwrite status differences. And it took repeated local rebellions[14] and a radical agrarian reform of the 1970s to eliminate the most salient forms of this exploitative relationship in rural Peru. Nonetheless, as we shall see, it has reemerged in other ways that underscore dependency and redraw ethnic boundaries.

Ceremonial Exchanges

In Tangor, sponsors of *fiestas* recruited dancers using *manay, minka,* and *waje-waje* relationships in order "to bring joy to the village." The process started during a family affair known as the *llanta takay* ("firewood cutting"), when the sponsor organized a work party four or five months in advance to cut firewood from trees growing on communal land. After the wood had dried, it would be used to bake great quantities of bread and to cook large banquets. About a week before the actual cutting, the sponsoring family recruited the workers among brothers-in-law, sons-in-law, grandparents, and *compadres* by going from house to house to notify them. To make the commitment more binding, the sponsoring family made the relatives drink some cane alcohol (*aguardiente*). This form of recruitment amused Tangorinos, who called it "going around with the bottle." In most cases, the request was a mere formality; but I observed other instances in which the recruiting was insistent, with alcohol almost forced on relatives—leading to rising tempers. Once the drink had been accepted, the person was obligated to help cut firewood on the appointed day.[15] This kind of recruitment was of the *manay* type. The enlisted relatives had the obligation to help but waited until the sponsor came to them personally to claim this obligation. While they cut firewood, the relatives were fed an ordinary meal and given coca, *aguardiente,* and cigarettes by the sponsor. Two days before the festivities, every person who helped cut wood or carry it to the village had a claim to a portion of dough when the sponsor's family kneaded the flour. It was called the *manay* dough.

The cycle of exchanges ended with the *cumplimiento,* a banquet served at the conclusion of the *fiesta.* Tangorinos fully understood that the sponsor owed nothing to anyone after that. Nonetheless, the day might come when the roles were reversed, such that the person who helped chop wood would be the next sponsor and the ex-sponsor would have to help his relative. The latter might show up voluntarily; but if he didn't and instead found excuses when the other one come around and requested it, with bottle in hand, negative consequences might ensue.

The night after the *llanta takay,* the sponsor and his relatives would stay around to chew coca and choose the possible dancers, *mayordomos,* and other players who might perform during the fiesta. As one Tangorino put it: "They look them over to consider if they are capable of fulfilling the role or not." Those secretly chosen were later invited to a meal and, without being clearly aware of the motive, were given a lot of *quemado,* a special concoction of *aguardiente* with cinnamon, to smooth the way toward persuading them to accept the obligation to dance for the fiesta. As a sign of acceptance, the designated persons each took home a bottle of "hooch."[16] The dancers had to spend their own money to rent or buy the expensive costumes. In return, they would be given their rights by the sponsor: full meals during every day they danced, a given quantity of freshly baked bread,[17] and a banquet in *cumplimiento* with a public display of gifts hung in garlands from their necks when they went home after the last dance.

Those persons who accepted their recruitment in such *minka* obligations would be, in the words of a sponsor, people "who feel sympathy for the sponsor and for the fiesta who are 'llano' to help the sponsor."[18] For dancers who agreed to be in a *minka* for such an event, this acceptance completed the obligations between them; but those who insisted on *waje-waje* would expect, when they became sponsors, to be able to claim that the owed service be returned. Such instances illustrate that a *minka* could sometimes be seen as half a *waje-waje.* To build up a group of dancers, the sponsor (much like farmers in the recruitment-to-work parties described above) would have to build up his team using several denominations of the reciprocity currency. Those who came in *minka* would not be owed anything after the event, those who owed *waje-wajes* from past events would have to pay off long-standing debts, and those with initiated *waje-wajes* would incur a new debt. In one case, a dancer had to come back to Tangor all the way from Lima to discharge his *waje-waje* responsibility. As Sahlins

(1972) and Mauss (1954) note, recurring interdebtednes is the hallmark of genial social relations, whereas prompt repayment signals that the friendship is in trouble.

Examples of *voluntad* as opposed to *manay* include first-haircutting ceremonies for male children and house roofing for married couples. The first haircutting, whose purpose was to raise a capital fund for the child that would grow as he developed toward adulthood, was one of the few instances I observed in which reciprocity entailed the transfer of money instead of personal services—even though the act of cutting hair could be considered a service and people clearly understood that the funds they were giving were gifts. Although it was in the parents' interest to increase the number of contributing guests, the latter could not be openly forced; indeed, as one parent said, "attendance and contributions are strictly *de voluntad.*" Yet parents did scout the village in search of people known to have money and enticed them to come with the promise of food, drink, and a good time, much like charity events in the United States. Contributions were supposed to increase each time a round of haircutting was undertaken, so participants started off with small gifts. It was the father's role to auction off locks of hair, and hints (some subtle, some not) were dropped to shame the guests into giving more each time around. The boy's hair was left uncut from birth to the day of the ceremony, usually four or five years later. As the day approached, a portion of hair was allowed to become matted and entangled; this dreadlock, called the *tankash*, was reserved for a couple of specially chosen guests, the *padrinos de cortapelo,* who would cut it at the moment they give the most substantial gift. The resemblance to cutting an umbilical cord was unmistakable and much commented upon. *Minka* relationships clearly found their ultimate expression in ritual co-parenthood, or *compadrasgo,* which established a kinship-like bond between nonrelatives—but one that was definitely hierarchical and asymmetric.

Here is an example of how a widow who lived in Lima switched from one form of reciprocal transaction to another, breaking the rules of etiquette because she was desperate. She had returned to Tangor to provide her house with a tin roof instead of the traditional thatch. Had she used thatch, her relatives would have had clear-cut roles that specified material contributions and work obligations, all delivered *de voluntad.*[19] But with a tin roof, the work requirements changed: The labor was less overall, but awkwardly shaped timbers and sharp metal sheets had to be carried up the steep hill to the village from the road. Since the widow had been away from the village for so long, her relatives did not feel like collaborating with her, so she fell back on the more explicit *manay* method. She tried to persuade her relatives that transportation from the road would cancel out other obligations, and she stated that she needed workers for the actual construction job. This is how she described her desperation.

I left my house searching for helpers, asking myself: "Who could help me? We do not have any relatives."[20] I thought to myself that those whom I would ask would not come, since they would say to themselves: "We help those Lima people in vain." [The implication was that Lima people do not return owed favors, so it was useless to help them.] I spoke to all, to Don Flavio I said, "Hurry up *maéstro*," and when I met him again, I insisted. Despite all this pressure, he did not come. Were he not my relative, I would not have asked him in that tone. I also went to Tiburcio and to Simón, who is my husband's nephew. I begged all of them vehemently, almost picking a fight. I went to one, to another. I went everywhere without much success. Afterward I went to Wilson with the bottle in my hand, I went to the upper and the lower half of the village, all over, searching for help.

Her nephew responded:

Sure aunt, if you don't *waje-waje* with people, nobody helps you. How can you expect help now, if neither you nor your husband Josefo have ever gone to other house roofings?

But the lady had the last word: "You are just beginning to have children. By and by, you will build other houses for them, then I will let my sons know so that they may help you." It is interesting to note that she was also unable to recruit wage labor for the job.

Reciprocity, Redistribution, and Symbolic Capital

The aggregation of several dyadic,[21] asymmetric (*minka*) exchanges with one single person as a focus reveals the elemental forms of a redistributive system. As shown in Figure 4.4, at Time 1, A accumulated goods and services. These were distributed to the whole community in the form of food, drink, amusement, and sociality during a named feast at Time 2. When the *fiesta* had been successfully completed, at Time 3, B, C, D, and E were given social recognition in the form of a *cumplimiento*. They also shared the prestige that the whole town awarded A for his efforts.

In this way the energy and material goods provided by B, C, D, and E were accumulated by A, who disbursed them to the whole community. B, C, D, and E received token but "generous" acknowledgments for their participation, but there was no equivalency in terms of what they gave and what was returned to them by A. Billie Jean Isbell (1978: 167–177), in her study of Chuschi, Ayacucho, showed that the contributors recruited by A were relatives that constituted a special group, the *kuyaq* (a Quechua phrase meaning "those relatives who love the sponsor"),[22] and each house-

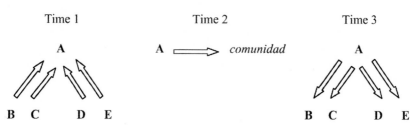

FIGURE 4.4   Redistribution

hold contributed amounts that varied according to rules of kinship distance, affection for the sponsor, or the giver's economic circumstances. A assumed the obligation "to serve the community"—an obligation known by the Spanish term *cargo,* which translates into English as "burden"—and then passed it on to another person, whose turn it would be to organize a similar or, perhaps, even more spectacular event next year (see Figure 4.5). Whole kinship groups were thus engaged in competitive systems of prestige feasting.

In Tangor the changeover from one sponsor to another was represented in a dramatic way. When the feast had ended, the sponsor baked two large breads shaped like human figures (one man and one woman), with an *ají* pepper nose, raisin buttons, and other decorative elements. (Collectively, these pastries were called *trukay wawas,* which in Quechua translates as "exchange babies." (Note, however, that *trukay* has a Spanish origin: *Trocar* means "to barter.") The breads would then be given away to the family that would assume the responsibility to finance the next year's feast.[23] This moment, known by the Spanish word *cambio* ("turn over"), was a public event in the plaza, where, alongside the large breads, other miniature items were on display: Smaller shaped breads, each with a name reminiscent of each element of the feast ("hands," "sheep," "bananas"), *ají* peppers, onions and cabbage, a pair of live guinea pigs, a sheep's head to make soup, cooked food, a small jar of *chicha,* and a bottle of *aguardiente. Trukay* things were considered "seed" for next year's event, which the new sponsors would transform into the great quantities needed to feed everyone, get them drunk, and entertain them. The family that received the *trukay* checked the items to make sure they were all there. If not, the family demanded that the missing things be given to them the next day, because, as was explained to me by a sponsor, "when the present sponsor makes his *trukay* he has to 're-turn' the things (to the future sponsor) in the same way that I gave it to him." Return, here, should be interpreted as passing on the symbolic capital to a third party in a system of generalized exchange (Levy Strauss 1969; Bourdieu 1987: 3–4).[24]

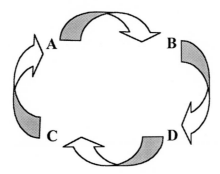

Figure 4.5   *Cargos*

Speeches were made by the past sponsors to the effect that they had *cumplido* with the community and had found two other sponsors to take on the obligation for next year. The new sponsors, in turn, repeated their promises while the authorities praised both sets of sponsors, reiterated community values, and warned against defaulting. The new sponsors sat gloating with their breads while admiring people came over to look at the display, and then drinks were served. Afterward the breads were taken home where they were cut up and distributed by the future sponsors to their relatives and friends, among them several who, in all likelihood, would be asked to accumulate the goods needed to organize the next *fiesta*.

On another occasion, the man who had accepted a *trukay* subsequently felt that he could not afford to finance it—and since he refused to postpone it for another year, he baked the *trukay* and handed it over to another man. As others phrased it, he did not have *voluntad* to do the feast and handed over his *cargo* to another. In this case, however, the *cargo* had been properly passed on. When another person defaulted altogether without baking the breads, people said that that person "had eaten the *trukay*." [25] In a third instance, the sponsors of the Christmas feast could not find anyone willing to take it on for next year. After waiting for two weeks, they baked the *trukay* and presented it to the authorities, explaining their predicament. The authorities sent some boys to ring the bells to summon everybody to an assembly. They then cut up the breads into small slices and distributed them to all the people who came. By dissipating the *trukay* capital, they indicated that the Christmas feast was suspended.

Taxation

Family labor and material resources were the subject of community taxation in Tangor. The ideology of reciprocity, encoded in the meanings of *vol-*

untad, manay, and *minka,* permeated the sphere of taxable contributions. Tangorinos often made reference to the notion that their individual contributions were for the good of all, that the *comuna* benefited. Chapter 5 of my dissertation reflected my considerable efforts to demonstrate that different kinds of services to the community could be fitted, more or less neatly, into the six forms of reciprocal exchange depicted in Figure 4.3. These are further discussed below.

To begin with, the very notion of service to the community was understood fundamentally as a contribution in labor, in skills, or in services, rather than as the surrender of a portion of one's crops, of goods in kind, or of money. (Although money quotas were levied, they were deemed exceptional, and authorities tried to make them appear as if they were a kind of service.) Service contributions were of two kinds, *manay* and *voluntad. Manay* obligations took two forms, of which the responsibility to contribute work was the more basic. (Although I never heard the term *manay* used in this context, the reason may very well be my inability to completely follow conversations in Quechua.) Formal request was the hallmark of *manay,* and summons to work parties (known by the Spanish word *faenas*) were always made by means of the village bells and shouted orders from the towers; the whole village had to attend. When two sections of the villages (*Urin Barrio* and *Hanan Barrio*) organized separate affairs, the officers of these units made the rounds with their bottles. At these events, authorities always distributed coca, cigarettes, and alcohol—though no food.

Communal work projects were undertaken frequently, about one Sunday out of every three or four, or as needed in emergencies. Paths were cleared and maintained, and the old water canal for the village was cleaned once a year in what they called the *faena real* (the "royal *faena*"). This procedure became unnecessary when the canal was replaced by a piped water system. Although the latter was built with government help, the villagers contributed their labor force to dig ditches and cart sand, gravel, and cement on their animals, taking turns for a job that lasted two years. Authorities worked out a roster in which every group, subgroup, and individual was assigned a portion of the task in the most equitable way; this was the household's *mita,* a Quechua word which translates as "turn" but also means "assigned task." Following this elaborate schedule, men from each of the four *barrios* worked one day a week for two years to provide a steady supply of rotating labor. Each household was notified as to what day a person should show up, where, and with what implements to comply with that household's *mita.* People often complained. Authorities used friendly persuasion to demonstrate to each person that it really was his turn, asserting that the agreed-upon schedule had to be obeyed, that postponements were not allowed. In similar undertakings the church was roofed, school buildings were built, and the bell towers were rethatched.

Failure to attend, which happened frequently, was met with a fine in the form of money or *aguardiente*. Attendance was variable, and it depended greatly on how important the people considered the task, how much enthusiasm could be generated, and how long it could be sustained. Attendance was also affected by the defaulters' sense of how much they could get away with. Loud complaints about work shirkers (*faltones*) were frequent, especially among those who did the work. Assessment was based on one man per household, not on every adult male in the community. As replacements, households could send sons but also *minka* servants. Some rich families, much to the chagrin of others, regularly substituted alcohol contributions for work obligations (paying the fine in advance and subverting the work atmosphere by supplying too much drink). People temporarily away were excused, as were the old, the sick, and the infirm. The really old were considered retired. Households that did not have male adults present were also excused, although wives, in order to avoid negative gossip, would often attend or send material contributions.

Since the village often had to buy materials or services with cash (e.g., to hire lawyers to resolve land disputes), assessments in money were collected, but these were given very reluctantly—and, then, only when the emergency was declared and when alternative ways of collecting cash were found to be unworkable. Each section of the village owned communal lands that were worked in *faena* whose harvests, when sold, were supposed to defray community expenses. In the Tangorinos' minds, this was the correct way to cover the community's money needs; but as proceeds from these enterprises were irregular and insufficient, quota levies were imposed. Neither system was an efficient way to raise funds. A regular unspecified community tax in money, which the government tried to impose in 1969, was fiercely resisted.

At the second level of *manay,* each male head of household had to serve, by turns, in authority roles as *varayoq*. Literally, *varayoq* means "staff holder," and the staffs (*varas* in Spanish) they carried were symbols of authority. The office was assumed by male heads of household on a rotational basis that entailed responsibilities for one year on behalf of the community. The *varayoq* system is the Andean version of the Latin American civil religious hierarchy.[26]

In the past some thirty men per year were involved in the *varayoq* system, which entailed ceremony, pomp and circumstance, and respect—all expressing a clear sense of hierarchy. Lower-ranking men had to learn from, serve, and obey the higher-ranking ones, who in turn responded with institutionalized generosity during carnival festivities. These authorities also oversaw the recruitment of *faena* labor, controlled agricultural activities, were allowed to have whips and used them occasionally to punish petty crimes, mediated domestic and inter-family disputes, and oversaw the proper performance of *fiestas*, ceremonies, and processions. As a moral force, they supervised religious events and made sure that children were baptized, the dead were properly buried, and the church was kept in good condition.

Introduced to the villages in the sixteenth century by the Toledan *reducción* reform, the *varayoq*'s activities were a meld of civic duties bolstered by European corporatist thinking and by popular Catholicism, which harked back to the strong political, religious, and social control that the colonial system had installed in the rural areas (Abercrombie 1998: 213–261). At the time of my fieldwork in Tangor the distribution of *chicha*, alcoholic drinks, coca, food, and honors, as well as the signs of rank ordering, still marked hierarchical relationships. The reciprocal obligations of serving and being served fit well into the patterns of labor exchanges and reciprocity. Officials from the town expected obedience and submissive public behavior from the *varayoq* office holder.

The *varayoq* system has been in decline throughout the last five decades in Peru, but it is being revived in Bolivia. With half the village migrating out of Tangor, the prominence of agricultural concerns declined, and as individuals aspired to successes beyond the local world, the *varayoq* system became associated with embarrassingly quaint country customs. The state's development bureaucracy and the modernizing Catholic church also discouraged the system. In 1930 Tangor took advantage of national legislation to became an officially recognized *comunidad de Indígenas*, and Tangorinos, in order to comply with the law, reorganized their internal government. The law stipulated a democratic assembly and elected officers such as president, treasurer, and secretary. During my fieldwork, the two systems were uneasily integrated, with the *varayoq* system clearly secondary to the official system; it was also in disarray. Half the positions were vacant in 1969, and the role of the remaining positions were filled by the poorer villagers. Whereas the *varayoq* system fit well with the Tangorinos' notions of reciprocity and redistribution, the modern offices and positions of authority—though a quicker route to power and prestige—did not.

Most Tangorinos remembered the time before the water system was installed when, at the royal *faena*, all members of the community would get together at a certain place during a break and go through a list of people who had served as *varas* to consider those who had paused long enough from their previous post to now be ready to take on the next office in the hierarchy. Somebody would suggest the name and qualities of a candidate for an office. The proposition was then loudly discussed by all, with expressions of approval or disapproval; and if approved, the named person would stand up and, after much demurring, would finally accept, knowing that sooner or later he would have to serve in that office. If he felt that he was not up to the responsibilities it entailed, he would request a postponement. Private backstage politicking kept inept persons and unpopular candidates out of the system, and outright refusals marginalized families in community standing. But during my time in Tangor, the authorities had great difficulty making the new appointments. They made their decisions in private and went from house to house trying to persuade candidates to accept. I was told that they used considerable pressure. Although the *varayoq* service still conferred prestige to some Tangorinos, office holders liked to portray their turns as a terrible burden. One of them complained to me, saying that he had been elected out of revenge and would be saddled with a millstone at the urging of envious neighbors. There was perhaps a bit of false modesty in this complaint, but it clearly reflected the ideology of the *varayoq* system. Serving was considered a troublesome *manay* obligation. One did it only when insistently asked.

Women had their own parallel *varayoq* hierarchy, with duties such as sweeping and maintaining the church, decorating the altars with flowers and candles, washing and ironing the saints' clothing, and directing the ritual activities during Easter celebrations. The top-level hierarchy was the *alcaldeza,* who had to be an elderly widow, and all members of the hierarchy had to be unmarried—that is, celibate. The reason given to me for the celibacy requirement was that unmarried woman would have more time to perform their duties; but given the small effort required in fulfilling them, perhaps an imitation of chaste Catholic convent life would be a better explanation.

The third level at which notions of reciprocity and public service were linked concerned the sponsorships of religious feasts for Catholic saints. Tangorinos called these sponsorships *cargos* and distinguished them from the *varayoq* system by emphatically stating that the decision to sponsor a fiesta was entirely an act *de voluntad*—volunteered and generously offered in devotion to a saint and for the happiness and benefit of the community. No one forced a person to sponsor a feast. One sponsor was emphatic in his statement (contradictory as it may seem, it was a correct expression within the range of options available in the repertoire of Tangor reciprocity): "When one organizes a *fiesta*, no one obligates one; nonetheless, one does feel the obligation to bring happiness to the people once a year."

Taxation by outsiders, so long a feature of Tangor's economy (as described in the previous two chapters), was mercifully absent during my fieldwork. The Indian head tax was abolished in 1854, Indians started refusing to give free labor in mestizo towns in the 1930s, and older people remembered how happy they were when President Leguia's Indian labor draft law to build roads, the *Ley vial*, ended in 1930. In 1969 Tangorinos were tax exempt and free from *hacienda* serfdom. They relished their long independence and had unfavorable opinions of the recently formed communities that had arisen out of the collapse of *haciendas*, whose inhabitants were thought to still have a serf mentality.

Counting and Sharing

Two additional concerns related internal taxation to reciprocity. The first was to ensure that everyone's contribution was publicly acknowledged. The second was to ensure that everyone shared equally in the tasks the community imposed. Work performed had to be counted. From an individual's point of view, the concern with equity was a matter of making sure that the others contributed as much as oneself or, from a more selfish perspective, that one contributed only as little as others would let one get away with. The village was full of self-righteous and self-appointed truant officers.

Being counted, and thus accounted for, was important to Tangorinos. It conferred important rights such as community membership, village citizenship, and privileges, and it marked community boundaries between outsiders and insiders. When migrants returned to their villages, authorities told them they had to pay up their missed *faenas* before full community membership could be restored to them. *Vara* and *cargo* holders had the opportunity to make office holding part of the public record.

During the *chacra jitay* ceremony, an event that opened the agricultural cycle by "throwing open the fields," the *varayoq* nominated two men to perform the *morocho*. These men gathered a lot of pebbles and sat before a poncho spread on the ground. Everyone who had served a *vara* or a *cargo* was counted by placing a pebble on the poncho. The men counted systematically from house to house, street by street, and *barrio* by *barrio*. For each person who had passed a *vara* or a *cargo*, they placed a stone on the pile. If the *cargo* was a major one, requiring the distribution of food and drink, a second one was placed for the wife. If the son had also served in a minor *vara,* it was counted separately. Women *varas* were also counted. When the two men were done, they counted up the stones and informed the highest-ranking authority of the total. Then the whole procedure was repeated again, with another pair of commissioned men.

At the time I observed the ceremony, I was mystified, because the arithmetic did not make sense to me. The team that came up with a larger total was said to be the winner (which is not necessarily the way to arrive at a correct number, nor did I feel that accuracy was served by declaring winners and losers). But no one paid much attention to the proceedings, and there was no public acknowledgment of each person's listing or any visible disputation or contentious argument. Further questioning brought some clarification. A friend remembered that in the past three piles were made: one for those who had passed *cargos* and *varas*, another for those who had not yet served, and a third for those who had died in the interval since the last count. In an article that described the procedure (Mayer 1972: 339–365), I concluded that this form of census taking had become an empty ceremony, devoid of its real function, which was to assign land. Thirty years later, I want to revise this conclusion.

What I saw was social behavior consistent with *quipu* record keeping, without using the actual knotted strings that served the Incas as a mnemonic device. The commissioned men were not only counting, they were memorizing the names and the services rendered. Their memories constituted the record, and they remained available as expert witness in case of disagreements. Although the men did not actually place a pebble on a separate pile for each dead person, they did review the status of each household one by one, noting changes, additions, and subtractions. Although little public attention was paid to these proceedings, the enumerators were surrounded by persons who helped them when they could not remember a name or office, when they skipped a house, and when they disagreed. Pebbles had replaced the knots of the *quipu* strings, and the Tangor system in 1969 anteceded the obsession with written record keeping that is associated with public reciprocity in villages in the Andes.

In a study of the village of Tupicocha in the Province of Huarochirí, in the Department of Lima, Frank Salomon (1997: 6) refers to this skill as "verbal literacy." The expansion of writing skill had an impact in Tupicocha, and what in Tangor was a memorizing by counting with stones became in Tupicocha the process of writing records of attendance and recording decisions. As Salomon (1997: 16) notes, villagers write during the course of village self-management:

> Every corporate entity [in Tupicocha], as everywhere in Peru, legitimates itself by producing manuscript books containing constitution and *actas*, i.e., minutes constructed as performative documents and signed by members. All schoolchildren learn *acta* format, and even the smallest details of community action bring their own chroniclers with them. If three villagers go out to mend a canal leaking in the rain, one of them will huddle under a sheet of plastic to inscribe the act on a soggy scrap. Secretaries aggregate such notes into *padrones* and *padroncillos*, that is, data tables about membership, chronology and participation, which eventually enter into narrative records. When multiplied by the number of entities that make up Tupicocha's intricate formal structure, this process yields a huge bibliographic harvest.

In Tangor, the ideology of reciprocity stressed symmetrical reciprocity. In harmony with its principles, individuals exchanged services with each other while striving to reach equivalency. At the communal level, the obligation to serve the community was transmitted from one person to another, so that for each person the opportunity to serve would present itself in due course. The Quechua word for this process was *mita* ("turn"). At the personal level, two individuals who exchanged work helped each other by turns; first A helped B, and then it was B's turn to help A. At the communal level, the turns or *mita* services unfolded over a longer time span, during the life stages of a person. At each step in life, individuals were

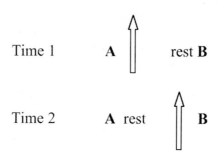

Time 1   A ⇑ rest **B**

Time 2   **A** rest ⇑ B

Figure 4.6   *Mita*

served and served the community. At both levels, their "true" notion of reciprocity was one of taking turns to help each other.

Asymmetrical forms of reciprocity contradicted this principle by substituting gifts in kind for the return service. Because there was no devolution of expended energies, the higher-ranking partner could accumulate wealth by using such forms. In matters of taxation, asymmetric forms—namely, *minka*, *manay*, and *voluntad*—were always used. A symbolic transformation of unequal exchange turned these into forms of equality through the use of the *mita* concept. Equivalency between individuals ensured that the burden placed on all would be equitably shared by each through the taking of turns. Taking turns thus became a pseudo-*waje-waje* relationship between two groups in the following way: In Time 1, A (e.g., *Hanan Barrio*) served the community and B (e.g., *Urin Barrio*) rested, whereas in Time 2, B worked while A rested. This relationship is depicted in Figure 4.6.

A computed B's "turn" of work as the cancellation of the *waje-waje* A was owed by B. Since the *waje-waje* relationship carries an implicit element of competitive rivalry, it was used by Tangorinos to egg each other on to outperform each other. A closely watched how well B had performed the task, and B, in an effort to defeat A, made sure that the "revenge" would be an even better performance. This is an ingenious solution to the free-rider problem, one that so often plagues voluntarism in communal action. Andean people are very aware of this possibility. Here is a nice example taken from an article by Salvador Palomino (1971: 78). In it, he mentions an origin myth that explains the reason for the division of the village of Sarhua in the Province of Victor Fajardo, in Ayacucho, into two *ayllu* halves or moieties known as *Qullana* and *Sawqa*:

Before, when there were no *ayllus* and everyone was equal, the people had gone to Jajamarca to carry the church bell "María Angola" and some rose-wood beams for the construction of the church. Since everyone was equal, no one had any energy to work; so then they thought—*let us compete with each other*. Well, you are going to be *Qullana* and we *Sawqa* and the governor divided them. (Emphasis added.)

That the myth is full of colonial references on how the village built its church, shows that the manipulation of Andean reciprocity was useful to Spanish masters as much as it had also served the villagers' previous conquerors, a point stressed by Paul Gelles (1995). Accumulation and exploitation cloaked as reciprocity has been a feature of the Andean economy for ages.

The Limits of Reciprocity

Any social relation has its limits. In Tangor the lower limits of formal male reciprocity coincided with the outer boundaries of the independently constituted household. In my field survey (Mayer 1970), I found a father and son who still lived with his parents, who themselves worked together and when I asked about the kind of arrangement that existed between them, the father answered, amazed, "But he is my son!"...Indicating that the work of a household member did not fall within the range of formal reciprocity. Sons were ordered around by their fathers, not formally asked to perform a *waje-waje*.

As economic flows within the household belong to a domain different from that of formal reciprocity between households, a different approach for studying them is required. Within households we could talk of pooling, the assignation of tasks, and the households' products for consumption. Production is organized according to the division of labor by gender and age, and consumption also varies on the basis of gender, age, and role-specific contingencies such as differential treatment of ill people or of daughters- versus sons-in-law. For Stephen Gudeman (1990: 45) these are *base-base* movements that stay within the confines of the "house" and do not go outside the "door." The flow of energy, material goods, and symbolic prestige that decidedly goes out the door of one house and into the door of another is governed, principally, by the rules of the game of reciprocal exchange.

I tend to be rather skeptical when relationships within the household, particularly those between husband and wife, are described in reference to models of reciprocity. Of course, I do not deny that there are complicated give-and-take interactions between husbands and wives. This is made clear by Tristan Platt (1986), Olivia Harris (1978) and Catherine Allen (1988: 72–77), who stress the unity and complementarity of the husband-wife pair, and by Billie Jean Isbell (1977), who describes the relationships between and across genders and age within a household. Rather, my point is that the formal, public, culturally constructed relationships described here are for the most part inapplicable within the household context. And this observation is consistent with the fact that formal reciprocity directs the flow of services and goods within the kinship system, which is composed of many independent households linked to each other.

The game of reciprocity began when the sons and daughters started to configure their own households. Elaborate and complex rules of reciprocity governed the exchanges between the new household and those of the spouses' parental households—with *ayuda* if members of the household were closely related through descent and with *waje-waje* in more formal relationships by marriage (Mayer 1977b: 64–65). If the household dissolved and portions of it reintegrated with a parental household, the rules would again lapse as these people regrouped to form a single domestic unit.

At the other extreme of the social field, there were limits as to how far social relationships could be stretched and still be considered by the actors to belong to the domain of reciprocity. Either of the partners could begin to feel the inadequacy of the formal pretense that hid the real negotiations, and they could attempt to bargain and dicker more openly, and when this happened, the relationship changed in nature and scope into something else. Options included a formal contract, a partnership, a share-cropping arrangement, even a procedure whereby money was used as the medium of exchange with open bargaining, thus taking a large step toward depersonalization.

In Chapter 7, I report on fieldwork that took place fifteen years after the Tangor study. It compares potato production in two regions of Peru: the Tulumayo Valley, which was more modernized and more integrated into the national market in Central Peru, and the Paucartambo Valley in Cusco Department, which was more traditional and less integrated. In the Paucartambo Valley, more than half the extra-household labor was recruited through reciprocal arrangements; in the Tulumayo Valley, reciprocal recruiting accounted for only one-third of the total. The remaining two-thirds were paid wages. The limits of reciprocity were different in the two valleys inasmuch as labor was becoming more proletarianized in the Tulumayo Valley and farmers were finding it harder to convince other people to help them out in their commercial business ventures (Mayer and Glave 1992: 131).

The transition from *minka* to wages was a sign that the limits of asymmetric reciprocity had been reached, because one of the negotiating parties, no longer content with the exchange, began to question the whole ideology of reciprocity. Those exploited by it worked hard to redefine the relationship, stopped being grateful when the *patrón* gave gifts, and began to demand more, seeking ways in which a change of attitude could be imposed on the *patrón*. Instead of relying on subtle social pressures to shame him, they formed peasant leagues, organized boycotts, went on strikes, invaded the *patrón's hacienda* lands, behaved like James C. Scott's (1985) resistant, irreverent, foot-dragging peasants, and became militant *campesinos* instead of humble *indios* as part of a vigorous contestation against the traditional understanding of asymmetric reciprocity. Indeed, the most important twentieth-century social revolution in the Andean highlands of Bolivia, Peru, and Ecuador has to do with the construction of a liberating redefinition of the rules of the game in Andean asymmetric reciprocity. However, liberation is not complete.

César Fonseca left field notes on changes in ethnic relations after the agrarian reform in the Paucartambo Valley, which I edited and published (Mayer 1988: 59–100). His evaluation was quite pessimistic, arguing that the long-established exploitative relationship (couched as reciprocity) between Indians and mestizos was reestablished in the new contexts (cited in Mayer 1988: 86):

> Once power has been ceded to the *Mestizo* the Indian community assembly loses any capacity to decide or to act. More important to the *comunero* is the *Mestizo compadre* who can intercede in his behalf with the police, the local judge or the agrarian bank manager. It is worth more to have a powerful ally in town than to rely on the united power of the community, because the community has not been able to get a single person out of jail. A *Mestizo* sees in his Indian *compadre* a subordinate who can be easily exploited, and the *Mestizo* asks for shares in all that the peasant produces, and the peasant accedes, with the hope that in the not so distant future, he can count on the *Mestizo's* support.
>
> There is a double coincidence of interests between peasants and *Mestizos*. Because of insecurity, ignorance of alternatives, and in their strategy in investing in long-term social relations, Indians constantly seek to personalize economic relations by cultivating alliances with *Mestizos*. While *Mestizos* despise the Indians (they said to Fonseca: "the Indian has to die an Indian, an Indian is always an Indian"), they continually use their networks of Indian contacts and personalized transactions in a dragnet of personal gifts and favors which finds its maximum expression in the relationships of *compadrazgo*. The power that the peasant class could thus exert becomes diffused and without direction. It has been wrapped in small gifts of potatoes and eggs and has been handed over to a parasitic class that inhabits the small towns and villages of southern Peru.

The rules of the game were also changing between the villagers and its migrants. At the time I did my fieldwork, fully half the villagers of Tangor were living in the Lima shantytowns. Although I did not study the flow of material goods and services between the village and the city, remittances constituted an important dimension of the village economy. Rich families in Tangor were considered rich because they sent out surplus labor and imported consumer goods. They had money and could deploy social relations in more flexible ways than those families unable to export their labor to the money economy. Food sent from Tangor was used by migrants in Lima to organize *waje-waje* and *minka* work parties with which to construct their houses. It was not directly consumed as food but, rather, was used as symbolic capital that converted it to more labor. In the process, the contents and extent of mutual obligations between relatives in the village and those who had migrated were constantly redefined.

Sarah Lund Skar (1994), describing the process of migration from the Department of Andahuaylas community of Matapuquio, writes about the bonds and emotional ties that people take with them as they migrate, struggling to maintain relationships with relatives at a distance. Arrangements have to be made for the care of property (land, animals, jobs, houses, and inheritance claims) that will be left behind. And some individuals must agree to serve as couriers of gifts, letters, and news to relatives and villagers at the other end. Appropriately, these missives are called *encargos* in Spanish. The delivery of letters can lead to tense moments because the bearer of the letters is also the interpreter of the messages therein and, often, the political agent of the desired outcome of the sender (as when the sender has entrusted the bearer with the task to "make sure my son returns home to take care of me"). Each letter, each gift of precious home-grown food, is a compressed and emotionally charged cultural artifact that makes claims, collects on past obligations, and purposefully plucks the emotional strings of the receiver.

A theme I was unable to broach as well as Billie Jean Isbell did in her 1978 study of Chuschi concerned the manner in which migrants living in the city redefined obligations and reciprocal arrangements to help each other out in the city. As Isbell (1978: 185) reported:

> Mutual aid has been a key factor in the success of the migrants' adaptation to their self-constructed community [in Lima]. . . . They constructed temporary mat shelters first and then built one-story cinder-block shells without roofs, flooring, plumbing, or electricity. . . . Adequate living space is the first consideration. A second story is added on as the migrant family is able to pay for the materials. Most often mutual aid is utilized for part of the construction labor, but wage labor is used for special skills such as brick laying. Communal labor is essential for the later priorities—sewers and electricity.

Similarly, Susan Lobo's 1982 study of migrants in a shantytown in the port area of metropolitan Lima, a literal desert in a cement environment, describes how the migrants of Corongo village from Ancash recreated the whole *cargo* fiesta system of their home village, celebrating, of all things, the cleaning of an imaginary irrigation ditch where no water flowed. Lobo (1982: 174) described the *cargo* holder's "exaggerated hospitality toward all who attended, his overseeing of the serving of the meals, his insisting that all of the plates be heaped with food and his exuberant commands that more cases of beer be brought out." The *fiesta* activated the network of reciprocal obligations that were continually utilized during the year in the form of loans, advice, support, crisis management, and business connections—all crucial to survival in a very competitive and hostile urban capitalist environment.

Though not unconscious of gender differences, my study in Tangor centered, for obvious reasons, on the male domain of reciprocity. I am convinced, however, that there is a whole other world of reciprocity between women (one I have been unable to tap) centering on the kitchen where food is prepared and cooked. Mary Weismantel (1988: 175–176) addresses "kitchen life" in her marvelous ethnography of food and gender in Zumbagua, Ecuador. The following quotation clearly shows how the game of reciprocity between women differs from that between men—because goods enter into the calculations of exchange in different ways. The context here is the preparation of the daily breakfast consisting of *máchica* ("barley mush").

> It is easy to make *máchica* like this, freshly prepared from scratch in a big household, with one woman to do the first grinding and another to do the second, fine grinding and sifting, leaving the senior woman to toast and boil and fill the bowls, handing them to a young granddaughter to carry to the men. A woman who runs a kitchen by herself, with only young children to help her, must grind the barley the day before. Many newly established kitchens do not even have a *kutana rumi*, the grinding stone; the woman still goes back to her mother's or mother-in-law's in midafternoon to make *máchica* for the morning meals. Or the gift of labor may be reversed: after so many years, as a young bride, of grinding barley at the older couple's home, now she may be awakened herself by a child bearing a bowl of warm *máchica* from the "big" house, ground by a grandchild or a new daughter-in-law. For years after a new kitchen is established, neither household cooks anything without sending a small pot to the other, a visible sign that affective ties still bind. The movement of cooked food between households is also the mark of ongoing exchanges of labor: the families that share food are those who also share agricultural tasks.

Postscript

This chapter is a synthesis encompassing not only my dissertation (1974a) but also three chapters (of which I am the co-author, principal author, or sole author) that appeared in Spanish in an edited book by Giorgio Alberti and Enrique Mayer—namely, *Reciprocidad e intercambio en los Andes peruanos* (Alberti and Mayer 1974a; Mayer 1974b;

Mayer and Zamallóa 1974). Both the thesis in English and the book in Spanish were well received and widely cited. In the present volume I include new citations, clarifications, and debates with the authors of other studies on Andean reciprocity that have been published since then. Although I have not modified my original ideas, they are updated here.

In the 1970s, my publication of a book in Spanish on reciprocity gave familiar practices a new theoretical twist—one that proved to be very popular. By importing "scientifically validated" European and American concepts of reciprocity that tied in with Murra's work, my ethnographic reports on *waje-waje* and *minka* provided good arguments for the growing intellectual "Andean" movement that linked past to present, giving new breath to writings on the communal nature of the *ayllu* "primitive communist" economy about which *Indigenistas* and socialists such as Hildebrando Castro Pozo (1924, 1936) had written four decades before. Since then it has been difficult to prevent a romanticized interpretation of my writings suggesting that "Andean" reciprocal exchanges are more virtuous than money-mediated exchanges in the market or more egalitarian and less exploitative than capitalist relations. And recurring critiques of my supposedly romantic, ahistorical, ideologized, and functionalist view have surfaced as well, most notably in the work of Rodrigo Sánchez (1982: 62) and Orin Starn (1992a: 157).

The publication of *Reciprocidad e intercambio en los Andes peruanos* came at a propitious time since peasant mobilizations, land occupations, and agrarian reform made debates on the nature of peasant economies very current. As editors, Alberti and I added a section on the policy implications of our findings to aid the agrarian reform process—implications that today sound trite (Alberti and Mayer 1974b: 31–32). We defended the right of peasants to maintain a subsistence sector over which they had greater control. We feared that peasants might lose this autonomy, as the cooperatives that the agents of the reform installed on newly adjudicated land had a strict commercial orientation. And we raised the specter that the penetration of impersonal market forces might dissolve away the fundamental values that underwrote the sociocultural configuration of Andean communities.

The edited book, to a greater extent than the dissertation, presented reciprocal relationships as if they were isolated and out of context. The book also did not account for the complexities involved in the interaction between reciprocal exchanges and the penetration of the monetary market (and, by implication, dominant capitalism), thus provoking debate. Harold Mossbrucker (1990) argued that I had revived the specter of dualism between two spatially separated economic systems—insisting, instead, that the two coexist side by side in city and countryside. I indeed emphasize this issue in Chapters 5 and 7, although the question of coexistence remains problematic.

The 1980s were also the years that Marxist theories entered anthropological debate in Peru. Mechanical applications of modes of production made their inroads, and Alberti and I succumbed as well. In the introduction to *Reciprocidad e intercambio en los Andes peruanos*, we editorialized that reciprocal exchanges as described therein represented a fundamental element of the communitarian-based mode of production—an idea that provoked derision.[27] Rodrigo Montoya (1978), arguing that peasants as petty commodity producers articulated with a fundamentally dependent capitalist economy in which reciprocity appeared only as survivals from the past, was later quickly dismissed as representing a primitive version of vulgar Marxism. (On this point Montoya has in later years reversed himself completely.) More interesting, but ultimately not as useful as hoped for, was the Marxian distinction between use value and exchange value. Some of my colleagues argued that nonmonetary exchanges such as reciprocity or barter represented use values whereas money mediated exchange values of commodities. This proposition cannot be sustained, however. Every exchange described here is by definition a transaction of exchange values, although not all are necessarily determined by market mechanisms. In addition, Jürgen Golte and Marisol de la Cadena (1983) proposed that nonmarket relationships guaranteed the reproduction of the household and community economy whereas participation in the real market as it presented itself in the countryside did not. The two spheres existed because market economy and village economy "co-determine" each other in social ways. Household strategies were organized according to a double process of co-determination: to secure a subsistence sphere and to increase the flow of monetary income at the same time. Choice and strategizing in production and exchange were necessary in order to combine the relative advantages and interactions between both spheres. I hope that the preceding description of how Tangorinos used reciprocity as an analogue of currency to strategize between options to achieve their goals has been clearly described.

Reciprocal relationships in the Andes will not succumb to impersonal market forces because they offer advantages, such as refuge from exploitative markets, and, in some cases, even underwrite the production of commodities below their real market value. Moreover, they will persist for social reasons and may, as in Western society, become aspects of consumption. But they also represent an expensive currency. The following is an indirect comment on my work by Gregorio Condori Mamani, a philosophically inclined, Quechua-speaking, rock-bottom poor urbanized Cusco Indian whose testimonial life story has circulated widely in Peru and the United States thanks to the efforts of anthropologists Ricardo Valderrama, Carmen Escalante, Paul Gelles, and Gabriela Martinez. Influenced by Murra and Mayer, Valderrama asked Gregorio's opinion about *ayni*. Gregorio responded (Valderrama et al. 1996: 44):

Such is life for the poor *runa* peasant: if you don't have a lot of kinfolk, you suffer, and then you are always having to exchange or sell your labor in *ayni* or in *mink'a*. When you swap *ayni* favors, you have to put your heart into it, and when they come to help you, you have got to treat them right. If there isn't any warmth in your house, few people will come and help you, because some villagers go work the fields just so they can drink corn beer and liquor. That is why being the host of a work party in the fields is a lot like sponsoring a small *cargo*. It is expensive; for one day's work in the harvest you have to give a bundle of potatoes to each villager who came by and helped you.

He could not afford it.

Notes

1. Formal economic behavior is defined by Plattner (1989: 8) as follows: "The rationalizing or *economizing* actor will select those opportunities that yield the maximal good (or a given level of good for the least cost). This assumption is called the *maximizing* assumption and has been the heart of micro-economics for many years. It assumes that people (1) are calculating beings who use forethought before acting and understand their own values; (2) have the necessary knowledge (which may be probabilistic) about costs, incomes, and yields with respect to all options; and (3) have the necessary calculating ability to solve the maximization problems." These strictures fully apply to the actors engaging in reciprocal exchanges. The only persons without sufficient information are the foreign anthropologists struggling to understand the system, who are often tempted to find such practices irrational.

2. I am grateful to César Fonseca, who pointed out to me that the correct expression for this type of exchange is *waje-waje*—not *waje*, the term I had originally used. In view of this exchange's tit-for-tat nature, the duplicated term makes eminent sense.

3. Mauss (1954: 62) astutely noted that in German, *Gift* is both a present and poison. It also works in Latin: With regard to ". . . the etymology of gift as coming from the Latin *dosis* . . . [d]osis has the same root as *donum* or French and Spanish *don*" (1954: 127).

4. Allen (1988: 92) describes it thus: "Similarly, injuries are also repaid in *ayni*. When angry word matches angry word, blow matches blow, rejection matches rejection—that *ayni* is of a negative kind." See also Abercrombie (1989: 516).

5. In the Cusco dialect this relationship is called *yanapay*, meaning "to help without requiring repayment" (Allen 1988: 263).

6. César Zamallóa was an anthropology student at the Catholic University during the first year I started teaching there. He accompanied me to Tangor to do quantitative surveys, and we co-published an article with the results in Mayer and Zamalloa 1974.

7. Reciprocity between women is a realm unto itself, but owing to my deficient Quechua and the strong gender separation in Tangor, I was unable to enter this realm. *Ayni* between women is described by Allen (1988: 75) and Gose (1994:

279). And *minka* between women is described by Fonseca (1974: 105–106). A year before a family assumes the obligation to sponsor a fiesta, the wife of the sponsor distributes bread and other treats among women relatives and friends, and in return is later given one or two balls of spun wool, which, when accumulated, is used to weave the *ponchos* and other finery worn during the celebration. The *cumplimiento* takes place the day they all gather together to participate in preparing the warp, a female festive occasion. This relationship, termed *auliskuy*, is also manipulated by rich peasants who accumulate textiles for sale: "The wives of rich peasants distribute food to women spinners during hungry times (generally poor widows) in exchange for spun wool which are then converted to finished textiles."

8. Gade and Ríos (1972) wrote an exemplary article on the Andean footplow, a "primitive" ancient tool, still used today, whose remains have been found in archaeological sites; early Spanish writers described how it was used. And as Pierre Morlon (1996: 39) observes, it has become a picturesque Andean symbol. Morlon's compilation shows in great detail what can be achieved in terms of the manipulation of earth and moisture with this footplow, termed a *chaquitaclla*. The steel tips are made out of truck springs in local forges, where a variety of shapes and sizes are available. They can also be made according to personal preference or to fit a particular type of terrain or task. Each man makes his own plow and shows up at the worksite with it. Fields consistently worked with the footplow over a long period gradually become slope terraces. The point here is that it's not the tool but the athletic wielding of it, along with teamwork, that achieves these astounding terraced hillsides. Tourists frequently ask whether Inca terraces were built by slave labor; the answer is that they were built by *ayni*. Indeed, the archetype of symmetrical *ayni* is teamwork with the footplow.

9. In Tangor such a team is called a pair (*un par* in Spanish) because it requires two plows and one puller or *rapador*. The latter does not "count," I suspect, because this role is performed by a woman in many regions of the Andes other than Tangor. A field can be measured in terms of how many pairs are required to plow it in a day. In my article on kinship (Mayer 1977b: 76–78), I make a distinction between pairs made up of equal elements (such as plowing teams), which are called *masintin* in Quechua, and pairs in which one element is different from the other (as with the two halves of a mirror image), which are called *yanantin* in Quechua. Platt (1986: 228–259) and Harris (1986: 260–279) further elaborate on this basic contrast. For the purposes of this chapter, it might be useful to think of symmetrical *waje-waje* as a *masintin* relationship and hierarchical *minka* as a *yanantin* relationship, though for Harris and Platt the root notion is the husband-wife team. I have also applied these concepts in the kinship sphere. Note, however, that there is a mistake in my 1977b article. *Lumtshuy* and *masha*, the kin terms for "brother-in-law" and "sister-in-law," are erroneously described on page 75 as reciprocal and *masintin* when, in fact, they are decidedly *yanantin* and hierarchical. See also Ossio (1988) for a further analysis of affinal relationships.

10. Twelve *soles* are equivalent to US$0.32. A day's wages bought half a kilo of sugar in a local store. The rates were based more or less on the notion of "just" price and were evaluated according to how much sugar, lard, or other cash items cost in the regional markets. When the price of these items rose, wages were eventually forced up too, and these had to be agreed upon in local assemblies. Nominal wages had been going up over the past twenty years, as people remembered having

earned five and then ten *soles*, congruent with a creeping inflation. In 1969, each village in the region had a rate that varied from 10 to 30 *soles*. Interestingly, wage differentials did not tend to equalize between neighboring villages, despite labor shortages during peak times. Some Tangorinos did take advantage of higher wages in other places by going there for a few days, but the exodus was never massive. One Tangorino explained that the differences in wages resulted from the fact that some villages were richer in cash than others. Tangor farmers justified lower wages in their village by saying that because they didn't produce commercial crops, they had less cash income and therefore could not afford to pay that much. This is an example of noncommunicating labor markets, a feature of the protectionist barriers that peasants build to defend themselves from the impact of the monetary sector. Further discussion of protectionism is provided in Chapter 5.

11. Using a reputational scale to establish a measure of wealth differences, I independently asked four trustworthy informants to classify all persons in the village along a continuum that gave *alto* (high), *medio* (middle), and *bajo* (low) as possible choices. Agreement among the four judges was remarkable. Part of the evaluation consisted in assessing productive resources available to families (animals, migrant sons who sent money, good jobs, lots of production) rather than possessions. This method provided me with a workable measure, and I have used it successfully in other studies. The difficulties of gathering sensitive quantitative data in Tangor are discussed in Mayer (1972).

12. More details on being paid in kind during harvests are provided in Chapter 5. See also Gose (1994: 190).

13. A serious problem in Gose's book is the fact that appropriation, so crucial to his argument, is never clearly defined or delimited. For him, appropriation can mean "taking the harvest home," or it can mean an arrangement whereby one person benefits more from a relationship than another, or it can be symbolized by a roof with its cross. In other words, appropriation in Gose's book is sometimes synonymous with private property and at other times synonymous with the process of consumption.

14. For a discussion of peasant rebellions, which are principally about land but also concern abusive labor and servitude conditions in the rural Highlands of Peru, see Alberti (1970), Barnett (1969), Favre (1976), Gow (1981), Handelman (1975), Kapsoli (1977), Martínez Arellano (1962), and Quijano (1967).

15. According to Allen (1988: 144–145), "The hierarchical and asymmetrical nature of drinking etiquette makes *trago* (low-grade cane alcohol) especially suited for purposes of requesting a favor. The solicitor, as the one who asks the favor, compensates for his subordinate position through his superior position in the drinking ceremony. The person solicited, as recipient of the *trago*, can only reciprocate by accepting the request." In Tangor the use of liquor in these circumstances was as close to a legal instrument as one could imagine. Furthermore, drinking and libations (the sharing of drink with Mother Earth and the mountain spirits) are important in that they involve complex "obligating" relationships between humans, their ancestors, spirits and gods—as shown by Abercrombie (1998: 317–362) and Gose (1994: 194–224).

16. Fonseca (1972a: 70) mentions an apt local metaphor involving *shokay*, which is what people in Chaupiwaranga call this way of obligating others to collaborate: "*Shoka* is also the egg that one puts in the nest of a chicken to force it to lay more eggs. It consists of a quarter bottle of *aguardiente*, a handful of coca and

a packet of cigarettes. My informants say '*carguyojpa tragun chichumi*,' which means that the person who drinks the quarter bottle has become pregnant and in consequence has no alternative than to help the *carguyoq*."

17. Weismantel (1988: 110) stresses an important category of food known as *wanlla* (which means "treats"): "Bread is the *wanlla* par excellence. It is the appropriate gift, the favorite treat. The distribution of bread is critically important in many social and ceremonial contexts. Large amounts of bread are necessary for certain formal gift-giving exchanges . . . . In Zumbagua minds, bread has none of the qualities of a staple. It is truly a *golosina*, a treat, a luxury."

18. The Spanish expression *llano* is a delightful word meaning "plain," not just in the geographical sense but also in reference to a person's character as straightforward, accessible, and honest. Contributions often include money given as a gift. Sponsors parade around town dressed in their finest clothing, and *llano* friends come up and pin high-denomination bills on their lapels—in full view of the whole village.

19. Details on house roofing can be found in Mayer (1974a: 156–172 and 1977b: 69–78). Note, however, that Gose (1991, 1994: 74–90, 266–267) provides a different interpretation of the symbolic meanings of house rethatching.

20. Many students in the Andes note that the Quechua word *waccha* means not only "orphan" but also "a person who is poor." The lack of a support network of relatives is seen as the *sine qua non* of indigence in this society.

21. Wolf (1966: 81) uses the term *dyadic* in his discussion of how peasants seek coalitions with other people to counteract selective pressures. See also Foster (1967), who describes as dyadic those coalitions that take place between two people or groups. The latter, he notes, epitomize reciprocal relationships between individuals in Latin American peasant societies.

22. According to Isbell (1977: 81–105 and 1978: 13), the Quechua term *kuyaq* (literally, "those who love me") means "my group": "For reciprocal exchanges, 'my group' encompasses a wide network of consanguineal, affinal and spiritual relatives. For marriage purposes 'my group' is defined as *ayllu*, a bilateral kindred with sexual bifurcation and genealogical distance as principles of organization." The web of relationships between relatives can be identified in terms of the way they practice reciprocity, a theme discussed not only by Isbell but also by Mayer (1977b) and Allen (1988: 91–119).

23. Both Fonseca (1974: 100–103) and Ossio (1988, 1992: 106) describe *cambio* exchanges between families during maize planting. Gifts are displayed and have to be passed on in exactly the same way to the next year's sponsor.

24. Economists conceptualize capital as goods and services that are not consumed but used to create more goods and services. However, Bourdieu goes beyond this strictly economic definition; for him, capital refers to those aspects capable of conferring strength, power, and consequently profit on their holder. He goes on to say that "symbolic capital, which in the form of the prestige and renown attached to a family and a name is readily convertible back into economic capital, is perhaps *the most valuable form of accumulation* in a society . . . " (1977:179; emphasis added). *Trukay* breads have both meanings: As economic and symbolic capital, they are goods that produce more goods, but they principally deal with honor and reputation as currencies. Why Bourdieu needed to transform older anthropological wisdom about the role of prestige in complex systems of exchange into symbolic

capital is a mystery to me; his doing so may be an example of shifting scripts (Gudeman 1986: 44) from one discipline to another without necessarily creating anything new. For that matter, *trukay* breads may be a good example of scripting the meaning of symbolic capital, given that Bourdieu deliberately extends the word *investment* beyond the economic sphere—because symbolic capital, he says, comes from "investments and over-investments (in both the economic and the psychoanalytical senses) which tend, through the ensuing competition and rarity, to reinforce the well-grounded illusion that the value of symbolic goods is inscribed in the nature of things, just as interest in these goods is inscribed in the nature of men" (1977: 183).

25. Personal communication with César Fonseca (1974).

26. The civil religious hierarchy, or *varayoq* system, has been amply treated in many ethnographies of the Andes. In particular, see Mishkin (1946), Stein (1961), Fuenzalida (1971), Isbell (1971, 1978), Rasnake (1988), Mitchell (1991), and Abercrombie (1989).

27. It was a politically imposed fashion in those times to describe social formations as being composed of various modes of production in articulation. The debate was fierce because the correct characterization of the "dominant" form called for specific types of political action, and this theory was a convenient way to accuse rival Marxist factions of being in fundamental error, if they did not "get it right." One position argued for predominant capitalism with feudal leftovers, thereby placing the proletariat at the vanguard of revolutionary change; the other, eventually imposed as dogma by Maoists (including Shining Path), insisted on predominant feudalism with a weak overlay of dependent capitalism, giving the rural peasants the privilege of being in the vanguard. The proposition that there was an Andean mode of production also circulated for a while. Apart from that one sentence about the "communitarian-based mode of production," I avoided getting pinned down on this ideologically charged issue of those times.

5

Aspects of Barter

*This chapter describes various forms of barter and explains
how they relate to transactions that involve cash. Barter represents a sphere of exchange separate from that of reciprocity as
well as buying and selling. Indeed, people create barter networks in order to protect themselves from unfavorable relationships involved in monetary transactions. The discussion of
money introduces a theme that is further developed in the next
two chapters, which describe how the flow of money through
markets and households perversely influences household resources, playing a role in the peasant economy similar to the
one that foreign exchange plays in national economies.*

Impurities

In real life there is no such thing as pure barter. In order for barter to be a
viable economic form, it needs to be stabilized by other contingent social
relations. Caroline Humphrey and Stephen Hugh-Jones (1992: 1), in a recent overview of barter, note its basic features as follows:

(a)The focus is on demand for particular things which are of a different
kind. . . . (b)The protagonists are free and equal, either can pull out of the
deal and at the end of it they are quits. (c) There is no criterion by which,
from the outside, it can be judged that [a widget is equal in value to the gad-
get]. Some kind of bargaining is taking place, but not with reference to some
abstract measure of value or numeraire; each simply wants the object held
by the other. (d) The transaction is simultaneous, but there are also situations where it can be separated in time. (e) The act is transformative; it
moves objects between "regimes of value" (Appadurai 1986) sustained by
the two actors.[1]

I agree with Humphrey and Hugh-Jones that barter is separable from other types of exchange—gift exchange, credit, formalized trade, and monetized commodity exchange—even though they may shade into each other at the boundaries. Still, barter is a distinct and irreducible form. It is ubiquitous and has moved material objects between humans for a long time. Formally conceived, pure barter is so unstable that only when institutionalized in what Humphreys and Hugh-Jones (1992: 8) call "barter systems" can it be viable and interesting for ethnographic study.

Barter systems exist when goods tend to be repeatedly exchanged with known people at particular times and places. Thus there is an in-built tendency to act fairly, so that the opportunity to repeat the exchange is not spoiled. Barter is also a very direct and uncomplicated affair in contrast with the complexities involved in, say, gift giving, where the viscosity between object and person enriches reciprocal relationships (as discussed in Chapter 4). Pure barter is therefore a myth or a conceptual construct that, in its very features, exhibits the mark of instability ("tit for tat and goodbye"). But exchanges exist in a social context, and people labor to ensure that this context is established. In the examples that I describe below, one can think of barter as an electrical wire that connects traders to each other: The wire energizes the movement of goods between people from time to time, but it is insulated by a coating of sociability, such as hospitality, which, although it adds to the transaction costs, nevertheless permits the transaction to continue to take place.

One complexity, however, revolves around the issue of value between the objects, which may be so dissimilar as to be noncomparable. Humphrey and Hugh-Jones (1992: 9) put it this way: ". . . [I]t would be a mistake to think that the consumption or use values of the objects are measurable by some common abstract standard held in the heads of the two parties." In institutionalized barter systems, known and quotable equivalencies are often established between commonly bartered objects; but these are not proxies to measures of economic value, nor are they some kind of price. Equivalencies serve as reference points for bargaining to take place, but it is not possible to aggregate equivalencies in a manner that reconciles all objects against each other. In established barter systems a given range of objects can substitute for each other, and people often categorize them with a descriptive term such that commonly demanded objects fall within a particular category. For example, Antoinette Fioravanti Molinié (1982: 220–221) describes barter in the Urubamba Valley of Cusco. In each climatic zone one primary crop serves as the main crop against which other equivalencies can be stated—maize in the valley, potatoes in the next level up. Coca, which comes from the tropical lowlands, is more ubiquitous throughout. There are equivalencies of other items against maize or potatoes or coca in each of the weekly markets in different climatic zones, where women can barter them against each other. These equivalencies set up the common ground that starts the bargaining process, and often the bargaining is about quantity rather than equivalency.

Because each exchange tends toward a "perfect balance," given that the parties "call it quits" when both sides are satisfied, the relationship tends to be unstable—but one that, "in principle at least, is one of equality" (Humphrey and Hugh-Jones 1992: 11). Humphrey and Hugh-Jones also note, however, that many instances of barter within wider relations of inequality can be cited, including examples of coercion, but they state that these are maintained by forces outside the exchange itself: "Barter itself, as a mode of exchange, is a struggle against enforced transactions, though frequently a puny one" (1992: 11). For example, people who barter within strict rationing systems subvert these systems and are often punished. And if barter attempts to struggle against other kinds of exchange, then it survives in an uneasy relationship with them. In other words, one often finds barter side by side with other forms of exchange, carving out a niche for itself; thus, in the appropriate context it can be another weapon of the weak (Scott 1985).

That is why barter systems are found even where money systems and established markets exist. Humphrey and Hugh-Jones (1992) give examples of international barter with the ex-socialist bloc and underdeveloped countries, of swap societies in middle-class America, and of barter systems where a common currency exists but people prefer not to use it. Barter frequently occurs where there is not enough money to go around, and it quickly becomes ubiquitous in situations involving economic crisis, currency crashes, inflation, or war-induced chaos. And in rural societies, such as the Andes, cash is an extremely scarce foreign resource, and its scarcity promotes barter transactions in the interstices where money has not yet spread. For these reasons, barter cannot be explained without reference to the market systems with which it coexists.[2]

Thus, there is no pure barter. Nor are the barter relationships described in connection with my field data in Tangor in 1969 about barter alone; rather, these data reflect a variety of contexts and practices in which people bargain without money to exchange goods.

Harvest Failure

In May 1969, many farmers in the peasant community of Tangor had a bad potato harvest, and they were worried. The harvest was indeed poor. One farmer, pointing to small tubers that came out of the ground, said that he had planted potatoes but harvested grapes. Another one, more disheartened, abandoned the harvest altogether, because his yields were so bad it was not worth getting them out; thus, he lost the seed as well. The lack of potatoes presented these farmers with many problems. Not the least of these was how to satisfy their family's food needs. But another was their inability to reciprocate their work obligations with other farmers (here it was customary to serve steamed potatoes and a *llocro* potato stew). Potatoes were also necessary for compliance with social obligations, which always involved generous presentations of cooked food. A proper social meal required that the hosts serve large plates of specially selected and good-tasting potatoes to be eaten with savory peppery *ají* sauces and soups. Despite the bad harvest, Tangorinos did not refrain from consuming potatoes that year. How they did so is what this chapter is all about.

Tangor is one of twenty-six recognized Indigenous or *campesino* communities in the Chaupiwaranga region (see Map 5.1) in the Departments of Pasco and Huánuco in Central Peru. It is situated in one of the valleys that form the headwaters of the Upper Huallaga river system. The Chaupi-waranga River starts in the high *punas* near Lauricocha and flows in a northeasterly direction, creating a deep and narrow valley as it passes the provincial capital of Yanahuanca at 3,000 meters above sea level and joins the Huariaca River at Ambo at 2,000 meters, some 70 kilometers down-river. On both slopes, about halfway between the river and the ridge, are the villages—among them Tangor at about 2,500 meters above sea level.

For purposes of production, each individual community, and each peas-ant farming family within it, attempts to have direct access to land in each of the different ecological zones that make up the landscape of the com-munity territory, as these zones enable production of the variety of crops that make up the basic diet. This scenario has been termed by John V. Murra (1964: 428; 1967: 384; 1968: 121; 1972: 427–468) the "ideal of vertical control of a maximum of ecological zones," or "verticality" for short. In Tangor, the alluvial terraces near the river experience warmer temperatures and can accommodate the production of maize, whereas the higher-lying and colder slopes produce potatoes. In 1969, all Tangorinos had access to high potato lands, which were favorable to the production of the most appreciated "floury"-tasting but slow-growing varieties. They also had access to lower-lying potato lands, which were worked in a secto-rial fallow rotation system. After fallow, in the first year, they all planted the main crop, potatoes; the second year they repeated the potato crop, but this time with early-maturing varieties; in the third year they planted other Andean tubers such as *ocas, mashuas, ollucos,* and fava beans; and in the fourth and sometimes fifth year, they planted wheat or barley. Then the sectors entered another fallow period for six or seven years. Each farming family was simultaneously working several very small fields scattered in five different sectors, which changed location and crop rotation each year as one new sector was brought under cultivation and another began its fal-low period. Each family also had lands lower down, where an annual crop of maize, squash, and beans was possible for seven or eight consecutive years before it entered one or two years of fallow. About half the fields be-longing to the Tangorinos were in fallow at any one time. Fallow lands

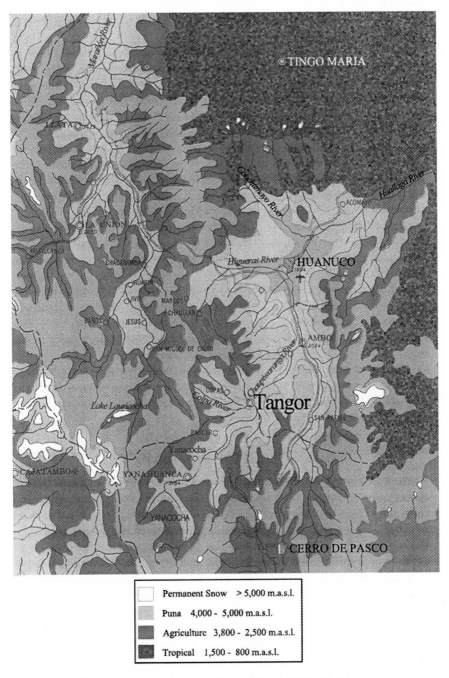

Map 5.1   *The Chaupiwaranga region. (From Mayer 1974: 19.)*

were used as open free pasturage for cows, sheep, goats, donkeys, mules, and horses. The latter were necessary for transportation but not necessarily affordable by every family.

Even though each community, in theory, was capable of providing for its needs, the uneven geographical distribution of highlands and valley lands is such that different communities in the region specialized in producing a surplus in those kinds of crops for which they were best endowed. Thus, the villages near the headwaters of the valley with its abundant pasture lands were more specialized in raising animals, whereas Tangor, with its more ample maize lands, specialized in producing a surplus in maize. Although animal raising was an important activity in Tangor, portions of Tangor's distant *puna* lands were available for the community to rent them out to herders from other communities; however, maize was intensively cropped with no more land available in that production zone.

The harvest that failed the Tangorinos that year was the "main" potato crop in one of the big sectorial fallow systems; other harvests in other rotational sequences, including the maize crop, were adequate. And among some farmers, especially those who had planted earlier, the potato harvest wasn't all that bad; early rains had provided them a fair-sized harvest, compared with those who had planted later and suffered from a late-season drought. Likewise, whereas some fields were infested with pests that finished off the crop before the humans could get to it, others escaped the blight. In short, agricultural production in Chaupiwaranga, as elsewhere in the Andes, is irregular, uneven, and unpredictable, but scattering fields at different elevations and with varying cropping schedules minimizes the probability that crop failures will affect the totality of production (Morlon 1996: 178–194; Goland 1992).

Strategies Intended to Overcome the Crisis

As the bad harvest was becoming apparent and the subject of much lamentation among Tangor farmers, one of them, Don Eulogio, disappeared from the village for two weeks, and when he returned, he told me that he had been to the villages nearer the headwaters of the Chaupiwaranga River, where the potato harvest was just beginning, and had obtained four sacks for his *gasto*—that is, for his regular food expenditure. Don Eulogio was the first farmer to travel north to explore. He explained to me that he initially went to the market in the town of Yanahuanca to find out which villages were actually ready to harvest, and was told that in the community of Yanacocha and the annexes of Yanahuanca the potato harvest was in full swing. Don Eulogio remembered that in Yanacocha he had a friend with whom he had done business before.

Carrying fresh corn on the cob and some squashes he had brought from Tangor, he set out for the house of his friend in Yanacocha. The house was locked, because the friend was away digging up potatoes. After a two-hour climb above the village, Don Eulogio found his friend who had set up a camp next to his fields. Don Eulogio was well received. His friend accepted the gift corn and squashes and invited him to stay on. Don Eulogio helped his friend harvest, and he was given half a sack of potatoes for every day he worked—or, in Don Eulogio's calculations, two days of work for one full sack. In 1969, the monetary value would have totaled 60 *soles* per day, since a sack of potatoes was then selling at 120 *soles*. In Quechua, the arrangement Don Eulogio made with his friend was called *allapakuy* ("to help harvest"). It was also described as *costumbre* (Fonseca 1974: 92–95), a Spanish word, translatable as "custom," that in this context referred to old usages based on reciprocal obligations that were valid among Chaupiwaranga villagers. Don Eulogio had certain *derechos* ("rights") based on this *costumbre*. With the corn and squashes he had brought with him, he earned the acceptance of his friend, who, by a customary obligation known as *yawasinakuy*,[3] (Quechua for "to open up each other's home"), was obligated to extend the courtesies of hospitality to Don Eulogio. As maize and squashes were not yet available in Yanacocha, they were welcomed by his friend's wife as a treat. The present obligated Don Eulogio's friend to reciprocate, but this went beyond the rather trivial affairs of returning small food gifts. In this case, both understood Don Eulogio's explicit, though polite, request: that the friend should respond in some way, as a big favor, to his need for a substantial quantity of potatoes.

To greater advantage, the Yanacochino could have either harvested the fields with his own labor and that of his family or hired a wage worker for only 12 *soles* a day, one-fifth of what it cost him to accept Don Eulogio's request to help harvest. It was the *costumbre* that obligated the Yanacochino to accept Don Eulogio's offer to help in the *allapakuy* arrangement. There was a moral obligation involved; indeed, it would have been difficult to reject the request from a person in need. And based on notions of reciprocity, it was not altogether improbable that the harvest might someday fail in Yanacocha, forcing the Yanacochino to look elsewhere for the needed potatoes—including, perhaps, the village of Tangor, where he might find a recourse to the established reciprocities with Don Eulogio, who would be indebted to him.

Don Eulogio's help also yielded more immediate advantages to the Yanacochino, given the scarcity of nonfamily labor that happens during harvest times. As everyone in the village sector harvested the crops at the same time, farmers who lagged behind ran the risk of losing the harvest to human theft or animal damage. In addition, a quick harvest minimized the threat that bad weather would delay the task and released labor for other important agricultural activities during those busy months. In sum, despite the higher cost, the *allapakuy* arrangement was an agreement of long-term mutual benefit, based on traditionally accepted practices that created social relationships among the inhabitants of the separate villages of the region.

Don Eulogio's success was widely commented upon by other people in Tangor. More people traveled south in search of potatoes, resulting in a veritable exodus. Some Tangorinos traveled by bus or truck; others went on foot, driving their donkeys and horses before them. Not all Tangorinos were successful in establishing a favorable *allapakuy* arrangement. Some had to buy the potatoes with cash—although they paid a lower price than the market rate that the wholesale buyers were offering because they were buying them directly from the fields. Moreover, Tangorinos sought the inferior potatoes: the smaller ones and those with blemishes that commercial buyers tended to reject. But the same generalized obligation to help out villagers from the region whose harvests had failed also contributed to their agreeing to sell them at a lower price. Those Tangorinos who had brought their donkeys offered their services to transport the potatoes to the Yanacochinos' houses. They, too, were paid in kind, rather than with money, at established customary rates for each trip.

Other Tangorinos went to the city of Huánuco to sell maize and squashes; and with the money they obtained, they bought baskets, pottery, lard, sugar, textile cloth, needles, and other manufactured products. They then rode the bus to Yanahuanca and from there set out on foot to the villages in the region to barter these products for potatoes. For some products they used old and established exchange rates. Earthenware pottery was exchanged for potatoes by filling the pot twice with potatoes for the value of that pot, whereas the baskets, being cheaper, were traded with only one filling. One pound of lard was exchanged for one *arroba* (25 pounds) of potatoes. Other, poorer Tangorinos, among them women, skipped the intermediate step of going to Huánuco and bartered their maize and squashes directly for potatoes. These labor-intensive, small-scale transactions—called *menudeo* in Spanish—enabled the women to cover basic needs but not much more. César Fonseca (1972a: 111–114) describes one such case involving four trips, minute quantities, and minuscule profits.

Tangorinos combined several exchange strategies in their efforts to secure the needed potatoes. For example, Don Francisco took two donkeys loaded with corn on the cob, which he exchanged for potatoes. He offered his donkeys to transport potatoes from the fields to the villages or road head, and he worked in *allapakuy*. And a weaver took advantage of this trip to obtain, in addition to potatoes, some wool for his trade. He worked in *allapakuy* to accumulate the sacks he needed for food; continued working in *allapakuy* with other farmers until he had collected three additional sacks, which he then sold to a buyer; and with that money he bought the sheep pelts. With the remaining money, he also bought sugar, noodles, rice, coca, and lard in the stores of Yanahuanca.

The harvest failure in Tangor was a rather exceptional event. Nonetheless, I must emphasize that the customary relationships in the region existed for the purpose of overcoming such eventualities—and, indeed, were used by the peasants from Chaupiwaranga many times. This fact can be demonstrated with the case of Tangor, which never was self-sufficient in potatoes, because what the farmers there harvested from their own fields usually lasted only until December. At that time, the villages to the north of Tangor, along the Colpas River basin, began to harvest their early-maturing potatoes, and Tangorinos usually went there in trips that combined the barter strategies I have described above, to secure potatoes until their own early-maturing varieties were ready for harvest in March. On their trips to the Colpas villages, *allapakuy* relationships were less common, because Colpas farmers "paid" much less in *allapakuy* than the Yanacochinos did. The rates in the Colpas Valley ranged from three to four days of work for one sack, depending on the good will of the owners and on how well the fields had yielded.

Barter: A Generalized Exchange System

In normal years Tangorinos preferred making barter trips rather than seeking out *allapakuy* relationships exclusively, taking with them such items as bread, lard, sugar, rice, maize, numia beans (*Phaseolus vulgaris*), and, in some cases, even money. They went to these villages not only to stock up on potatoes, which they needed to fulfill consumption needs, but also to trade—that is, to make a profit in money. They bartered for potatoes with the items they brought with them and then sold the potatoes in the Parcoy Sunday market.

Parcoy is a small village, located on the road to Huánuco, where a crowded market was held every Sunday, attended by people from all around the region. Potato buyers from Lima went there with their trucks during the harvest, and Tangorinos who carried out this trade speculated there. They ran the risk of not covering their initial investment in bread, or lard, because the price that the wholesale buyers paid for the potatoes fluctuated widely depending on the conditions of supply and urban demand in Lima; in contrast, the barter rates tended to be fixed. The Tangorinos' aim in these trading trips was to make a cash profit, taking advantage of differential exchange rates between cash and barter transactions, as well as absorbing transportation costs from field to road. One pound of lard had a price of 7 *soles* in a store in the region, and was exchangeable for one *arroba* of potatoes which, when market conditions were favorable, could be sold for 20 *soles*.

Barter trips to make a cash profit were very common among Tangorinos, who regarded themselves as seasoned traders in the region. A good example of such trips was the tale of adventure recalled by Don Federico, whom

I interviewed in Tangor. He started the business by borrowing 400 *soles* from a Tangor neighbor, at a monthly rate of 5 percent interest (60 percent annual rate!), and went to Huánuco where he purchased a number of manufactured goods, mainly enamel plates, pots, and pans. Other Tangorinos bought plasticware, sewing equipment and supplies, and ready-made clothing. They also carried highland products such as wool, dried meat, freeze-dried potatoes, and llama grease (used for medicinal purposes), which they obtained in barter from highlanders. Don Federico traveled with a partner for company, protection, and mutual aid, but both engaged in their own separate business. After spending a night in some very cheap lodgings at 2 *soles* per person, locally known as the "wild *tambo* of Huánuco," they rode the bus toward the tropical lowland settlements on the Cordillera Azul of the Tingo María region in the Upper Huallaga drainage. From there Don Federico set out to visit the coca- and coffee-producing farmsteads. He traveled on foot, carrying all his merchandise on his back along the muddy and difficult trails, offering his wares to the women in the farmsteads, and exchanging them for coca, coffee, or annato seed (a food dye and spice).

Don Federico worked with a 100 percent markup for his wares; that is, he charged double the price he had paid. But he did not take money. Instead, he collected the value in coffee or coca, calculating the exchange ratio according to the going market value of an *arroba* of coffee in the producing area, which was always less than the price offered by the wholesale buyers at the road head. Since the coffee had usually not yet been picked or dried, he most often left the items that had been exchanged after reaching a verbal agreement to pick up the bargained amount of coffee on his way out. Once he had disposed of all his merchandise, Don Federico and his companion worked for one or two weeks as day laborers for cash or kind, picking coffee, weeding the plantations, picking coca leaf, or whatever job presented itself in the area, until he calculated that his clients had the coffee or coca ready for him to pick up. On his way back to the road, he collected his contracts until the load he had to carry on his back (one *quintal,* or 50 pounds) became too heavy for him. Normally Don Federico would then have hired a pair of mules to carry the commodity out to the road; but this time, he was lucky to find another middleman in the interior who paid a good price and relieved him of his burden. His sale was for 1,030 *soles.* On the cost side he calculated 400 *soles* for the initial investment loan, 60 *soles* in expenses, and 20 *soles* in interest. The net profit was 550 *soles,* not counting the wages he was paid, in cash or in kind.

Don Federico regularly traveled to the lowlands two or three times a year in June, July, and August, during the months of the coffee harvest in the Tingo María region and whenever there was a relative slack in agricultural tasks in Tangor. In addition, he often went to the highlands of the Oyón region in the Department of Lima to collect the wool and dried sheep and llama meat that he bartered in the lowlands. On one such trip, just after he had funded an expensive fiesta in Tangor that required the ceremonial distribution of bread, he had some left over, which he took to the highlands. There he bartered the bread for wool, using an exchange rate known as *unay precio* ("old prices"). The bread was worth 10 *centavos unay precio,* and the wool pelts were worth 30–40 *centavos unay precio,* depending on their quality. (One pelt was equivalent to sixteen breads.)

Forms of Barter

There were three main methods of bartering in the Chaupiwaranga region, each involving a different way of determining equivalency between products: by weight, by volume, or by counting. After the partners decided that they would barter with each other, by weight, say, they had to agree on how they were going to weigh their products. There were may different systems of measurement in Tangor, derived mainly from Spanish colonial standards.[4] One option was a weighing device, known as a *romanilla,* involving a spring calibrated to a dial that measured *arrobas* and pounds on one side and kilos on the other; it could be hung from a nail or held in the hand and had a hook at the bottom for attaching a basket or sack holding the contents to be weighed. Another option was the use of traditional containers that indicated amounts in weights but actually measured volumes. These containers were arranged in groups from small to large. The smallest amounts were measured in gourds that also served as serving plates and were used by women to barter delicacies or very fine grains such as quinoa or flour. Ceramic cooking pots measured amounts of fava beans, wheat, or barley. A third option involved special baskets woven out of *chogo* grass (called *chicra* in Quechua and *cereta* in Spanish). These came in three sizes: one *arroba,* one-half *arroba,* and one-quarter *arroba,* respectively. For bulky items such as potatoes or corn on the cob, there was one set of three *ceretas;* for finer grains, another set of *ceretas* with a smaller volume capacity. A fourth option was the *lata,* a rectangular tin container that manufacturers used to pack and ship commercially manufactured lard. Empties, which could be bought at stores, were very convenient measures of volume and good storage containers in the home. A smaller *lata* measure was the one-gallon can that originally contained soybean oil shipped from the United States as food aid (a warning stamp printed in English on the outside stated "Not to be sold or bartered"). And, finally, since so much transportation was by pack animal, the sack was a ubiquitous measure. In olden times it was woven out of fine alpaca wool, but nowadays it is more often made from jute or sturdy plastic thread. To facilitate barter, I myself collected alpaca sacks, which had markers, woven into the fabric, that indicated measures for fine and bulky grains.

Unay precio was one method used when the agreement to exchange involved counting. An established exchange rate used in barter transactions between products from different ecological zones, it used the terminology of a coinage that had been valid in Peru since the early years of this century, with 10 *centavos* as the most popular reference. Ten *centavos* were also called 1 *real*; 5 *centavos* had a Spanish synonym, *medio* ("half a *real*"); and an alternative term for 20 *centavos* was a *peseta*. At the time I was doing fieldwork, the actual coins to which this system referred were no longer in circulation; however, as a school boy in Huancayo in the 1950s, I was given one *peseta* if I did my chores.

As a reference pricing mechanism, *unay precio* allowed barter to take place with fluctuating exchange ratios. In Tangor in 1969, the base of *unay precio* was twenty pairs of ears of dried maize on the cob (*huayuncas*)[5] at a cost of 10 *centavos*. This price had nothing to do with the then-current market prices in *soles*, whereby one single ear of dried maize was worth 75 cents. It would have been a ridiculous proposition to offer maize for money at *unay precio* rates.

Unay precio existed only for barter transactions and was generally used in exchanges between valley peasants and highland peasants. Looking to barter for maize, highlanders traveled to the Chaupiwaranga Valley to exchange wool, cheese, meat, freeze-dried potatoes, and textiles such as woolen sacks and llama ropes. They quoted the *unay precio* rate at which they were willing to barter these items—say, 30 *centavos* for a pelt of wool, 20 *centavos* for a leg of lamb meat, or 20 *centavos* for a half-pound mold of cheese. If Tangorinos found this price acceptable, they gave twenty times three (i.e., sixty pairs of maize ears) for the woolen pelt and twenty times two (forty pairs of maize ears) for the leg of lamb or the cheese. In short, *unay precio* was a measure of relative prices between maize and the highland products.[6]

There were years when the highland herders decided, for various reasons, to raise their prices—from 30 to 40 *centavos* for a pelt, say, and from 20 *centavos* to 30 for meat or cheese. Conversely, there were years when maize production yielded less and Tangorinos decided to alter their offering price—say, from forty to thirty or even twenty pairs of maize ears for ten *centavos*. Indeed, during barter times each year, there was a lot of haggling between the highlanders and the lowlanders, until they reached a mutually acceptable exchange rate. *Unay precio* allowed barter with fluctuating exchange rates rather than fixed ones, but they remained within the category of what can legitimately be called customary rates. One farmer explained this situation to me as follows:

> When the *puna* people wish to barter with *unay precio*, then we too employ the *unay precio* system, and we have to give twenty pairs for one *real*. If they open up the bargaining session by asking for 1 *sol* for their cheese, instead of

twenty *centavos*, then we too have to fight and give five ears of corn for *medio* or ten for one *real*. In an assembly we discuss the matter and decide at what price we will give our maize to them.[7]

But the important thing to note is that whatever exchange rate was established in any given year, it was always less than the monetary value that could be realized if the highlanders sold their sheep, and the valley farmers their maize, in the real market at the then-established prices with real contemporary national currency. For example, a sheep was valued between 300 and 350 *soles* among meat buyers. Given that one sack of maize on the cob was worth 140 *soles*, if the highlander had carried out two monetary transactions he would have gotten two sacks of maize for his one sheep instead of the one he got in the barter transaction. One highlander said to me, after I pointed out this calculation to him, that he nonetheless always brought some sheep to barter for maize because "they [valley people] too like to eat meat, and if we do not supply it to them in this way they would not be able to obtain it." Old reciprocal relationships continued to hold sway in the region despite the penetration of the monetary market. Highlanders felt the obligation to provide meat at an unfavorable exchange rate, without taking into account the real market prices.

One should note, nevertheless, that highlanders do sell a sizable proportion of their wool and animals in the monetary market, allocating only *some* of their production for less profitable barter (Fonseca 1972a: 113). With the then-current exchange rates, maize producers stood to gain from this barter relationship, but they justified it using the same reason. The valley people said that they continued with the barter relationship, instead of selling maize for money, because "*puna* people also like to eat maize." *Unay precio* as an institution existed because highlanders and lowlanders gave each other "favored nation" status and created a special protectionist market that stayed somewhat immune from the fluctuations and market trends affecting the national monetary sector. Also interesting was the use of the features of a pricing system with a reference currency that guided the transactions. The important function of coinage, as a measure of relative values, was performed for the peasants by referring to the standards set by an obsolete currency.

Data on the historical evolution of relative exchange rates between animal and agricultural products in the region suggest that a shrinking maize production and perhaps an increased demand caused the price of maize to rise relative to that of mutton. When Fonseca (1972a: 113) collected *unay precio* exchange rates valid in 1939, 1940, 1949, and 1965 in his native district of Puños in the province of Huamalíes, Huánuco, he found that in 1939 a highlander from Puños could obtain three sacks of maize with one slaughtered sheep; and in 1949, two. But by 1965, the same quantity of meat fetched only one and a quarter sacks of maize.

In June 1969, after the maize harvest, I observed many barter transactions as groups of highlanders arrived in Tangor with their llama trains full of cheeses, wool, and meat. Tangor women rushed out to offer their homes as resting places in order to have the privilege of trading with their owners first. They competed with each other with offers to feed and house the travelers, and once their offers were accepted, a customary exchange of *yawasinakuy* hospitality took place. Highlanders presented gifts of *pachamanca* roasted meat, gourds containing delicious freeze-dried potatoes, packets of lake algae, and other highland delicacies, and they were served the best foods from the lowlands such as chili peppers, fresh herb sauces, toasted maize, squash stew, and maize hominy.

Hospitality aside, though, haggling was loud and insistent, because the highlanders stated that they preferred to sell their meat for cash and also to buy maize for cash—transactions that would have been unfavorable to the maize producers. However, competing Tangor offers began to drive upward the barter exchange rate of maize for meat and cheese, as Tangorinos began to tempt highlanders with better maize rates than those initially stated; yet they always demurred to accept real money. Even after agreeing to trade, they continued to haggle with gusto. Apart from the haggling that arose from efforts to establish a mutually acceptable *unay precio* rate, the driving of hard bargains created disagreements about the size and quality of the products. There was always room for argument that the maize cobs selected were smaller than the standard, that the fleece was too long or too short or of third-rate quality, and that the forequarters of the mutton were too skinny for the asking price. The deals that did get struck were those for which the *unay precio* quotes moved up and down, as when a haggler said, "I'll give it to you for 32 cents instead of the customary 30."

In one case, a man and his highland partner had agreed to exchange a sheep for 1 *sol* and 20 *centavos* in small-sized cobs of maize. When counted, the cobs filled one sack to the rim, but the highlander showed his disappointment by counting them all over again. (The smaller the cobs, the less volume they occupied by fitting better in the sack.) When he finished, the Tangorino asked him whether he was satisfied, and the man said "yes" (meaning that the cobs were correctly counted) but pleaded for an additional *llapa* ("extra above the agreed amount"), which is also part of Andean bargaining. So the Tangorino gave him a good *llapa* and the two remained friends.

Toward the end of June, a man and his son arrived in Tangor driving twenty llamas from Quichas (Oyón District, Cajatambo Province, Lima). The son said that it had taken them two and a half days to get to Tangor, staying with friends and acquaintances along the way. They planned to accumulate fifteen *tercios* (a balanced load to be carried by one pack animal) of maize, which converted to twenty llama loads (the llama can carry less than a donkey), all of which was intended for *gasto* consumption at home.

They brought cheeses, which had already been bartered for maize (at 25–30 *centavos unay precio* each), which would come to four sacks of maize, more or less, since they had not yet collected the maize. More maize was due them since they planned to collect the wool given to the Tangorinos during last year's trip. They had already contracted with several farmers to use the llamas to transport the maize from the fields to the Tangorinos' homes, at a rate of one sack for every eight transported. In addition, the boy's father had agreed to buy some maize for cash from the communal field of the lower *barrio*, and they were looking to buy some more of it with cash. I saw them working and trading in Tangor for a week, and when they left, their llamas were loaded to the hilt.[8]

The discrepancy in the exchange ratios between barter and the cash nexus worried me more than it worried the Tangorinos or the highlanders. Neither group perceived the situation in those terms, since they figured that the highlanders were obtaining all the maize they wanted anyway, by using several methods at once (as in the example of the Quichas father and son); thus the exchange ratio between meat and maize was only part of the whole trading trip. Small differences in exchange ratios make a big difference when large quantities are involved, but only a small difference in small-scale barters.

Why Barter?

Barter was important to peasants in the Chaupiwaranga regional economy. Its trade covered great distances and, as we have seen, was controlled by elaborate sets of rules and behaviors. What accounts for this extensive movement of goods within and across the region? In theory, barter should not have been necessary if we bear in mind that every community and every peasant family sought to cover its needs through direct production with access to the resources guaranteed by community land tenure. Murra's (1956) response to evidence for barter was that barter represented a second alternative to direct production and colonization. But more to the point, from our current perspective, is the question as to why barter was relied upon if these goods were also available in the regional marketing system and anyone could have bought these products with money.

Barter, as it was practiced in Chaupiwaranga in 1969, can be explained in terms of the following five factors. First, specialization leads to the so-called double coincidence of wants ("the low likelihood that I have what he wants and he wants what I have") that the authors of economic textbooks cite when discussing barter. Second, differences in the timing of harvests reflect a situation in which peasants seek products they themselves produce but have not yet harvested. Third, barter in 1969 followed ancient trade routes integrating disparate ecological regions in ways different from those affecting the marketing network of the national cash economy. This cash market network extracted commodities from the countryside and distributed urban manufactured products, so there were reasons why peasants would have wanted to avoid using this network. Fourth, barter networks constituted an economic sphere that was separate from the cash sphere, constructed and maintained by the peasantry who, for their own purposes and to their own advantages, tried to isolate it from the cash nexus. Barter in this region was a form of protectionism. Peasants isolated a flow of goods to favor a self-selected group of other peasants, who used cultural norms to create a separate circuit of goods for their own benefit. Norms governing whom to barter with and how to barter controlled the behavior of those inside the group and reserved privileged trading opportunities to partners. Such networks attempted (albeit not very successfully) to exclude agents from the money market for money accumulation. Together, these four factors are the very opposite of an open free-access market, which in turn is regarded by economists as a precondition for the efficient operation of supply-demand-price allocation mechanisms.

The fifth factor relates barter to shortages of money. Such shortages cause people to rely on barter in much the same way that collapses of national currencies create renewed conditions where barter surfaces, even in monetized economies such as those in Thailand and Singapore during the Asian economic crisis of the late 1990s. In this connection, I will consider how Paul Bohannan (1959, 1963) and Frederick Barth (1967) use the concept of economic spheres. In both models, entrepreneurial activity seeks to destroy the barriers that separate the spheres. In another vein, Barth (1969) made the more general point that all boundaries are porous; therefore, despite efforts to keep the economic spheres separate, they are constantly being penetrated by the very agents that seek to keep them apart, creating the mixed forms of barter and money exchange previously described.

The first factor, as suggested above, hinged on specialization in production. There were two distinct lifestyles evident in the Chaupiwaranga region: agriculturalists and highland pastoralists. The agriculturalists were producers of potatoes, maize, squashes, barley, and fava beans in the valleys. They lived in nucleated settlements, and their fields were a few hours' walking distance from their homes. They produced a surplus in agricultural products that they exchanged for animal products. The highland pastoralists, by contrast, lived mainly in dispersed temporary homesteads in the treeless highlands and raised sheep, llamas, alpacas, highland cattle, and horses.[9] They tended to concentrate along the headwaters of the Chaupiwaranga basin and near the high mountain ranges between the deep valleys. Expansion of sheep raising was also a feature of the national economy as Peru became a wool exporter and the urban market increasingly consumed mutton. As noted by Gordon Appelby (1976a, 1976b), Benjamin Orlove (1977a), and Alberto Flores Galindo (1977), the internal market system expanded as a phenomenon subordinate to that of the wool export economy.[10] Most herders were affiliated with peasant communities, and some were tied to *haciendas*, although this bondage did not hinder them from establishing similar barter relationships for agricultural products. As a secondary activity, herders also produced small amounts of highly valued but low-yielding high-altitude crops such as frost-resistant potatoes, which they converted into freeze-dried *chuño*. In addition, they wove cloth with their wool, twisted llama hair into ropes, and collected eggs from wild birds. The highlanders had a surplus of animal products. The pastoralists adopted a more independent, aggressive, and self-confident posture in contrast to the quiet, humble valley farmers (Bradby 1982).

As mentioned in Chapter 1, R. Brooke Thomas (1976: 390) demonstrated that the highland agro-pastoral system in the high *punas* of Ñuñoa, Puno, did not generate enough energy resources for self-sufficiency. The export of meat and wool brought in higher-carbohydrate-content grains through trade and barter. For pastoralists the exchange system of protein and fiber for carbohydrate grains was an absolute necessity. Valley agriculturalists and highland pastoralists were in a symbiotic relationship with each other, each producing a surplus of products with the resources in which they were better endowed and exchanging these with each other. In Tangor the maize-meat/wool exchange network extended toward Cauri and further afield to the Cordillera Raura region in the Department of Lima. Every year, the same pastoralists came to Tangor with their llamas, donkeys, and horses bringing wool, *chuño*, mutton, and cheeses. They stayed with friends, plied their trade, and returned with their animals loaded down with grains.

It is in this relationship that *unay precio* was most prevalent. As described, barter transacted with *unay precio* was an elaborate game, revealing a historical relationship of long-term partnerships based on reciprocity, governed by moral sanctions, and shared and understood by the inhabitants of the whole region. The rules of the game included, as a matter of course, the pursuit of self-interest through open bargaining. Hypothetically, if the highlanders had decided to boycott the Tangorinos and refused to exchange meat for maize, the Tangorinos would have described them as selfish people who lacked any compassion with their fellow peasants. Likewise, moral outrage would have been expressed by the pastoralists if the Tangorinos had decided to sell all their maize in the money market, leaving the highlanders without *cancha*—that is, without food. In my dissertation (Mayer 1974a: ch. 6), I argued that although exchange of goods was very different from exchange of services, barter relationships with distant trading partners were an aspect of long-term established reciprocal ties bonding the region together in solidarity networks that extended beyond the local community but tried to exclude the national monetary market system.

Regarding the second factor noted above, barter can be explained in terms of trade in goods that farmers themselves produced but were available at different times and places. Climatic variations led to differences in timing among the agricultural seasons in the region. In Tangor, for example, fresh corn on the cob was available in June, whereas in communities to the south it was still green. In June of every year, agriculturalists from farther upriver came to Tangor to exchange wool for fresh corn and squashes. Areas in the upper reaches of the Colpas Valley, at about the same altitude as the potato-growing areas of Tangor and its neighbors, were about two months ahead in their agricultural calendar. Since Tangor families often ran out of their own store of crops before the next harvest was ready, they could obtain the same crops that they produced by barter—though sporadically they had to buy them with cash. Schematically, one village obtained its early products from the north but gave its products to partners and friends in villages that were to their south. During normal years, Tangorinos went for potatoes to the northern villages in the Colpas Valley, where the harvest was always ahead of theirs; in the year that their own harvest failed, they went south, where the harvest was behind their own, in order to harvest in the fields of others, accumulating vaguely framed but fully respected debts to be collected in the future.

The third factor, also of a historical-ecological nature, had to do with the long-standing relationships that highlanders had with the tropical *montaña* regions with pre-European historical roots. A convenient way to express this point is to employ the concept of ancient trade routes. Using the 1549 and 1562 *visita* documents, Murra (1967: 384–386 and 1972: 3–11) has shown that even in colonial times the ethnic groups of this region directly controlled the production of lowland products through the maintenance of colonies rather than through trade. My own reading of the same sources, discussed in Chapter 2, showed that barter exchanges went alongside direct colonization to the same areas. In addition, it is known that since early colonial times Spaniards and mestizos began an expansive trade in peasant products for money profits, especially coca, expropriating the Indians of the lands suitable for the development of these products. Finally, since 1900, when roads began to be built into this jungle region, these lands have become areas of intense colonization and of cash crop production, with coca as a peasant commodity and coffee as the main export crop, even before the coca/cocaine boom (described in Chapter 6) changed the character of this region once again.

It is clear that economic factors have fundamentally changed the relationships between the highlands and the tropical *montaña*. In 1969 Tangorinos were actively settling in the same area to grow cash crops that we know they used to colonize in pre-European times. As we saw in the case of Don Federico, he peddled manufactured products in exchange for coffee, which then entered international trade. But the relationships between the two regions is a persistent and old one. The Tangorinos' success as coffee buyers is partly due to the fact that they also took potatoes, wool, meat, *chuño,* and other highland products that were in great demand in the hot and humid lowlands, because, as in pre-European times, the colonizers in 1969 were from the highlands and desired these goods. For many centuries peasants from the Chaupiwaranga region have consumed tropical products—chiefly, coca. Circumstances in the 1970s made the discussion of coca contraband a touchy subject, and I did not insist on pursuing it; but I am sure that Don Federico came back to Tangor carrying some *arrobas* of coca, which he then used for further trading ventures in Tangor and the highlands in patterns described in Chapter 6. (See also Burchard 1974.)

Why does barter persist as a method of trade in place of buying and selling with money? I argue that the operation of the cash nexus creates and maintains the barter sphere of exchange. Though the patterns may be ancient, and also colonial, their utility in the present needs to be explained. One initial observation is that monetary transactions far outweigh barter in both frequency and the volume of goods traded. Barter is a marginal activity covering perhaps 5 to 10 percent of household production (Figueroa 1984: 39; Gonzales de Olarte 1994: 117). An exception is the village of Tapay in the Colca Valley in Arequipa (Paerregaard 1997: 99), where barter predominated over monetary transactions. However, such a small percentage should not be dismissed, because, as we saw, barter covers crucial gaps in the subsistence sphere. Why it has not disappeared altogether is what has to be explained.

Toward this end, it is necessary to observe how Tangorinos obtained and used cash. In general terms, money was procured through permanent and/or temporary migration to Lima, the mines, and the tropical areas in the quest for wages, trades, or commerce. Literally the men had to get out of Tangor to earn money. Migrants maintained relatives to look after their interests in Tangor or periodically returned to take care of their fields during planting and harvest times. Cash income from the sale of agricultural products was almost insignificant in the Tangor economy in 1969. Tangor, like the rest of Chaupiwaranga communities, was an exporter of labor to the national economy and an importer of money. A perceptive old man in Tangor told me that Chaupiwaranga was "the nursery for mine workers" (Laite 1981). (Fifty-four percent of the men and 45 percent of the women were absent from the village at the time I took the census.) In that sense they were integrated into the national economy, but in a partial and deficient way and not as producers of agricultural commodities for the national market.

Tangorinos used the cash income to buy manufactured goods needed for their daily consumption, such as sugar, lard, kerosene, candles, noodles, bread, vegetable oils, condiments, and salt. Money also circulated to buy the products needed to comply with festive social obligations: liquor, beer, cigarettes, coca, the hiring of musicians, the rental of elaborate costumes, and so on. Money was further needed to purchase more durable consumer items such as ready-made clothing, shoes, hand mills, sewing machines, and radios. School supplies, uniforms, and the boarding costs for children studying away from home constituted a sizable cash expenditure for some elite families. Farmers used cash to pay some laborers in their fields and to supply them with coca, liquor, and cigarettes. Money was also invested in trading trips, and savings were oriented to convert it to animal raising, to house construction or improvements, to the purchase of house plots in the village and, until the agrarian reform law was enacted, to the purchase of additional small agricultural plots.

Following Paul Bohannan's (1959, 1963) discussion of economic spheres among the Tiv in Nigeria, I have found it useful to distinguish two kinds of trading transactions: those that link the peasant to the money market or the cash nexus and those that involve the exchange of goods within a subsistence sphere. Bohannan (1963: 246) introduced the concept of economic spheres in the context of what he termed a multicentric economy, as "one in which a society's exchangeable goods fall into two or more mutually exclusive spheres, each marked by different institutionalization and different moral values." Exchanges within one sphere were morally neutral and legitimate; Bohannan called them conveyances. Exchanges between spheres were more complicated, because they involved breaching the moral rules that kept them separate; Bohannan called these conversions. The main point about them was that ". . . given the moral ranking of the spheres, such a situation leaves one party to the exchange in a good position, the other in a bad one" (Bohannan 1963: 251). Conveyances were regarded as boring, unimportant activities that adjusted supply and demand between items within a sphere, whereas competitive conversions were the real economic aim of each Tiv. In short, the goal was to convert goods from the lower and less important sphere to a higher more prestigious one by transacting with a few selected items that overlapped the spheres.

A close reading of the case, however, shows that in order to successfully complete a conversion, a person often had to move beyond the immediate moral group, to find a distant hapless victim who could not easily retaliate the ignominy of having converted down in the same exchange that improved the eager converter's position. This was one step toward fulfilling the condition of impersonality that made markets operative. Much of Bohannan's discussion of spheres is not germane to Tangor; however, I make the case that the peasants of the Chaupiwaranga region did try to maintain a subsistence sphere separate from the money market, although they also purchased a lot of items that entered the subsistence sphere. Further discussion about the morality of the two kinds exchanges follows.

Bohannan pointed out, in his discussion of economic spheres, that the mode of transaction, the reason for the transaction, and the social relationships between traders are distinguishable from one sphere to another.

In the Andes, one kind of transaction, which I also call conversion, inevitably involved the cash nexus, the purchase with money of some kind of manufactured product, or the sale of a commodity, including labor, to obtain cash. I borrow the term *conversion* from Bohannan to point out that peasants in most cases come out as losers in such transactions. They converted down in terms of social prestige and self-worth, and, often (but not always), in terms of unequal exchange as well. Barth's (1969) suggestion about the porosity of ethnic boundaries is useful here because conversions do cross the boundaries between Indian peasants and mestizo intermediaries.

In Chaupiwaranga, in order for a conversion to take place, cash was almost always a necessary element; it implied establishing a different kind of relationship with a commercial intermediary. Likewise, conversions existed when Tangorinos sold their labor, sold a few agricultural products for cash, or bought products with cash to resell them for cash, seeking to make a profit. If a Tangorino were to sell his potatoes at the marketplace in Parcoy, he had to deal with a mestizo intermediary, who in turn dictated the price at which he would buy the commodity and paid for it with national currency. The Tangorino dealt with a person who was his social superior and had to humble himself before him. The relationship was impersonal, stereotypical, brief, and strictly business oriented; it was often patronizing, but sometimes also notoriously abusive. Tangorinos always suspected that the buyers cheated with rigged scales or that they colluded to buy at lower prices.

A related situation obtained when a Tangorino bought manufactured products in a store in Parcoy, Yanahuanca, or Huánuco. In all these transactions, the context of the exchange was strongly tinged by power and class relationships, and the conditions of exchange, such as price, quality, and packaging, were dictated by the superior mestizo, with little bargaining ability left to the Tangorino purchaser. In a study of the Cusco city market, Marisol De la Cadena (2000: 227) singled out the practice of *trato,* which refers to the way one is treated by, and how one treated, others in marketplace encounters. Insisting on being treated with "respect" also permitted "disrespecting" others (*faltar el respeto*). "Frequently, . . . " in order to defend one's place, De la Cadena says, "market women deliberately display a crudely discriminatory behavior," a pattern patently obvious in Chaupiwaranga as well. Most often, trading was conducted in Spanish, dictated by the mestizos' preference and placing the Quechua-speaking Tangorinos at a disadvantage. Their only option was to choose between one or another merchant.

Abusive trading practices in rural Peru abound, because the market extracts food resources for urban consumers. For example, Appelby (1976a: 157–158) describes conditions in Puno before 1940: "Market abuses were unfortunately common. Local police collected the municipal market tax. Political authorities might confiscate a chicken or a sack of potatoes for their personal use. Townspeople could force the final sale price on vendors because they had the political clout. . . . Market abuses made countrymen reluctant to sell their produce in town. This reluctance reinforced the townsmen's coercive behavior." And Fonseca (1972a: 140) describes the characteristics of the "mestizo" economy in Central Peru: Those who lived in small towns surrounded by Indian communities, where they kept stores, organized Sunday markets where hundreds of Indians attended. Mestizos bought up local produce to be resold to higher-level markets, or to be sold back to peasants in times of scarcity. They gave credit in exchange for work and used Indigenous economic institutions to collect handicrafts that they then sold. They lived by share-cropping arrangements and extorted Indians on the basis of their literacy in Spanish, knowledge of legal procedures, and office holding. Clientelistic relationships bound the Indian partner to his mestizo compadre. Fonseca further observed that Indians always tried to socialize economic relations, whereas the mestizos endeavored to mercantilize the social relationships of spiritual kinship. Nonetheless, Indians frequently fought the mestizos' monopoly control of stores and marketplaces. Ricardo Claverías (1978), for example, describes a massive political protest movement in Puno to open more markets to break monopoly control of local storekeepers and *hacendados*.

In stark contrast, a conveyance was an exchange within the peasant economic sphere. In a Chaupiwaranga conveyance, buyer and seller were owners of the products they traded, and they carried out the transaction for immediate consumption purposes. The mestizo intermediary was shunted out of the picture. The rates of exchange were established through a reference to established equivalencies and there was ample room to haggle in Quechua, the language in which they were all fluent. The social relationships in conveyances permitted peasants some degree of control over the transaction by allowing ample time to conduct the deal and creating a social context conducive to bargaining and seeking better exchange rates. From a Tangorino's perspective at any one time, a conveyance had variable exchange rates that he could try to influence in his favor, whereas a conversion had fixed exchange rates that gave him less options.[11] In a conveyance, the relationship between buyer and seller was personal and was maintained over a long time, governed by social conventions, hospitality, etiquette, and mutual obligations—even while it allowed each partner to pursue their self-interest. Finally, buyer and seller came from the same social class and understood each other intimately. I thus argue that there were social and economic advantages for peasants to invest in sustaining a separate sphere for the exchange of goods between social equals, and to avoid the cash nexus when possible. Although Olivia Harris (1995) has argued that money exchanges in the Andes are not seen as "immoral," just as barter is not seen as "virtuous," I maintain that sociability of the mode of exchange does count. To put it in an economist's terms, the preference for a more relaxed environment where bargaining does take place has to be taken into account when choosing among trading options. One can add a final clincher: that human beings will inevitably try to avoid exploitative situations if alternatives are available. Barter networks provided such an alternative.

Peasants always suffered from a shortage of cash, but at the same time they were very dependent on a regular supply of manufactured products. In this situation it was obvious and logical that they should reserve the few coins at their disposal to purchase in conversions those products they needed most, rather than dispersing their hard-earned cash for agricultural or animal products that could be obtained without a cash outlay.[12] Cash was therefore reserved for conversions in market transactions. Scarcity of cash created the possibility for alternative kinds of transactions that avoided the use of cash, and barter conveyances filled the spaces where conversions were unnecessary. Given the opportunity to choose between them, the separation of cash and barter spheres was a rational allocation of scarce cash resources.

Other advantages, too, explained the preference for barter. In some cases, as demonstrated by Glynn Custred (1974: 279), barter trade was more profitable than cash transactions, particularly if it absorbed long-distance transportation costs and more than one transaction. Since conveyances were less integrated into the national economy, exchange rates tended to be controlled by peasants themselves and remained more stable and predictable, even though there were yearly variations and also, as we have seen, long-term changes. As the collective and institutionalized creation of the peasant sector, the barter sphere was less vulnerable to negative influences on the national economy such as inflation, devaluation, currency collapse, and central-bank bankruptcy. In this connection, Orlove (1986) points to a resurgence in barter transactions in the Lake Titicaca region during national economic crisis of the 1980s. Maize producers in Tangor benefited from barter conveyances in their exchanges with highlanders and were therefore keener defenders of the barter system than the highlanders—a situation the maize growers could maintain as long as they continued to produce the much-appreciated maize and to withhold some of it from the conversion market for cash. Highlanders, despite their apparent isolation, were much better integrated into the national market system through the sale of wool and meat, but nonetheless also reserved some of their production for the barter sphere.[13] As Orlove (1977a: 124) notes in his study of Alpaca herders: "It is quite simple for both pastoralists and agriculturalists to shift between barter and cash modes of articulation. This is favored by an unusual characteristic of the region. Cash crops are the same as the traditional crops consumed locally."

The use of conversions and conveyances as concepts thus "thickens" the descriptive cultural and social contexts that a simple typology of cash or barter transaction otherwise tends to oversimplify. But there are problems with Bohannan's (1963) presentation of economic spheres, which Barth's (1967) treatment of the Dafur case resolves. For Barth, the spheres become circuits, and at several points a Fur man or woman has choices between alternative pathways. First there is the millet-beer-labor circuit, which is not involved in the market. Another circuit involves labor-cash crops-money-consumer goods-labor. And a third circuit involves cattle, which can increase and be resold for money. Barth identifies theoretically possible barriers in each circuit that limit expansion or growth. These barriers allow for the coexistence of discrepancies in returns between the circuits. As an example, Barth cites local wage rates compared to much higher government wage rates that do not tend to equalize, much like the situation in Tangor reported in Note 10 of Chapter 4. Barth also discusses entrepreneurs, those who seize on such discrepancies to realize material gains but, in so doing, rearrange the circuits themselves and cause other people to reassess their original situation. The entrepreneurial breaking of porous barriers is an innovation—not a conversion, as Bohannan (1963) would have it. For Barth (1967), conversions constitute net drains in the economy, since these materials are exchanged for feasts, or pilgrimages to Mecca, which bring prestige to the person but do not form circuits. In Barth's scheme, one person's conversion does not create another's diminished status.

Barth's scheme is helpful to our case because it suggests that we should search out the circuits rather than be obsessed with the mode of transaction as the indicator of a sphere; it also alerts us to the role that choice plays between alternatives. Pastoralist-agriculturalist exchanges constitute one such circuit and its associated choices, but the choices are not between barter or cash as a mode of transaction, since the different modes are built in to each circuit; rather, they concern which part of the harvest will be apportioned for cash sale and which part to barter. In addition, entrepreneurs will seize on the discrepancies to find short- or long-term gain by breaking the barriers and altering the social and institutional arrangements, which do cause conflicts and, indeed, are often expressed in terms of moral outrage because they upset the way things are usually done.

Don Federico's peddling trip to the *montaña* illustrated the entrepreneurial breaking of barriers because it combined aspects of both the cash and the barter circuits. Don Federico was extending the tentacles of the international commodity market in coffee to its furthest extremes. In this case there was a chain of transactions that began with one market transaction (the purchase of merchandise in the Huánuco market); continued through a series of barter transactions in which manufactured products were exchanged for agricultural commodities but transacted in the manner and polite mode of barter conveyances; and ended with another transaction that converted the commodity back into cash. We saw that the purpose of the trip was to make money profits through an initial capital investment—profits that were possible because these traders carried out important functions in peasant markets (bulk breaking, distributing of manufactured products, and bulking and transporting agricultural commodities to a central accumulation point at the road head [Mintz 1959]). Federico's entrepreneurial skill was also evident in the fact that he took advantage of the social conventions of barter-like conveyances to transform them into economic profit. Peasant colonizers bought from Don Federico because he brought the merchandise right to their doorstep, because he could forecast the things they might demand, because the transaction took place in a friendly and relaxed manner among social equals, and because he provided the important service of bringing, along with manufactured products, those highland products that a mestizo coffee buyer could not.

However, this kind of peddling, which combined the features of barter and cash transactions, was nothing more than the furthest tentacle that linked the peasant producers to an international commodity market. Indeed, Appelby (1976b: 291–307) describes the marketing system in the Department of Puno as a finger-like dendridic system (Smith 1976: 34–36) that suctions food products out of the hinterland to feed the central cities:

Agricultural produce in Puno is bulked through outright purchase of pound lots and through the tedious piling together of handfuls of staples obtained from countrywomen in exchange for such petty household needs as dried chilies, bread, oranges, bananas, candy and plastic bags. This form of bulking, known as *chala* locally, is widespread in the agricultural areas, where it is associated with urban items of consumption needed daily in the rural homes, and with a scarcity of disposable cash among countrymen. It is eminently rational in that the countrywoman receives in her rural market the urban market value of her staples. Although *chala* involves purchase-with-commodities, it is definitely not barter; rather, it is a disguised purchase.

Should we quibble with Appelby? Is it not barter because the circuit is different? Is it not barter because the woman bulker is not the final consumer of the product? Is it not barter because the exchange was determined by monetary prices hovering in the background instead of by the dealing of two parties who meet in the marketplace? Conversely, should we insist that it *is* barter because no money mediates the exchange of the commodities at that time and place? And should we persist in classifying it as barter because the woman uses her gender, social, and ethnic status to conduct her transactions in a manner amenable to her woman clients? In a study of the disposition of fish from Lake Titicaca, Orlove (1986) finds that cash or barter options do not offer great opportunities to break barriers in terms of profitability, because the exchange rates between them tend to be about the same (1986: 94). Rather, a greater proportion of fish were bartered in house-to-house transactions than in the marketplace. In addition, the less preferred bony fish, the *carachi* (considered by all to be "poor people's food"), was more likely to be bartered than to be sold for cash—a clear indication of a conveyance where one food item is exchanged for another, each item to be directly consumed by both households.

And yet barter transactions in Cahupiwaranga were part of the traditional peasant construction of their livelihoods, which in its operation reflected and created social relations among the inhabitants of different villages in the region. The barter networks integrated the region and provided an alternative organization of space and movement of goods and peoples. This peasant sphere existed within a more powerful and more complex market system of extractive and exploitative market relations that also characterized the peasant economy. Money transactions were pervasive and quantitatively greater than barter and have received far greater attention in studies of peasant economies as an aspect of peasant's partial or exploitative integration into the national and international capitalist market. Despite the overwhelming power of the market to dissolve away more ancient economic relations, barter trade was explained in this chapter as evidence of repeated and sometimes relatively successful attempts by peasants to create, within their capabilities, their own protectionist internal trade niches as a defense against extractive market penetration.

Postscript

My report from the field on forms of barter was an instant success; it became required reading in anthropology, sociology, and economics classes in Peru and was frequently cited in scholarly works abroad, most notably in David Lehmann (1982), Benjamin Orlove (1986), and Karsten Paerregaard (1997). Its catchy title, *Un carnero por un saco de papas* (erroneously describing a nonexistent form of barter), was so popular that I hesitated to correct it.

The unintended uses to which my report was put are interesting in themselves. It was critiqued by some Marxists because barter seemed to point to the existence of pre-capitalist forms in Peru's "dominant capitalist formation." For others, evidence of barter validated the Marxist distinction between use value and exchange value. Though contrary to my intention, the report was applauded by those who adhered to the propositions of dualism—that is, who argued for the survival of curious ancient archaic systems not yet displaced by modernization. The presence of barter represented for still others a bit of exotica and proof of isolation and underdevelopment. Finally, the report provided support to those interested in asserting cultural and ethnic specificity to Andean culture and civilization, despite colonialism and capitalism—support that was definitely my intent.

Peruvian economists, however, took the issue more seriously, noting that barter transactions, though ubiquitous, constituted a very small proportion of total transactions. My response was to say that salt is also a small proportion of total consumption, but a very necessary one. Economists also provided frameworks to analyze such transactions. The economist Christopher Scott (1974), in a comment on anthropologists' work published in Alberti and Mayer (1974), directed the readers' attention to Barth's circuits and transaction chains, which I have now incorporated properly into the body of this revised text. I am grateful for these suggestions and agree with his conclusions: that "entrepreneurship" and "arbitrage" eventually eliminate the discrepancies in exchange ratios between barter and cash transactions, leading to situations in which cash and barter prices reach equivalency. But not inevitably. Protectionism is always an option in Tangor—and anywhere else in the ancient or modern world. Scott also called attention to issues of transport and transaction costs assumed by peddlers in taking advantage of regional price differences.

In a recent review of this issue, Gonzales de Olarte (1997: 40) refers to barter networks and reciprocal labor exchanges as *proto-markets*, meaning ". . . those forms of exchange that do not yet have the characteristics of the impersonality in the transactions, that have barriers to entry and exit, and that do not function in a regular manner. In addition, they function in situations prior to the formation of proper markets." As Gonzales further notes, barter exists, strictly among peasants, and its rationale appears to originate in a scarcity of cash, in the small quantities transacted, and in the high transaction costs required to convert them into cash. Also important is the scarce urban demand for their products. Gonzales adds that lack of information about market prices may also explain barter—a comment that seems to be derived from theory; many observers agree that the exchange ratios tend to converge, so misinformation is hardly the issue. Gonzales notes, too, that the preference that allows the possibility for flexibility in bargaining over amounts and weights—as well as personal ties between women buyers and sellers—may promote barter. The real market passes these by since it is not the appropriate institution for regulating this minuscule trickle of goods. Consequently, he ends, barter and cash can co-exist in a sort of unequal symbiosis. In short, barter is seen by Gonzales as residue—what the market cannot, or will not, pick up. Maybe the revision and re-publication of the article can serve to continue the debate. Without doing violence to the original version, I hope to have reiterated the non-residual, unproto, positive features of barter that articulate Andean peasant households to each other, despite its small scale and uneasy coexistence with the ever-expanding globalizing markets.

Notes

1. This quote was changed to fit my example rather than that of Humphrey and Hugh-Jones, but it retains the wording of the theory exactly as in the original.

2. It is worth noting that Humphrey and Hugh-Jones (1992: 2) disagree with the common supposition that barter is a precursor to the invention of money and hence the origin of modern capitalism. They state that it is a creation myth perpetrated by classical and neoclassical economists. The famous and oft-quoted proposition that the invention of a common medium of exchange overcomes the "disutility" of barter by reducing the double coincidence of wants that therefore leads to more trade underlies a strict model that does not allow for the element of time to enter into the exchange. An article in their edited volume by two economists elaborates upon this point (see Anderlini and Sabourian 1992). Credit—that is, trust that a promise will be kept at a future date—relaxes the strictures of the model, as does adding more than one trade opportunity to the strict binary extreme case. In cases where people are willing to take on a commodity they do not want, so that they can then engage in a second transaction to obtain the one they originally wanted, the difficulties inherent in the model are also relaxed. With a medium of exchange, traders need two transactions to get what they want; in barter, one is enough. Common to both ways of stabilizing barter, then, is the possibility of recurring transactions in the future. Humphrey and Hugh-Jones point out that the institutionalization of barter systems has provided the social settings in which not only can the possibility of future transactions be assured but information can circulate and trust can be generated.

3. Fonseca (1972a: 109–111) describes hospitality between acquaintances from other villages as follows: "One has to serve the best, those things that others crave, what they call *cilu* which is derived from the Spanish *celos* or envy, a word which, as we know, connotes the suspicion that something has been grabbed from one. *Cilu* is probably the translation of the Quechua word *tushu*, which is better understood as the ardent desire to eat exquisite things which, if not satisfied, can cause illness of the heart. It is also a translation of the Quechua word *munay* which means to fall in love or to passionately desire something, which manifests a degree of covetousness or envy. My informants express these sentiments very objectively when they say to their guests: '*yawaikuy kay ichiklatapis tushulaikaipapis*,' which is to say: 'try at least a little bit, I do not want you to get sick in the heart because of me.' The person being served disarms this bit of magical evil by saying: 'May God bless you and may you have good harvests every year.'" Further discussion of rivalry in the context of reciprocity can be found in Chapter 4 of the present book. And for the cultural meanings of food in the lives of Andean peoples, see Weismantel (1988).

4. Valencia (1982), influenced by Inca revival ideology, describes Spanish Colonial weights and measures but insists that they are organized by Incaic categories. See also Concha (1975) and Casaverde (1977).

5. A *huayunca* is a pair of ears of corn tied together by their husks and hung from the rafters of the house for storage. A gourd cap prevents mice from getting at the grains.

6. Old denominations used in barter transactions are also described by Concha (1975), Casaverde (1977: 178–180), and Paerregard (1997: 121).

7. Another example of collectively negotiated barter rates is given by Paerregard (1997: 103), who explains that during harvest times in Tapay, the fruit-growing village in the Colca Valley in Arequipa, highland traders bring urban industrial products and pastoral products to be bartered for the harvested fruit: "A villager in each settlement is appointed to organize an auction in which everyone is summoned to exchange the fruit for the goods brought by the herders. Before opening the auction, the appointed villager and the traders negotiate the rate of exchange. Now acting as an auctioneer, the appointed villager writes down the names of those who wish to acquire a share of the goods."

8. Long-distance trading trips undertaken by pastoralists to obtain valley agricultural products are ubiquitous in Southern Peru and Bolivia. They have been studied by Casaverde (1977), Custred (1974), West (1981), and Love (1988).

9. Studies of pastoralists include Flores Ochoa (1968), Flores Ochoa (ed., 1977), Flannery et al. (1989), and Orlove (1977a).

10. On the expansion of the wool export market in Central Peru, see Long and Roberts (1978), Mallon and Rénique (1977), Manrique (1987), and Mallon (1983). On the expansion of this market in Southern Peru, see Flores Galindo (1977), Orlove (1977a), Burga and Reátegui (1981), and Jacobsen (1993).

11. Here, the term *fixed exchange ratios* is meant literally, inasmuch as prices were fixed elsewhere and controlled locally by middlemen; the point is not that they couldn't fluctuate. In conveyances, peasants had the opportunity to exert some control over exchange rates.

12. When coinage was in short supply, even *hacienda* owners, mestizo traders, and other businesses resorted to barter (or "disguised sales," to use Appelby's phrase). Here is a mid-nineteenth-century example from Puno, reported by Jacobsen (1993: 72): "By establishing long-term commercial partnerships in which one essentially paid for goods bought from a trade partner with other goods, the need for cash was reduced to a minimum."

13. Bradby (1982) notes a trend in her description of a pastoral community in the Central Highlands, Department of Huancavelica, that gradually broke its dependent relationship with the dominating valley community of Huayllay. As part of the pastoral community's bid for independence, it deliberately withheld meat and wool products from valley agriculturalists in traditional barter situations through which they would otherwise have obtained maize. Instead, the members of this community sold their products in a wider commodity market, imported industrial grains such as flour and noodles, and drank distilled cane alcohol instead of brewing their own maize beer.

6

Coca as Commodity:
Local Use and Global Abuse

This chapter is about luxury goods and commodities. It describes coca as a means of easing inter-household relationships. By stressing the differences between coca as a local commodity and cocaine as a global commodity, it develops the theme of how things become commodities. It then discusses the negative impact of the cocaine economy, although a modest proposal is made to expand the legitimate consumption of coca in Peru and elsewhere. The chapter ends with a discussion of the concept of illegitimate cultural appropriation, which is always an issue in the conversion of objects into commodities.

For millennia there has been a legitimate way of consuming coca in the Andes. This way is, however, becoming discredited and threatened through the association that Western people have with cocaine. In fact, the reality and the image have very little in common with each other. I take the position that if coca production were to disappear as a result of international pressures, then once again, as the Spanish expression goes, *justos pagan por pecadores:* "Just people pay for sinners." I am also responding to botched policy attempts to stem an enormous illicit international cocaine traffic through campaigns to eradicate coca cultivation in Peru and Bolivia.

To make my position clear, I must first emphasize the enormous difference between coca use in the Andes and cocaine use in the modern Western world. In terms of potency and danger, coca use is as different from cocaine use as transport by donkey is from transport by airplane; therefore the conclusions valid for cocaine are not applicable to coca (Grinspoon and Bakalar 1976: 87–93). Second, after having read the literature on the medical effects of coca mastication in the Andes, even though I am not in the medical profession, I concur with the general opinion that, unlike cocaine consumption, coca use is about as injurious to the health of its users as the use of coffee or tea, and is certainly less dangerous than cigarettes.[1]

Third, my position in defense of the right to masticate coca is based on the role it plays as a nexus in social integration. Traditional coca use is a culturally defined symbol that expresses group membership. It sends a clear message of the will of Indians to maintain their ethnic identity by sharing this uniqueness. For this reason, I believe that the medical arguments over whether coca is beneficial or harmful to the individual user are of less importance than the social reasons for its use. More to the point, attempts to suppress coca use constitute paternalistic interference from denizens of the outside world who imagine the Indians of the Andes to be like infants incapable of making decisions for themselves. The elimination of coca use can even be construed as an attempt to destroy Andean cultural patterns and lifestyles. A policy advocating the eradication of coca use thus deserves—at the very least—a discussion and evaluation of the consequences that such a policy would produce. Indeed, we must listen carefully to the opinions Indians themselves may have on this matter.

Almost all cultures in the world endorse one or more forms of stimulation, whether through pharmacological or other means. In Western culture, we have alcohol, tea, coffee, tobacco, and a host of over-the-counter medicines such as stimulants and tranquilizers—not to mention illegal drugs. Among nonchemical means we have television, the thrill of speeding in cars and roller coasters, and the stimulation provided by crowd participation in spectator sports. In the Andean world, coca is one of the main stimulants—and has been for four thousand years or more.[2] In no sense has coca been an impediment to sociocultural development or caused the degeneration of Andean culture or society. Indeed, the Andean culture is one of the great civilizations of the world. If Andean culture is in decline today, one need only look at centuries of Spanish conquest, Western domination, concomitant societal disintegration and population destruction, land and resource expropriation, forced acculturation, and imperialist exploitation to fully understand the sources of the problem. To lay the blame on the harmless coca leaf is to seek a simplistic and convenient scapegoat.[3] Indeed, as proof of this fallacy we may consider Ecuador, where, despite the eradication of coca use in the last three hundred years, Indian groups continue to live in miserable conditions (Gagliano 1978: 789–805; Gagliano 1994).

Coca's Economic Functions

All cultures classify consumption goods according to a scale on which three categories can be distinguished: basic necessities, luxury goods, and prestige goods.[4] Those goods that satisfy the primary needs of humans, such as food and shelter, and that guarantee normal continuity of life are basic necessities. People have a pragmatic attitude toward these goods (e.g., they tend to provide food to others who clearly need it), although this attitude has been shown to encompass the domain of primary kinship groups.[5]

The second category comprises luxury goods, relatively scarce goods that provide personal gratification and pleasure. They are used not only to indulge but also, when shared and given as gifts, to establish ties of friendship and goodwill. This function is possible precisely because such goods possess a quality that provides personal satisfaction. People hold a different attitude toward these goods than toward basic necessities. Moreover, it is a learned attitude. In our culture we teach our children this attitude. For instance, when we give candy to children, we tell them that they should not eat it all by themselves but instead should share it among siblings and friends. We can also observe how a luxury good becomes a medium of exchange: One child may barter the candy for a toy, whereas another may use it to gain a permanent ally. Luxury goods are socially valuable as well as personally gratifying. It is necessary to point out that in all societies, no matter how simple, there is a category of luxury goods; thus it makes sense to talk about the *need* for luxuries as universal. This is how coca is used in the Andes. It is considered not a subsistence good but, rather, a luxury and is treated as such.

The above discussion leads us to our first conclusion: that the mistaken joining of coca and food is a travesty of reality. In the Andean world, food belongs to a category of goods entirely different from that of coca. Coca is never confused with food and never treated as a substitute for it. For this reason we have to reject the implicit assumptions, so frequently made by observers of the Andes, that coca replaces or displaces food, that people prefer coca over food, and that many people masticate coca because coca removes hunger pangs and that is why coca chewers are malnourished.[6] In any case, of course, the suppressed hunger pangs return after the effects of coca have worn off.

The third category of goods is that of prestige goods. These are symbols of power and recognition of status. Attitudes toward these goods are intertwined with attitudes toward positions of status and persons with power and prestige. The use and circulation of prestige goods is thus determined by the changing contexts of power and prestige of the persons involved. A Western example illustrates this point. The hierarchy of bureaucrats in an office is expressed in terms of the privilege to use such exclusive status symbols as well-furnished offices with original works of art on the walls, executive bathrooms, corporate dining facilities, company cars, and so on. Access to these goods does not even depend on the purchasing capacity of the individuals in question (since the goods are provided by the corporation). Rising within the hierarchy is the way in which access to these goods is achieved, and for that reason the circumstances in which these goods are consumed reflect changing power and status positions of the individuals involved. In Andean culture, textiles provided this function (Murra 1962).

The view that coca use was restricted to privileged classes in the Inca empire can be traced to the colonial debate about coca. As Joseph Gagliano (1994: 14) notes, colonial abolitionists tended to cite those chroniclers who wrote from an anti-coca perspective (e.g., Garcilaso 1996 and Santillán 1927), inasmuch as these authors described coca as reserved for the elite who used it exclusively in rituals. This argument is often repeated because the colonial debate about coca "shaped the perspective of twentieth-century abolitionists in Peru" (Gagliano 1994: 14). But it is an argument that lacks validity. It reflects a Spanish misinterpretation of what I believe did take place in the empire—namely, that the privilege to distribute coca was a fundamental way of differentiating a "noble" from a "commoner."[7]

Let us return to the category of luxury goods in the Andes, among which coca is prominent. Precisely because they are defined as such, luxuries are exchanged, distributed, given away, and converted to other goods with great exuberance. They are therefore goods among which the manipulations of exchange—such as reciprocity, gift, credit, debt, and convertibility—intervene with more force and clarity than is the case with other kinds of goods. I would venture to say that along with other luxuries, coca is the first commodity in the Andean world. Coca is a commodity because it has exchangeable value and because it circulates widely in the peasant economy. But coca is not just any commodity; it is the one with the most liquidity. Coca functions in the peasant economy as a quasi-coin and, as such, competes with national currencies.[8] It is a quasi-coin because it is capable of fulfilling all the functions of real coinage, such as being a medium of exchange, a standard of value, a means of deferred payment, and a way to accumulate wealth. It is also easily convertible with money, and can often substitute for it. One peasant expressed this opinion: "With coca there is no lack of anything. Coca brings food into the house. With coca everything is available" (cited in Burchard 1974: 251).

Roderick Burchard (1978: 809–834) has shown in a study how coca can be bartered with just about all the products that circulate in the peasant economy. Interestingly, the exchange rates between coca and various commodities are different from their monetary terms of exchange, even though in the peasant society of the contemporary Andes all goods can also be exchanged for money. In one example, Burchard shows how it is possible to convert one sack of potatoes into eight, using coca as the medium of exchange. The chain begins in the highlands with three sacks of potatoes. One sack is sold for money to pay the busfare to the lowland tropical region where coca is grown. In the jungle, one sack of potatoes is bartered for twenty pounds of coca. And up in the highlands again, coca can be converted back to potatoes at a rate of three pounds for one sack. Discounting the expenses incurred, one can accumulate up to eight sacks of potatoes in this manner.

Such barter is possible with a whole range of products. By judiciously manipulating barter relations, people can reap sizable profits, whether in accumulated goods, food, or even labor obligations. In a second example, Burchard (1974: 209–251) demonstrates a different mechanism: A woman with insufficient land borrows some coca and distributes it on credit among her neighbors during planting time (the time of most demand). She does so with the promise of being able to claim the equivalent of the loan, plus interest, during harvest time in food products.

Coca barter is very important in the peasant economy. It unites and creates relationships between diverse regions that produce a very different range of goods, thus creating regional networks of exchange. The exchange rates are favorable to peasants, and in this way they can avoid unfavorable contacts with profit-seeking intermediaries of the national marketing system. Not surprisingly, the defense of coca trade led to rebellions in the Huanta region of Peru in the 1820s (Méndez 1991 and Husson 1992).

Social Roles of Coca

As detailed in Chapter 4, throughout my studies of peasant economy in the Andes I found that reciprocity plays a crucial role. Access to additional labor and to the resources of other families are part of a complex system of reciprocal relationships with other families and with the community. In the context of the present chapter, I should add that there is no reciprocal exchange in which coca distribution, together with that of cane alcohol and cigarettes, is not present.

Given the connotations of generosity, pleasure, and confraternity associated with coca, it plays a very important role as lubricant of reciprocal exchanges, facilitating and propitiating the climate in which these exchanges take place. The reason is that coca is not only offered but also consumed at that very moment. The ceremonial and often ritual act of consuming fresh coca leaves in a group, surrounded by friends, creates an atmosphere of solidarity that is indispensable for carrying out reciprocal exchanges. Note that the phrase *coca chewing* is actually a misnomer, as the leaves are kept in a wad in the cheek and rolled over. Indeed, chewing them is considered bad manners. Because chewing gum is so popular in the United States, the negative connotations associated with the word *chewing* need to be avoided. In Quechua, there are three terms for coca consumption—*aculli, chacchay,* and *hallmay* (Allen 1988: 127–130)—all of which describe the social context of coca consumption as approximating that of the English *having dinner.* Let me give some examples.

In Tangor, when a farmer is going to plow a field, he asks the help of relatives, friends, and others. These individuals come to his assistance knowing that there will be a return of equal labor in the future. Before the labor task begins, coca, cane alcohol, and cigarettes are distributed by the owner of the field. These are received by the helpers with thanks. The coca leaves are not immediately consumed. Rather, a ceremonial procedure and etiquette are followed, as admirably described by Catherine Allen (1988: 125–140). Each person chooses three leaves, called the *cocaquintu*, from his allotment. The essence of the *cocaquintu* is offered to local gods, such as the mountain gods (*Apu*) and Mother Earth (*Pachamama*), by means of a small ritual in which one blows on the *cocaquintu* from different directions. Frequent sharing and exchanges of *cocaquintu* take place among the participants during this ritual. Then each participant carefully places a few coca leaves in the mouth. The coca wads get built up by patient and measured ingestion of the leaves, mixed from time to time with lime or other additions containing calcium oxide. The lime is needed to release the alkaloids that give coca its mild and temporary stimulant effect. It is extracted from a small gourd with a spatula that has been whetted with saliva so that the lime adheres. Conversation flows, and the atmosphere is one of tranquillity and sociability. The field owner, meanwhile, makes an offering to the gods and the ancestors (who are the "real owners" of the field) by hiding coca, liquor, cigarettes, and candy in a corner of the field and inviting the ancestors to participate in the *chacchapakuy* (the ceremonial partaking of coca). He then prays that the work will be easy and come to a finish without problems (Allen 1981: 157–171).

The agricultural workday is divided into two parts, each of which is further subdivided. Each of the four segments is marked by a rest period. During the first rest period, the coca wads are renewed. Food is served during the second, and coca is distributed as dessert. During the third break, coca is again consumed. Then, at the end of the day, before everyone goes home, there is a final coca distribution. A basic measure of work duration consists of the time between coca breaks. There are also community-wide work parties, organized by the community leaders. Coca breaks are common during these parties, where the community authorities themselves distribute coca. On such occasions, community affairs also get discussed. In this way, coca plays an important role in organizing work patterns.

Another example demonstrates the role of coca in the planning and organization of complex political tasks. In Tangor, frequent reunions take place in order to plan out a series of actions for the future, such as organizing a *fiesta*, constructing a house, or even deciding on the best strategy to pursue a land litigation with a neighboring community. Such events often last all night. On these occasions, coca is placed on a table covered with a cloth and participants help themselves. Throughout the evening, practical goals merge with social, ceremonial, and ritual behaviors. Even while people talk and plan out their actions, coca is used to divine the outcomes of the actions and to detect whether there are any likely pitfalls along the way to success. One of many methods of divination involves the taste of the coca juices: "Sweet," "bitter," and "boring" tastes respectively provide positive, negative, or noncommittal oracular answers to the questions posed. Other more specialized methods include "reading" the coca leaves as they fall on figurines and symbols that have been placed on a cloth. A leaf that falls with the shiny side up has one meaning; the reverse of the leaf, another. The patterning and shapes of the leaves scattered among the symbols also offer avenues for interpretation. Reverse rituals of harmful doings through witchcraft involve the same procedures but utilize the worst coca, the crumpled and broken shreds that are found at the bottom of every person's coca bag (Bolton 1974).

Thus created is a sacred atmosphere that not only generates group cohesion but also seals the pact of collaboration. During these meetings, coca serves the additional purpose of sharpening the senses, permitting concentration, and, when consumed with care, creating a sense of internal peace and tranquillity that is indispensable for intellectual work. Alcohol is less evident on such occasions because it tends to befuddle the mind and produce conflict.

Here is a third example. Before battles with members of rival communities are to take place, abundant coca is distributed and then consumed in all-night sessions. During these, the periods between renewal of the wads is shortened in order to enhance the stimulant effect of the alkaloids and to build up the courage needed for success in the coming battle (Mayer 1974a: 56–57). These nocturnal vigils not only create the solidarity needed by the group but also enhance the nervous tension felt by the participants. Accordingly, Tangorinos say that "fierceness is having a green mouth."

Thus, it is not surprising to hear Indians say that coca gives them energy, wisdom, and courage. Contrast these qualities with the negative, mestizo-propagated images of the coca-chewing Indian. One is that the Indian is solitary and taciturn. This stereotype is negated by the fact that, in the Andes, coca is almost always consumed in groups. Coca's context is one of prescribed courtesies, etiquette, and good manners, all of which serve to socially regulate its use. Allen (1988: 127–130), in her study of how coca is tightly interwoven with issues of Andean identity, devotes an entire section to the etiquette of coca use. Another mestizo myth is that coca stupefies the Indians (Gutierrez Noriega and Zapata Ortiz 1950: 22–60). This is untrue because, as we have seen, coca is utilized precisely in those moments when there is a need for clarity of thought and incisive analysis. A final, incorrectly ascribed attribute of coca is that it creates apathy.[9] If that were so, the Indians would not have been able to survive as an integral component culture in the Andes in the face of almost five centuries of ex-

Photo 6.1 Ceremonial coca use during the Laraos irrigation canal-cleaning ceremony in May 1975. (Photo taken by Enrique Mayer.)

ploitation and cultural domination. Andean culture has endured because of the fierce will of its native people to maintain it—an accomplishment made possible by internal solidarity, group integration, and feelings of belonging. In this effort, coca has been judiciously used.

If it is necessary to choose among stereotypes, I prefer those that come from the people who speak with the voice of direct experience with coca and who underscore that coca use gives them strength, wisdom, and courage. What remains to be established is whether this power comes exclusively from the alkaloids in the coca leaf, or, as I believe, also from the solidarity, shared experience, and *esprit de corps* generated in sessions in which *chacchapadas* take place.

In assessing coca use in the Andes, I believe that we have allowed ourselves to be excessively influenced by American-European images of the lone and furtive drug taker who, hiding in a garret, ingests cocaine in uncontrolled amounts and abandons himself to hallucinations. In the Andes, the mild coca leaf is not used in this way. Instead, as we have seen, it is used collectively and ceremoniously in specific contexts and amounts and in prescribed customary and moral ways. In short, its use is culturally sanctioned and supervised.

Access to Coca
and Ethnic Domination

I have shown not only that coca use is well integrated into Andean communal life but also that its use actively generates this integration. There is hardly an important event in the life of individuals, families, and neighborhoods that is not ceremonially marked by the use of coca. And thus integrated, surrounded by formalities and controlled by communal forces, coca is unlikely to be abused (in the sense that its consumption could cause harmful effects in the health of individuals). This argument is identical to the one we commonly accept for alcohol: that in well-integrated communities, widespread alcohol abuse is unlikely to occur.

But there are undeniable circumstances in which coca is abused. These are associated with communal disintegration, with feelings of social alienation, and with the manipulative and exploitative use of coca by *hacendados* (owners of large landholdings), merchants, and mine owners.

Hacendados, merchants, and mine owners have always generously distributed coca (perhaps it is the only thing with which they ever were generous), thereby creating monopolistic channels to coca access in exchange for unpaid work obligations or ridiculously low money wages. As Mario Vásquez (1961: 31) notes, "In some regions *hacendados* provide the peon with a ration of coca (one ounce) for each day of work."[10] It is in response to this situation that the *Indigenista* movement (*Indigenismo*)[11] pronounced itself as an anti-coca lobby in the 1930s and 1940s; indeed, coca use was regarded as similar to opium use in Europe-invaded China and even to the fictional *soma* use in Aldous Huxley's (1946) *Brave New World*. Coca has been used to keep Indian workers and Chinese indentured workers quiet and submissive, and it has been used to avoid paying proper wages. Today coca continues to be used by unscrupulous merchants to develop debt obligations that create a captive clientele.

There are two important dimensions to take into account. First, the act of distribution of coca confers power over the users—a contingency that goes back to pre-Spanish times. Given the social importance of coca, users frequently fall into the hands of those who distribute the leaf. In exchange, they give services, work extra hours, sell cheaply, and buy dear. As in everything else, the Indian has been exploited—in this case, for access to coca. But it must be remembered that this exploitation is not limited to physical needs, as in supposed drug addictions; it is also based on the exercise of monopoly power over scarce goods. The Indian has been exploited in the same way for access to alcohol, land, irrigation water, pastures, mediation services at courts of justice, church sacraments, and medical and educational services. Coca distribution lends itself to exploitation in a vast system of general domination that is characteristic of colonial and neo-colonial situations of exploitation (Cotler 1968).

The second dimension to be emphasized is that a rootless individual, torn away from the community and its solidarity group, suffering in a mine or on a plantation, alienated from home and facing strange surroundings such as a prison, is likely to abuse coca in the same sense that a European in similar circumstances is likely to abuse alcohol. But, again, the crucial factors are rootlessness and the erosion of communal and solidarity ties; these explain the abuse of coca, not addiction, as has been argued all too frequently.

On the other hand, it is worth remembering that the very act of using coca is a clear signal that immediately identifies a person as Indian and thus the object of discrimination by urban and rural mestizo elites. The revulsion[12] that the habit provokes in the latter group spills over into the Indian. Coca thus also functions as a discriminatory stigma (Goffman 1965). A coca-using Indian is immediately excluded from a series of social contexts and situations, regarded as filthy and put in his place, and treated either condescendingly or in a brusque manner, provoking a defensive reaction on the part of the Indian.

Accordingly, Oscar Núñez del Prado (1965: 196) speaks of the double behavior of the Indian:

> With Mestizos he is suspicious, silent, withdrawn, and nearly inaccessible; he offers a passive and systematic resistance. He is humble, fearful, and inattentive; reticent and evasive in his answers, indecisive in his attitudes. He suppresses and hides his emotions and rarely reveals his disagreement even when he finds himself in fundamental opposition. He is obsequious at times, but this attitude implies that he wants something very specific, that he expects almost an immediate reward. With other natives he is open, communicative, fond of practical jokes, he makes a display of his industry and is ready and willing to cooperate; he shows his feelings and states his opinions without reserve. He is fond of *fiestas* and enjoys himself in them. When he is drunk he is impulsive and courageous in a fight; he bears grudges, is vengeful, astute and often mocking. He is sober and moderate in his sex life, frugal in eating and tranquil in daily affairs.

It is obvious that this reaction arises from the exploitative and abusive context of interactions between Indians and Mestizos and, most emphatically, not from the effects of coca use. No wonder, then, that these character traits have been enshrined in the literature, and that ascribing them to the generalized effect of a drug has become so convenient. Given these conditions, paradoxical situations tend to occur that can be explained by the discriminatory effect implicit in coca use. On the one hand, there is self-deprecation, as astutely observed by Núñez del Prado (1965: 105):

In all three countries [Peru, Bolivia, Ecuador] contempt for everything Indian is habitual. No one wants to belong to this class, and it is very nearly an insult to suggest to a Mestizo that he has an Indian relative; the Indian himself, when he has passed to the *cholo* social class, wishes to wipe out his Indian connections and cover them up as much as possible because he knows that society condemns the Indian to an inferior position and that even his legal rights are obstructed. He becomes ashamed of his language and even abuses his relatives who maintain their Indian status.

On the other hand, since coca use is a stigma, those who use it openly and in defiance of the discrimination it provokes are affirming among themselves ties of brotherhood and solidarity against the discriminatory mestizo world. The circle is thus closed again. The act of *hallmay* (with coca) is a defiant act against the outside world and, as we have seen, also integrates into a cohesive group those who share it. Those who do not use coca exclude and are excluded at the same time. Hence my conclusion that coca use is a powerful symbol of social identity that clearly separates those who are with the Indians and those who are not. Hence, too, the frustration and feelings of impotence felt by the dominant classes when they confront coca use, since they acutely sense that its use functions as a major barrier against capture of the Indian's imagination. And that is why we have such violent attacks on coca and such exaggerated claims about its harmful effects on the Indian populations.[13] Attacks on coca use thus constitute an attempt to undermine the very basis of Andean culture and the internal solidarity of an oppressed group. These negative campaigns are an attempt to break through the barricades in the defense of the so-called *Perú profundo*[14] in the hope that coca and the Indians will disappear and that the floodgates for massive Westernization will be opened.

The debate over coca use (for or against) has indeed reached surrealistic dimensions. Both proponents of coca's continued use and abolitionists see themselves in the same camp, for both are would-be defenders and protectors of the Indians against external aggression by mestizo and white oppression. The abolitionists find themselves in the situation of having to save the Indians from aspects of their own culture (such as coca use). The obligation to save the Indian implies making him less of an Indian in that very same process of salvation. The abolitionist position of the ambiguous *Indigenista* movement arose out of these sentiments. As a movement, the *Indigenistas* proposed to upgrade the value of the Indians and their image in the country, and to integrate them into the mainstream of national life—but only as individuals, not as an integral culture. That is why the *Indigenistas* insisted that Indians get rid of the stigma causing them to be objects of discrimination: that they abandon coca use, the Quechua language, and, by implication, all other aspects of Andean culture. Properly shorn of their own culture they would perhaps be allowed to integrate into Western culture—though once an individual has timidly entered this world, constant reminders of an Indian background are nonetheless used to mark distances and keep hierarchies.

In affirming the Indians' right to use coca, I defend the right of Indians not to have to integrate into the dominant culture individually as a precondition of nondiscrimination. I defend the right of Andean culture to survive in its integrity. And my utopian vision includes a kind of cultural pluralism of mutual respect between all cultures. Until the conditions that would permit such pluralist integration are forged, my perspective implies that I must continue with the defense of Andean cultural patterns. I also contend that inter-ethnic strife is necessary for the survival of Andean culture until such a day as when conditions of equality in power relations and the control of productive resources have been achieved. Under those conditions, coca use will then again be thoroughly "domesticated"[15] and abuse of coca use will correspondingly diminish.

In assuming this position, the defenders of the right to use coca occasionally find that they are in the same camp with those who distribute coca, exploit the Indians, encourage its indiscriminate use, and inculcate its use outside the social controls that limit and channel its use. Even worse, defenders may be lumped with those involved in the narcotics trade, since they appear to provide a convenient ideological base for the criminals to justify themselves. Obviously, it is necessary to combat those who, because they want to profit from coca or cocaine distribution, are promoting indiscriminate use of the leaf or encouraging the use of a recognized world menace—cocaine.

Coca Substitution

We are facing a situation in which it is likely that, because of external pressures, attempts will be made to substitute coca in the Andes.[16] The pertinent questions then are: What can replace coca? And what effect would substitution have on legitimate users?

In order to attempt answers, we must first ask: Which of coca's multiple functions will be affected by substitution? If coca leaf is (erroneously) considered a drug, then the solution to its substitution seems relatively simple. Pharmaceutical companies could market a product, such as a mixture of chewing gum with caffeine, aspirin, or even steroids, that would reproduce the slight pharmacological effects that coca has on its users and provide the necessary oral gratification. But could this measure also replace all the other functions of coca use?

I believe that I have demonstrated here that the perception of coca as a drug is a short-sighted vision of the problem and, as such, ignores a number of issues more important than its slight pharmacological effects on users. In the first place, given the characterization of coca as a luxury good within the scale of its users' consumption items, a substitute for coca would have to be not only another good in the same category but also one that could serve as a token of generosity and hospitality. This good would probably be alcohol[17]–either cheap cane alcohol or expensive beer–whose consumption in Peru is on the rise. But encouraging the substitution of alcohol for coca would, in my opinion, be a reprehensible act of social irresponsibility with ample and unfortunate precedents in terms of European settlers' actions against Indian populations on the continent—as Peter Mancall (1995) shows for the North American case.

We must also ask: What would substitute for the economic functions of coca? In today's context it would probably be national currency. But the effect of this substitution would be a drastic devaluation for the peasant economy. The exchange rates would have to equalize upward to currency exchange rates. In addition, the multiple trade routes that peasants have created would collapse, leading to a greater degree of regional disarticulation. Moreover, the expansion of the national currency marketing network would not be to the peasants' advantage, given the system of advances, the manipulation of prices, the systematic cheating in weights and measures, and the high interest charges that are all too well known. It is precisely because of these disadvantages that the peasants have built the alternative of barter networks as a defensive mechanism in which coca plays a very important role. It is probably true that barter networks could continue to exist even without coca, but a great deal of flexibility and efficiency would be lost with the disappearance of the quasi-currency that facilitates exchange.

However, regarding coca's social functions as a mechanism of social integration and solidarity, it is not substitutable with *anything*—given its mystic and mythic significance.

If coca were replaced, then, a symbol with profound and important significations and millennial, deep-seated traditional roots transmitted from generation to generation would be wrenched away. Also lost would be a unique non-Western way to value and enjoy human relationships. A rich vein of cultural content would disappear and, with it, the sense of leading a contemplative and philosophical way of life that is implicit among those who use the sacred leaf. Denial and denigration of the social roles of coca use are essentially acts of ethnocide, deculturation, and disarticulation, perpetrated repeatedly not only today but throughout colonial history against defenseless cultures of the Third World. (In Japan, the daily use of tea, and its ceremonial aspect, expresses the essence and quintessence of Japanese cultural values, but it has not yet occurred to anyone to forbid the use of tea, or to replace the tea ceremony because in another country certain aspects of tea production and consumption (such as caffeine addiction) are regarded as harmful. Similar examples include wine in France and Italy, betel nuts in India, jat in Yemen, and the use of tobacco and peyote among American Indians.)

In short, Andean culture has contributed to the Western world a whole series of useful plants such as potatoes, quinoa, mashua, oca, olluco, cotton, *ají* peppers, tara, quinine, and coca (National Research Council 1989). In some cases, as with potatoes, cotton, and quinine, the West knew how to benefit from them. In others, as with mashua, oca, and olluco, it has ignored their potential. But coca, alone, has been misused by others outside its native context. Concentrated into a dangerous powder, divorced from its cultural context and the etiquette of its use, it has become a menace. One has to question whether the vengeful destruction of coca fields would not also bring far-reaching and profoundly detrimental consequences for Andean peoples. As we have seen, coca—within its cultural context—is a valuable resource. Who will pay the consequences when this resource is lost?

The New Context in the Late 1990s

As of this writing, sixteen years have passed since I began participating in the campaign to defend traditional coca consumption. During the decades of the 1970s and 1980s it seemed important to highlight two points: first, that traditional coca consumption is not a "toxicomania" (Dr. Fernando Cabieses [1980] and other scholars have published several studies affirming the impossibility of demonstrating that prolonged traditional coca use has any negative effects on the organism); and, second, as a nexus of social and cultural integration in Andean culture, coca has such an important role that it is difficult to imagine this culture without its coca. These points were largely accepted as the twentieth century drew to a close.

In the interim, certain topics have acquired greater importance in today's context of U.S.-inspired drug wars. Specifically, I am concerned with the position that defenders of the right to use coca will have to take in confronting the negative effects that the growing illegal narcotics trade and ways to combat it are having on Andean society and culture. Is it necessary to reevaluate my position? I do not believe so, but I do think it is important to change the emphasis in the way the argumentation is presented.

In 1978 I edited a special issue of the Journal *América Indígena* (Vol. 38, No. 4) devoted entirely to the defense of the right to consume coca. It quickly sold out and was reissued as a book (Boldó y Clement 1986) that had an important impact. The contributors to the latter volume supported this right from various points of view: biomedical, political, cultural, historical, and religious. Baldomero Cáceres (1978: 769–785; 1990: 31–72) demonstrated how the supposed biomedical arguments against coca use lacked any scientific basis whatsoever. And an article by Roderick E. Burchard (1978: 809–835) cited the works of Carlos Monge (1946), who stated that coca was necessary to the physiological processes of people who live at high altitudes. Burchard tried to corroborate this argument by highlighting the role that one of the chemical components of the coca leaf (ecgonine) has on the digestive process. Other papers have demonstrated the importance of the coca leaf in traditional medicinal practices (Hulshof 1978: 837–846; Gagliano 1978: 789–805). Cultural anthropologists such as myself (Mayer 1978a: 849–865), Catherine (née Allen) Wagner (1978: 877–902), and Javier Zorrilla (1978: 867–874) argued that coca is an instrument of social integration and a symbol that serves as a marker of membership in a social group, such that its use expresses the will that this group exercises to maintain its identity. Contributors to the volume also protested the elimination of coca use as part of an attempt to destroy Andean religious beliefs and values. Zorrilla (1978: 873), in particular, argued that coca's "destruction violates human rights in general, and in particular against religious freedom. It can be considered as a new extirpation of idolatries, an act of ethnocide and a negation of the practice of cultural pluralism."

In 1989, the Interamerican Indigenous Institute in Mexico published the results of a new research effort carried out in Peru, Bolivia, and Northern Argentina, where the above-mentioned points were amplified and further corroborated (Instituto Indígenista Interaméricano 1989). In its conclusions, presented and debated at a special conference on inter-American traffic in narcotics in Rio de Janeiro in 1986, the Institute, with the backing of the United Nations' Inter-American Consultative Group on Coca Leaf Problems (UNFDAC), recommended that

> [t]he right to the cultivation and use of the coca leaf in the traditional Andean culture must be effectively recognized in any legislation about drug control in the Andean countries, which must spell out the conditions under which it can be cultivated and legitimately consumed by that sector of the population that shares in this cultural tradition. (Cited in Carter 1989: 29.)

In the international context of those years, we did achieve a small victory. It became accepted that traditional coca use in the Andean countries was different from the activities of coca production for the illegal international narcotics trade. In 1988 the United Nations' Convention for the Control of Illicit Narcotics and Psychotropic Substances, within the framework of its drastic recommended actions to eradicate these substances at the source, nonetheless stressed that these measures "... *shall respect fundamental human rights and shall take due account of traditional licit uses, where there is historic evidence of such use, as well as the protection of the environment*" (emphasis added). The repressive anti-drug forces have not attacked traditional coca users; nor has the incapacity of these forces to control the expansion of coca production for cocaine diminished the supply of coca for traditional consumption, even though demand for the leaf as a source of cocaine paste has continued to increase exponentially. It is nonetheless also true that in Peru and Bolivia, the commercial channels of legitimate coca trade were subjected to tighter controls and suffered the local abuses and extortion that such measures inevitably produce. It is also true that these measures had absolutely no impact in curtailing the illegal narcotics trade, but instead created points of friction among various military forces, police forces, government officials, truck drivers, passengers, coca merchants, and consumers.

In some respects, however, this victory was not all that important. Anti-drug forces quickly realized that even if they were to eliminate traditional coca use, doing so would have no impact on the international flow of narcotic substances consumed in the First World. The fight was not against traditional coca consumers. And in any case, the political costs of enraging several million Andean coca consumers would have been high, especially given the anti-imperialist overtones in the arguments in defense of traditional coca consumption. Leaving traditional coca users alone and licensing legitimate trade in coca have had positive results. For example, only very few of the producer committees that arose to defend themselves against U.S.-sponsored eradication campaigns in Peru and Bolivia have used the cultural relativism argument to protect their illicit participation in the incredible boom of cocaine production of the last four decades.[18] It is also interesting to note that none of the famous Colombian cocaine entrepreneurs have ever defended their profession with cultural arguments and positive propaganda about the virtues of the coca leaf. In general, and thus far, the world of coca and the world of cocaine have kept to their separate paths without affecting each other very much.

Nevertheless, several new contexts emerged in the late 1990s. First, the narcotics trade expanded greatly, wreaking havoc on the Andean countries. Narco-money, narco-politicians, narco-kidnappings, narco-money-laundering operations, and narco-influences crept into every crevice of society, corroding its whole fabric. The cost in terms of corrupted institutions and induced violence in the Third World has been enormous, greatly surpassing the cost of maintaining or rehabilitating incapacitated addicts of the First World. Until recently, traditional coca consumers could justifiably say that those problems were not theirs and that they were not directly affected by them. Today this is no longer true. There are many Andean peasants who have benefited from working as *pichicateros* in the clandestine growing, collecting, manufacturing, transporting, and selling of cocaine paste (*pichicata* in local parlance). Edmundo Morales (1989) is a dissenting voice. He argues that the impact of cocaine traffic on peasant societies is negative, owing not so much to the effect of the drug but to the fact that illegally obtained money has been unwisely spent. There are many who have profited from the cocaine boom, but scores have also died, assassinated by the greed that the white powder rush has created; and it has to be admitted that there are many cocaine-paste addicts who end their lives miserably in the drug-consuming quarters of cities in the Huallaga Valley of Peru, named by the locals as the "Chicago" of Tingo María. Narcotics and terrorism are linked factors that have profoundly affected peasants in the rural zones of the subtropical regions. The extent to which the narcotics trade has armed terrorist groups in Peru and Colombia is not well documented, but they are certainly armed. The narcotics industry has induced the highest levels of violence known in rural areas for many decades. Counternarcotic military operations add yet another dimension to the corruption and violence, which escalate in ever-expanding spirals.

At the same time, the inflow of dollars through the sale of cocaine paste has negative impacts on the national economy and contributes to an economic crisis that also smites the peaceful traditional coca consumers (Alvarez 1998). The pretense of people in the Andean countries that they do not have serious problems caused by the narcotics trade is like the ostrich who buries its head in the sand so as not to see what it does not want to know. It is urgently important to create and implement an intelligent and effective anti-cocaine policy that can make clear distinctions between legitimate traditional coca consumption, on the one hand, and the growing local consumption of cocaine paste among urban populations, along with cocaine exports to the metropolis, on the other. As a minimum requirement, coca-producing committees who demand that they be exempted from eradication campaigns must participate in the combat against the narcotics trade and honestly promise not to leak any of their production toward cocaine.

The second new context concerns the United States, which is beginning to understand that its "Drug War" policies, created during the Reagan-Bush era and half-heartedly continued by the Clinton administration, are a failure (Cotler 1999: 231–242). This new context demands more of the anthropologist than the assertion that traditional coca consumption has nothing to do with the narcotics trade, and it is indeed time to propose viable policies that originate in the Andean nations and involve all sectors of the local society and its global partners in the resolution of the problem. The typical attitude of people in Andean societies not to take U.S.-sponsored anti-drug policies seriously (e.g., by signing agreements with the United States under pressure and accepting its funds but passively subverting its programs) is obsolete and dangerous. In contemporary Peru, Colombia, and Bolivia this is especially serious, because arms and military resources that enter the country under the cover of anti-drug war efforts likely end up being used in illegal and undemocratic contexts.

Third, the economic crisis in Peru and Bolivia in the 1970s, 1980s, and 1990s pushed hundreds of thousands of peasant families into coca production for cocaine, owing to a lack of viable economic alternatives (Parkerson 1989). In terms of economic anthropology, the conversion of subsistence-oriented peasants to cash-cropping commercial agriculturalists seeking the highest possible returns is the best demonstration of the rational-peasant argument one could ever wish to find. Newly established peasant communities in the Huallaga Valley of Peru and the Chapare of Bolivia have become politically active in defending their economic interests. In Bolivia they seek representation at the highest levels of political institutions, whereas in Peru political terrorism has become involved in protecting and exploiting the cocaine trade.[19] In Colombia the drug trade takes the form of an illegal capitalism that is violent to the extreme.

Fourth, today's world is moving beyond prohibitionism. Decriminalization of drug use is being seriously proposed in order to mitigate the high social costs of violence that comes with illegality. Prohibition and police persecution are being questioned as the model that combats drug use and trade, because it is ineffective and incapable of resolving the problems that result from consumption of pleasure drugs. As cocaine products begin to lose their appeal, consumption patterns in the cities of the First World are beginning to decline, leading to a decrease in the associated criminality of cocaine distribution—although many police chiefs think that this decline is due to their policies of zero tolerance, increased surveillance, and high levels of incarceration. In the Andean countries, military and police forces created to carry out the drug war are plagued by corruption; and through this all-too-human correlate of illegality, the narcotic trade infects all other aspects of civil society (Cotler 1999).

Fifth, the social context of oppressed cultures has changed. Recall that 1993 was the International Year of Indigenous Peoples. This was the decade in which cultural claims became politicized and cultural and ethnic warfare was ubiquitous. In Latin America, new forms of respect for traditional cultural practices were insisted upon, as were an expansion of identity politics that transcended previously rigidly defined ethnic boundaries and affirmation of the value of preserving traditions for their own sake. Defending coca remains a wonderful political weapon in cultural and ethnic conflict in the Andes. Thus while cocaine becomes a global phenomenon, the defense of coca production and consumption becomes its local manifestation.

Sixth, there is now a surplus of coca production. Coca producers have organized and acquired political weight. Like any other industry in crisis, these producers are now turning to the government for institutional support. Colombian, Bolivian, and Peruvian governments have to navigate the tempestuous cross-currents that are brought against them both from abroad, to eradicate the crop, and from resistance generated by producers and dealers within their own nations.[20] As a result of this push and pull, the peasant coca producer of today is not defined as a narco-criminal or an illegal producer and is immune from prosecution. Prosecution under narcotics law is reserved for those who accumulate coca leaf for concentration, process the leaf, transport the leaf or source chemicals needed for cocaine production, transport, sell, or distribute the basic cocaine paste or its refined products, and, more recently, launder the profits.

The Peruvian coca monopoly known as Empresa Nacional de la Coca (ENACO), recently privatized as part of structural readjustment policies, is under the obligation to buy at below-market prices any coca leaf offered to it, in order to divert the leaf away from cocaine production. As a consequence, ENACO has enormous surpluses of coca leaf that needs to find legitimate and legal market outlets. This situation reflects the fact that overproduction of coca now characterizes the Peruvian and Bolivian industry, as a result of the relatively static or even diminishing demand for coca leaf as it applies to traditional consumption patterns. Many think that drug consumption is now entering a period of decline. Cocaine is in competition with other narcotic substances in the world, and because Colombia has increasingly become a direct coca producer for its own lucrative international manufacturing and distribution network, the prices of coca leaf in Peru are in decline.

ENACO, under the influence of neo-liberalism, issued a call for a marketing campaign to sell this growing inventory and invited me and other international experts to participate in the Second International Forum to Re-valorize the Coca Leaf held in Cusco, Peru, in June 1993. Some of the issues I raised at that symposium are discussed in the next section.

Aggressive Marketing

What can we do to organize an effective marketing campaign to valorize and legitimize coca leaf as a commodity? I offer seven suggestions.

Defend Traditional Uses

Coca consumption is still stigmatized in the Andes, and therefore it is necessary to continue to insist that traditional coca use is a harmless way of consuming coca. Research that conclusively demonstrates this fact is also still necessary. As Cáceres (1978: 775–780; 1990: 51–56) has clearly shown, the biased scientific research of the 1940s and 1950s unfairly established an equivalence between coca use and cocaine "toxico mania." Numerous questions about the physiology of coca chewing and the absorption of its chemical components through the mucous membranes of the mouth and the digestive tract remain unanswered,[21] and there are many hypotheses that have not been subjected to rigorous unbiased testing. It is also important to reach beyond the limited scope of the professional literature to educate the public about the results and implication of these studies. Toward this end, communication with the Quechua- and

Aymara-speaking peoples is necessary, as they are the most directly concerned with this issue. It is also necessary to change what gets taught about coca in rural and urban schools. The prejudices stemming from the years when coca consumption was included in the same category as cocaine addiction still condemn all Indians as drug addicts; nor are these prejudices free from the racist idea that the degeneration of the Indian race is due to coca consumption. Though demonstrably false, such prejudices continue to run rampant and are widely diffused among the population. Cáceres (1990) insists that the ideologically powerful psychiatric language of "toxico manias," which includes "cocainism," should be banished as pseudoscientific. ENACO does not yet dare to advertise legal coca teabags in newspapers or on radio or television, and it would not think of organizing a campaign for the ready-to-chew coca leaf. Though coca sales are legal, the leaf is not available in middle-class urban supermarkets.

Expand the Groups That Consume Coca

Through advertising and the changing of social mores, a greater consuming population needs to be created. In practice, this means that the social contexts in which coca is legal, legitimate, and socially approved need to be expanded. Also implied is an expansion of the conscious practice of Andean culture by its members. This practice must begin to emerge from its hiding places in urban crevices and semi-clandestine conditions into new public spaces. Representations of such behavior in the public media, such as soap operas that show normal people consuming coca leaf as an ordinary activity, are also important. For example, what is happening among the new generation of Andean migrants' children born in cities with respect to their attitude toward coca consumption? And are the millions of fans of urban *chicha* music[22] going to adopt coca chewing as part of their newly created identity of urban Andeans, or will they, too, succumb to the allure of other products of the coca leaf?

Twenty years ago, in communities, villages, and towns of the Andes, public consumption of coca—and abstention from it—clearly marked ethnic and class boundaries. These boundaries have undergone remarkable changes since then, and the people who use coca have also changed (Jordán Pando et al. 1989: 79–107; Roth and Bohrt 1989: 171–230). The remarkable resurgence of coca leaf tea consumed by the middle and upper classes is but one example of these changes. A modern marketing study is necessary to evaluate the potential for expanded rural and urban markets for diverse forms of coca consumption. Here the distinction between private and public spheres plays a role. For example, how many middle-class families of the highlands and coastal cities in the Andes do not ordinarily consume coca leaf but do so at wakes? In Salta, Argentina, coca leaf is served as a treat after meals in restaurants and middle-class homes. When was this practice abandoned in Cusco? Is it possible to revive this and other customs for mestizos in the highlands?

De-Andeanize Coca

In other words, export the habit of coca leaf consumption to other cultures. Introduce legitimate and pleasant ways to consume coca leaf or coca products as part of the world trade in mild stimulants. Starbucks Coffee and Godiva Chocolates could and should stock nicely packaged coca leaf and coca products in every outlet in the United States and around the world. Just as there are different ways and reasons to consume coca in various Indigenous cultures in South America, it should not be difficult to introduce exotic coca consumption into other stimulant-consumption cultures around the world. Tobacco, tea, coffee, and chocolate have become world commodities, but coca leaf has been unfairly and unjustly prohibited.

Accredit and Legitimate Coca As Part of Official Culture in the Andean Countries

Official organizations and public spokespersons need to develop ways of communicating to the public that governments and trendsetters of fashion and taste approve of and support the legitimate consumption of coca leaf. For example, apart from propaganda and the inclusion of coca use in public ceremonials, municipalities can create special places where coca products are sold. International tourists arriving in Cusco, who are offered an obligatory coca leaf tea to mitigate the effects of altitude sickness, can also be taught more traditional ways of consuming coca such as the relaxed *hallmay* ritual so beautifully described in Allen's (1988) book. Finally, anti-drug consumption campaigns directed at youth groups should carry the message "Say yes to coca, no to cocaine" or "Consume the coca but leave out the cola."

Join the International Natural Foods and Medicines Market

Coca is unfairly excluded from this growing international market. Research and information campaigns need to extol the virtues that the biochemical components of the leaf, singly or in combination, offer to natural-medicine consumers of the world. Coca is distinctly suited for this purpose, since it acts as a stimulant and enhances the energy levels of those who use it. Nor are the other known virtues of coca leaf properly promoted. For instance, it is an effective local anesthetic as well as a pain killer for stomach and menstrual cramps. And coca's well-known capacity to temporarily suppress the sensation of hunger should be taken advantage of by the scores of people who are dieting to lose weight.

To take this route is, of course, to return to a trend that was well under way at the beginning of the twentieth century but abruptly stopped when cocaine became a proscribed substance in 1914 (Gootenberg

1999). Coca and cocaine products were widely sold all over the world at a time when coca was being promoted as one of the wonder plants of the world. The French apothecary Angelo Mariani was a marketing genius then, popularizing various over-the-counter tonics that contained coca and/or cocaine in exclusive patented packages and with recommendations printed on the labels from eminent physicians and important personalities (among them Pope Leo XIII, the Czar of Russia, and the writer Jules Verne). Also available were Vin Mariani (wine with coca leaves), Elixir Mariani (containing stronger concentrations of alcohol and more potent cocaine), Pastilles Mariani (for persistent coughs with alcohol extract of coca), and Thé Mariani (extracts of the leaf for hot-water infusions). An imitator, John Styth Pemberton of Atlanta, Georgia, patented a medicinal tonic drink similar to Vin Mariani in 1885. The next year he took away the alcohol and added caffeine-rich cola nuts; then, in 1888, he mixed it with carbonated water because the latter was perceived to be more medicinal than ordinary water. Finally, he changed the name—to Coca Cola. The patent was sold in 1891 to Asa Griggs. The company's advertisers had consumers believing that drinking Coca Cola is the essence of being a *gringo*. Thus coca had contributed once again to identity formation. If these entrepreneurs were so successful at marketing coca products, there is no reason why the same cannot be done again, assuming that the prevailing attitudes and legislation can be changed. There is a huge potential global market for coca products—a market whose dimensions are difficult to envision. Who would hold the patent rights to these products is a question that has not yet been raised, but it would certainly have to be considered.

Eliminate the International Restrictions

While the prevailing ideology of neo-liberalism that is bringing down trade barriers lasts, it is necessary to pressure the international drug control organizations to eliminate the old-fashioned restrictions that impede international trade in coca and its legitimate products and to permit its beneficial and peaceful consumption. Even though the Drug Enforcement Agency (DEA) of the United States and other international organizations now recognize that coca consumption is innocuous, Bolivia's request to the International Narcotics Convention to strike coca leaf from its list of prohibited substances was once again denied in 1992.

Teach the World to Use Coca

Even more daring is my proposal that the Andean cultures have something to teach the rest of the world. Traditional coca leaf consumption is practiced in the Andes in a relaxed, contemplative, social, nonviolent, and peaceful manner. Consumed in this way, coca causes no harm to anyone, so let the Andes promote coca-chewing practices as a natural alternative to the harmful and dangerous consumption of cocaine products. Andean culture can broadcast to the world that there are socially acceptable, tranquil, and harmless ways of consuming "drugs" that pose no threat or danger to anyone. The only caveat is that coca chewing stains the teeth and has a rather unpleasant smell—but so, of course, does tobacco.

It is time to take an offensive stance, and to propose to the world that the Andean way of consuming drugs is socially beneficial, psychologically stimulating, and a "natural" means of benefiting from one of nature's gifts. It is not only a matter of pride for the Andean civilization to have discovered the properties of the coca plant and to have domesticated it; it is also the responsibility of the Andean peoples to show the rest of the world how to consume it. Let Andean peoples teach the world how to do *hallmay!*

Respect for Coca

Scholars defending the right to use coca have insisted that an offensive against coca consumption implied an attack against the Indigenous Andean culture in its essence and integrity. We defended the right of Andean culture to follow its precepts and practices as a fundamental principle of cultural relativity and found that unfair criticism of coca use was yet one more manifestation of ancient prejudices and discrimination. And we affirmed that coca was the sacred plant of the Andean Indians and therefore appealed to the basic freedom of worship. Although still valid, this argument now appears exaggerated to me because it leads to a somewhat ridiculous posture. The reason something is considered sacred in one culture is not the same in others, and to represent coca as a revered object, similar to the most holy objects of other religions, is somewhat laughable. Coca *is* the sacred leaf of Andean Indians, but its sacredness is different from that of religious objects or symbols in other cultures; consider, for example, the representations of the host in Christianity and the rituals that take place in front of it. Indeed, coca's sacredness is expressed in less dramatic ways.

Coca is the faithful companion of an Andean man and woman. Coca is spoken to, and a person's most intimate secrets and yearnings are confided to it. Coca responds and tells. It communicates with human beings. It can reply to inner doubts with its taste or through other divinatory devices. Used in this way, coca helps one to think through dilemmas in daily life, to mull them over until a way out is found, to ponder options and alternatives. Its effect is the very opposite of the escapism and hedonism sought by the cocaine or crack user. Coca does not stupefy; on the contrary, it generates wisdom and helps find solutions to problems that involve the interaction of unknown factors. It helps resolve problems. It has mysteries, which are learned with patience and experience, and eventually convinces even the most agnostic doubter (Henman 1978). Because coca chewers talk and think about their problems as they take a break, they may even be less in need of psychiatric help.

Here is a story told to me by a very skeptical migrant from Tangor. He had successfully moved to Lima, where he distributed and sold clothing that his relatives manufactured in the informal sector of the shantytown of El Agustino. His personal documents (electoral, military, and tax cards) were forged. He was in Tangor for a few days to visit family and to celebrate the carnival. When he found out that I was interested in coca, he told me in all seriousness that coca really had the ability to "tell." He had lost his precious documents and was worried about it. His grandmother saw him in this state and said that something was wrong with him and that she would consult the coca leaf. After doing so, she gave her opinion. She said that the young man was in love. And with that, the youth found his documents under the mattress of his girlfriend's house.

Thus coca "communicates" with humans in mysterious ways. Its magic is manifested in important rituals such as the *despacho* and the *mesa* (used to cure a sick person), in the many songs in which it is addressed, and in the exchange of cattle (where coca leaves represent the animals that are bought, sold, or given away).[23] Coca has subtle forms of permeating the thoughts and sentiments of each user, and that is why it is a loyal companion on the path and in life. As Allen (1988) says in her book, coca has the hold on life. It is a way of being and, hence, an expression of a person's identity. Coca has a special kind of sacredness; it is intimate and familiar, quotidian and subjective. Coca is thus an expression of a minimalist religion. It is not the majestic or inexplicable mystery that requires a leap of faith; nor is it the thunder or the lightning or the ultimate enigma of the universe. On the contrary, coca is humble and serene—and it is at this level that its virtue is to be found. Coca use does not produce grand visions or changes in the senses or experiences of pleasure or terror. One does not get high on coca, but neither does one suffer a "down," the profound and desperate sensation of depravation that causes the cocaine user to seek ever higher doses of the stuff.

This is the paradigm that I think is worthy of acculturation to other peoples. It seems to me that in this use of a stimulating chemical substance, Andean users have discovered a way of being and a way of doing things in life that are worthy examples to teach the rest of humankind. If coca can teach humanity something, it should be this: that the collective sharing of leaves during a pause for a few moments from the activity one is undertaking, to reflect, to be contemplative, attuned, and attentive, is a philosophical moment that produces wisdom and calm. It is during such calm and thoughtful moments that the guidelines for future action are generated. And this power does not derive solely from the biochemical processes during which the active ingredients of the leaf are mixed with saliva and lime and absorbed in the body. It derives as well from the social way that coca is consumed. In the daily rhythm of activities, one takes time out to sit down, to have a conversation, and to think about big and little things in life with one's companions and with spirits, mountains, and other mysterious forces also participating. Indeed, coca is a great socializer.

I thus propose that if coca is to be valorized in its totality and integrity, the context of the culture that created it and uses it must be taken into account. To value coca means to accept the validity of Andean culture, and this in turn implies that we accept the practices of its most humble practitioner, the *indio coquero*. Herein lies a viable behavioral model that can be adopted and used by the rest of humankind.

Undue Appropriation

Authenticity does have to be questioned here, for artificial cultural situations could conceivably be created through the introduction of coca to groups that have not used it before. However, as with McDonalds hamburgers in Beijing, if an innovation sticks, however strange and inauthentic it may have seemed when first introduced, it may soon become fashionable and in time even achieve the status of a tradition. This aspect of creativity accounts for the diffusion of cultural patterns around the world. As Eric Hobsbawm and Terence Ranger (1984) have noted, many traditions that people consider unshakable and fundamental were at one time arbitrarily created.

A Peruvian example is the contemporary Cusco pageant of *Inti Raymi* that glorifies the Inca past for urban Cusqueños and tourists every June 24th, admirably studied by Marisol De la Cadena (2000). In its present form, it is a creation of Cusco intellectuals of the 1940s that soon became tradition and acquired more and more authenticity as time passed. Coca itself did not appear on the stage until 1993, when Baldomero Cáceres pointed out its omission to populist mayor Daniel Estrada. The latter ordered the choreographers to include it in the representations, whereupon great baskets of coca were carried on stage by pages and priests waved the leaves in the air.

Now that it is important to expand the spheres of coca consumption, we enter into the social and cultural terrain of extending, expanding, and changing the parameters of a tradition in the name of safeguarding that very same tradition. To be sure, when innovators break social boundaries, there is always the risk that they might be creating something spurious. And if this were to happen, there will immediately be a flurry of accusations to the effect that what is being proposed or practiced does not constitute an authentic expression of this tradition. What is truly spurious will then come out in the wash, while genuinely interesting innovative inventions and extensions of this tradition will flourish. Baldomero Cáceres in Peru and Silvia Rivera in Bolivia, both recognized intellectuals (oftentimes lovingly described as eccentric), are two of the very few middle-class professionals who openly and defiantly masticate coca in public and in front of TV cameras. Other supporters of pro-coca campaigns, especially Bolivian diplomats, prefer to wear an enamel inlaid silver lapel button in the shape of the leaf as a sign of support of coca they themselves do not use.

To valorize a cultural process is to recognize that which has value in its given context, in the respect it shows to its antecedent models, and in the integrity of its intentions. For example, valorization of Andean traditional medicine implies recognition that the tradition exists and has its own set of values and merits. Extension of this traditional medicine to clients from other cultures can also be valuable and lucrative.[24] But there are occasions and opportunities in which some aspect of a culture is yanked out of its context and used with other intentions. Take, as an example, the reading of coca leaves to divine the cause of an illness or misfortune—a procedure that is part of curing ceremonies.[25] If anthropology students from Cusco were to go to hotel lobbies and read coca leaves in order to promote tourism, one could say that this is an undue appropriation of a genuine tradition.

Undue appropriation can here be defined as the extraction of one aspect of a culture for uses totally different from those for which it was originally created. As such, it is one of many factors in the tense relations that exist between ethnic and cultural groups under situations of domination, dependency, neocolonialism, and imperialism—relations that characterize contemporary cultural clashes. The practice of undue appropriation involves a kind of stealing or plagiarism of the essence of one culture by agents of another. The appropriating culture ends up enriched, whereas the other feels in some way diminished, cheapened, deprived, or abused.

In fact, an alkaloid contained in the coca leaf was unduly appropriated by the Western world—a context alien to the integrity of the plant and its cultural uses in the Andes. Showing no curiosity or interest in learning how people use the coca leaf, and indifferent to the horrible consequences resulting from the use of cocaine, narcotics traffickers are truly the agents of undue cultural appropriation. Their motivation is their addiction to profits. Peruvians, Bolivians, and Colombians who participate in this trade do so in what can only be described as a form of prostitution, because they permit valuable resources from their own lands and from their intimate and private lives to be used in wrongful ways.

As we think about the opportunities of expanding the legitimate coca trade on a global scale, it is pertinent to ask: What is it that we really want to export? Is it respect for Andean culture? And with it, a legitimate way of enjoying a natural product? Or are we merely interested in selling a refined chemical substance? If the answer to the second question is affirmative, then we will once again have allowed the external agents of globalization to perpetrate an undue appropriation of something that is valuable in Andean culture; indeed, we will have dishonored the very Andean culture that invented and created a legitimate use of the coca leaf.

Postscript

This chapter consists of two articles. The first appeared in Spanish in *América Indígena* (Mayer 1978a); the English version, translated and revised, was titled "Coca Use in the Andes" (Mayer 1989b), with Edmundo Morales as guest editor. The second article was published as *"Factores Sociales en la Revaloración de la Coca"* (Mayer 1993) and is reprinted with permission from the journal *Debate Agrario*. For this book I have merged the two articles, eliminated repetitions, updated references, and thoroughly revised the text once again.

As coca eradication campaigns become increasingly confrontational and violent, as the United States steps up the role of military and secret services in carrying out these campaigns, and as illegal drug profits continue to grow and corrupt Latin American society, I hope that this modest proposal contributes to a more sensible approach toward legalization and normalization of one more Andean export commodity.

Notes

1. The debate about the health effects of coca chewing, though old and venerable, has not commanded the attention among responsible researchers that it deserves (see the useful summary in Grynspoon and Bakalar 1976: 120–129). Especially unjustified are the medical profession's shrill judgments about the supposedly "noxious" effects of coca chewing. An example is the comment by Dr. Fortunato Carranza Sánchez, who said that coca mastication produces "[a] disorientation towards the present and a moral anesthesia towards the future" (*La Prensa,* November 11, 1977).

2. Lanning (1967: 77) notes that the use of coca (accompanied by lime, carefully stored in gourds and dispensed with fine bone spatulas) dates from the Preceramic era (2,500–1,800 B.C.). See also Plowman (1984, 1986), who is a botanist with expertise on the coca plant.

3. In a discussion of scapegoating, Gantzer, Kasischke, and Losno (1977: 66) underline the tendency to blame coca use for the miserable material conditions of the Indians today. See also Ricketts (1952: 310–322; 1954: 113–126) for a classic example set in Peru.

4. Spheres of exchange are discussed in Chapter 5. First presented by Salisbury (1962), they are further analyzed by Bohannan (1959: 491–503).

5. Sahlins (1972) shows how necessities circulate according to the norms of generalized reciprocity, whereas goods classified as luxuries circulate according to the norms of balanced reciprocity.

6. Gutierrez Noriega (1948: 73) asserts that people use coca because they do not eat well, and then they do not eat well because they use coca. Malnutrition does exist in the Andes, but it is due to the lack of proper means to produce and distribute food.

7. Murra (1986a) dismisses the argument that access to coca was restricted to the Inca nobility, asserting instead that commoners had access to coca through distribution of their headmen or *curacas* who, in turn, obtained it from their respective archipelagoes where people were sent to cultivate, harvest, and transport it to the populated areas. In each of the five cases of vertical control analyzed by Murra (1975: 59–116), coca production, bulking, and distribution occurred at different levels of complexity and scale. Murra (ed., 1991) also notes that coca producers in Sonqo had a share in the coca produced for the Inca state. And as Gagliano (1994:19) points out, the chroniclers concur that access to coca was mediated by the state as a reward: "Coca leaves were awarded to individuals regardless of social rank, as a quasi-divine gift from the emperor."

8. The use of commodities in scarce supply that perform most of the functions of money is common in many parts of the world. As Bartolomé de Las Casas (1967, vol. I: 365) reports, during the early days of Spanish contact with Amerindian peoples, Peruvians used coca in lieu of coinage. Romano (1986: 333–338) also provides a lengthy discussion on the quasi-coin functions of coca in the Andean "natural economy." Here it served as a medium of exchange, as a means to accumulate, as a store of value, and as an important means of payment for labor. For centuries it has also enriched coca merchants and provided the church and state with tax revenues.

9. An example of drug-induced apathy is provided by Wright–St. Clair (1970: 224): "A nation of addicts, undernourished and apathetic, was easy prey for the ambitious and well armed *conquistadores*." In contrast is the following chronicle of a more realistic action: "In the haciendas of Chinche and Huarautambo, where the exploitation of the peasants had reached acute extremes, agitation and discontent [were] endemically characterized by violence. In the same way the communities of Michivilca, Yanahuanca, [and] Quillacocha acted with more violence against their aggressors in revenge for abuses committed against them over long years" (Kapsoli 1975: 123–124).

10. Coca was also distributed to Indians to get them into debt. An older example is the complaint of the *Lupaqa* Indians in the Altiplano of Puno in 1567: The *Cacique*, don Martin Cari, declared that "in this village there are thirty Spaniards more or less, who trade and engage in farming and selling coca and wine to the Indians which is not to their benefit because the Spaniards give them baskets of coca and wine on credit and other things like expensive maize and *chuño* and afterwards they take for this sheep, llamas and silver and if the Indians do not have the means to pay, they put them in jail . . . " (in Murra [ed.] 1964: 26). Colonial and republican coca trade has also been studied by Mörner (1985: 47–48), Gagliano (1994), and Romano (1986).

11. The coca debate within the context of Indigenismo is reviewed by Gagliano (1994: 119–163).

12. Europeans' revulsion over coca chewing has long historical roots. Bartolomé de las Casas (cited in Cáceres 1990: 43) quotes reports from sixteenth-century

Spanish observers who said that coca chewing "is a very dirty thing and it creates great disgust seeing them thus."

13. Because it is a symbol of cultural resistance, coca use is vehemently attacked by many non-Indians; yet the biochemical reality is innocuous. As Grinspoon and Bakalar (1976: 218) note, "This is an exceptionally clear example of a situation in which the pharmacological effects of a drug are less important than the symbolism that surrounds the habit of using it."

14. *Perú profundo,* a phrase coined by Peru's eminent historian, Jorge Basadre (1947), is much quoted today to indicate hidden but profound Andean cultural elements that pervade the nation. Presumably, it contrasts with the image of (legal) Peru as trying to be a carbon copy of a European nation—a tendency against which Basadre fought. Further analysis of *"Perú profundo"* can be found in Mayer (1992) and Note 2 of Chapter 10.

15. Grynspoon and Bakalar (1976: 233) note that one way of dealing with drugs is to "domesticate" them—that is, ". . . to create a social situation in which they [drugs] can be used in a controlled fashion and with moderation." Coca use in the Andes is a clear example of such a "domestication."

16. The United States has funded repeated attempts to reduce the cultivation of coca in the producing areas, aimed at cutting off supply for the narcotics trade. These attempts have been met with opposition and resistance, and several agents of the program have been shot. Moreover, they have had little effect in reducing the supply of cocaine for the narcotics trade. On this point, see Strug (1986); in addition, Cotler (1999: 239) shows a displacement of coca production from Peru (down by 43 percent between 1990 and 1997) to Colombia (up by 98 percent in the same period). Current short-term policies have not reduced coca consumption in the traditional areas, although the insatiable demand of cocaine merchants has increased the price of coca available in these areas, and there have been periods of shortages. Nevertheless, Peru signed a 1950 UN recommendation to control the expansion of coca production and to carry out a campaign that would gradually reduce coca consumption in the traditional areas in twenty-five years. The deadline was 1975, but consumption was barely affected. For a study of coca consumption patterns in contemporary Bolivia, see Carter and Mamani (1978) and Roth and Bohrt (1989: 171–230).

17. It would be difficult to imagine the important game of reciprocity in Andean culture using chewing gum as the token and expression of the social relationships that link people together. When Carter and Mamani (1978: 932) posed a similar question in a survey in Bolivia, 74 percent of the respondents said that nothing could substitute for coca. Other answers included food (11 percent), alcoholic beverages (11 percent), and candy (17 percent).

18. Keeping up with the literature on the impact of coca leaf production for drug export is an almost impossible task. The following sources are nevertheless recommended. A useful but no longer up-to-date compendium can be found in Pacini and Frankemont (1986). Healy (1986: 101–143) studied the politicization of coca producers in the Chapare of Bolivia. An update on production and its problems is provided by Parkerson (1989). An early political analysis of the effects of the cocaine trade in Bolivia at the time that Bolivia had a narco-dictatorship can be found in Canelas Orellana and Canelas Zanner (1983). Julio Cotler (1999) describes how

U.S. anti-narcotics policy shored up the autocratic Fujimori regime. Viola (1995, 1996) describes the failure of substitution programs in Bolivia as well as the Indigenous ethnogenesis and anti-*Gringo* sentiments that eradication programs have created there. Bigenho (1998: 114–122) has found musical expressions of nationalism in the defense of the right to consume coca. A comprehensive study of coca-cocaine links in Bolivia can be found in Jordán Pando et al. (1989). Diego García Sayán (1990), a member of the Andean Commission of Jurists, has edited a volume that analyzes the international dimensions of the cocaine trade, its environmental impact on the producer regions, and the effects of the narcotics trade on the national societies of Bolivia, Peru, and Colombia; also discussed are the politics of the narcotics trade, the violence and revolutionary movements it has spawned or supported, the judicial and legal problems it has created, and the financial havens of Panama and the Caribbean. The Comisión Andina de Juristas (1994) has edited a volume that examines the criminological implications of applying anti-narcotic laws in the Andean countries. Finally, León and Castro de la Mata (1989) have edited a volume dealing with cocaine-paste consumption in Peru.

19. The connections between narcotics trade and armed revolutionary movements in Peru are reported in Tantahuilca (1990), Gonzales Manrique (1989: 207–222), Tarazona-Sevillano (1990), and Kawell (1989). In addition, the *New York Times* currently carries almost daily stories on the tax on coca that armed revolutionary guerrillas extracted from producers in Colombia.

20. The power of drug lords to hold nations hostage is illustrated in García Márquez (1997), in which he tells how Carlos Ochoa staged a kidnapping in order to negotiate with the Colombian government, turned himself in to the authorities, and was sent to live in a golden prison—from which he later escaped.

21. In one of the few respected studies on the physiology of coca ingestion, Hanna (1974; see also Hanna and Hornick 1977) reports slight physiological changes in core body temperature among coca chewers. Jerí (1980) emphasizes more recent medical and pharmacological studies of coca and cocaine use in a volume that attempts to substantiate negative effects, prove addictions, and thereby justify eradication policies.

22. *Chicha* music is the urban musical expression of children of migrants from the Andes. Using modern electronic instrumentation, it imitates rock groups in dress and presentation, combining Spanish lyrics and Latin rhythms with Andean melodies and themes. It is immensely popular with teenagers who attend crowded dance halls known as *chichódromos*. The self-referential non-stigmatizing term they use to refer to their music is *música tropical andina*. The invasion of Andeans into urban spaces has been jeeringly described by Matos Mar (1987), and a more serious, though also more unfriendly, analysis of this musical phenomenon can be found in Turino (1993: 178–179).

23. See Quijada Jara (1957, 1977) for a discussion of the rituals practiced by the pastoralists of Huancavelica.

24. Hollywood film actress Shirley MacLaine (1983) is a devout follower of out-of-this-world experiences. One such experience occurred in the Andes, where she consulted Eduardo Calderón, a Peruvian Moche shaman who was also anthropological informant to Douglas Sharon (1978) and manufacturer of "authentic" Moche pre-Hispanic pottery reproductions. In his later years he performed

shamanistic ceremonies on the mysterious Nazca Lines for first-class elite tourists seeking authentic new-age experiences.

25. See Paz (1989: 232–381), a scholarly expert on divination rituals that include the reading of coca leaves.

7

Alguito Para Ganar ("A Little Something to Earn"): Profits and Losses in Peasant Economies

WITH MANUEL GLAVE

This chapter is about the concept of profit in peasant economies. It uses the results of a survey of potato fields in two comparable valleys in Peru to clarify the differences between a strict business accounting procedure to establish profits or losses and the method that peasants use to evaluate the profitability of cash crops. It also looks at how farmers evaluate the status of their subsistence crops, showing that they require important cash investments but do not necessarily account for them. A central part of this chapter is the presentation of a cultural model of householding that monitors the flows of resources and of money, relating these to Stephen Gudeman's house economy.

In this chapter, we try to establish what peasant agriculturalists in the small-scale family-based production of potatoes in the Peruvian highlands mean by "profits" and "losses." This is an important issue, since profits or losses, according to economists, are the signals that induce economic agents to modify their activities, without which there is no self-regulation through market mechanisms. We will show that the actors' understandings of profits and losses are complex, "profits" being a constructed cultural category arrived at by socially established (accounting) procedures. For that reason, "profit" may have not have a single definition.

We proceed by a series of approximations in three stages. First, we begin as economists would if they were sent to evaluate the development potential of potato cultivation. We examine the results of a survey of 153 potato fields that we carried out in two field seasons between 1984 and 1986 in two valleys in the eastern slopes of the Peruvian Andes (Tulumayo in Central Peru and Paucartambo in Southern Peru). In the analysis of this survey, we calculated profits and losses according to strict cost (business) accounting procedures. Our results show that Peru's generalized economic crisis of the mid-1980s, which led to rapidly rising production costs and decreasing potato prices, caused alarming losses in the peasant agricultural sector. Though aware of their losses, the peasants evaluated the crisis in less alarmist ways than we did.

Second, closer to the peasants' point of view, we observe that peasants divide production into cash and subsistence crops. We show that they use different criteria than those of economists to establish profits or losses on cash crops. Specifically, we suggest that peasants evaluate profits or losses of cash crops in terms of a simple cash-out and cash-in flow, ignoring household inputs and family labor. This kind of calculus carries an implicit subsidy (by not counting family labor and household resources) that enables market participation but provides little or no long-run benefit under prevailing productivity conditions and price levels. When evaluating subsistence crops, peasant farmers also ignore the cash expenses necessary to produce them. Profit calculations are irrelevant to the farmers in subsistence calculations, but attention to the flow of resources that produces crops is highly relevant.

Our study focuses on the profitability of a single crop within peasants' diversified activities. We chose potatoes because they have been the main source of subsistence as well as the main cash crop of many households over the past fifty years. The initial impetus for this study was our desire to understand the economics of genetic erosion in potatoes, so as to determine whether improved "green revolution" (higher yielding and therefore more profitable) varieties drive out older land races. Because the Andes are the center of potato domestication, there is a high degree of genetic diversity there. This diversity is now being threatened by rapid introduction of improved varieties, causing the displacement of native varieties—a process known as genetic erosion (Harlan 1975).[1] Our findings indicate that despite the unprofitability of native varieties, they continue to be cultivated (though on a very small scale).

Third, we become ethnographers. Following Stephen Gudeman and Alberto Rivera (1990), César Fonseca (1972a), and Sutti Ortiz (1979), we describe accounting procedures in Andean peasant households. In peasant accounting, we find that "profit" is not a relevant category. Dividing their income and expenditure into three streams—expenses, money, and service—members of households are more concerned with monitoring flows within each stream than with evaluating outcomes of past ventures. In this schema, then, the question of whether profits have been realized is a feature of the flow of money but not of the total resources needed to procure money. Although this schema may prove practical to household members, it masks underlying resource flows that often impoverish peasants.

The ways in which individuals must struggle to gain access to money is the opportunity to have *alguito para ganar* ("a little something to earn"). In local usage, the Spanish verb *ganar* refers primarily to ways in which money can be earned. For example, to work for wages is to *ganar un jornal,* to sell in the market is to *ganar en el negocio,* and *alguito para ganar* is a phrase one often hears poor people say when they bargain or ask for an opportunity to provide a service in exchange for some coins, even if it is only to clean the windshield of a car stopped at a red light. But *ganar* also translates as "to win," and therefore *ganancias* are profits; *pérdidas* are losses. A profitable business is *un negocio rentable.*

Ganarse la vida is how one earns a living. In this usage, the notion of profit is not always present. It includes living on a farm whose members often describe their activities as a state of being such as *estar en la chacra nomás* ("just being on the farm")—a state of being they themselves belittle as something of trivial consequence, an altogether unimportant aspect of their lives, because it is a place where the opportunity to make profits is rare. This expression finds its way into academic textbooks as relating to the question of how the peasantry reproduces itself and, much more elegantly, appears in Gudeman and Rivera's (1990) recent discussion of the "house" model, which focuses on how peasants struggle to maintain themselves in the remote Colombian countryside beyond the margins of profitability.

Overall, we are more concerned with peasants' everyday meanings and understandings of "profit" than with the way in which the discipline of economics defines the term *maximization* (the rational pursuit of optimizing solutions) or with the basic motivation known as the profit motive, which makes businesses run. In this regard, we concur with Alain de Janvry (1981: 104), who warns that we should not "confuse the inability of peasants to capture profits with their presumed nondesire for profits." As we will show below, we are in basic agreement with Gudeman and Rivera's notion that there are fundamental differences between the ways in which businesses pursue profits and the ways in which peasant households operate. But this distinction should not be allowed to obscure the fact that peasant farmers are interested in earnings and in pursuing gains wherever they can.

Alexander Chayanov (1966) pioneered this debate by claiming that the economic concept of profit made no sense in a peasant economy (since profits are calculated after deducting wages and land rent from gross income). In a peasant economy, there is no separation between what constitutes land rent and what constitutes family wages, since the crops people consume embody rent and wages. Therefore, it is not easy to know how to subtract wages and rent from gross income. That is why Chayanov (1966: 5) proposed the term *labor product* to describe total income minus costs incurred. Subsequent interpretations of the Chayanovian position popularized the notion that peasants were not profit seekers. Extensions of the Chayanovian way of thinking led to a generalized theoretical affirmation that peasant families have an inner drive to satisfy family needs first (as if the rest of us did not have the same motivation) rather than to seek profits (as if one objective were not dependent on the other). The conceptual separation that economists tend to make between the profit-seeking firm and the household that puts its needs first obscures the fact that in agricultural contexts households are also like firms, and their members must pursue both objectives.[2]

A very different approach to peasant studies comes from Marxist class analyses of peasant economies. Such analyses have dominated the theoretical literature of the past two decades; their authors argue strongly that relations of domination, surplus extraction, and the struggle to compete with capitalist agriculture eliminate profit from peasant households. Our critique is that throughout this body of literature, it is the analyst who creates definitions and identifies contexts and constraints under which peasants operate. For example, Carmen Diana Deere (1990: 266) distinguishes petty commodity production (which reproduces the household with no possibility of profit) from capitalist accumulation (arising out of profit). We agree that physical and social constraints such as land scarcity and poor resource endowments, exploitative market structures, and domination are at the roots of the peasant predicament, and we endorse the position that peasant profits in commodity production are often negative because of competition with large-scale capitalist agriculture. But more relevant to our concern here is that, although this large body of literature addresses the question as to why peasant agriculture is not or cannot be profitable, it defines profitability as if the concept had universal meaning. Our study focuses on how farmers understand profit and how they calculate profits or losses. As we will demonstrate, these issues do not always arise in the ways one would expect, inasmuch as people consider profit and loss only in the context of their cash nexus. We will show that small-scale farmers tend to conceive profitable activities in simple ways that maximize cash returns on money invested.

Cash is an important component in production and consumption, but the flow of cash in a peasant economy often has a perverse impact. As an external and scarce resource generated through linkages with urban and national markets, money affects a peasant economy in a way similar to that of foreign currency on a national economy. Peasants use currency to import products that they cannot produce locally, such as fuel, clothes, liquor, food, and agricultural inputs. When the terms of trade are unfavorable (i.e., operating against peasants), in desperate attempts to continue to export products they devalue the elements of the economy that are under their control. In order to continue to operate, peasants must sell their products below production cost, absorbing the losses at home. In the long run, this leads to impoverishment.

Academic interest in the economy of Peru's large and impoverished peasant sector in the mountain regions has an interesting trajectory. Ethnographic descriptions by Stephen Brush (1977a), César Fonseca (1972a), Jürgen Golte (1980), Enrique Mayer (1974a, 1985), and Benjamin Orlove and Ricardo Godoy (1986) focused on the role of ecological complementarity in a harsh, diverse, and resource-poor environment as well as on the collective control of resources. Mayer (1974a; see also Chapter 4) examined reciprocity in labor exchanges, and Mayer (1971; see also Chapter 5) and Orlove (1986) compared barter and cash sales. These authors examined all such issues as features of a fairly isolated, nonmonetary subsistence system that supposedly characterized the Andean peasants in the remote mountains. William Mitchell (1991) showed how resource insufficiency accounted for diversification into nonagricultural activities and heavy outmigration. Though none of these scholars ignored the role of market penetration, their analyses tended to treat markets as an extraneous variable that affected the patterns under consideration.

This approach changed when, in 1974, Peruvian economist Efraín Franco published the results of a detailed peasant farm income study (completed in the northern Department of Cajamarca in 1973). This remarkable survey permitted Carmen Diana Deere (1990) to carry out an insightful analysis of peasant household survival strategies. Highly unequal distribution of resources (land, capital, and market access) in the region led Deere to break her sample into five groups: near landless households, smallholder households, middle peasant households, rich peasant households, and petty bourgeoisie. We will consider her near landless, smallholder, and middle peasant households because they are comparable to the households in our study. Income for these households was derived from a variety of sources. Farming activities accounted for a low proportion of this income (20 percent for the near landless households, 24 percent for the smallholder households, and 55 percent for the middle peasant households), showing that peasants do choose between alternative ways of making a living depending on how much can be earned from each (Deere 1990: 275). Only a quarter of the Cajamarcan peasant households attempted to generate their livelihood as petty producers of agricultural products, and these were concentrated in the upper strata. The Cajamarca Study (Franco 1974: 22) shows that, during this time period, net average annual income from agriculture was US$17 for the near landless, US$64 for the smallholders, and US$166 for the middle peasants. Slim pickings! Our findings, a decade later, were similar: US$7, US$41, and US$33 for the Tulumayo Valley and US$24, US$65, and US$87 in the Paucartambo Valley.

Deere was concerned not with profits or losses but with the question of whether this small net income from agriculture was sufficient to reproduce household labor power. She used two proxy variables, the official minimum wage and the "going" local wage, thus defining a "moral and historical" level of subsistence against which to measure farm income (Deere 1990: 278). The results were dismal. Only 6 percent of the smallholder households and 5 percent of the middle peasant households netted enough from their agriculture to match the standard of living defined by official wages. When Deere calculated this ceiling with the lower "going" wage rate, she found that 9 percent of smallholders and 4 percent of middle peasants could cover their needs from agricultural activities alone (Deere 1990: 278).

The Cajamarca Study had an important impact in the 1970s and 1980s, leading Peruvian economists to enrich the debate with detailed quantitative monographs of peasant household productive and exchange activities. Following Theodore Schultz (1964),[3] Adolfo Figueroa (1984) constructed complex matrix tables that detailed income and expenditure streams of a whole range of activities typical of the diverse "portfolio" that characterizes peasant systems. He distinguished monetary from self-produced income, which, when added, gave a total book income. Of this total, he found that 49.2 percent was derived from monetary pursuits, whereas agricultural and animal production accounted for 50.8 percent (1984: 43). However, the sale of agricultural products contributed only 10 percent of monetary income; animal products, only 20.7 percent; and the sale of labor, only 29 percent (1984: 49). Figueroa also showed that consumption was heavily monetized; 68 percent of monetary income was spent on regular food, clothing, and educational expenses (1984: 50). Daniel Cotlear, Figueroa's student, replicating his teacher's methods, analyzed the impact of intensification of agriculture, of green revolution technology, and improved education of the farmers. He showed that green revolution technology was profitable and predicted that its adoption would lead to development (Cotlear 1989). Our study, three years later, showed that profitability of potato agriculture had changed for the worse. From 1990 to 1995 it was important to assess the impact of the generalized crisis in Peru's economy on the peasant sector including such issues as inflation, regional market integration, and government policies (Gonzales de Olarte 1987, 1994). Javier Escobal (1994) startled the academic community with his conclusion that the poorest and least monetized peasants fared better than wealthier farmers in the aftermath of the infamous structural readjustment policies imposed by President Fujimori in 1991.

Tulumayo and Paucartambo Valleys

Tulumayo Valley, the first of the two valleys we studied, is easily identified as the more developed. It is located on the eastern slopes of the Department of Junín (Concepción Province) in the central highlands, a narrow valley with abundant and early rainfall that makes it particularly propitious for potato production.[4] Roads link the Tulumayo Valley to the larger markets of Huancayo and Lima. Most of the region's agricultural land is in the hands of twenty-three peasant communities with a total population of 12,818 that is growing at a moderate annual rate of 0.8 percent.[5] Agricultural innovations (improved potato seed, fertilizer, and chemical inputs to combat pests and diseases) began in the early 1950s. These innovations were rapidly adopted and underwrote regional prosperity at a time when terms of trade were favorable for peasant producers. In the 1970s, annual potato exports to metropolitan Lima, Peru's mining centers, and the city of Huancayo averaged two to three thousand tons. This green revolution did not necessarily mean that cultivation of native potato varieties was abandoned (Brush and Taylor 1992). Indeed, these varieties, along with a range of other crops grown mainly for local consumption and family subsistence, still play an important role in the regional agricultural economy. Potato exports make up 70 percent of the total potato crop, which occupies about 60 percent of the cultivated land.

The second valley, the Paucartambo Valley, is in the Department of Cusco (Paucartambo Province) in the Southern Andes. As in the Tulumayo Valley, the population is concentrated in the upper zones of the region's drainage system. The valley's population was 20,209 in 1981, and the growth rate has been a very modest 0.4 percent. Until Peru's agrarian reform of 1969, the *hacienda* system dominated the province of Paucartambo. By 1985, however, the province's 169 *haciendas* had been converted to 73 peasant communities. Though expanding, the potato market is still weakly developed. It is overshadowed by contract farming of barley for a beer company. Potatoes from Paucartambo Province supply the city of Cusco, a smaller market than the combined metropolitan Lima and Huancayo outlets that farmers from Tulumayo Valley enjoy. Although green revolution technology was introduced in the Paucartambo and Tulumayo valleys at about the same time, its extensive adoption by Paucartambo Valley small-scale peasant farmers is more recent and as yet incomplete.

We chose to study specific fields as our unit of analysis and asked farmers to provide us with detailed information (not estimates).[6] Overall, profits and losses in one or two fields do not represent the total balance of a household's income and expenditures, and this study does not pretend to repeat the analyses of Figueroa and Cotlear. In particular, we were interested in whether the proceeds of the harvests from our sample covered costs.[7]

We collected data during multiple visits to farmers' fields. We selected eighty-five fields in the Tulumayo region and sixty-eight in Paucartambo. These fields were chosen from ten representative communities in each region that showed diversity of potato cultivation. With the farmers, we gathered detailed information on each step of the production process. We quantified the inputs that required a monetary outlay as well as those that came from the farmers' own resources, for which we imputed a monetary value based on local market prices. The results are presented both in averages and in *intis* (a now defunct Peruvian currency). There was a high inflation rate while we carried out the project, and we corrected our calculations accordingly. All comparisons are in constant *intis* for April 1985, at a conversion rate of eight *intis* to the U.S. dollar.[9] Specifically, we developed a stratified random sample to provide us with enough variance to study three variables that are important determinants of productivity. The variables include environmental determinants, botanical variance, and socioeconomic factors. Environmental determinants include location along an altitudinal gradient. Such determinants are expressed in three production zones (following the methodology established in Mayer (1985; see also Chapter 8), with different productivity potential in each. From the poorest to the most productive lands, these comprise the high zone (HZ), which represents the upper limits of possible agriculture; the intermediate zone (IZ), where the bulk of the potato crop is grown; and the low zone (LZ), an area where potato production is expanding in response to market demand. Botanical variance entails the varieties of potatoes cultivated. For our study, we grouped similar varieties of potatoes into three categories that represent differences recognized by the local population: improved varieties (IV), selected varieties (SV), and native varieties (NV).[10] The latter are grown for household consumption, whereas the former two are sold and consumed in varying proportions (as shown in Figure 7.1). Finally, socioeconomic factors characterize the resources of the peasant producer household. These categories are rich farmers (RF), middle farmers (MF), and poor farmers (PF).

Figure 7.1 compares, along all variables, the quantities of potatoes sold versus the quantities retained for home consumption and seed. The first set of bars on the left represents regional averages; the second set, the allocation between consumption and sale among the different variety types; and the last set, sales and subsistence production by farmer type. It is immediately apparent that the Tulumayo Valley sells greater quantities of potatoes than the Paucartambo Valley. Rich farmers have the greatest proportion of marketed production, and improved varieties are the most popular varieties for sale; this relationship holds in both valleys. In three categories—native varieties, the middle level, and poorer farmers—lower sales are shown, along with a higher proportion of production retained for home consumption.

Real Losses (Total Balances)

As we conducted our research, producers insistently told us that for several years they had been losing money on their commercial potato production.

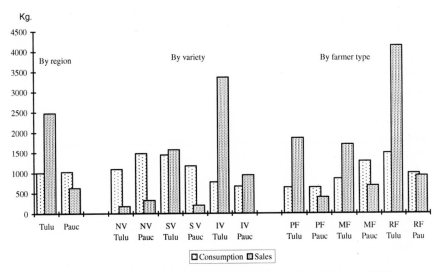

Figure 7.1 *Average Potato Home Consumption and Sales: Tulumayo Valley (1984–1985) and Paucartambo Valley (1985–1986)*

We then attempted to measure their profits and losses. But how does one measure these for peasants?

A firm's accountant calculates profits by subtracting incurred costs from total income. A positive balance indicates profits; a negative balance, losses. We call this method of calculating profits and losses the "total balance" because it takes all resources into consideration and follows strict business procedures. But very few farmers in our sample reckon profitability in this way. Instead, they use resources that are not accounted for in the "cost" side of the balance sheet; therefore, it was difficult to find out how they knew whether they had profited in an agricultural season. For this reason, we had to make the methodological decisions discussed below.

Total balance is calculated as total income minus total costs. Total income is the value of all sales plus the value, calculated at regional market prices, of the harvest retained for seed and home consumption. To determine costs, we added an imputed value for all inputs derived from a household's own resources (labor, animal manure, animal transport, seed, and so on) to all cash expenditures incurred in working a specific field. Careful decisions were made in giving a monetary value to these imputed resources.[11]

The results of our survey are shown in Table 7.1. Almost two-thirds (62 percent) of the fields in the Tulumayo Valley show negative total balances compared to one-third (35 percent) in the Paucartambo Valley. The average losses for a field planted with 100 kilograms of seed were 89.42 *intis* in the Tulumayo Valley, whereas the average profits were 207.76 *intis* in

Table 7.1   Total Balance: Tulumayo Valley (1984–1985) and Paucartambo Valley (1985–1986), Showing Distribution of Cases with Losses

| | By production zone | | | | | |
	Region		High		Intermediate		Low	
Tulumayo	53	62%	23	72%	25	56%	5	62%
Paucartambo	24	35%	3	43%	14	47%	7	23%

| | By crop variety | | | | | |
	Improved		Selected		Native	
Tulumayo	31	61%	13	54%	9	99%
Paucartambo	13	37%	3	38%	8	32%

| | By farmer stratum | | | | | |
	Rich		Middle		Poor	
Tulumayo	14	54%	25	63%	14	74%
Paucartambo	3	27%	13	37%	8	36%

| | By field size (quantity of seed) | | | | | | | | | |
	< 100 kg		100–200 kg		200–300kg		300–400 kg		> 400 kg	
Tulumayo	17	81%	18	62%	9	60%	4	66%	5	36%
Paucartambo	6	35%	5	25%	7	39%	2	33%	4	57%

the Paucartambo Valley. Total losses in the Tulumayo Valley were 39,440 *intis* whereas total profits came to 34,181 *intis*, showing that the whole sample of Tulumayo Valley fields lost more than it gained. In contrast, farmers in the Paucartambo Valley did better, even though this is the less developed of the two regions. Total losses there came to 9,005 *intis* whereas profits came to 39,383, showing a net gain of 30,378 *intis*.

A breakdown of the variables shown in Table 7.1 demonstrates that the intermediate and low zones of the Tulumayo Valley, where most commercial crops are planted, were more profitable than the high zone. Nevertheless, the intermediate and low zones had high rates of loss (more than half the total balances showed losses). The improved, high-yielding crop varieties were slightly less profitable than the selected commercial varieties. Growing native varieties in the Tulumayo Valley always produced loss. Rich farmers were better endowed with agricultural resources and skills, and their performance showed fewer cases of loss. By and large, very small fields were less profitable. (The range is less than one-tenth of a hectare for small fields to one-half of a hectare for large fields. All fields are terraces on very steep hillsides.) The data showed economies of scale, but larger fields were subject to greater fluctuations in losses and gains.

In the Paucartambo Valley, things looked much better during the 1985 and 1986 season compared to the Tulumayo Valley's poor performance during the previous agricultural season. The more commercial intermediate and low zones had a lower percentage of fields showing losses (47 percent and 23 percent respectively, compared with the Tulumayo Valley's 56

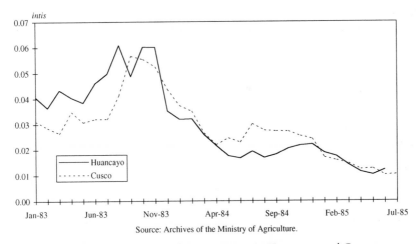

Source: Archives of the Ministry of Agriculture.

Figure 7.2   Wholesale Improved Potato Prices in Huancayo and Cusco, Adjusted According to Consumer Price Index (base year 1979). (Source: Archives of the Ministry of Agriculture.)

percent and 62 percent). Although improved varieties were not profitable for two-thirds of the Tulumayo Valley farmers, only one-third of farmers in the Paucartambo Valley suffered similar losses. Producing native varieties was also a profitable venture for 68 percent of the cases we studied in the Paucartambo Valley. In the Tulumayo Valley, native varieties resulted in a loss in all cases but one. These findings startled us since we expected the less integrated region of Paucartambo to show greater losses than the more integrated Tulumayo Valley.

Three macroeconomic factors that influence the terms of trade between agricultural and nonagricultural goods explain the high percentage of losses and the differential performance between the two valleys in those years: variation in sales prices, increasing costs of chemical inputs, and high rates of inflation.

Small-scale farmers in the Andes have no influence on sales prices. They must accept the prices set by regional marketing structures. These prices fluctuate widely, as they are ruled by the interplay of supply and demand in a speculative, but competitive, market for perishable staple foods. Gregory J. Scott (1985: 114) shows that between 1960 and 1980, potato prices (held constant against inflation) manifested a slow decline. As shown in Figure 7.2, which compares the potato prices for the Cusco and Huancayo markets over time, potato wholesale prices fell further during the final years of the Belaúnde government (1983 to 1985).

In 1986, after years of poor prices and protest, the newly inaugurated populist government of Alan García sought to curry favor with farmers by introducing guaranteed support prices for potatoes and increasing subsidies for government distributed fertilizers. Only the Paucartambo Valley farmers benefited from this policy. In constant *intis*, potato prices throughout Peru rose by 45 percent. To a great extent, this rise explains the Paucartambo Valley's better performance. In the two years subsequent to our fieldwork, Andean farmers benefited from García's policies. These benefits dissipated, however, under the hyperinflation that became rampant during the later years of his administration (1988–1990). Support prices, easy credit, and subsidies were totally eliminated in 1991 by the Fujimori administration. As a result, the 1995–1996 agricultural season was the worst in recent memory. Potato prices were so low that farmers let their crops rot in the fields.

Even if one eliminates the effects of higher prices, the data from the Paucartambo Valley show fewer losses than in the Tulumayo Valley. At price levels comparable to 1985 and in constant prices for both valleys, the Paucartambo Valley would have had an average profit of 82.25 *intis* compared to an average loss of 89.42 *intis* in the Tulumayo Valley. With this adjustment to the data, only 44 percent of fields in the Paucartambo Valley would have had losses, compared to 63 percent of Tulumayo Valley fields. Lower levels of losses for the Paucartambo Valley are related to lower levels of investment that reduce costs and offset the fall in income derived from decreased yields.[12]

During the 1970s and 1980s, the price of chemical inputs, principally fertilizers, rose steeply even though they were subsidized by the government. Since chemical fertilizers and pest controls are the largest components of monetary costs (about 33 percent), the rising tendency of inputs against falling trends in sales prices contributed to the high incidence of losses in the two regions. Our study foreshadowed the general tendency of farmers to reduce drastically the amounts of chemical inputs as inflation, and the structural readjustment programs of the Fujimori regime caused the prices of these inputs to skyrocket.

Inflation also contributed to farm losses. From November 1984 to June 1985, rural inflation in the Tulumayo region was 52 percent, whereas urban inflation reached 150 percent. Prices of chemical inputs, fertilizers, and transport also increased 150 percent, whereas local costs such as wage labor and food rose considerably. The result was an enormous loss in income for producers. Gonzales de Olarte (1987: Appendix 3) shows that between 1977 and 1988 the annual rural inflation rate for production in the Pampa de Anta (Cusco) was 109.7 percent. If inflation is corrected by calculating the replacement of cash outlays to begin a new cycle of production in the Tulumayo Valley, the number of cases with losses goes up by 26 percent (from 18 percent of cases with nominal losses to 44 percent when adjusted for inflation). By 1988–1989, hyperinflation was rampant throughout Peru. Most peasants were forced to liquidate their cash reserves and drastically decrease their consumption of purchased goods.

Our data from 1984–1986 foreshadowed the strategies peasants would employ to defend themselves against the ravages of the national crisis that came afterward. These included a reversion to greater reliance on subsistence production to help them tide over the losses of money. Monetary investment in chemical inputs and wages were reduced drastically (Paucartambo Valley farmers invested 11,510 *intis* for improved varieties compared to 33,760 *intis* laid out by Tulumayo Valley farmers). Paucartambo Valley producers spent one-third less than their Tulumayo Valley counterparts on pesticides and fungicides. Though this strategy reduces productivity, it is also a cost-reduction strategy. Another interesting example of micro-level adjustments is the use by Paucartambo Valley farmers of 12.63 fewer labor days to produce 100 kilos of potatoes in the lower zones than Tulumayo Valley farmers did. And only 19 percent of the total labor was paid wages in the Paucartambo Valley compared to Tulumayo Valley's 30 percent. In short, a drastic retreat from the market, a de-intensification of agriculture, and a serious reduction in marketable output were characteristic defensive strategies against short-term national monetary crisis. Any gains in productivity and technological innovation that the two regions had made in past decades became unprofitable, whereas a return to the traditional systems of production seemed to provide better defenses against the crisis.

Monetary Balances
and the Illusion of Profits

It is well known that peasants and artisans rarely include the value of their own labor in their cost calculations and that they tend to sell their products below cost. Because the total balance includes a monetary value of labor, we feel that it does not accurately reflect the way peasants calculate profits or losses. In this section, we therefore introduce a different way to calculate profitability and demonstrate that this procedure more closely approximates the way peasants reckon gains and losses. We call this new calculus the "monetary balance."

Much like a cash register, the monetary balance measures the cash flow through a field in one season. The monetary balance is calculated by taking monetary income (product of sales) minus all cash spent on production during the season. Potatoes retained for seed or home consumption, the family's labor, and other home-based inputs are not counted here. Since farmers dedicate so much effort to produce a cash crop, they seek to maximize cash returns.

To be fair, we eliminated all fields destined exclusively for home consumption—a factor more easily determined in the Tulumayo Valley than in the Paucartambo Valley because, when we concluded our survey, over half the farmers in the Paucartambo Valley still had not sold any portion of

*Table 7.2   Monetary Balance: Tulumayo Valley (1984–1985) and Paucartambo
Valley (1985–1986), Showing Distribution of Cases with Losses*

	Region		By Production Zone High		Intermediate		Low	
Tulumayo	31	44%	12	60%	16	36%	3	43%
Paucartambo	7	21%	-	-	4	31%	3	14%

	Improved		By Crop Variety Selected		Native	
Tulumayo	20	41%	8	42%	3	100%
Paucartambo	4	16%	2	100%	1	14%

	Rich		By Farmer Stratum Middle		Poor	
Tulumayo	9	39%	16	48%	6	40%
Paucartambo	2	33%	3	19%	2	17%

their crop. This outcome reflects the marketing strategy of Paucartambo farmers: They prefer to hold onto their harvest and await better prices later in the season while selling only such small amounts of potatoes as their need for cash dictates. In contrast, Tulumayo farmers sell their cash crop immediately after the harvest, which they try to time to coincide with moments when they expect prices to be high.

Table 7.2 gives a summary of monetary balances and shows the breakdown according to our variables. For obvious reasons, the monetary balances look much better than the total balances for both valleys,[13] even though the poorer performance of the Tulumayo Valley is still apparent. By this calculation, the average monetary profit in the Tulumayo Valley came to 61.94 *intis*, whereas it was a negative 89.42 *intis* in the total balance. The average profit of Paucartambo Valley farmers remained unchanged, but the number of fields with losses decreased from one-third to one-fifth. Table 7.2 shows that only 21 percent of the Paucartambo Valley sample lost money, in contrast to 44 percent of the Tulumayo sample. And whereas 41 percent of Tulumayo Valley farmers lost money on improved varieties, only 16 percent did so in the Paucartambo Valley. The three strata of farmers (rich, middle, poor) always did better in the Paucartambo Valley than in the Tulumayo Valley.

Which of the two balances is correct—total or monetary? For the economist, actuality is found only in the total balance sheet, which takes into account all the resources involved in the productive process. From this perspective, farmers calculating the monetary balance carry out only a partial accounting of their costs and seem to be making erroneous calculations. But the economist's calculation shows that peasant losses are greater than those that peasants themselves calculate.

Small-scale farmers may have another perspective, and cost calculation has different nuances. Money is their scarcest resource and the most difficult to obtain. Money losses are the ones that really hurt because a loss of "working capital" (as they call it) affects their future production possibilities and reduces their capacity to consume. But losses in the total balance manifest themselves principally in the gradual decline of their own resources (poorer nutrition, soil erosion, etc.). Even though peasants perceive this resource depletion, they do not feel it as acutely as chronic cash shortages and the disappointment experienced directly at the end of a season when they might lose sizable quantities of cash.

For these reasons, we assert that small-scale farmers seek to maximize their monetary income from commercial production, and they generally evaluate profits and losses by considering only the monetary balance. For them, reality is reflected in the monetary balance whereas the total balance is, in certain respects, an illusory calculation. Perhaps the word *illusory* is appropriate if we use it to refer to an ideal but unreachable goal, rather than simply as a euphemism for *erroneous*. Peasants are conscious and rational about the deployment of their own nonmonetary resources in the productive process. They know that these resources can be assigned a monetary value. Proof of this is the fact that, as we conducted our survey and explained the differences between the two balances, farmers clearly understood our reasons for proceeding as we did. When we showed them that according to the total balance calculation they had lost even more than they had estimated with their monetary calculations, we received whimsical smiles in response. One farmer said, *"En vano trabajamos"* (We worked in vain).

Thus we conclude that when Andean peasants calculate profits and losses, they do so in different ways than commercial firms. The monetary balance determines their investment decisions for the coming seasons in the short (season-to-season) run. This is the level of normal profits that economic textbooks indicate as necessary under perfect competition to induce the small firm to remain in business. With characteristic modesty, these peasants seek only to maximize monetary income in their commercial production and are willing to tolerate returns close to zero.

Comparing the monetary and total balances shown in Tables 7.1 and 7.2, we find that 61 percent of the rich, 52 percent of the middle, and 60 percent of the poor farmers in the Tulumayo Valley had positive monetary balances; the comparative figures in the total balance are 46 percent, 37 percent, and 26 percent, respectively. The monetary balances were reasonable and compared well with small firms in the business world where high rates of failure characterize "mom-and-pop" shops. That is why it is reasonable (and not surprising) that in the following season, despite their complaints of losses, peasants in the Tulumayo Valley decided to sow areas virtually equivalent to those pertaining to the year of our survey. Many farmers hoped that the new government would do something about prices—which, in fact, it did. After government intervention, farmers' profits improved. And in the Paucartambo Valley, the results were even more encouraging: 67 percent of the rich, 81 percent of the middle, and 83 percent of the poor farmers made cash profits on their invested money.

Nevertheless, as sympathetic outsiders, we are obligated to state that this form of calculating profits creates an illusion, because it leads farmers to make erroneous decisions about how unprofitable their cash crop ventures really are. In the long run, if important structural changes that positively affect profitability of cash crops (no matter how profit is calculated) are not implemented, the crisis of the peasant farmer in the Peruvian Andes will worsen. In the long run, peasant production under such conditions is unsustainable. Our study captured two years of instability and crisis that affected the whole nation in the 1980s, but the same trends relentlessly continue to aggravate the agricultural sector. If product prices continue to fall and those of inputs continue to rise, commercial potato production by peasants must decrease, and they will retreat from the market to greater subsistence strategies. These factors will result not only in a decline in peasants' contributions to national food production but also in increased emigration rates as other opportunities entice people off the farm.

Subsistence Production Costs Money

Contrary to old and persistent notions that subsistence production and consumption are carried out only with local resources, our results show that subsistence agriculture also has a strong monetary component and that this cash investment is often lost. Figure 7.3 demonstrates that the proportion of the harvest retained for household consumption is roughly the same in both valleys. It fluctuates around 800 kilos per field. Note the choices, however: Native and selected varieties are preferred over improved varieties for household use. The less productive high zones are devoted more to subsistence production than are the agronomically favorable intermediate and low zones. Contrary to expectations, rich farmers retain more for home consumption than middle farmers who, in turn, keep more than poor farmers.

Table 7.3 shows the average quantities of money lost in fields without sales by zone, crop variety, and peasant stratum. It should be noted that the losses recorded in this table were not explicitly lamented by farmers, since there was no intention to recuperate the invested money through sales.

In the Tulumayo Valley, production of native varieties always generates a loss, no matter how returns are calculated. Production of native varieties for home consumption is considered a luxury, and only some farmers (predominantly the rich ones) can afford it, knowing full well that this production is subsidized by their commercial activities. The category of native

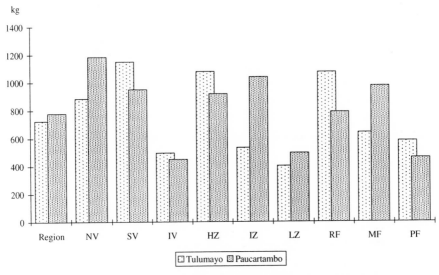

Figure 7.3   Home Consumption in Tulumayo Valley (1984–1985) and Paucartambo Valley (1985–1986): Net Production Minus Production Sold (averages)

Table 7.3   Monetary Losses in Tulumayo and Paucartambo Valleys: Cases Without Sales (April 1985), Showing Average Losses by Zone, Variety, and Stratum

	Cases Without Sales (April 1985), Showing Average of Losses by Zone, Variety, and Stratum			
	Average Money Lost *		Number of fields	
	Tulumayo	Paucartambo	Tulumayo	Paucartambo
By Production Zone				
Region	401	226	14	34
High zone	432	270	12	7
Intermediate zone	296	173	1	17
Low zone	99	219	1	10
By Crop Variety				
Improved varieties	197	236	2	10
Selected varieties	565	137	5	6
Native varieties	337	257	7	18
By Farmer Stratum				
Rich farmer	427	155	3	5
Middle farmer	506	269	7	19
Poor farmer	187	176	4	10

*In 100 kg of seed; in constant *intis*

includes a great number of varieties grown for local use. The Land Use and Genetic Erosion Project research team found sixty-five genotypes in the Tulumayo Valley and sixty-nine in the Paucartambo Valley (Brush and Taylor 1992: 246). These varieties are planted in mixed patterns. In the Tulumayo Valley, they are known by the Spanish word *regalo* ("gift") or by the Quechua term *chalo* (best translated as "assorted"), and this assortment is what farmers look for when they plant a field in native varieties. Each variety has a distinct taste, color, tuber shape, and genetic aptitude. In the Tulumayo Valley, consumers say they prefer these potatoes because they have a "floury" rather than a "watery" texture and taste. In the Paucartambo Valley, native varieties exhibit a broader range of taste and consistency. In addition to the floury types, they include bitter frost-resistant potatoes to make *chuño* ("freeze-dried") and boiling potatoes, varieties that have virtually disappeared from the Tulumayo Valley. In both valleys, native varieties are mainly for home use, to be consumed in ceremonial meals; hence they are designated as gifts. Karl S. Zimmerer's (1988b) accurate observation that very few farmers had a high degree of assortment of native varieties is worrisome for those concerned with genetic erosion.

Farmers from the Paucartambo Valley had twice the number of fields without sales than their counterparts from the Tulumayo Valley. In part, this was due to the different marketing strategies mentioned above. It also reflects the importance of the alternative cash crop and, above all, Paucartambo farmers' lower degree of market integration. Not all fields generated losses in total balance calculations, and some losses could be recuperated by selling part of the harvest. More commonly, cash needed for subsistence production was paid with income obtained from other pursuits such as wage work, handicraft production, and the sale of animals.

Thus another set of conclusions from our study concerns the monetary component of subsistence production. This conclusion has important implications in survival strategies, for peasants need money to invest in food production, and this money is not easily recuperated. An extreme example would be the migration of peasants to cities in order to earn money to invest in subsistence production that then loses money. Just as commercial production is subsidized by family resources, subsistence production is subsidized by cash expenditures derived from the monetary income of their household economy. We use the term *subsidy* advisedly, since it implies assistance that will not be returned. Discounting the value of one's labor from the selling price of a product is akin to ignoring monetary inputs to subsistence production. The two sectors are in a dynamic and complex interrelationship and should not be conceived as simple zero-sum options of alternative allocations—such as those posited in the often-mentioned but poorly researched "subsistence first" strategies that supposedly characterize peasant economies (Lipton 1968).

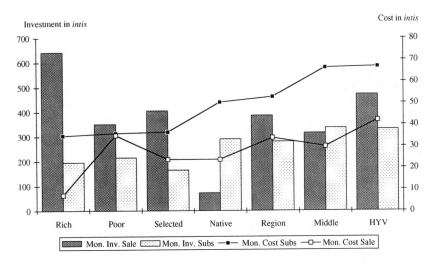

Figure 7.4 *Comparison of Monetary Investment and Monetary Costs in Subsistence Production Versus Commercial Production: Paucartambo (1985–1986)*

One such complexity is shown in Figure 7.4, which indicates the amounts of money invested in producing 100 kilos of potatoes in the Paucartambo Valley as a function of farmer stratum and crop variety. In each pair of bars, the left bar represents money invested in commercial production and the right bar represents money invested in subsistence production. (The case of native varieties is dubious because it is not clear how strict the subsistence/sale distinction is.)

Because cash is in short supply and farmers know that money invested in subsistence production cannot be recuperated easily, they tend to invest less money in subsistence than in commercial production. Less monetary investment (as in the purchase of fertilizers) implies lower yields and therefore higher unit costs, represented in Figure 7.4 by the lines corresponding to the scale on the right side. The monetary costs of subsistence production are higher than the monetary costs of commercial production (except for the coincidental case of poor farmers in our small sample).

This inefficient allocation of resources arises from cash scarcity and the logic of recuperating cash through market activity. Cash-poor farmers have to decide how to allocate expensive fertilizer and pesticides. Seeking to maximize their monetary returns, they put more of these items into commercial production and less into subsistence production, thereby raising the unitary monetary cost of subsistence crops. The most favorable lands are set aside for commercial production, the poorest and most distant fields for subsistence. Commercial production is prioritized over subsistence production, which ends up being less efficient and more expensive than commercial production. Furthermore, farmers' desperate need for money forces them to sell their cash crop below cost in order to recuperate their cash outlay. No "subsistence first" rationale is evident here.

Our data suggest strange dichotomies in production efficiency. Often commercial fields, especially those of middle farmers in the Tulumayo Valley, tend to be overfertilized and treated with excessive pesticides and fungicides, whereas subsistence fields are underfertilized and inefficiently worked. Market distortions force less than optimal solutions on input allocation in peasant agriculture. Further research is needed to estimate the ecological consequences of this dual pattern.

Another important conclusion from the data is that native varieties are more expensive to produce than high-yielding varieties. This outcome was in keeping with the intent of the green revolution, which introduced high-yielding varieties in order to lower production costs. But biologists are now concerned with maintaining genetic diversity by encouraging farmers to keep their nonimproved varieties alive. Biologists and ecologically minded development organizations have to understand that, compared to the genetically bred and selected high-yield cost-reducing varieties, native varieties are indeed more expensive to produce. If peasants were entirely the rational-choice actors of the textbooks, seeking only to maximize profits or calories, they would have to abandon production of native varieties. That they have not fully done so has to do with taste preferences, culinary choices, and other cultural factors that favor the home-grown gift potatoes (Brush 1986; Zimmerer 1996). Genetic diversity is conserved by highland farmers through hefty subsidies originating within household economies.

Tulumayo Valley farmers are clearly aware that native potatoes are luxuries. And luxury consumption depends on the overall well-being of the farm family. Thus the best hope for maintaining genetic diversity lies with rich farmers who can better afford to subsidize production of a variety of potatoes. Rich farmers can better assume the expense to produce small amounts of culturally valued native varieties because of their success as commercial farmers and their technical efficiency and monetary skill in investing in high-yield varieties. Poor farmers cannot afford such luxuries and have to resign themselves to eating chemically contaminated high-yield varieties that, in their opinion, are bad-tasting and watery. On-site conservation of genetic diversity in land races requires a profitable commercial foundation established by high-yield improved varieties, favorable prices, and strong, culturally sustained values in the subsistence sector. As Tulumayo Valley farmers scrutinized their potato portfolio in 1984–1985, they came to the conclusion that their commercial varieties were unprofitable whereas their native varieties were not for profit.

Ethnography of Accounting

To this point, we have attempted to approximate how peasants calculate profits or losses by offering a comparison between two kinds of balance sheets. In these balance sheets, we have followed economists' standard practice of imputing market monetary value to those household resources used in production in order to arrive at a single commensurate measure of costs and income. Andean farmers, however, do not normally do this. Rather, their reckoning system tends to keep things separate, and they do not use money as a standard measure of value. In this section, we follow the fascinating discussion of the "house" model proposed by Gudeman and Rivera (1990) whose research in the highlands of Colombia parallels the work of our late colleague César Fonseca. Fonseca's work is not widely known outside Peru, but his dissertation, written a decade earlier (1972a), in many ways corroborates the careful attention paid by Gudeman and Rivera to the concepts that farming people actually use when they think about their economic activities.

Andean peasant accounting involves three categories or stocks (as per Gudeman and Rivera 1990: 116) that, in daily life, peasants attempt to keep separate (Fonseca 1972a). These three categories, which we will also call "ledgers" (though no physical record-keeping devices are used),[14] keep track of gasto ("subsistence needs"), money, and services rendered through reciprocal labor obligations. The three ledgers are a means of tracing changes in stocks and flows of goods and services; each one has its own accounting unit. Accounting on the gasto (literally, "expense") is done in real quantities: so many sacks of potatoes, pairs of corn ears, and arrobas of fava beans. The gasto ledger also includes kilos of sugar, bags of noodles, packets of salt, and quarter-liter bottles of commercially produced alcoholic drinks. A woman member of the household (usually the wife) controls this ledger.

The unit of accounting in the money category is kept in currency denominations, and this is the man's domain. It includes not only the actual currency but also those resources earmarked for the production of money. The field to be planted in cash crops, the potatoes to be consumed when that field is worked, and the reciprocal labor obligations assigned to plowing the cash field are part of the money category, or para plata—the same term that Colombian farmers use (Gudeman and Rivera 1990: 46). Household resources allotted to this sphere are converted to cash via the market. Men's and women's labor costs incurred in these activities are not valued. Assigning the different spheres to different gender domains probably helps keep the ledgers separate from one another.

Service accounts are remembered by the farmers as the number of obligations in favor of or against the household in terms of wajetes or ayni, the local terms for reciprocal labor obligations (Mayer 1974a; Mayer and Za-malloa 1974; see also Chapter 4).

In a household economy, other kinds of resources are considered stocks; these include animals, houses, land holdings, and household items (radios, bicycles, furniture, etc.). They are under joint husband-wife control. Gude-man and Rivera (1990) highlight the concept of *la base* (the house, land, and other material resources that constitute a household's patrimony). Peasants' long-term objectives are to increase *la base* through judicious management of all elements of the house economy. If harvests have been good, family consumption prudent, and the surplus carefully recycled, then *la base* grows, whether in the form of new land acquisitions, an extension added to the house, or a greater stock of animals. In difficult years, when resources have to be consumed or sold, *la base* shrinks.

Money, considered a dangerous element because of its inherent liquid properties and its tendency to flow out of the household, has to be care-fully managed and insulated from other flows. In her studies of the Laymi in North Potosí, Bolivia, Olivia Harris (1982, 1987, 1995a) describes var-ious social mechanisms that keep money separate from food and family re-sources. She also mentions actions people take to limit the circulation of money inside their "ethnic" economy. In this connection, Harris (1982: 251) notes:

> It seems that women who are responsible for the household budget oppose the conversion to money if they don't have in mind an immediate purchase to complete the circuit. This practice serves as a protection against inflation but is also a strategy to prevent men from converting money's excessive liquidity to drink, that is, drunkenness. (Translation by Mayer.)[15]

At the same time, Harris observes, money is understood as yet another means to generate the wealth and fecundity actively sought by peasants. Thus when they make their libations (*ch'allas*), a libation for money (*phaxsima*) is always carried out in conjunction with other libations to in-crease the fertility of animals and crops:

> Far from being treated as antithetical to the sources of fertility on which the economy is based (agriculture and livestock raising), money is closely identi-fied with them. Placed in a wider setting, the ritual priority given to money and metals in the month of August forms part of a cycle in which all the sources of well-being and increase are honored. (Harris 1995a: 315)

This is why the ledgers for *gasto*, money, and services are not tallied in any single measure of value. Fonseca (1986: 380) uses the term *economic spheres* to describe the relationship between ledgers and efforts to keep them separate: "In each sphere the relationships of production and the cultural values are different." For Fonseca, the separation of spheres does not imply, for example, that money or its products do not enter into the *gasto* sphere. The consumption of goods in the *gasto* sphere includes, in addition to harvest retained, all mercantile goods that are consumed as well as the "ceremonial fund" (Wolf 1966), comprising the expenditures necessary to fulfill the religious *cargo* obligations. Likewise, the "for money" sphere includes the reciprocal labor exchanges that are applied to mercantile production: "The peasants finance their economy on the basis of traditional exchanges and on the basis of the advantages that they can achieve, here and there, in the mercantile sphere" (Fonseca 1986: 380).

Men are expected to give women money on a regular basis to cover *gasto* needs. In addition, women often engage in petty trade by selling small portions of household products to make some money on their own. Brewing *chicha* beer and cooking food for sale on market days are good examples (Núñez del Prado Béjar 1975). In woman-headed households, it is the woman who can easily assume the management of the money ledger; the existing literature on successful women traders (mentioned in Chapter 1) allows us to modify the assertion that handling money is an affair exclusively in the hands of men. In doing so, however, we do not invalidate our main point: that the flow of money constitutes a separate sphere in the household's economy whether handled by men, by women, or jointly by both.

Nonetheless, transfers between the spheres do occur at times. Consumption goods bought in the market lose their monetary value when they enter the subsistence sphere and become, say, kilos of sugar. The money assigned to purchase these goods is called *para el gasto* ("for subsistence"), and it passes from men to women to signal the transfer; numerous observers throughout the Andes (e.g., Bourque and Warren 1981: 125,144; Deere 1990: 288) show how difficult it often is for women to persuade men to hand over the money. Likewise, in the productive process, resources are clearly transferred from one sphere to another, as when potatoes are taken out of storage to feed wage earners working on a cash crop. These transfers are not clearly accounted for in the costs of production, which is why resources from the *gasto* sphere are not clearly evaluated in the money sphere. This is not to say, however, that *gasto* resources have not been counted. Women know how many resources under their jurisdiction have been used for different agricultural activities, and they carefully plan how to replace them. The transfer from one sphere to the other implies a passing of control from women to men. In the process, the changing value of these goods and services goes unnoticed, partly because of the morality of kinship. Husbands should not treat their wives as if they were market women, nor should transactions typical of the marketplace characterize their relationship.

Recent studies of the agricultural and ceremonial calendar reveal that seasonal rhythms have a quotidian praxis as well as economic, ritual, and ideological structures (Fonseca 1972a; Gose 1994; Poole 1982; Urton 1981). Each activity has its season, its associated ceremonies, and its intimate familial way. As the time approaches when certain activities have to be carried out, family members begin planning how to marshal the resources needed to accomplish these activities. Women assign items from the *gasto* pool, and men figure out how to procure needed money. Women and men make a careful listing of who should be asked to help, and they use ceremonial occasions to renew commitments for inter-household labor exchanges. In all these activities, careful calculations (accompanied by detailed memorization and sometimes even record keeping) and planning are necessary to replenish amounts withdrawn from the various stocks. For example, the quantities of harvest to be set aside for seed and food must be budgeted. In their study of the "house schema" in Colombian peasant areas, Gudeman and Rivera (1990; see Chapter 1) have decoded a simple and efficient system for assigning products—a system that divides them into *para* and *sobras*—"for" and "remainder." The first "for" is seed; the rest is "remainder." Out of that, the next "for" is food, and so on through successive iterations. Portions of the product are allocated for sale, feeding animals, and other uses in proportions that depend on the size of the harvest and budgeted needs. Fonseca's (1972a: 120) schema breaks up a hypothetical harvest as follows: 10 percent for seed, 50 percent for *gasto*, 10 percent for barter, 10 percent for payments in kind, and 20 percent for *plata* (money).

In an excellent analysis of farmers' skills in tracking economic information in rural Colombia, Sutti Ortiz (1979) provides an interesting perspective on how farmers employ shorthand mechanisms to register the magnitude of the flows in these ledgers—an aspect Gudeman and Rivera do not discuss. Rather than remembering real quantities, Ortiz (1979: 69) writes, peasants describe harvests as being "bad, not very bad, not very good, good, or very good." Such relativities leave implicit questions of time and context ("last year?" "needs?" "expected?" "my other field?"); but once the context is known, such information can function effectively. In the same manner, prices are remembered in categories that exhibit similar evaluations. For example, a barely sufficient price "brings in a minimum," whereas a good price "pays" [expenses?] (Ortiz 1979: 68). When asked to remember past prices, rather than to give the actual amount received when the coffee was sold, farmers provided evaluations: "Prices are judged as good or bad in terms of what they did for the farmer, rather than the actual amount" (Ortiz 1979: 71). The *sobras* and *para* scheme reveals how such nominal categories provide the players with criteria with which they can make decisions each time a stock or a flow is monitored in any of the three ledgers. Subsistence production can thus be judged simply as "sufficient" or "insufficient" (Ortiz 1979: 72) in any of the several stages during which it is allocated for seed, food, or other purposes.

Money is husbanded (note the familial term!) so that cash is available when expenditures are due. In the Tulumayo Valley, the proceeds from the sale of one harvest are often used to finance the next planting. A poor farmer from the Tulumayo Valley explained that the fundamental rationale behind his commercial production was to be able to pay for the fertilizers he needed in all his fields, including those earmarked for home consumption.

Certain monetary needs are less pressing, or at least perceived in less anxious ways than others. Consumption needs are always in competition with productive uses. Money is invested in the productive process in amounts that vary throughout the agricultural cycle. The costs least felt are those associated with harvesting and transport to the market, because these costs can be offset immediately by proceeds from sales. Conversely, outlays at the beginning of the season worry farmers the most. Expenditures for fertilizer and wages tend to occur during the period of greatest cash shortage. In moments of crisis, the household has to liquidate some of its *base* stocks to replace a depleted cash reserve. For example, the economic crisis that affected the Tulumayo Valley caused many farmers to sell their animals in order to invest in potato farming that turned out to be less and less profitable.

The role of money in a peasant economy is analogous to that of foreign currency in a national economy. Both the peasant's money and a nation's foreign currency are kept in their own separate domains, surrounded by complex cultural and symbolic constructs. In both cases, moreover, special strategies are employed to keep monetary or foreign currency reserves replenished; priority is often given to "foreign" over local currency; and depletion of foreign reserves often precipitates a crisis situation.

It is not out of ignorance that peasants disregard the assignation of value to their labor and resources as part of their production costs. Rather, this neglect is the result of a conscious strategy to separate commercial and subsistence spheres. When commercial production is limited or when most production inputs come from household resources, farmers can feasibly sell cheaply because these transactions do not produce any monetary losses. However, now that the production process is heavily monetized due to changes in technology and the monetization of labor, a new accounting category has entered peasant economic ledgers. Andean peasants call this category *capital de trabajo*, or "working capital," which they know needs to be replaced each season through market activities. Working capital is made up of contributions from all three spheres, even though consumption and production needs are not neatly separated or explicitly accounted for in this new sphere. Monetization of the productive process has made the category of working capital more explicit. Given these developments, farmers need to learn to keep accounts of this fourth ledger with greater care. They must record in a single valuation the transfers made to it from the *gasto*, money, and service spheres.

There are other fundamental differences, too, between the structure of information management of a firm and a peasant household, as Gudeman and Rivera (1990: 121) have shown for Colombia and as corroborated in the Tulumayo and Paucartambo regions. A firm reviews its profits and losses, whereas peasants anticipate theirs. They hope that this year's cash income will be able to finance the next year's fertilizer purchases. They eyeball the harvest to estimate future consumption possibilities. When peasant farmers calculate monetary profits, they probably compare present levels of sales in currency with sales from the previous year (yielding Ortiz's categories of "bad, not very bad, not very good, good, or very good"). Business accounting procedures would find this practice unacceptable since the figures come from different production cycles and different sales. From the standpoint of the peasants, however, such comparisons allow them to determine whether they have fared better or worse than the previous season.[16] Ortiz (1979: 75) also discusses how these categories allow peasants to formulate expectations for the next season: "Peasant farmers do not base their choice on a single forecast or a carefully weighted set of probable outcomes, but on a range of expectations, some of which are more familiar than others."

We can conclude, then, that each growing season farmers embark on a risky commercial venture with the triple expectation that climate, pathogenic factors, and prices at the end of the season will be in their favor. They hope that, other things being equal, their monetary investment will provide a monetary gain—which most often is not the case. One destabilizing factor is the wildly fluctuating value of currency in underdeveloped countries. The ethnography of accounting thus has to take into consideration the instability of national currency in the Andean countries and its dubious role as a store of value or, more relevant here, as a measure of value.[17]

The Question of Subsidies

We have shown how production for the market needs the support of home-based resources such as labor, seed, manure, draft animals, and food, which are not accounted for in the monetary balance sheet. Home-based resources are a farm-based subsidy for commercial production without which it would be impossible to participate in the market and bring in needed currency. Likewise, subsistence production requires a hefty contribution of resources from the monetary sector. Money sunk into a field for subsistence production cannot be recuperated directly from that particular field. It must be replaced from other sources that generate cash.

These findings should alert social scientists to the need for modifying deeply held perspectives about peasant economies. Academics usually imagine that peasants cover their subsistence needs first and only later sell their surplus. Eric Wolf's (1966) terminology, for example, points to the priority that *caloric minima* have in the peasant economy. His discussion of the problems related to surplus (i.e., its disposition and claims to it) comes after his discussion of calories. He uses the term *replacement fund* (1966: 6) to designate those calories necessary to reproduce the farmer's animals, family, and seed for the next season. Gudeman and Rivera's (1990) house model also privileges maintenance and physical growth of *la base* above those of cash accumulation. In the house model, according to Gudeman and Rivera (1990: 47), money should be kept away from the house to the extent possible. V. Gómez (1986: 31), summarizing various theories of the peasant economy writes, "The central objective of the majority of the peasantry is to *guarantee the reproduction of the family*, and therefore this excludes the fundamental objective of maximizing profit rates" (original emphasis). The image that comes to mind is of horizontal layers of material wealth, with a broad base of subsistence goods at the bottom, fewer surplus market goods on top, and the market layer implicitly but securely positioned over the subsistence layer. Gudeman and Rivera (1990) write that peasants insist on having a gate that keeps farm products "inside" the doors of their "houses" and on carefully controlling what goes out of their doors and what comes in—all of which makes them sound rather like protectionist politicians. Perhaps peasants invoke this model so often because it no longer works.

Instead, our findings suggest a two-sector model (with the two sectors side by side). One is a market-oriented money sector (*para plata*), and the other is a home-based, food, and consumption house sector (*para el gasto*). The two sectors are mutually interdependent and subsidize each other, but they also deplete each other. For example, Figueroa's (1984) study of peasant economies in Peru shows that 74 percent of monetary income is spent on consumption and only 10 percent on investment, of which 5 percent is for agricultural inputs. We argue that the interdependence is neither as symbiotic nor as smooth as the horizontal subsistence and surplus model suggests. Negative feedback relationships between the two sectors may have profound influences on each other that tend to worsen the situation of the peasantry. Gudeman and Rivera (1990: 48) raise similar issues: "The house cannot persist as a pure market participant but is increasingly forced to do so, with the result that it must lower its consumption or raise its work input." As we have also shown, the monetary sector plays the dominant role, and it may have deleterious effects on subsistence production, consumption, nutrition, resource maintenance, ecological stability, and even sustainability.

How are anthropologists to interpret the fact that peasants do not value labor and home-based resources in their calculations of costs? Are these home-based resources a subsidy that peasants provide to the urban sector? Or do peasants grow poorer as they absorb these costs? The value of household resources is large. In the Tulumayo Valley, it accounts for about one-third to one-quarter of total costs; for the Paucartambo Valley, the figure is approximately one-half.

A standard political economy argument states that by not taking into account household resources used in commercial production, peasants are able to sell at lower prices, thereby transferring benefits to the urban sector in the form of cheap food. Viewed from this perspective, cheap food policies that have characterized Latin American economies for centuries are, in effect, a rural subsidy to urban and industrial sectors. Lower food prices permit lower urban wages, which in turn benefit industrial sectors by allowing them to compete in the global market. The urban bias in agricultural policies implemented since the 1930s provide an incentive toward industrialization, as has been discussed by Michael Painter (1987) and Alexander Schejtman (1988). Schejtman further notes:

> Primordial undervaluation of peasant products is inherent in the very structure of relative prices (as between peasant production and capitalist production), formed over generations, on which the reproduction of the economy as a whole is crucially dependent, because of the well-known relationship between food prices, wage levels and the rate of profit. (1988: 379)

The foregoing argument would be correct if the peasant sector still had an ability to set prices for food crops, but this is no longer the case in either the Tulumayo or Paucartambo valleys. Potatoes produced by peasants make up only a small proportion of the total urban supply. Large enterprises in the Mantaro Valley and on the coast produce the bulk of potatoes consumed in Lima and therefore play a leading role in price formation (Mayer 1979: 91–97; Scott 1985: 131). In Cusco, too, producers from the Paucartambo Valley compete with large-scale firms located in the Pampa de Anta. Only 18 percent of high-yield varieties and 9 percent of selected commercial varieties sold in the Cusco market come from the Paucartambo Valley (PRODERM-MAG 1985). Large enterprises enjoy ecological, agronomic, and technical advantages. They are located closer to markets and benefit from economies of scale that enable them to produce at unit costs lower than peasants can manage.[18] They also have enough political clout to affect the market and government policies when prices are not to their liking.[19] In other words, low potato prices originate in the agribusiness sector, not with peasants who sell below real cost. Agribusiness does not have to compete against peasants who undercut them. Instead, peasants must compete against agribusiness and therefore have to sell below cost to compete for a market share. Peasant undervaluation of produce does not translate into cheap food in urban centers; rather, it is a result of unequal competition between agribusinesses with favorable natural and economic resource endowments, on the one hand, and marginal, small-scale producers with low productivity potential, on the other.

As improved technology spreads, potato prices fall worldwide (Horton 1987). Alain de Janvry (1981) points out that the centuries-old trend toward cheap food produced by peasants for cities has changed in the past four decades due to technological innovations, government incentives, and food security policies to feed ever-growing urban populations. This change has placed industrialized agribusiness in competition with peasant-produced food, both in quantity and price: "The peasantry is ousted from the production of agricultural crops when it cannot compete with large-scale capitalist production of those crops or with the undervalued imports of foodstuffs via overvalued exchange rates and price subsidies" (de Janvry 1981: 173).

Thus peasants have to absorb losses or, in G. Scott's (1985: 61) unfortunate terminology, "internalize" them:

One might argue that small producers do not lose money because they undervalue their labor and non-purchased inputs. This approach seems perfectly legitimate. However, this does not necessarily mean that peasant producers' surplus value is then transferred out of agriculture by monopsonistic middlemen. It is argued here instead that since peasant potato producers generally sell such a small percent of the potatoes they produce, they "internalize" most of this surplus value.

Calculating the probability that harvest retained for consumption could compensate for this kind of internalization, we found that compensation is possible only if profits in one balance sheet (either total or monetary) can offset losses in the other. In the Tulumayo Valley, this offset was not possible in fully half the fields under consideration; in the Paucartambo Valley, it was not possible in one-fourth of the fields studied. Where it was impossible to compensate, losses were absorbed by other activities in the subsistence or monetary sectors of peasant household economies.

Although peasant farmers frequently lose money in commercial production, they sometimes make a profit. The difference in performance in the two regions demonstrates this fact. Under certain conditions (available land, opening markets, reasonable prices, and favorable government policies, among others) the family-based peasant farm is viable, as Reinhardt (1988) has shown for the pioneer colonization area of el Palmar in the Colombian tropics. But issues regarding negative long-term prospects and sustainable development under current neo-liberal policies are also forcefully raised by our data. Neo-liberalism puts enormous emphasis on the self-regulating mechanisms of the free market. A key component of this mechanism is the role that profits and losses play in the system, inasmuch as they act as incentive and disincentive to production decisions and entry or exit from the sector. In this context, an important question has not been adequately answered: How are peasants to react to these incentives? Generally, the prices of their products are so low that productivity in the marginal regions where they live and work is, from the business point of view, not profitable. Because losses can be absorbed by the subsistence sector and hidden by "erroneous" accounting procedures as well as by transfers mediated as gender relations within the household, peasant farmers can continue as players in the market for the time being. But farmers also experience a slow and continuous deterioration of their real resources. It is not surprising that the peasant sector is also the poorest in Peruvian society.

The irony of neo-liberal ideas is that their leading proponents (who favor unregulated market economies and the elimination of subsidies in debt-ridden Third World economies) are from countries that heavily subsidize their own agricultural sectors. First World farmers also lose money in agricultural production, but they are bailed out by state intervention. In 1990 alone, the governments of developed countries spent $176 billion in agricultural subsidies. The European Economic Community subsidizes grain with 36 percent of its farm cost prices, Japan with 97.7 percent, and the United States with 44 percent (Escobal 1991). Third World peasants, on the other hand, habitually must assume negative profits as a normal condition.

Postscript

My second postdoctoral research project (Mayer 1988) was a collaborative project on agricultural change, land-use, and genetic erosion. Funded by the National Science Foundation, it included Stephen Brush, Enrique Mayer, and César Fonseca as co-directors; Karl Zimmerer as field director in the Paucartambo Valley; and Manuel Glave as participant in the field research, data entry, analysis, and writing of phases of my part of the project. In 1986, César Fonseca died in an unfortunate accident in the Cusco airport as he was finishing his stint in the field in Paucartambo. I have endeavored to incorporate his singular contributions into this chapter. Part of the write-up phase took place during my fellowship year (1988–1989) at the Woodrow Wilson Center for International Scholars in Washington, D.C. My edition of Fonseca's notes on the aftermath of the agrarian reform in Paucartambo Valley was published as Mayer (1988); in Mayer and Glave (1990) preliminary findings were presented to Peruvian colleagues at the Seminario Permanente de Investigación Agraria in Cusco; Glave's dissertation dealt with aspects of our field research (Glave 1992); and an edited book, *La Chacra de Papa: Economía y Ecología* (Mayer, Glave, et al. 1992), was published in Lima. Brush's and Zimmerer's other publications from this project are cited in the present book. Chapter 7, which originally appeared in *American Ethnologist* (Mayer and Glave 1999) and is reprinted with that journal's permission, completes my analysis of various forms of exchange of goods in the articulated peasant's economy; however, this chapter stresses the money circuit.

Notes

1. On the issue of genetic erosion in the Andes, see also Ochoa (1975); Brush, Carney, and Huamán (1981); and Hawkes and Hjerting (1989). Results of our genetic erosion study have been published in Brush (1986, 1989); Brush and Taylor (1992); Brush, Taylor, and Bellon (1992); Zimmerer (1988b, 1991, 1996); and Zimmerer and Douches (1990).

2. Caballero (1984: 23), in our view, correctly critiques the notion that peasants do not seek to maximize. Sol Tax (1963) noted long ago how Guatemalan peasants were always chasing even the smallest marginal profit in their pursuit of cash. In *Penny Capitalism*, he called it "turning a penny" (1963: 12, 18). Tax anticipated current debates about formal and informal economies and raised the question of maximization in a forceful way. Harris (1995a: 309) gives as an example the Laymi of Bolivia, whose concept of profits uses biological models (as did Aristotle, cited in Gudeman and Rivera 1990: 147). The Laymi say that money (invested in trading) "has given birth" to more money.

3. Schultz is best known for characterizing peasant agriculture as "poor but efficient," a notion he derived from an appreciative reading of Tax (1963).

4. At the time of our study, Shining Path, the Maoist guerrillas, and the guerrillas of the Movimiento Revolucionario Tupac Amaru (MRTA) were present in the valley, but political violence did not occur until three years after we left. Part of Shining Path's policy was to starve the cities by forbidding market production in rural areas. They burned stockpiles of fertilizer, killed truck drivers, blew up bridges, and threatened farmers if they produced more than what was needed for subsistence. For three years (1988 to 1991), potato exports out of the valley ceased. During this time, in the province of Concepción (which contains the Tulumayo Valley), 88 attacks were recorded, resulting in 140 deaths (SEPAR 1992). In 1990, violent imposition of Shining Path terror-based policies provoked a reaction in the Tulumayo Valley, and, together with military support, peasant groups formed armed *rondas* (vigilance groups) and managed to expel the guerrillas by 1992 (Starn 1991). The Paucartambo region was not affected by political violence during our research period.

5. The data for both valleys comes from the 1981 census. The rate of growth concerns the period 1961 to 1981.

6. Goland (1992) used this method to study risk reduction through multiple-field scattering strategies.

7. In the endeavor to calculate costs, we were immediately confronted with several alternate ways of accounting for costs. For example, what value is to be assigned to family labor? Sen (1966: 442–443) cites a case study in India: "*The Studies in the Economics of Farm Management* (1954–57) came to the frightening conclusion that much of Indian agriculture is being run on losses [if labor is assigned its market value]." Sen thinks that imputing market values to family labor is too high since household labor is less productive on the farm than wage labor in industry off the farm. Peasants stay on the farm due to a dearth of opportunities. Schejtman (1988: 366) offers conclusions comparable to ours when he says that for Latin America "an evaluation of economic results achieved by peasant units over one or more cycles, using conventional 'factor cost' concepts, will show in the vast majority of cases that these units systematically incur losses."

9. Peru's former currency, the *sol*, was changed to the *inti* in 1984 (1 *inti* = 1,000 old *soles*), which later became the *nuevo sol* in 1989 (1 new *sol* = 1,000 *intis*).

10. Brunel (1975), Brush, Carney, and Huamán (1981), and Zimmerer (1988a) pay careful attention to folk taxonomies of potatoes, the principles by which they are organized, and their correspondence to scientific taxonomies. The three categories we use here are derived from marketing strategies, patterns of commodification, and consumer preferences. Farmers, middlemen, and consumers know varieties by name and by specific characteristics. Each one of our categories contains a number of similar varieties.

11. In order to impute monetary values to household resources, we tried to establish the going market rate for them. In general, there is an active regional market for labor and other inputs, and the farmers could easily supply us with a monetary value of what it would have cost them to buy an input. We checked these prices for accuracy in each village. When prices changed, we adjusted them. For example, in response to inflation, wages doubled during the time of our study.

The "real" value of a family's labor is, of course, the most troubling issue in peasant economics. We assigned the going village rate for day labor for every task performed by household labor. Women earn two-thirds of a man's wage; children, half of their gender's wage rate. We tried to approximate opportunity costs, which are defined as the income that individuals could have earned in alternative activities. In agricultural labor, the obvious alternative is to work as a laborer in someone else's field. We also calculated the returns to labor to see if they were comparable to regional wage rates. (Returns to labor = total income minus total costs [except labor costs] divided by the number of labor days used in the field. The calculated returns to labor were close to the going wage rates, giving us confidence in our procedure. In all cases, owners fed their workers during the day's work. We imputed a value to the resources taken from the family's food storage and carefully tracked the monetary component of other expenditures such as alcohol, cigarettes, coca leaf, and purchased foods. Labor paid in kind was evaluated according to the cash value for which the produce would have sold, a price that was always higher than the wage rate. Seed and other material inputs were assigned their respective market values at the farm or village level. We tracked with great care the costs of packing the product (gunny sacks, string, and nets). We did not, however, assign a value to the proportional depreciation of agricultural tools because this is a negligible cost, nor did we assign a value to the opportunity cost of land. Though theoretically relevant, the ethnographic situation of the local land tenure system, an imperfect land market, and the near absence of a rental market did not allow us to find a proper monetary measure for land. (Further discussion about imputing market value on nonmarket resources can be found in Barlett 1980 and Chibnik 1978.)

12. The relationship between yields and levels of fertilization is curvilinear and at upper levels reaches diminishing returns. Whereas lowering levels of fertilization reduces yields, unit costs do not increase proportionately to the lowering of yields. It is also possible (with adequate rotation) to farm without fertilizers and pesticides, thereby lowering costs even more.

13. The monetary balances appear more advantageous because they exclude family labor costs on the positive side of the balance, but they also exclude the value of the potatoes retained for food. On the issue of whether to include or exclude household labor in cost calculations, Kula (1976: 41–42) observed: To arrive

at the conclusion that half of mankind is constantly engaged in a productive activity that operates at a loss represents a *reductio ad absurdum*. . . . [It seems] that to draw up a balance-sheet of the peasant plot according to capitalist norms makes no sense and can only lead to the conclusion mentioned above (deficit if we take into account unpaid labor and interest; surplus, if we do not)."

14. Note that Andean peoples during Inca times were very careful record keepers, using *quipus* (knotted string cords) to keep track of stocks and resources.

15. Harris's (1995a) revised translation of the 1987 Spanish edition omits this paragraph. We concur with her revised opinion that "money as such seems to have a neutral value; the flow of cash is limited for practical rather than for cultural or ideological reasons" (307). The point we wish to stress is that money flows through the household in channels separated by gender. Harris herself notes this: "Men in general are said to be more civilized than women since they have more experience in handling money (echoing liberal discourse)" (1995a: 304).

16. Businesses do construct time series that rely on past events to assess future trends, but each point in their graphs is a backward-looking calculation.

17. Unstable national currencies in the Third World lead some businesses to use the dollar in their accounting practices, whereas peasants rely on real goods as stores of value. Farmers, truckers, and middlemen develop their own terminology for blocks of currency. One million *soles* was "a stick" during our fieldwork. Chapter 5 describes a set of prices (*unay precio*) with which farmers bartered but which had nothing to do with national currency. They used older, defunct denominations as reference to prices to establish equivalencies between products from the highlands and the lowlands.

18. G. Scott's (1985: 41) survey showed that in 1976 small potato farmers had unit costs that were 71 percent higher than those of the large commercial agribusinesses in the Mantaro Valley. The medium-sized farms had unit costs that were 20 percent higher than the large ones. All Tulumayo Valley farmers are comparable to Scott's small farmers. Small farmers in Scott's study cultivated less than 0.75 hectares in potatoes and sold small quantities. Medium producers ranged from 0.75 to 3 hectares, whereas large commercial producers ranged from 3 to 100 hectares.

19. Peru's national lobby of potato growers, *Comité de productores de papa*, includes predominantly coastal producers and large highland seed producers. The thousands of peasant producers do not play any significant role in the group, which successfully lobbied for potato support prices in the first two years of the García administration (1986–1988). Still, potatoes are less prestigious foods in urban areas, where many people rely on staples of rice and wheat (bread, noodles, and sugar). The rice producers' lobby was more influential than its potato counterpart, which has suffered some setbacks. With high inflation in 1989, the potato lobby threatened to withhold deliveries to urban markets in an effort to force the government to index the price of potatoes to the inflation rate. Neither event took place; deliveries were not interrupted, and the price was not indexed to inflation.

8

Production Zones

*This chapter is about how households manage their commons.
I use the term production zones in this context because it gives
us a concrete and direct understanding of how environmental
variation in mountain ecosystems is handled by the local population. The chapter describes the importance of village-based
management of resources, giving a vivid picture of how collective aspects directly impinge on household autonomy in terms
of decisions about where and how productive activities such as
planting, irrigating, or grazing should be allowed to take place.*

A Myth

The native people of Cupara village survived just by channeling some water
from a spring to their fields, and they were suffering greatly for lack of water
at that time. [This spring flowed from a tall mountain that rises above San
Lorenzo village—a mountain that today is called Suna Caca.] In those days
there was a native woman of that village named Chuqui Suso, a really beautiful woman. This woman was weeping while she irrigated her maize plants because they were drying out so badly, and because the water supply was very
scarce. When Paria Caca saw this, he obstructed the mouth of her little pond
with his cloak. The woman started to cry even more bitterly when she saw
him do that.

"Sister, why are you crying so hard?" he asked her.

"Sir, this little maize field of mine is drying up on me for lack of water!" she
replied.

"Don't worry about it," Paria Caca said to her. "I'll make water flow from
this pond of yours, plenty of water. But first let me sleep with you."

"Get the water flowing first, " she retorted. "When my field is watered,
then by all means, let us sleep together."

"Fine!" said Paria Caca, and released an ample amount of water.

Overjoyed, the woman thoroughly watered all her fields. After she had finished irrigating, Paria Caca said, "Let's sleep together."

"Not right now," she replied. "Let's sleep together tomorrow or the day after." Paria Caca, who desired the woman ardently, thought, "I wish I could sleep with her right now!" and promised her all kinds of things.

"I'll fix this field of yours with a water source direct from the river," he said.

"Do that first, and then we'll sleep together," the woman replied.

"All right," Paria Caca said.

He widened an irrigation canal that had belonged to the Yunca people, a little ditch that descended long ago from the ravine called Coco Challa to the small hill overlooking San Lorenzo. He extended this canal down as far as the fields of Lower Cupara. Pumas, foxes, snakes, and all kinds of birds cleaned and fixed that canal. Pumas, jaguars, and all kinds of animals vied with each other to improve it, saying, "Who'll be the leader when we lay out the watercourse?"

"Me first! Me first!" exclaimed this one and that one. The fox won, saying, "I'm the chief, the *curaca*, so I'll lead the way first." And so he, the fox, went on ahead.

While the fox was leading the way after he had laid the watercourse out halfway up the mountain over San Lorenzo, a tinamou suddenly darted up, whistling "Psic psic." Startled, the fox yelped "Huac!" and fell down the slope. Then those animals got indignant and had the snake lead the way. If the fox hadn't fallen, that canal of theirs would've run at a higher level. But now it runs somewhat lower. The spot from which the fox fell is clearly visible to this day. In fact, the water flows down the course the fox's fall opened. (From chapter 6 of *The Huarochirí Manuscript*, translated from the Quechua by Salomon and Urioste [1991: 62–63].)

Introduction

The work of John V. Murra on Andean production systems certainly has stimulated new research ideas and interpretations. One can trace the intellectual origins of his thinking on "verticality" to his thesis in 1956 in which, in the chapter on rite and crop, he draws a clear distinction between two kinds of agriculture simultaneously practiced in the Inca state to produce the delicate but prestigious maize as well as the lowly but crucial subsistence Andean tubers and grains. On a more regional scale, discussing the evidence for or against the existence of trade in the Inca state, he offers the following speculation:

One aspect of Andean trade which may or may not be Pre-Incaic is the tendency for highland people to stabilize the bartering situation between climatic zones by transplanting colonies of their own kin at the other end of the exchange. . . . Thus the *coca* and *uchu* [pepper] growing settlements "subject" to Xauxa Valley dwellers sound from the description like village or most likely tribally sponsored projects. (Murra 1956: 238)

Subsequent archival and fieldwork in Huánuco and in the *altiplano* generated a clearer and more precise formulation of how the mechanisms of verticality actually could work in terms of an articulation of productive capacities between different climatic zones. This system allowed not only for the satisfaction of subsistence needs but also, in Murra's vision, for the enhancement and growth of autonomous and ever more expansionist *señoríos*, or ethnic polities (Murra 1968, 1972). In this chapter I discuss three main points concerning subsequent interpretations of Murra's work. First, in his 1972 article, Murra uses four key terms—*control, maximum, vertical,* and *ecological levels*—but it seems to me that anthropologists have focused on the latter two to the detriment of the others. The concept of control is derived from the domain of politics and thus is not an ecological but a political variable. Power, geopolitics, and organizational capacities are central to Murra's (1972) thinking on verticality. It follows that *maximum* is dependent on the capacity to control, implying that the more powerful the group, the more zones can be controlled and also the farther apart these can be from each other. Distant colonies can produce valuable goods and revenues that further enhance the political and economic possibilities of the controllers. The control and exploitation of colonies are mechanisms of accumulation, both political and economic, that underwrite these *señoríos*. Murra's early suggestion that these were tribal projects (as quoted above) is sustained and expanded in the later formulations.

Another question I address here deals with a more precise formulation of what is actually an ecological tier or *piso ecológico*. I propose that we superimpose the concept of *production zone* as a human-made thing atop the natural variations of the environment. When we think of production zones as artifacts, rather than as adaptations to the natural environment, our attention is directed to how they are created, managed, and maintained. Then the importance of the political aspects of control by human beings over each other, in relation to how they are to use a portion of their natural environment, will again come to the fore.

A final consideration concerns the distinction between different levels of organization. A close look at the historical evidence used by Murra reveals that we have to consider at least three levels of social organization, all of them neatly nested together but nevertheless conceptually and practically distinct. The first level is the domain of the agricultural productive peasant household. The second level concerns locally aggregated groups of households residing in a given place and exploiting a common set of resources. (In the sixteenth-century *visitas,* the latter are called *pueblos*, or villages; dwellings near their fields [*chácaras*] are their most obvious indicators.)

The third level of social organization concerns the larger kinds of units capable of mobilizing local groups as well as individual households. As noted, Murra terms these *señoríos,* or ethnic polities. Despite the diversity between them, these ethnic groups shared some common characteristics as yet not completely understood. For example, anthropologists used to assume that these ethnic groups, like tribes in the ethnographic record of other parts of the world, defended clearly demarcated territories; but this assumption becomes infinitely more complex once we realize the implications of vertical control. Furthermore, today's concept of ethnicity may be very different from the way identities operated in pre-conquest times.

Under the verticality regime, each household was clearly affiliated with an ethnic group. It also seems that the villages and hamlets were subject to particular ethnic polities. At the same time, the hamlet could contain within it people who were active members and beneficiaries of village organization but affiliated with different ethnic groups. I suggest that we still know too little about village organization to understand the full implications of ethnicity or verticality. This is surprising because scholars believe that substantial features of local village organization have survived into the present, despite the destructuring and restructuring actions imposed by the Spanish colonial administration, which interacted with the internal dynamics of villages to produce present configurations. The inadequate understanding of village-level organization is also surprising, given that it has been extensively studied by ethnologists in the last four decades. What has been lacking is the framework that allows us to integrate this level into the larger ethnic or *señorío* level.

I am particularly concerned here with the interaction between the household and the village—or community level—of productive organization. Without an understanding of local village organization, we cannot fully comprehend the complexities of the verticality model. It is my contention that the household alone cannot by itself deal with all the technical and organizational problems of production in a given zone; it needs the concurrence of other instances of "supra-household" (Guillet 1978: 89–105) organization, which must be locally organized regardless of the ethnic affiliation of its members.

My work is with contemporary Andean peoples, and, indeed, the household and village levels are far more in evidence today. The third, or ethnic, level is elusive because it was largely destroyed during four centuries of colonial rule. Even so, at the first two levels, many aspects of the Andean productive system are still operative—even if they form only part of the expansive vision of a system that has served the Andean people well.

Organization of Production Zones

Given the enormous diversity of microclimatic and ecological conditions, the technological task for Andean peoples is to create conditions for stability and security of production. This implies a process of simplification of nature's diversity (Brush 1977a: 9). The real technological challenge in the Andes is in the effort to adapt needed staples and desired luxury crops to as many of the varied micro-environmental conditions as possible. I argue that there is a specific Andean collective form of organization of production that, under varying and changing social and ecological conditions, will constantly generate technological solutions that bridge the gap between desired crops and the local environmental conditions that favor, limit, or impede production. An understanding of the features of this productive organization can be achieved only through a comparison of how various crops are grown along an ecological gradient.

César Fonseca and I began such a task in 1974 as part of a long-term project that transected the Andes from the coast to intra-montane valleys and down again to the lowlands where highland colonization stops. Specifically, we were able to survey and map the production zones in the Cañete Valley (see Fonseca and Mayer 1978; Fonseca 1978; Mayer 1977a, 1978; Mayer and Fonseca 1979; De la Cadena 1977, 1980; Fonseca and Mayer 1988).[1] A second (but incomplete) survey of the transect was done by me in the Mantaro Valley (Mayer 1979). The next stage of research to the lowlands was concluded in a project that examined the eastern slopes of the Andes in 1984–1986 of the Tulumayo Valley in Central Peru and the Paucartambo Valley in Southern Peru (Mayer, Glave, et al. 1992; Zimmerer 1988, 1996; Mayer 1988). The overall aim was to seek out and study the basic patterns of Andean productive organization to see if common Andean organizational principles could be elucidated. My colleagues and I are nowhere near a satisfactory solution, but we have begun to organize data collection in certain ways that seem promising.

The first step was to clarify Murra's concept of *piso ecológico*. What we were really dealing with was a contrast between human concepts, on the one hand, and manufactured things, on the other. The latter we call *production zones*. Various criteria have been used to conceptualize such zones on a continuous ecological gradient as stress factors make conditions for biological life more and more difficult (Odum 1971). Steep environmental gradients such as those in the Andes favor a zonal approach since the gradients are characterized by discontinuous plant communities—not only because of abrupt changes in the physical environment but because of boundaries sharpened by competition and co-evolutionary processes between interacting and interdependent species (Odum 1971: 145). The recognition, description, and utilization of these natural clusters, or *ecotypes* (Troll 1968), take many different forms, depending on the criteria by which they are judged, the internal characteristics that make one zone distinct from another, and the way that boundaries are determined.

Previous attempts at defining ecological zones in the Andes have not always been explicit in specifying the criteria used to define them. In general, however, three kinds of conceptual zonations are in use. The first employ

Western scientific criteria (Craig 1985) or follow the guidelines of Leslie Holdridge (1967) and the careful work of Joseph Tosi (1960) on the *Zonas de Vida Natural en el Perú* (reprinted by ONERN in 1978). Tosi's zones are descriptions of natural plant communities related to three climatic variables expressed in 1,000-meter altitudinal belts (theoretically at their climax stage in ecological succession). As a means of describing the natural environment, Tosi's scheme therefore does not take into account the profound modifications brought about by human activities. Attempts to refine the Tosi classification for ethnographic purposes have been made by Stephen Brush (1977a), William Mitchell (1976a), Glynn Custred (1977), Bruce Winterhalder and R. Brooke Thomas (1978), Daniel Gade (1967: 109–198), Mario Tapia (1996), and Karl Zimmerer (1988, 1996). See also Zimmerer (1999) for a critique of zonal approaches.[2]

The second kind of zonations are those made by the local Andean people; thus they describe their "subjective" (Valée 1971) criteria of relevance and importance, or, as Zimmerer (1999: 137) puts it, their "models for" representations of space. Pulgar Vidal's influential though flawed *Las Ocho Regiones Naturales del Peru* (n.d.) is an extrapolation of such Andean concepts as *jalka* ("high *puna* grasslands"), *kichwa* ("valley"), and *yunga* ("low valley"), with geographical, climatological, vegetational, landscape, and other criteria added to varying degrees. Fonseca (1972a: 318–324; 1981) has pointed out that Andean thinking about the natural environment is much more gradient-like in its approach, in that Andean people use terms such as *jalka/kichwa/yunga* in relation to each other, with reference to a midpoint or line (*chaupi* or *taypi* [Harris 1985]), rather than as absolute descriptions of particular environmental regions. It is the contrasts (which really interest farmers) that can be applied to geographical areas, things, people, food, music, and so on, ranging in magnitude from very large areas such as the whole of the *puna* (which would be *jalka*) to smaller areas such as the valley of Chaupiwaranga (which would be *kichwa* in relation to *jalka*). Within the valley there would be further *jalka/kichwa* distinctions, down to such small contrasts as when two prickly pear (*tuna*) plants growing near each other are compared, the lower one being the *kichwa tuna* and the upper one the *jalka tuna*.

Another set of zonations has emerged from government offices that seek to delimit areas of influence into "recommendation domains": "A group of roughly homogeneous farmers with similar circumstances for whom we can make more or less the same recommendation" (Shaner, Philipp, and Schmehl 1981: 44). I used these zonations in the Mantaro Valley study for the International Potato Center, distinguishing between "agro-life zones" and "subzones" (Mayer 1979: 35–55).

In contrast to these conceptual schemes are real production zones, which is where farmers grow their particular crops in specific ways. In each community these zones are clearly identifiable, with precise boundaries (in some cases even communal fences) and, for the most part, a characteristic type of field that adjusts slope to the requirements of the plant (e.g., in terms of the way it receives its moisture or accommodates the needs of the grazing animals that eat it). Examples of these fields would be slope terraces, irrigated terraces, meadows, and orchards. These distinct field types have the advantage of forming easily recognizable patterns for mapping from aerial photos, a technique that has been used to map all the production zones in the Cañete Valley (Mayer and Fonseca 1979; see Map 8.1). Clifford Smith, William Denevan, and Patrick Hamilton (1981: 25–50) have identified abandoned raised fields in the Titicaca Basin in the same way, and Pierre Morlon (1996) provides a complete compendium of Andean agricultural systems that pays close attention to field types in relation to slope, frost mitigation, flood control, crops, and production intensity. Since any one type of field occupies a specific territory, production zones form bounded ecosystems that permit rigorous ecological study. We must recognize, however, that these microenvironments are modified by human action.

For each production zone there is a specific form of social organization among people who have access to it that permits the production of crops. A formal definition of *production zones* is as follows: a communally managed set of specific productive resources in which crops are grown in distinctive ways. These zones include infra-structural features, a particular system of rationing resources (such as irrigation water and natural grasses), and rule-making mechanisms that regulate how the productive resources are to be used. Complementing the management of these resources are individual production units (such as households) that hold access rights to specific portions of these resources. They have full rights to all products obtained by them from their labor, and they have the right to transmit them to others.

Despite the great natural diversity in the Cañete Valley, production zones are fairly uniform. In a land-use map (Mayer and Fonseca 1979), Fonseca and I identify only ten distinct types.[3] Descriptions of these zones as well as the crop assemblages, rotation systems, mechanisms of water distribution, and ways in which crops are grown in each one can be found in our several publications reissued as a single monograph (Fonseca and Mayer 1988).

Our map allows us to estimate that the total cultivable hectarage of the Cañete Valley is twice as large as that estimated previously by the Peruvian National Office of Resource Evaluation (ONERN): 68,000 hectares versus 34,000 hectares (Mayer and Fonseca 1979: 8). The difference arises because ONERN had largely ignored *sierra* agriculture, a reflection of the low value that government agencies give to this important group of farmers. Also shown in our survey are a massive conversion of ancient maize terraces to a new type of alfalfa meadow on which cows graze to produce

246

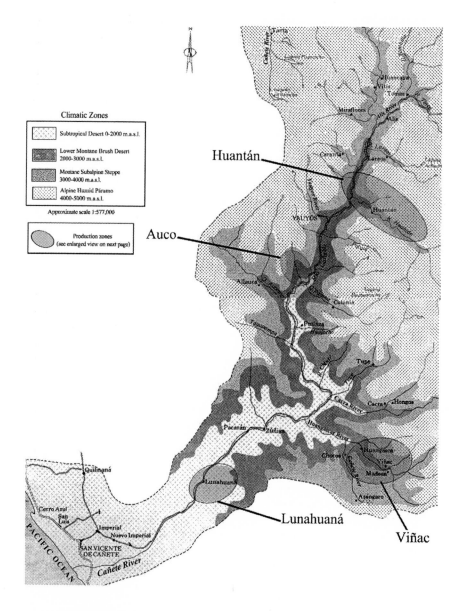

Map 8.1   Modified map of production zones in the Cañete Valley

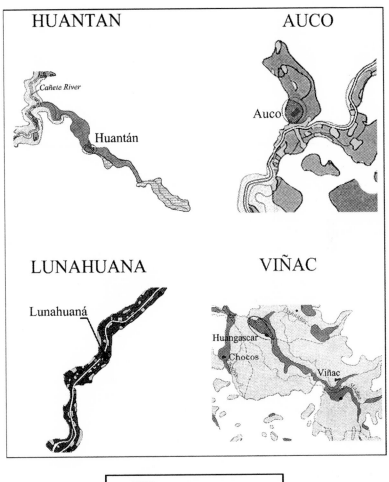

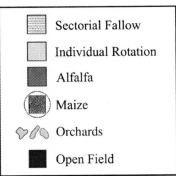

Map 8.2 *Production Zones for Selected Areas in the Cañete Valley*

cheese for the Lima market, as well as a dynamic expansion of the agricultural front into the highland desert to open areas for the cultivation of commercial fruit. These shifts, in favor of the national economy and in certain ways detrimental to peasant interests, nevertheless demonstrate the creative dynamism of these farmers, who are hewing, by hand, new productive areas out of rocks and boulders, intensifying production, and converting their resources to fit changed outside circumstances. This kind of expansion can only be achieved with a great deal of internal organization.

The social organization that characterizes the management of a production zone is diagrammed in Figure 8.1. It is a dual decisionmaking system. At one level the household is the unit producing the crops; at a higher level the community manages and administers the territory through the control it exercises over the households. Ideally, this body controls a vast and heterogeneous territory. A complex organization of authority delegates control so that different hierarchical positions are in charge of a local specialized segment of territory. Decisions about land management are both centrally coordinated and locally decentralized. Depicted in the center of the figure are the ecologically specialized production zones; depicted on the right are the levels of authority that administer and manage the territory. Each production zone is under the management of a local set of authorities ("3") who make decisions throughout the growing season and see that the rules are enforced by fining infractions and reporting problems to higher levels ("2" and "1"). Shown on the left side of the diagram are individual units such as households that have access to land in each production zone, but for whom the conditions for working the land are laid down by the authorities. It follows that in each production zone the rules will differ according to the agronomic requirements of what is grown there. This is not to say that there is blind conformity or an absence of individual interpretations of these rules. Ultimately, households can influence the conditions of land use through assemblies and political pressure on the authorities— or, even more effectively, by ignoring the rules and risking the consequences. In this system, production in the zones is specialized, but the production units are diversified. Farmers thus have the time, freedom, and ability to simultaneously cultivate land in other production zones, whether these are in the overall administrative domain of the local authorities or in other distant areas. Problems of scale are resolved, providing the household with external economies of scale that it itself cannot generate.

There is a dynamic, symbiotic, and conflict-ridden relationship between the constituent households at one level and the community at another. The households are autonomous production and consumption units, and the community comprises the association of households in a territory administered by them as a unit. This dynamic relationship manifests itself in a constant tension between the interests of the households, which push for as much autonomy and independence as possible, and the communal aspects

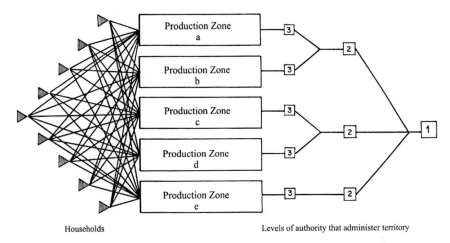

Households   Levels of authority that administer territory

Figure 8.1   Land Management Under Peasant Agricultural Systems

of their own collective selves, which impose restrictions and controls. At certain times and in certain production zones we can see a total absence of communal controls; at other times and places there are strict controls enforced. This tension, this constant debate, this push and pull generates individual technological solutions for each production zone and generalizes them as innovations for all.

The Dynamics in Production Zones

Let us observe, by means of some examples, how this individual/collective dialectic works in terms of the organization of production zones.

Crop Selection and Zonation

New crops are introduced and domesticated, and varieties are selected for use in production zones by individual households. Experimentation and adaptation is constant (Johnson 1972), belying all the talk about unthinking traditionalism. New plants are sown in kitchen gardens (Fonseca 1972a: 319) out of curiosity and are paid serious attention only if they produce viable seeds. Indeed, another important feature of the agricultural system within the domain of households is the maintenance of genetic diversity through careful management of the family's stock of seeds (Brush, Carney, and Huamán 1981; Brush 1986; Zimmerer 1996). There may also be a period of experimentation in actual fields that involves intercropping the new crop in an existing production zone. Some farmers may have enough faith in the new crop to grow it as a full field crop in a given production zone, ignoring existing rules and practices as well as skeptical neighborly comments.

If this kind of experimentation produces successful results, a process of persuasion of the collective group must take place in order to assign a portion of the territory for the introduction of the crop. Zoning and rezoning of community territory occur frequently. For instance, the villagers of Putinza, the first apple growers in the Cañete Valley—once they had convinced themselves of the agronomic and economic viability of apples—decided to convert all but one of their maize zones into apple orchards (Mayer and Fonseca 1979: 32; Fonseca and Mayer 1988: ch. 3; Eresue et al. 1988). In Laraos, grazing rights are clearly zoned according to animal type: Sheep are permanently grazed in the high *puna*; cows alternate between pastures in the lower *puna* and pastures in the *maizal* after the harvest. Hence only the cobs can be harvested, as the *chala* ("stalks") are a communal resource; horses and donkeys are allowed on the fallowing sectors of the sectorial system; goats and other smaller ruminants are restricted to the lower uncultivated mountain slopes (Mayer 1977a: 61; Fonseca and Mayer 1978: 32; Brunschwig 1996: 380). Comparative analysis in the valley has revealed considerable variation in these rules, showing again how the dialectic individual/community works out its particular solutions in each place.

The factors that ultimately determine the collective decision as to what and where to produce depend on (1) what the people want to consume and sell; (2) what is being produced in adjacent production zones; and (3) ecological limitations concerning particular varieties and species. Because maize is the more delicate crop in any given community, it always gets the priority of lower zones, even though potatoes and Andean tubers would bring better yields if they were planted in these zones. Thus, the decision to reserve one zone for maize also determines where the potato zone will be. Within a regional framework there is a tendency to domesticate upward—for as new crops are introduced, they displace the existing ones to higher production zones. What also can happen is that one crop displaces another altogether and the latter is not shifted to a different production zone.

Gade (1967: 154) has distinguished between the "absolute" and "effective" limits of crops. The extremes of invested effort to which farmers are willing to go to raise the effective limits of crops can be shown by the example of maize. People in the Cañete Valley once considered having their own maize to be so important that they extended the effective limit of the crop as high as possible (3,600 meters above sea level). As a result, they had to invest in irrigation to extend the supply of moisture beyond the rainy season. (Since plant growth is slowed by altitude and lack of insolation in these narrow canyons, it takes ten months for the crop to mature this high above sea level.) This decision, in turn, necessitated the construction of very elaborate terracing and irrigation systems. Other crops, equally or better adapted to these altitudes, would not have required such heavy investments.

Expansion, Contraction, and Segmentation of Production Zones

The above process, considered over a longer period of time, produces the expansion or contraction of production zones in response to demand. There is reason to believe that the myriad of terraces and irrigation canals in the upper part of the Cañete Valley was a response to increased demand for maize, which we know was an Inca concern but not necessarily a colonial one. Current reduction of demand in maize has produced the outright abandonment of maize terraces (in areas where irrigation water has diminished) and the conversion of the majority of the remaining terraces into alfalfa meadows. Concomitant changes are the practically complete disappearance of *chicha* as a ceremonial drink and the substitution of bottled beer, which in turn has triggered the expanded growth of malting barley throughout the Andes. Yet all communities have preserved at least one maize zone for their home consumption of *choclo* ("corn on the cob"), *cancha* ("toasted corn"), and *mote* ("hominy"). Cañete Valley dwellers are as particular about their own varieties of maize products as Tulumayo Valley producers are about their gift potatoes (see Chapter 7).

Expansion of production zones implies the physical construction of needed infrastructure for a particular kind of crop. The kind of infrastructure built depends on the needs of the plant that is going to grow there. In the Cañete Valley, expansion and opening of agricultural land in the semi-arid subtropical desert—an ecological zone defined by Tosi (1960)—implies the cyclopean task of making the desert bloom. Community and individual interact. The main irrigation canals are built by communal labor, and anyone wishing to have land allotted in this new area must work on the construction of the canal. Individuals then clear their own land, construct access canals and private stone walls, and begin the process of soil formation and planting. It is probably not strictly necessary to be a member of the community in which this expansion is taking place to be permitted to work in the *faena* of canal construction. Once land is allotted, one becomes a member of the community and of the irrigation association of that particular canal. In all of the canals, membership is mixed, with individuals from all sections of the villages (*barrios*) and kinship groups. Heads of household have land along practically all canals of the communal system, as long as they or their ancestors participated in the construction of the main canal. In terms of the myth that opens the chapter, collected from the neighboring Huarochirí area, the fox, the puma, jaguar, snake, and bird *ayllus* would all have rights to cultivate maize in Huracupara. It would not matter that these *ayllus* have "home bases" in other communities. Today's community of Catahuasi is made up of members who are from other places in the valley as well as outside of it (De la Cadena 1980).

Individual participation in production zone membership is not difficult to achieve, regardless of origin or affiliation, although considerable variation both regionally and over time can be expected. More problematic is the establishment of a communal land claim over an area. Such claims are fiercely disputed and lead to complicated land disputes between communities, between communities and *haciendas*, and between communities and individual defensive associations made up of unaffiliated small property owners, all of whom claim rights to occupy particular pieces of territory.

Segmentation of production zones can take several forms in response to the process of intensification, which implies a progressive fine-tuning of increased technological and labor inputs. This process may result in the subdivision of a previously larger production zone into smaller ones covering the same area, where the upper zone is now worked as extensively as before and the new lower production zone is worked more intensively than the whole. In the Mantaro Valley this process has reduced production zones to very small areas. As one moves down the eastern slope, fallow is progressively reduced such that in higher areas one sees three crop years and four fallow ones, whereas lower down on the same slope one sees four crop years (potatoes/Andean tubers/grain/ grain) with three fallow years individually—rather than communally—rotated. Yet in some badly eroded hilly areas at the same altitude, individual rotations with two crop years (potato/grain or Andean tuber/grain) and two years of fallow occur in response to poorer soil conditions (Mayer 1979: 70).

Disintegration of Production Zones

Unlike abandonment, the process of disintegration implies a progressive dismantling of communal controls and the triumph of individualism in agricultural decisionmaking. Figure 8.2 depicts a fully functioning sectorial fallow rotation system. In Figure 8.3, I show the progressive dismantling that the sectorial fallow system has undergone in the Mantaro Valley, caused by, among other things, increased pressure on the land leading to an overall shortening of the fallow system. This disintegration took various forms and occurred in several successive stages (Mayer 1979: 67–71).

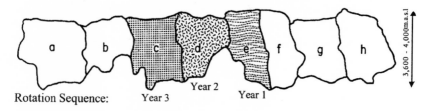

Rotation Sequence: Year 3   Year 2   Year 1   3,600 - 4,000 m.a.s.l

Figure 8.2 Sectorial Fallow/Rotation Systems

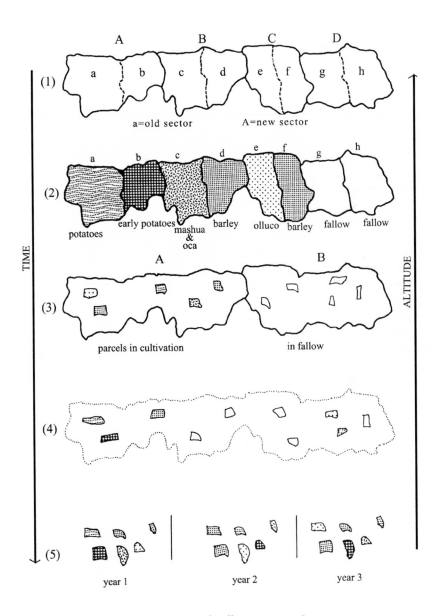

Figure 8.3   Distintegration of Sectorial Fallow/Rotation Systems.

Consider situation (1) in Figure 8.2. In response to community pressure, the size of each sector under cultivation was increased, eliminating several sectors and thus diminishing fallow years. An alternative would have been to lengthen the crop cycle without changing the size of the sectors or allotting more land, but just having more cropping years, some repeated in the rotation sequence. Land is cultivated longer at the expense of fallow years; this is situation (2) in the figure.

In situation (3), both processes combine to create a larger sector, although the community no longer decrees how, where, or what should be rotated. Only two sectors remain (one in crops, the other in fallow and allowing grazing rights). In this situation each family must have a large number of plots in each sector, since all crops must be produced in one sector only. When the community gives up regulation of land use and the whole territory is parceled out, situation (4) arises. Here, families privately decide rotation patterns and the years of fallow according to their resources, their needs, and the residual soil fertility of their plots. The unshaded parcels in situation (4) are those that have been left fallow. Progressively, fallow is abandoned between one rotation cycle and the next, depicted as situation (5).

This sequence of disintegration, based on historical process, also provides a geographical representation of the present-day situation, since the communities in the lower zones began the process of dismantling their sectors earlier than those in the intermediate and high zones. In higher-lying areas, fallow still seems to be a necessary biological process not substitutable by fertilization, because longer fallow characterizes all higher agriculture in the Mantaro Valley. Interestingly, the more tuber-oriented communities on the eastern side of the valley still maintain more of the sectorial fallow system in higher areas, whereas on the more European grain-oriented western side, all traces of communal sectorial fallow are gone.

The disintegration of production zones is often associated with the process of privatization, but the two should not be confused. Situation (5) in Figure 8.3 depicts full privatization with complete individual control. Throughout the Cañete Valley, full private ownership exists in the irrigated areas within viable and communally managed production zones, a situation Fonseca (1975: personal communication) liked to call "parallel land ownership."

Land Tenure in Production Zones

The implication of parallel property in terms of the individual/community dialectic is that individuals will try to gain as much control as possible over how to use their parcels, whereas the community will encumber this autonomy by imposing restrictions on how the land can be used. But *land tenure* must be carefully defined to avoid falling into the trap of ready-made categories such as communal or private property. I see land tenure as a bundle of rights and obligations (Royal Anthropological Institute 1954) held by different groups and actors over diverse privileges concerning land. The focus here is to ask who has the right to use what portions of land for specific productive purposes, rather than who has rights over land as property. We must pay careful attention to what the community allows the individual farmer to do.

Following this approach, I can readily show that use rights vary across production zones. In each zone the community imposes diverse restrictions on how individuals can use the land, depending not only on the conditions required by the cultigens in specific production zones but also on social factors that impinge on the productive process. In the next chapter I show how use rights vary in the five production zones in Laraos. They range from many restrictions imposed by the community in the higher *moyas* ("sectors") to practically complete freedom in the lower *potreros* ("meadows") and irrigated orchards. In a seventy-year period since the turn of the twentieth century, the imposed rules were repeatedly changed according to the particular interests of the group in power. Specifically, from 1900 to about 1950, when the *Libre Pensadores* were in power, restrictions on land and water tenure were considerably eased such that individuals gained much more control over their productive decisions in all production zones; then, from 1951 to 1970, a younger group of *comuneros* (*La Quinta Internacional*) reinstituted many, though not all, of the communal controls in three of the five production zones.

Is it possible at this stage to generalize about land and water tenure in the Andes? One widespread system, the sectorial fallow system, is associated in many communities with higher lands (3400–4000 meters above sea level), no irrigation, cultivation of tubers and hardy European grains, use of the footplow, or *chaquitaclla* (Gade and Rios 1972; Morlon 1996) as the main tool to break the ground, and creation of the communal controls described above. In some areas the sectorial fallow system is absent at the appropriate altitudinal level (e.g., in Uchucmarca [Brush 1977a]), probably as a result of particular climatic conditions. (In the Mantaro Valley, the system has been dismantled.) Many areas that once belonged to communities but were taken over by *haciendas* became pasture zones after displacing the local agricultural population. Since the agrarian reform restored land to the communities, people have reestablished extensive sectorial fallow systems in these areas.

Tentative generalizations can be made about the tenure arrangements in the sectorial fallow system, the production zone in which there are the greatest number of communal controls. The community intervenes decisively in terms of what, when, and where the farmer can cultivate. Because the community retains grazing rights on the sectors that are in fallow as well as, in many cases, the stubble grazing rights in recently harvested sectors, it also regulates the agricultural calendar by dictating the harvest date and scheduling the animal and plant cycles accordingly. The community also acts as a court to settle disputes between farmers, a function that arises out of having to set up a court system to punish individual farmers who are in contravention of the rules of use imposed by the community.

A system of authority is specifically assigned to the supervision of the production zones. In Laraos, the village officials in charge of the sectorial fallow system, known as *meseros,* serve their *cargo* for one year. Billie Jean Isbell (1978: 89–93) describes three interlocking *varayoq* (staff holder) systems, each associated with one production zone. Because one of the cargo systems was too much under the control of the local priests, the Chuschinos abolished it and replaced it with a new system that was supported by the government; thus they used agrarian reform to recuperate church lands. In Tangor (Mayer 1974a: 235–253), the *vara* system's primary function was to manage the rotation of the sectors and to settle disputes arising from its operation. In some communities, such as Miraflores in the Cañete Valley, land is still distributed annually by the authorities; in most communities, however, farmers return to their own family plots after the fallow years.

A careful look at the symbolic statements made during the *fiestas* associated with these *varas* shows that the rituals are also associated with different production zones (Isbell 1978: 139–145; Mayer 1974a: 40–45). It follows that a calendrical *fiesta* associated with agriculture will reveal which of the production zones is considered the most important for that community. Care must be taken, however; in the Laraos irrigation canal-cleaning *fiesta,* for example, much emphasis is placed on their *maizal,* even though it is actually the *puna* lands that are economically the most important. A case can be made here for ideological manipulation. Parallels also exist between the communal and individual levels mirrored in the ceremonial cycle. Household-level *fiestas* organized to sow maize (Mayer 1974a: 149–153; Fonseca 1974: 99–104; Ossio 1992: 109–111) and the famous animal fertility rites (*marca del ganado*) reported in the journal *Allpanchis* (1971) and by Hiroyasu Tomoeda (1985) clearly are individually organized concerns that bring family members together, in contrast to communally organized land distribution ceremonies (Fonseca 1972; Mayer 1974a) and communal irrigation canal *fiestas.*

Individual farmers hold a different bundle of rights over the productive process. They can decide how much land they are going to work (which is different from the amount of land they own, since they always have recourse to internal exchange arrangements between *comuneros*)[4] and how this land is going to be worked. Also up to the farmers are the kinds of plowing, furrowing, and drainage systems they will use, as well as the kinds of seeds, manure, insecticides (if any), and other plant care they need. Finally, it is the autonomous decision of the farmers to recruit their own labor (see Chapter 4). Within the limits set by the community, each can decide on the crucially important issues of early-, middle-, or late-season planting (Camino, Recharte, and Bidegaray 1981; Zimmerer 1988: 81–110).

Individual households have complete rights to the products that are the fruits of their labor; they also have the right to transmit rights of access to their heirs. They can buy, sell, and give away individual pieces of land to other parties, although there are kinship and communal controls as well as legal restrictions as to whom the buyers can be. Very few remaining communities periodically redistribute land, though the tendency is still visible. (In 1980, a government survey claimed that 44 percent of the communities still redistributed land [*Dirección de Comunidades Campesinas* 1980: 27.]) In general, today's rules reserve access rights to people who are members of communities, to their heirs, and to relatives. Total strangers have a more difficult time becoming established in a community, although their presence is not that rare. We must assume that in the past the right to assign land within production zones was not always within the sole domain of local communities.

It would be tempting to find in this sectorial fallow system the ideal model of pre-Hispanic land-tenure systems and to relegate all deviations to post-conquest colonial interference and to privatization.[5] However, my research has shown that the more intensively land can be worked (i.e., the longer it can be cultivated in a more permanent way), the more independence farmers want to have over productive decisions. Thus, the degree of communal control varies with the ecological gradient, since lower lands can be worked more intensively, and vice versa. For example, in the *altiplano* in Bolivia, land in more favorable niches is allocated in more "private" ways as *sayañas*, in contrast to the more collectively managed *aynoqa* (Carter 1973). In Marcapata, Peru, the contrast is between the *banda* and *kita chacra*, the latter being worked more independently than the former (Yamamoto 1981: 107). The upper part of the *banda chacra* is under the sectorial fallow system whereas the lower parts are more permanently planted with maize (Yamamoto 1981: 106). Tatsuhiko Fujii and Hiroyasu Tomoeda's (1981: 44) study of Cayrabamamba similarly reveals a more intensive cultivation of maize and potatoes in lower zones, which they call the *complejo chacra*, than in the *laymis* higher up. Because of the more restricted rotation patterns in the *laymis* and the nonexistent fallow in the *chacras*, communal controls are greater in the higher zones. In some cases these *chacras* are considered absolute private property, precisely because of the absence of communal restrictions.

Distribution of Irrigation Water

On the western slopes of the Andes another factor becomes crucial: the community's control of irrigation water. By rationing water in certain ways, the community determines the crops that can be grown in the various production zones. Thus, the distribution of water, a limiting factor, becomes the crucial factor in communal control as one moves from the *sierra* to the drier coastal areas in the irrigated zones of the Cañete. Many of the features described above for the sectorial fallow system are also applicable to irrigation systems under communal control.

Farmers gain access rights to particular portions of an irrigated production zone by having worked on the construction of the communal infrastructure features, such as the main canals. They maintain these rights by regularly attending the *faenas* ("obligatory work projects") that keep the canals in working order, as well as by serving as *cargo* holders in the associated *fiestas*. Water is allocated differently in each production zone, depending on the requirements of the main crops growing there. For example, in Laraos, *papas mahuay* ("early-maturing potatoes") require irrigation every two weeks in the dry season, whereas maize can grow even if it is irrigated only three times during the growing season—again, in contrast to the requirements of alfalfa meadows, which need water every week, or orchards, which have very complex irrigation schedules arranged in such a way as to produce a crop of fruit when the market price of the apples is highest (Fonseca and Mayer 1988: ch. 5).

In general, water-rationing systems are worked out as a result of individual interests that coalesce into pressure groups. The conflicting interests are resolved democratically in assemblies to allocate different amounts of water in different ways in each production zone. As in any democracy, the interests of more powerful groups may be better served than those of the general majority.[6] These rules then become the givens that determine a great deal of the agricultural practices for the individual farmers. Mitchell (1976b) shows how irrigation water is zoned in Quinua, Ayacucho, to extend the supply of moisture beyond the rainy season because crops need additional water in the upper zone. In the lower zone, water is needed because there is an absolute shortage of moisture throughout the growing season.

In Putinza, too, the supply of water is very limited, and water must be rationed very carefully. Water sources depend on underground filtration that emerges as springs, with maximum availability reaching a peak during the rainy season. Water can simultaneously be distributed along the four canals during this season, which is therefore the time when the greatest area of land can be irrigated. If the sources of water seem to be particularly abundant in a given year, water is sent to a special production zone where plots are cultivated in maize intercropped with beans and *cucurbits*. These crops can grow with little water; and when the amount available diminishes, water to this production zone is cut off altogether in favor of the more delicate, valued, and revenue-producing apple orchards. Later in the season, as the flow continues to diminish, all the water flows along one canal by *turnos* ("turns") rather than in all four simultaneously. During years when the community decides that water will be insufficient, a collective decision is made not to cultivate in the maize sector at all (Mayer and Fonseca 1979: 34; Fonseca 1983).

Systems of water distribution also vary by production zones and according to communities. Free water is known as *toma libre*; individuals may take as much water as they wish, when they want to. Distribution of controlled water can vary from fairly free to very restricted. In less constrained distribution systems, farmers who want water pay their fee to the official in charge of distribution, who then assigns it among those who came to ask during a particular week. More stringent communal controls are termed *mitas de agua* ("water turns"). *Mitas* can be assigned to individuals or groups of individuals, who then have water during a whole day to irrigate all of their fields scattered throughout the production zone along several of the canals. Or *mitas* can be assigned to the canals, in which case the order of irrigation can be from the last field at the end of the canal to the first, or from the first to the last, or some other variation—each with particular advantages and disadvantages to individual farmers or groups. The actual solutions worked out in each production zone and community vary, as local concerns are thoroughly hashed out by the most interested parties. Disputes about water take place frequently, and there is a court that settles water disputes in much the same way that crop disputes are settled in the sectorial fallow system. The threat of fines is far less compulsory than the threat to cut off the water supply of the offending farmer.

One new aspect of water distribution is the question of priority and hierarchy. In Huantán, as recently as thirty years ago, water was allocated to groups of four or five farmers along a canal, who became the *patrones* of that day. Other *comuneros* helped the *patrones* in the agricultural tasks during those days, and this help was returned on the day when the *comuneros* became the *patrones* (Fonseca 1978, 1983). The order in which these groups of farmers were assigned their water allotments predetermined the rest of the agricultural cycle: Those privileged by early water distribution could harvest sooner than farmers at the end of the roster. In Auco, another community in the Cañete Valley, there is an annual ceremony called *la asentada de la mita de agua* ("the assignment of water turns") (Fonseca 1978: 6–7). The authorities provide a big feast for all *comuneros*, because they receive the best choices for water distribution during their tenure—a privilege that is rotated among the *comuneros*. The amounts, periodicities, and groups of farmers who are to irrigate on a given day are decided on that day. Thus, the distribution of water privileges accurately reflects social hierarchies. Where irrigation is necessary, communal controls do not weaken despite the possibility of working production zones more intensively (Netting 1976), but communal controls shift from land to water.

What elements characterize communal management of production zones in the Andes? David Guillet (1978), in defining the "suprahousehold sphere of production," specifies the following agronomic productive functions: (1) factor proportionality, (2) creation and enforcement of production rules, (3) scheduling and coordination, and (4) labor recruitment to maintain production zones. In addition, he stresses the important fact of collective defense of land, which, though not directly associated with production per se, is nevertheless a very necessary precondition. To these productive considerations I must now add more social specifications. Community controls are usually concerned with matters of common interest: to protect the rights of other farmers (though not always in an egalitarian way) and to consider the long-range maintenance and use of natural resources. In addition, communal organization must deal with matters of priority and hierarchy: who has access to the production zone and under what criteria, who gets the choice pieces of land, who gets the water first. Individuals have rights and are concerned about agricultural inputs, the product of their effort, and the transmission of the rights of access to production zones to their heirs, though I suspect that in the past this issue was handled more stringently through such matters as kinship and *ayllu* membership. Individual interests tend toward autonomy of decisionmaking, seeking the reduction of demands that the community can impose on them.

A tentative generalization concerning all production zones that would be valid over time, thus allowing us to pose questions for historical and archaeological research, should include the following features: (1) recognition that production zones are communal creations that allow individual access; (2) acknowledgment that rights to access are controlled in part by the community, and that the concomitant obligations to these rights include the giving of labor and participation in the rule-making, rule-breaking, and rule-enforcing mechanisms of the local community; (3) communal and extra-communal control over the rationing process, setting up priorities and hierarchies of privilege; (4) control of the agricultural calendar, not only to ensure the proper scheduling activities, which are important in multizone exploitations (Golte 1980), but also to enhance the controls the community can exercise over individuals; (5) agricultural ceremonies associated with ritually ensuring a balance of appropriate climatic conditions; (6) the ritual validation of hierarchies and privileges that justify them in terms of appeals to higher ideological principles (e.g., appeals to the good of all); and (7) drinking and dancing ceremonies and rituals that serve as a means of recruiting labor, ensuring compliance, and achieving a greater degree of solidarity.

All of these communal controls also create the conditions for greater and more controlled labor exactions, which go beyond the maintenance or expansion of production zones. For example, the control of the agricultural calendar and the associated ceremonies are crucial in ensuring that the *curaca*'s, Inca state's, and *Huaca*'s claims on land and labor get assigned and worked first (in the sense that these have priority) in a given production zone, before individual commoners are allowed to work their own plots. State and *curaca* plots must be located within the locally created and managed production zones. There is also the communal right to distribute and redistribute access rights, although the latter are not always completely within communal control but, rather, are affected by land distribution policies of higher-level entities such as the *señoríos* and the state.

The Limitations of Village-Based Verticality

So far, this discussion has been restricted to considerations of how production is organized. However, certain factors go beyond these considerations, necessitating the following questions: How can surplus be generated from existing production zones? How can "supra-village" social groups gain control of the communal level of organization and reorient their productive capacities to their own social, political, and economic ends? How do production zones fit in with verticality? In this section I discuss the inherent limitations affecting the expansion of localized villages into many production zones.

Aggregation of Production Zones

The process of aggregation refers to the efforts made by villages as units to create and control as many production zones as possible. It is a different process than that implied when individuals from one village have access to production zones in other villages. There are many factors affecting the capacity of a local group of people to control a maximum number of production zones. One of these is distance. The number of production zones that can simultaneously be managed by all households within a village depends on how far these zones are from each other. Distance, in any case, should be conceived of in terms of the villagers' own criteria of near or far. Steepness of the gradient accounts for the ease or difficulty of movement between one zone and the next—a feature largely determined by the local and regional topography. Gade's (1967) and Brush's (1976a: 161–165) classifications of "compressed," "extended," and "archipelago" are examples of the application of this concept of distance. Distance per se is not useful as a measure. It must be combined with intensity of labor requirements in different zones and at different times. Agricultural zones seasonally concentrate labor inputs only during certain times of the year, while herding areas require constant inputs by a few people throughout the year. Jürgen Golte calculates that labor requirements in each production zone are not enough to occupy household labor on a full-time basis; and because productivity in each zone is low, several production zones must be combined in order to produce enough for subsistence needs. The number of production zones that a community can actually create and control further depends on the size of the village population. But more important, it depends on the size and complexity of the social organization of the locally productive households. The larger the farming unit (the more members it has), the greater the possibility of dividing the tasks among a larger number of production zones. A family that can permanently assign people to take care of herding animals in the *puna*, as well as have the necessary manpower to cultivate in different production zones, is more capable of exploiting all the resource possibilities in a community than a family that is short of the necessary productive labor composition (Webster 1980; Custred 1980). This is a matter of demographics and domestic cycle (Goody 1966; Lambert 1977), but also a matter of kinship and social organization. Progressive nuclearization of families as a result of European and Christian pressures is one important factor in the destructuring of the Andean political economy.

We must also consider whether there are tendencies toward specialization and division of labor within a village. The tendency is to assume that every family would desire access to all production zones, but an equally valid alternative is specialization of tasks within a village whereby some groups are more concerned than others with the exploitation of certain specialized resources in particular zones. Village organization ensures maximum control over all the production zones, with internal specialization and differentiation. Goat herders and cheese makers in Laraos are specialized groups, separate from the group that combines agriculture with wage work in the nearby mines (Brunschwig 1996). Specialization within a village permits the presence of people from other villages and zones to reside within it and yet have access to the production zones they are interested in on behalf of their home villages. Coordinating all these special interests is one of the functions of community organization.

Another indicator of multi-production zone management is the location of the village: Ideally, it will be situated nearest those production zones that require the most intense care. Given today's limitations on village organization, two common patterns tend to emerge: primarily agricultural villages located at the boundaries between potato and maize zones (Fonseca 1972a; Brush 1977a), and pastoral villages located between the limits of agriculture and their pasture lands (Custred 1977). In a useful survey of communities in Peru (*Dirección de Comunidades Campesinas* 1980: 28), José Portugal has compiled data showing that nearly half—46 percent—of the communities control only two zones, and that in this group the combination of pasture with agriculture is by far the most frequent (41 percent). Communities with three systems (irrigation, rain-fed agriculture [*secano*], and pastures) account for 22 percent, and 20 percent comprise communities with only one system—either irrigation (2 percent), *secano* (9 percent), or pastures (9 percent). (There were no data for 12 percent of the communities surveyed.) However, we must assume that within each of these official categories further production zones are differentiated.

Shifts in emphasis in production zones are associated with changes in location of the villages themselves. In the Cañete Valley there are new settlements in the lower fruit-growing areas, whereas the older and higher villages are suffering a marked decline in population (De la Cadena 1977; Wiegers 1999). In the famous case of Huayopampa in the Chancay Valley, the whole village moved to a new site (Fuenzalida et al. 1968, 1982). In many communities pre-Hispanic settlements are at a higher location than the contemporary residences. Archaeological and archival research that pays close attention to a chronology of settlement patterns in relation to production zones should reveal great historical shifts of villages up and down the slopes, depending on the particular productive emphasis in each historical period.

Within this framework we must also consider the process of creating *anexos*, or satellite villages, in terms of the ways in which a village can expand control over different and more distant production zones. *Anexos* are often situated in places where a different mix of production zones is available. *Puna anexos* are associated with many agricultural communities in Central Peru. And in the Cañete Valley there is a tendency to create *anexos* lower down to begin the process of orchard expansion; Putinza and Catahuasi started off as *anexos*. Portugal's survey shows that 25 percent of all communities have more *anexos* in the northern departments, where the Andes are much more broken (*Dirección de Comunidades Campesinas* 1980: 14).

The social relations between *anexo* and mother community are often characterized in terms of political dependence and domination. For example, Fernando Fuenzalida (1970: 36–49) and Henri Favre (1976) describe the relationship between the *mistis* of Moya in Huancavelica and their *chuto* (Indian) herders in the *anexos* as violent and exploitative, and Barbara Bradby (1982) explains how the herders liberated themselves from valley domination. In contrast, Tetsuya Inamura (1981) characterizes the relationship among agricultural *ayllus*, each one with their *anexos* in the *puna* in the district of La Puica, Arequipa, as "symbiosis" (i.e., rather than domination), given the close collaboration between *puna* and valley people through kinship, *compadrazgo*, barter, and complementary mutual aid such as using llamas for transporting agricultural produce.

Even if the *puna* and valley villages are not in a relationship of *anexo* to *comunidad madre*, indirect control by a group of villagers over other, more distant villages has larger historical significance. Here the relationships between agriculturalists and herders become important. In contemporary Central Andes, agricultural villages are in control of the *puna* lands, which are worked by a distinct group of people usually somewhat despised by the agriculturalists—even though the latter are dependent on the herders whose animals are herded alongside their own. The herders' dependence on agricultural products as well as on political representation explains their submission. Fujii and Tomoeda (1981: 51) describe relationships in Caraybamba in this way: "The high *puna* is exploited by the *punaruna* through a system of pastoralism, these people being indirectly controlled by the *llaqtarunas* (townspeople)." Conversely, historical examples from the *altiplano* in Puno and Bolivia reveal at least partial control by the herders over the agriculturalists (Saignes 1978: 1166). In any case, data on barter and privileged exchange relationships (Flores Ochoa 1968; Casaverde 1977; Caro 1978; Fonseca 1972; Mayer 1971) clearly show the interdependence between the two groups, leading us to view the domination-submission scenario as a gross simplification.

Given the inherent limitations of local village organization, the possibilities of vertical control that a local village is capable of mobilizing should not be confused with the potentialities of vertical control as organized by a *señorío*. Village organization is not a pale reflection (Murra 1985: 10) of verticality but, rather, a component of the whole system concerned with the local exploitation of resources. In short, a component of the whole should not be confused with the system itself.

Independization of Production Zones

Independization refers to the severing of the links between one or more production zones from the whole. Today, the overwhelming tendency is toward the separation of production zones from each other, but this process probably took place in other historical periods as well. The *puna* lands in the Cañete Valley are breaking away from their *comunidades madre*. The issue is complex; it concerns a three-pronged fight over the control of *puna* lands that are now a most valued resource (as further discussed in Chapter 9). On the one hand, there are the dependent herders who are severing their ties with the agriculturalists by refusing to herd the latter's sheep in order to expand their own herds. On the other hand, there are the old *libre pensadores* who were able to amass huge private *haciendas* within community territory as *comuneros*, but whose right to do so was challenged by the next generation of agriculture and mining *comuneros*. The reaction of the *libre pensadores* was to try to become an independent community by means of an alliance with the rebellious dependent herders. The third party in this dispute comprises the *haciendas* (who in the 1970s became cooperatives), seeking to expand their borders throughout the *puna*. It was easier to swallow up small and specialized purely *puna* groups at that time, just as it was more strategic to lead the battle against *hacienda* encroachment in alliance with the old *comunidad madre*, given that the latter had the original titles and a greater capacity to mobilize opposition (Mayer 1977a; Fonseca and Mayer 1978; Mayer and Fonseca 1979).

A similar process is taking place in the lower parts of the Cañete Valley. The new fruit-growing production zones, once *anexos* of a larger community, are cutting themselves off from their old communities and seeking the status of separate communities. Putinza and Catahuasi are examples; they once were *anexos* of Pampas and Tupe, respectively, but broke off from them because they found the labor exactions and other controls imposed by their mother communities too onerous while they were building and expanding their apple orchards. Further fieldwork will help us to understand how these newly independent communities have settled the water rights among themselves and their old villages, since irrigation water comes from land within the old communities.

In the Mantaro Valley, the process of independization has been brought almost to its ecological limits. Giorgio Alberti and Rodrigo Sánchez (1974: 49–58) describe the historical process by which Mito, once a Colonial *reducción* that had lands from the banks of the Mantaro River all the way to the *puna*, progressively lost territory until it had shrunk to its present small size in the low zone. The process was accompanied by the settlement of new areas, which in turn became villages that were elevated to the official status of *comunidades* and *puna haciendas* within a time span of one century. One way in which individual farmers have tried to reconstruct access to multiple production zones, apart from trade links, is by owning land in several villages—and this is possible given the advanced degree of privatization in the valley.

Recent government administrations have played an important role in this process of political fragmentation to single production zone communities, inasmuch as they readily elevated *anexos* to district status and provided any group that wanted it with papers recognizing them as *comunidades de indígenas*. Privatization of land, intensification of agriculture, the breakdown of sectorial fallow systems, and the growth of commercialism accompanied this process; another consequence was the multiplication of a number of micro-communities that no longer control much land at all. Thus, the current tendency is to destroy village-based verticality by breaking up the multiple production-zone management characteristic of Andean villages.

The Toledan *reducciones* profoundly modified village composition, location, functions, and integration into larger political territorial units (Gade 1991). From the very beginning the Spanish were concerned about the dispersion and what to them seemed a confusion in village organization—so much so that they soon started arguing about the need to *reducirlos* ("concentrate them"). It is our task to make sense of what to European eyes seemed so confusing and disorganized. The first simple question concerns village size and location in relation to production zones over time. Other questions include the following: Were villages much smaller but closer to their respective production zones in pre-*reducción* times? Was there a greater degree of single production zone specialization with local residences nearby, while what was then considered to be a village constituted a more dispersed unit? What shifts can we see in terms of creation and intensification of production zones by studying village locations and settlement patterns over time? What was the internal composition of villages in terms of ethnic, state, and local populations?

Individual Interest Groups in Villages

We now turn to an examination of individual interest groups and their concerns over how to use production zones. To be effective, an interest group must be capable of exerting pressure on the communal level so that its particular interests have a bearing on the outcome in the communal decisionmaking process. What one actually observes in a given production zone is the outcome of power struggles between the different interest groups represented in the village. If a particular group clearly dominates, its interests will be reflected in the way that the land is worked. But if power is more evenly distributed, the way a production zone is being used will be reflected in the outcome of several kinds of negotiations and compromises, as well as in shifts of power among groups within the villages. This approach takes for granted that the internal composition of villages is heterogeneous.

It also follows that we need not necessarily think only of families when we consider the individual level. Institutions and organizations can have access rights to lands within a given production zone—as is the case with the *yupanakuy* (communal) lands belonging to different barrios in Yacan (Fonseca 1972) and the *cofradía* lands in Laraos that were expropriated by the *Libre Pensadores* at the turn of the century. Such institutions have their representatives at the local level to ensure that the institutions' claims and interests are not forgotten. These representatives are the people who actually mobilize the work on the land for such organizations. The power that local representatives can exercise within the village derives not only from the one vote of its representative but also, and much more importantly, from outside the village—as is the case with the *cofradía* lands, whose expropriation by the municipality of Laraos was bitterly opposed by the church hierarchy. Though numerically inferior, such institutions can wield a strong influence on the way a production zone is to be used.

In analyzing these interest groups, we must distinguish between two factors that influence their decisions over how to use production zones: (1) direct influences, which have to do with how a particular interest group wants to use a production zone, and with what technology; and (2) indirect influences, which are also concerned with production decisions, except that the reasons for favoring one particular choice over another are related not to the production concerns themselves but to demands and obligations that impinge on that particular individual interest group and indirectly influence the way it wants to use the production zone. These latter factors are often termed "constraints" in the modern, agriculturally related social science literature (ICRISAT 1979). For example, in today's *campesino* world, one group of *comuneros* wants to use land as intensively as possible to produce the cash crop that brings the highest returns. But another group that earns most of its cash income from outside the community opposes such a move and favors a more extensive, less labor-intensive use of the same land to obtain crops for home consumption. The second group's interests in use of the land are indirectly constrained by their interests in the cash nexus.

Individual interests thus are torn between two kinds of demands. On the one hand, there are the demands inherent in being participant members of production zones. Communal labor demands relating to production zone maintenance, scheduling of tasks according to the established rules, serving *cargos*, and so on, are locally emanating demands. Following Thiery Saignes (1978), let us describe these demands as arising out of residence requirements. The other kind of demands has to do with an individual's membership in larger groups that may or may not transcend the local village; these latter demands arise out of the individual's affiliation. The demands placed on the miners in contemporary Laraos, for example, include compliance with a 24-hour work-shift schedule (which can interfere with agricultural tasks), support for the miners union, and the feasting of the mine's managers with lavish *pachamancas* in order to ensure that patronage relations provide employment opportunities and other privileges for Laraoinos. Thus, the miners' concerns over their time, money, and resources affect the decision they make about how to use their production zones. In my observation, miners are the most traditional agriculturalists of the Cañete Valley because they see in their agriculture a complement to their income; they produce food rather than cash crops, and this food includes the best local *choclos* necessary for the *pachamancas*.

In historical and pre-Hispanic times, an important requirement placed on the individual was compliance with tribute (*corvée*) labor obligations. Since these obligations could be partly discharged in the local production zone on state parcels, they became part of the residence requirements for individuals. But affiliation requirements also implied *mit'a* labor contributions in other places or even work at home in textile production (Murra 1956). The amount of labor time taken off for these purposes influenced the way a production zone was worked and the number of zones a family could work in.

Absorbing 30–40 percent of labor time on nonagricultural tasks is another way in which unused labor capacity can be utilized (Golte 1980). Tribute labor and multiple-zone exploitation can become contradictory demands if not carefully administered by competent authorities. The colonial rationale behind *reducciones* was to reduce family access to production zones, limiting them to those required for minimum subsistence levels in order to expand available labor time for tribute.

I propose that we think of villages as arenas where diverse interest groups interact and coalesce. Diversity of interests may also arise out of local internal situations and extra-village linkages that impinge on the village. They can affect land-use interests either directly or indirectly by imposing constraints on different groups and their labor times. The function of local community organization is to arrive at a consensus among diverse interests and to determine the rules and conditions under which production zones are going to be worked. The outcome as to which decisions are implemented depends on local-level politicking and does not exclude the clout that external groups can bring to bear on the situation.

My argument, however, is that outside groups need not necessarily control a whole village and its production zones in order to achieve the desired multiple vertical control in several production zones. I think that the structure of village organization today permits the participation of members of very diverse social groups in local production zones. (The same was true in the past.) Because village structure can accommodate the requirements of residence as well as affiliation of diverse interest groups, Murra's (1972) model of inter-ethnic sharing of resources comes to rest in the particular characteristics of Andean village organization and its production zones.

We can observe the communal level of organization as selecting from a whole range of technological choices, enhanced by the diverse provenience of its members, each of whom can bring along a particular cultural tradition. These traditions, in turn, must be adapted to local climatic and ecological conditions. Technology thus needs to be considered a means-end schema as well as a cultural tradition in which desired ends are made compatible with existing choices of means (Lechtman 1977). Village organization is an institution that creates appropriate technology within a given economic, political, and environmental context. It follows that technology is constantly changing and adjusting itself according to the demands placed on it by the human beings who are managing this complex machine that I have called production zones.

Some brief examples of local productive organization with multiple affiliation of its individuals are instructive. Throughout the Cañete Valley, outsiders who have lands along specific community-controlled irrigation canals participate actively in the *faenas* of irrigation canal maintenance, as well as in the membership-validating *fiestas* that accompany the maintenance work (Fonseca and Mayer 1978: 35). In 1969 several immigrant families tried to establish themselves in Tangor, and they were even more punctilious about complying with the *cargo* system than the local Tangorinos (Mayer 1974a: 260–261). And Tristan Platt (1982) as well as Olivia Harris (1978) note the phenomenon of double residence in the Potosí area of Bolivia that ensures the Machas and Laymis continued access to lowland areas in modern times. This phenomenon is also common in Peruvian communities; but, because it is illegal, it is a strategic datum not often revealed to inquisitive anthropologists. Silvia Rivera (1976: personal communication) also reports that in *hacienda* times in Pacajes, the *hacendado's* *parcelas* rotated along with the *campesino's* lands within the *aynoka*, which in turn was managed in common between the *hacendado* and the *hilacata* (village leader) of the *hacienda*.

Consider Saignes's description of the people living in the *yungas* of Ambaná in the seventeenth century. Although these people were affiliated with the *puna curacas* and paid tribute to them, as co-residents with the local *yunga* people they were required (like everybody else) to comply with their residence requirements. To the tribute obligations must be added

> ... the supplementary obligations that [were] implied in their membership in the social milieu of the valley: *corvees* on the haciendas, services to the *corregidor*, to the church, or at the *tambo*, the priest's salary, [and] participation in the fiestas (*cargos*) within the organizations of the town's religious sodalities. This part of the obligations resulted from the neighborhood solidarities and reactivated the rights to lands in the valley. (1978: 1168; translation by Mayer)

In addition, Maria Rostworowski (1985) describes how the *pachacas* in Cajamarca are distributed among practically all the *pueblos*, so that with the exception of the *pueblos principales*, each pueblo is composed of representatives of several *pachacas* in the Diego de Velazques de Acuña *Visita* of Cajamarca in 1571–1572. Finally, Murra (1975: 83) gives us an example of how at least three ethnic groups shared a few furrows of coca in Quivi. This arrangement was such that, to the former slave Rodrigo, they appeared to be *revueltos los unos con los otros* ("all mixed up with each other") (Murra 1975: 93; Rostworowski 1988). The shared production zone was carefully delimited so that each of the ethnic groups' representatives knew which furrows, terraces, and canals were assigned to whom.

They even collaborated in damming up lagoons in the distant *puna* in order to assure themselves of enough irrigation water. Yet the dispute about the control of these fields spanned centuries before the Inca and after the Spanish Conquest (Rostworowski 1988).

Conclusions

It would be a lengthy and complex task to elucidate the internal organization of villages through time in order to understand how the double requirements of affiliation and residence can suitably be managed through local village organization. Antoinette Fioravanti-Molinié's (1978: 1187–1191) study of contemporary Ambaná shows that moieties, as well as *vecinos, comuneros,* and *obreros,* are not only territorial organizations that coordinate access to diverse ecological areas but also endogamous organizations that perpetuate the three groups. These organizations permit the double requirements of residence and affiliation to interact, even though today the connections between the highlands and the *yungas* are very different from those of the past (as reported by Saignes 1978). I would also like to call attention to the symposium on *Ayllu, Parcialidad y Etnia* (Castelli, Koth de Paredes, and Mould de Pease 1981), which presented several excellent case studies on the issues of kinship, ethnic, and territorial affiliation of various groups with a historical perspective. Fonseca's (1981: 168–188) contribution is particularly relevant since he posits that the same principles that underlie the organization of production are also used to organize the groups that share these productive tasks without losing their distinctiveness. He concludes:

> The pre-Columbian criteria of social organization seem to be the same as those that characterize the organization of production that are still operative in traditional communities of the country. The classificatory elements of Upper/Lower, Left/Right were used to classify and to locate the *ayllus* within a larger unit which could have been the ethnic group as a totality. In the same manner, when the *ayllus* were reduced into *pueblos* during the Colonial period, the new *comuneros* used these same criteria to communally create production zones. (Fonseca 1981: 186; translation by Mayer)

Production zones need not be restricted to agriculture. Felix Palacios Ríos (1977) describes how specially inundated pasture lands for seasonal grazing of alpacas are created by irrigation in the high *puna*. Some communities in the Mantaro Valley have created a *cargo* for the purpose of controlling trout fishing; *comuneros* are allowed to fish for free, but outsiders must pay the community a fee every time they want to fish. Benjamin Orlove (1991) observes how villagers collectively manage *totora* reed production on the shores of Lake Titicaca. Regarding historical times, Pilar

Ortiz de Zevallos and Lía del Rio de Calmell (1978) report on saltwater lagoons near the coast, built and maintained by the communities of Coayllo, Chilca, and Calango, which were "owned" by the *curaca* of Mala. And Ana Maria Soldi (1982) describes how sunken gardens in the desert used low water tables to agricultural advantage. Further research will undoubtedly reveal the variety and magnitude of production zones in which resources are collectively managed and individually exploited in this way, both in the past and now.

However, not all detectable zonation phenomena are production zones. Some zones arise naturally out of the discontinuous way the environmental resources are distributed; and if humans exploit them in the absence of the social organizational features described above, they cannot really be called production zones. Furthermore, differential working of agricultural land, from more intensive to more extensive as distance from a market center increases, generates clear agricultural zones on a flat plain with uniform resource distribution without any communal or supra-household intervention, as Johann von Thünen (1826) showed many years ago. Esther Boserup's (1965: 85) schematic description of the process of intensification also implies the creation of different zones along an extensive/intensive diachronic axis. A decisive intervention by the participating units that are exploiting the resources is required in our definition of production zones. In the 1950s the *hacendados* of the agro-industrial part of the Cañete Valley were overusing pesticides, and this resulted in resistant strains of insects that were cotton-disease vectors, necessitating an integrated pest-control program. Each *hacienda* contributed a certain amount of money, which paid for construction of an experiment station designed to monitor insect activity. This station issued and enforced stringent rules on how and when cotton was to be planted and how it was to be sprayed (Boza Barducci 1972). I can talk of a production zone in this case since there was a supra-*hacienda* sphere of production that decisively intervened in certain aspects of the production process.

The existence of production zones as a form of production is not uniquely Andean. As Robert Rhoades and Stephen Thompson (1975), Stephen Brush (1976b), and David Guillet (1983) point out, many features of communal control of the productive process are also characteristic of villages in other mountain environments, such as the Alps and the Himalayas. Nor is the fact that villages communally manage resources uncommon elsewhere in the world. However, in all these cases the features in common reduce themselves to the village level, which has inherent structural limitations that expand multi-zonal agricultural production.

What *is* unique in the Andean production zone and village organization is that Andean social organization has been able to break through the limitations of village-based verticality. Villages in the Andes are organized in such a way as to include in their communal organization peoples and institutions from various and different *señoríos*—each with distinct interests and aims, yet capable of cooperating with one another on a day-to-day basis in the coordination, creation, and use of communally managed production zones. In this breakthrough in organization we find the dynamic, expansive, and transformational capacities of verticality that underlie the political economies of *señoríos* and the pre-Hispanic state. Careful study of this organizational capacity at the local level in historical times has been neglected, however, because of the initial enthusiasm leading anthropologists to search for the applicability of the verticality model in the Andes at all levels and throughout time.

My aim has been to show that some, but not all, of the very dynamic aspects of Andean social organization are still operative at the village level. Today we hear much about the low potential of highland agriculture and its inability to sustain development despite the fairly radical agrarian reform process that has taken place in the Andes. In Peru this process was not complete in the 1980s, since only the "top-down" phase had been implemented by then. But now that government-instituted cooperatives have failed and the land has truly reverted to the peasants, we will surely see progressively more and more actual control by the Andean people of their productive resources. Contrary to the opinion of Mario Vásquez, an agrarian reform official who once accused this kind of "Murrista" research of being "an exquisite flight into folkloric academicism," this chapter has shown that the search to understand how the Andean people organize production is of crucial importance.

Postscript

"Production Zones" (Mayer 1985) was my "coming-out" publication in English. In it I summarized the six years of postdoctoral research on ecological aspects of land use that César Fonseca and I had undertaken with generous funding from the Social Science Research Council in 1974 and additional support from the Smithsonian Institution (channeled through Betty Meggers and Clifford Evans, curators of South American anthropology). By that time Fonseca and I were established academics. We had support from our respective university departments in Lima and involved our students in field trips. We also had an opportunity to consult with both government and nongovernment organizations—in my case, the International Potato Center, which sponsored my study of land use in the Mantaro Valley (Mayer 1979). This study achieved worldwide circulation. The use of aerial photos and mapping techniques in the Cañete and Mantaro valleys greatly enhanced the acceptance of my findings. They were drafted by Fulbright Fellow Richard C. Shea. In 1983, when I became a faculty member in the department of anthropology at the University of Illinois, Craig Morris, Izumi Shimada, and Shozo Masuda invited me to participate in an interdisciplinary symposium (sponsored by the Wenner-Gren Foundation) that brought leading scholars together (one-third from the English-speaking world, one-third from the Andes, and one-third from Japan) to examine aspects of John Murra's ideas about the relationship between environment and the uniqueness of Andean civilizations. For this symposium, apart from ethnographic reporting, as I endeavored to find common themes, I focused on the dynamics of village collective action in managing natural resources. I still consider my symposium paper exciting and useful for future generations, since environmental issues in anthropology are now at the forefront of academic and activist concerns.

An extract of the paper was translated into French and included in Pierre Morlon's (1996) compendium, which eventually found its way back into Spanish when published in Peru. Another Spanish version was published in Lima, together with a paper by Marisol de la Cadena, as a pocketbook for students interested in development work in peasant communities (Mayer and De la Cadena 1989). Sophisticated techniques and technical training of geographers and agronomists have largely superseded any expertise I can bring to bear on land-use and landscape studies in the Andes. I happily refer readers to the oft-cited compendium by Morlon and to the work of Mario Tapia (1996) as showcases of the sophistication of the many scholars who now work on this topic.

Since "Production Zones" stressed how individual interests interact with collective action, it was able to make a strong case for how Andean Indigenous knowledge was maintained. The point was that this knowledge is democratically discussed, collectively applied, and capable of inducing dramatic changes. Production zones are consciously constructed objects that modify topographical features of the natural environment and, as such, embody collective knowledge. In the context of the 1980s this argument provided a powerful counterpoint against the prejudiced view that only outside (Western) technological intervention could introduce beneficial change. In those times I was called a *neo-indigenista*—a label I was rather proud of.

By the 1990s, however, this argument had become politicized, partly as a reaction to the phenomenon of globalization. A group of intellectuals with previous careers in the administration of agrarian reform (all of them my friends) began formulating an intransigent ideology of nativism with a strong rejection of Western neo-colonial interference dressed up as technical aid (they call it "occidentalism") that gives their discourse a vehemence and self-assurance characteristic of extremist ecological movements. Their writings are available in English (Apffel-Marglin 1998: xiv), and a statement of their aims is clear):

PRATEC [Proyecto Andino de Tecnologías Campesinas] is a small non governmental organization constituted by a core of technicians devoted to the animation of formative dynamics, to research and dissemination of the wisdom/knowledge of the Andean peoples. It is dedicated to Andean cultural affirmation expressing our own personal conviction as well as our culture's own excellence without any pretension other than contributing to the dynamics of cultural affirmation conducted by the Andean peasant communities themselves. The aim is to let Andean culture's own vigorous flow purge it from the distortions that colonization has caused in it so as to reestablish its wholeness.

In short, PRATEC seeks to fuse an Andean cosmology with a revitalization movement that has aspects of a program tinged with ethnic separatism. It seemed to me that my work was being used to back positions I cannot wholeheartedly support. PRATEC has become a Peruvian ideological version of Andeanism (Starn 1992).

In 1994 I debated with Eduardo Grillo, the founding member of PRATEC and leading ideologist in an open seminar in Arequipa, Peru (Mayer 1994: 510–517). In this debate I stressed that indeed it would be interesting to create and lead a mass movement to reinvigorate Andean agriculture, but that it would be unwise to associate it with withdrawal from national and international trends. I expressed surprise that the ideas of John Murra and his followers (myself included) had now become unquestionable ideology rather than research issues to prove or disprove. The members of PRATEC seemed to be more adept and vehement at bashing the Western scientific and development establishment than at producing better *chuño*. The seeming distance between Andean belief in harmony and conflict-riddled practice is puzzling, as in their writings there is no demonstration of how belief relates to practice nor are we given any understanding of how quotidian practice produces a sound ecological management of the landscape. On the other hand, I praised the efforts of PRATEC members to shore up Indigenous knowledge by providing a political forum for its debate, and I assured them that I support them in combating Western neo-colonialism.[7] I still think that it is important to renew Andean agriculture, but beyond ideology, it needs to be infused with a new research agenda, similar to the one that energized intellectual production two decades ago—an agenda that will inspire PRATEC's efforts at creating a new generation of organic intellectuals. (Ironically, much of the research that proved productive for PRATEC was conducted by foreign researchers with funding by Western institutions.) Eduardo Grillo ended up agreeing with me; and just two months before his death in 1995, he visited me in New Haven on a very cold, snowy day and we continued to converse amicably for many hours.

Notes

1. Subsequent studies in the Cañete Valley corroborated and amplified our initial findings. These include the work of French agronomists and social scientists working with Peruvian colleagues out of the Institut Français de Recherche Scientifique pour le Développement en Coopération (ORSTOM), the Instituto Francés de Estudios Andinos (IFEA), and the Universidad Nacional Agraria La Molina (UNALM). Among their accessible publications are the following: Morlon (1996), Eresue and Brougère (1988), Hevré (1987: 329–347), Wiegers et al. (1999), Brougère (1992), and Malpartida and Poupon (1987).

2. More recently, Zimmerer (1999: 135–165) has questioned the usefulness of the zone model in favor of a more flexible representation of the Andean landscape in terms of overlapping patchworks. Although I am in fundamental agreement with his finding that there is a high degree of overlap and patchiness in the process of Andean landscape formation, Zimmerer subordinates, perhaps correctly, the role of contemporary communal coordination in the creation of these varied Andean landscapes. My emphasis here is on the greater or lesser degree of inter-household coordination of agricultural and pastoral activities. A high degree of communal control may not necessarily account for greater uniformity or for a higher degree of patchiness of crop assemblages. As the ecological consequences of overlapping patchworks are different from those of uniform zones, Zimmerer's point is well taken, forcing me to relax the assertion made above, that production zones form bounded ecosystems permitting rigorous ecological study, even though uniform belts vertically arranged are visible in many narrow valleys with steep gradients under community (*comunidad campesina*) regimes. Zimmerer's article also contains a very useful summary of the major academic trends that have led, according to him, to an overemphasis of a zonal view of Andean landscape formations—formations that nonetheless resist ". . . the parsing tendencies of many modern scientific and cultural studies" (1999: 139).

3. The ten types of production zones comprise two types of rain-fed agriculture: sectorial fallow system and individual fallow rotation systems. Irrigation agriculture is subdivided into five open-field crop zones and three kinds of permanent orchards, distinguished on the basis of the dominant fruit crop growing in them (apple orchards, vineyards, and citrus groves).

4. Among arrangements that provide access to land even in the absence of direct ownership, Glave (1992: 191–214) describes an increasing trend toward sharecropping involving the landowning, labor-providing peasant, on the one hand, and a partner who supplies liquid capital, fertilizer, pesticide inputs, and technical know-how, on the other. The harvest is divided in equal shares.

5. Since the original publication of "Production Zones" (Mayer 1985), several interesting studies have been conducted on the sectorial fallow system, which exemplifies a commons in operation characterized by private appropriation of agricultural production with communal pasture in the same space. Morlon (1996) accomplishes a masterful summary, Orlove and Godoy (1986) published the first pan-Andean survey that went beyond individual case studies, and Campbell and Godoy (1986) compared the Andean version to medieval European examples. A comprehensive symposium on fallowing in the Andes was organized under the auspices of ORSTOM in Bolivia (Hervè, Genn, and Riviere 1994), focusing on

possible effects such as soil erosion and ecological degradation as well as on in-stitutional aspects of the management of common pasture lands. Kraft (1994 and 1995) compared two sectorial fallow systems, one in Peru and the other in Bo-livia, and examined the political processes involved in intensification, expansion, and reduction in years of fallow. Cotlear (1989), an economist, followed a strict Bosserupian interpretation that associates reduction in fallow with population growth and institutional change that removes the constraints against privatiza-tion; however, he provided no concrete evidence to support his view. Kervyn (1989), also an economist, used an interesting institutional economy model to demonstrate that the costs of privatization, such as those involved in the building of fences and walls and those involved in supervision, were too high to warrant full private management; this is why lower productivity makes communal arrangements with lower costs and lower yields more likely in more marginal zones. The point is that a well-organized community can make the costs of con-travening its rules and regulations very expensive indeed. Hervé (1987) and Wiegers et al. (1999) noted that in the Cañete the sectorial fallow system has be-come more extensive with less cultivation, longer fallow years, and even outright abandonment as emigration has reduced labor supply and agricultural intensifi-cation has taken place in other more productive zones in these communities.

6. Although small-scale locally managed irrigation systems on the drier west-ern slopes of the Andes are participatory and consensus based, it is important to note that they are also characterized by inequality in access to water and land. Guillet (1992: 46) assesses the water distribution system of Lari in the Colca Val-ley in Southern Peru as unequal, but adds: "What is anomalous, given these indi-cators of differentiation, is the lack of the perception by villagers of socio-eco-nomic inequality." The neighboring villages of Coporaque (studied by Treacy, 1994) and Cabanaconde (studied by Gelles, 1999) are similar to Lari in that they are characterized as gerontocratic systems that perpetuate differences in rank, privilege, and wealth (although poorer households are able to contest some of the rules and defend access to the means of their minimum subsistence). Trawick's study of the Cotahuasi Valley (1994) reveals the coexistence of highly egalitarian and nonegalitarian systems. The latter, however, breed conflict, resentment, and sometimes even violence. An example of a badly managed irrigation system is given by Seligmann and Bunker (1993) in the Department of Cusco, resulting in inefficient resource distribution, conflict, mismanagement, and the decay of the system. Hendriks (1988) describes the celebrated case of an existing canal built by landlords that was abandoned, under government orders, by local users who built a new one, which promptly collapsed; he also discusses the very slow reha-bilitation of yet a third canal in Mollepata, Cusco. The role of the Peruvian state intervention, and the conflicts and misunderstandings it creates, is a theme cov-ered by all the authors mentioned and further explored in a volume edited by Mitchell and Guillet (1993).

7. Although PRATEC is fiercely anti-Western, it is in alliance with Western "al-ternative" and postmodern critical movements. This, too, is an interesting aspect of globalization. Apffel-Marglin's (1998: 22) laudable effort at making available PRATEC's points of view in English includes in her introductory essay a discus-sion of my criticisms mentioned here, as well as some rather harsh comments about my "academic ivory tower" refusal to enter into a conversation with those

who advocate a postmodern, postcolonial-Western anti-Western-derived episte-
mology. My disagreements with Eduardo Grillo, however, are about something
totally different from the inability of Western science to recognize other forms of
knowing.

9

Land Tenure and
Communal Control in Laraos

This chapter follows up the previous one on production zones by focusing on one case study of communal control and land tenure in the community of Laraos. First, it shows how rules of use of land vary between different production zones and how these have been altered repeatedly over time, shifting from communal control to individual control depending on which power group controlled village politics. Next, it discusses the process of privatization of land that took place at the turn of the twentieth century, thereby addressing the issue of privatization of communal land currently being debated all over the world—an issue that is on the neo-liberal agenda.

This chapter expands on the issue of land tenure in production zones—an issue that was raised in a more general way in the previous chapter. It explains the characteristics of communal control over natural resources in the land-tenure system of one Andean community. My use of the term *land tenure* is the same as that in social anthropology, as defined in *Notes and Queries in Anthropology* (Royal Anthropological Institute 1954: 154): "Land tenure may be best understood in terms of the rights of persons and groups in land. The most fundamental of these are the right to use land in various ways, and the right to take a share of the produce of the land, either directly or as rent, without contributing labor. Other rights are: the right to transfer holdings, the right to alienate land (as in a sale or gift), [and] the right to grant rights of use to others. . . . " The foregoing definition differs from others, such as the one in *Funk and Wagnalls Standard College Dictionary* (1913): "the legal right to the possession, use, enjoyment and disposal of a thing." Instead of emphasizing the type of property, the latter definition centers on the act of possession or dominion.

Land tenure is a study of the rights and obligations that the owner has over the thing. The rights are socially recognized and legitimized in that the owner has the possibility to claim them against challenges by third parties. Land tenure thus refers to the bundle of rights and restrictions that various actors have over the use of land. I reject as typological simplification the European concepts of property (communal, feudal, private, etc.) precisely because these concepts presuppose the mutual exclusion of the items in the typology. By European definitions, property is either communal or private, excluding the possibility of combining the two. The use of the qualifier *semi-* (as in *semifeudal* or *semiprivate*) patently demonstrates the difficulties that researchers have in trying to force observed practices into one of the existing prearranged categories. When the concepts of tenure are distinguished from those of property, many confusions are cleared up because property is separated from control. Instead of blindly assuming that the person who has the property also has control, a study of tenure tries to establish who has control over what as a question of empirical investigation. Various possibilities open up: The one who has control also has the property (private property), or, as frequently happens in pre-capitalist, capitalist, and post-capitalist societies, control is partially separated from property. In any case, it must be remembered that in research the emphasis should be directed primarily to the question of control over the means of production, and only secondarily to the issue of property. In Marxist analysis, too, the crucial issue is the control over the means of production, not the label. By the same argument, the terms normally used in census material or bureaucratic reports that classify land-tenure regimes in categories such as "property," "leasehold," or "communal" are also rejected so that significant research about the social basis of these forms of land possession can be conducted. A final comment refers to the excessive emphasis that has been placed on the rights to dispose of the products from land in comparison to the scant attention given to the rights and obligations that concern the use of land, which are equally important in determining land-tenure patterns.

This chapter provides an ethnographic description of how land is used, how its use changes over time, who intervenes in the decisions concerning its use, and why they do so. It is based on observations of the agricultural practices of farmers and attempts to interpret their rationale: whether agricultural practices respond to botanical characteristics of the cultivated plants, climatic conditions, and quality of soils, on the one hand, or to communal rules that affect third parties or the whole community, on the other. A wealth of documentation made available by community members allowed me to reconstruct land use patterns in the past.

The theoretical thrust of this chapter is that agricultural practices and land tenure are intimately linked to each other. It follows Robert Netting (1976: 137), whose study of land tenure in the Swiss Alps demonstrated that "[t]he system of property rights in the peasant community will be directly related to the manner in which resources are exploited, the competition for their use, and the nature of the product produced—more specifically, land use by and large determines land tenure."

The Community

The community of Laraos in the Cañete River Basin, Province of Yauyos, is a *reducción de indios* from the sixteenth century[1] that has managed to keep its royally assigned territory intact throughout its checkered history. Its inhabitants have engaged in long and difficult judicial appeals, social pressures, and pitched battles from which they emerged victorious thanks to the political acumen of their leaders, who always knew how to adopt current national legislation to community interests. They have litigated against neighboring Huanca and Yauyos communities, against *haciendas* of *caciques,* and against private owners as well. They even disputed victoriously with the republican state. During the colonial period the communal possession of land was under legislation that protected *tierras de indios.*[2] In republican times, when such communal protection was abolished, the legal right to represent the community was transferred to the Municipal Council.[3] In 1937 Laraos was registered as a *comunidad de indígenas,*[4] to protect itself not so much from external threats to its integrity as from internal ones—that is, from certain groups interested in privatizing land.

The community of Laraos comprises a territory of 65,742 hectares, of which 96 percent is in the *puna* and useful only for pasturage. The remaining 4 percent is located in a narrow valley where the agricultural fields and the village are located.[5] There are three satellite villages (*anexos*), two in the *puna* and one near the main road that links Huancayo to Cañete in the areas of lowest altitude of the communal territory. The local villagers distinguish three natural life zones—*puna, quebrada,* and *bajillo*—that correspond nicely with the (1960) ecological classifications of Joseph Tosi, Jr.[6] In the agriculturally productive land, Laraoinos—since pre-Hispanic times—have created and maintained four production zones.[7] The *puna* constitutes a fifth production zone that is reserved exclusively for pasture of sheep, llamas, and alpacas. Note that this zone has always been the most lucrative for Laraoinos. Operative in each one of the five production zones is a different land-tenure system that regulates the rights and obligations to which a community member is entitled as he uses the different production zones.

The *Puna* and the Grazing *Estancias*

Since time immemorial the *puna* has been divided into smaller units called *canchas, estancias,* or *mudaderos* of approximately equal productivity, which the community has assigned to one *comunero* title holder in exclusive usufruct for himself, his family, and his heirs.[8] In exchange, at least since 1867, the community has had the right to charge a levy in sheep, money, or work obligations to finance expenditures in favor of community welfare, such as the collective payment of taxes, tithes, and the costs of territorial defense or public works to improve the village. As administrator of these lands, the community has always had the power to resolve conflicts between families on such matters as the boundaries of *estancias*, the rights of heirs, and so on. In addition, the community has had the power to remove usufruct rights from those families that disobeyed internal rules and regulations that the community made from time to time—such as the 1902 communal decision to remove usufruct rights from any *comunero* who did not have a minimum of twenty animals pasturing on an assigned *estancia*.[9]

Individual rights, which parallel communal ones, are concerned with usufruct rights, the right to administer the *estancia*, the right to exclude others from use of the assigned territory, and the right to cede partial-use rights to pasture by mutual agreement between the assigned use holder and his *wacchillero*.[10] Today some *estancieros* manage their lands through shepherds who have subsidiary rights to pasture some of their own animals in exchange for the obligation to take care of those of the owner. Other *estancieros* manage them directly. From time to time there have been discussions to promote regulations requiring exclusive direct management of communal *estancias*—regulations that were fiercely opposed by other interest groups in the community.

All these rights are transmittable to the heirs of the assigned usufructuary, who, when he receives the *estancia*, also assumes the obligations toward the community. There is an ambiguity in the regulations, in the sense that these rights are in theory partible among the heirs; at the same time, however, there is a partially enforced notion that *canchas* should not be subdivided but managed in common among the heirs who share in the inheritance. Various solutions have been worked out. In some cases, one member of the family assumes the role of *estanciero,* excluding other heirs. In others, the *estancia* is truly managed in common, with family members sharing the pasturing activities on a rotational basis (according to the number of sheep each one has). In still other cases, the *estancia* becomes an estate whose owners share in the profits of the operation, which is often managed by one relative and run by dependent herders.

I have data indicating that the community has proceeded to recover land that was illegally sublet to third parties (who were not community members). The community argued that these sublease agreements were "not right" and "abusive."[11] Alternatively, the community has the power to rent out *estancias;* or, with the same outcome, it can assign the revenue from such rentals to communal ends. The community can also donate or cede the revenue to institutions such as the church,[12] the communal ranch, or the school.[13] Today, individuals do not have the right to sell *estancias* to third parties, particularly noncommunity members. As we shall see, this has not always been the case.

The Agricultural Zones

As can be seen from Map 9.1 (drawn for me by the then-mayor of Laraos, who had worked as a topographer in the nearby mines), the agricultural zone is clearly subdivided into four distinct production zones: *aisha, mahuay, maizal,* and *huertas.*

Aisha

The highest zone is locally called *aisha.* It is characterized by rain-fed agriculture in which tubers (potato, *mashua, ocas, olluco,* and barley) predominate. The most common type of field in this zone is the "slope terrace" or *falderón* (see Figure 9.1). *Falderónes* are gradually shaped by the way they are plowed. All on steep slopes, they mold themselves to the local topography and the requirements of the plants to be grown on them.

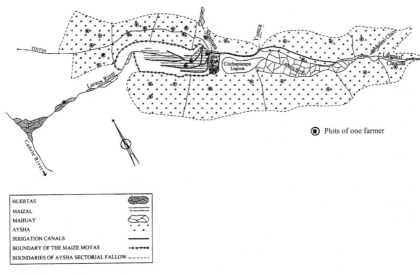

HUERTAS	
MAIZAL	
MAHUAY	
AYSHA	
IRRIGATION CANALS	
BOUNDARY OF THE MAIZE MOYAS	
BOUNDARIES OF AYSHA SECTORIAL FALLOW	

Map 9.1   Laraos

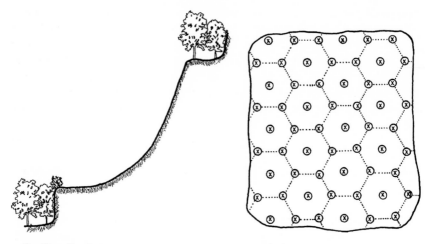

Profile of a slope terrace   Frontal view a slope terrace

FIGURE 9.1   Slope Terrace. Shown here are the profile of a slope terrace (left) and the frontal view of a slope terrace planted in tulpa style (right).

The terraces are cut from the slope at 15°–30° angles and have, in place of retaining walls, bushes and grasses that are allowed to grow on the bottom lip to contain downward erosion. Over time, by plowing deeper at the top, turning the sods downhill, and harvesting from the bottom up, farmers create a gently sloping field.

The *aisha* zone is cultivated in a sectorial fallow system; therefore, the community regulates the crop rotation and fallow of all fields. Each sector has its communal fence, called *moya*, maintained by all who will plant in it.[14] The community decisively intervenes in the productive process of this zone since it decides the sequence of sectors to be cultivated. It insists that every user plant the same crop within the *moya*. It also calls for the work party to repair the communal *moya* fence, thereby relieving individual farmers of the costs of fencing off each field. Physical damage to the slope terraces is avoided by prohibiting sheep and goats from pasturing on the *moyas* in fallow and permitting only the grazing of heifers, bullocks, donkeys, and horses.

The community also intervenes in the productive process by using its powers to permit free stubble grazing in the fallow *moyas*, by regulating the agricultural calendar, and by deciding on the opening and closing dates of plowing, sowing, and harvest seasons.[15] Individual freedoms are constrained by these scheduling decisions; yet they are also retained to some degree, given that farmers can decide on the exact dates of each activity according to their own labor resources, their calculations of climatic uncertainties, and the variety of cultivars available (whether rapid-maturing or slow-growing). At the household level, the organization of the calendar is quite complex. In any production zone, each crop within the communal framework may be planted "early," during the "main" planting, or "late" (Camino, Recharte, and Bidegaray 1981; Goland 1992; Franquemont 1988; Zimmerer 1988b: 81–110).[16] As Karl Zimmerer notes, production zones are primarily organized through the use of time as a scheduling principle rather than in terms of vertical space in the Paucartambo Valley, Cusco.

Another dimension of communal intervention is the court that resolves disputes between individual farmers, imposing fines and compensations for damages. In order to administer the zone, this court is empowered by the communal authorities to regulate use of the zone. The *mesero* serves as *cargo* for one year. He is supported by the village authorities, whose task is to watch over the crops growing in the sector and to punish or fine those who break communal regulations.[17]

Individual farmers, on the other hand, decide on the amount of land they will cultivate in a given season. As we saw in Chapter 4, they can choose the helpers with whom the various tasks will be completed and the method of transacting the labor exchange. They are also free to seek out the kinds of seed they will use, to choose the type of furrows that will be needed, and to decide how the harvest will be disposed of, once a basket full of potatoes is given to the *mesero* as a token of recognition for his efforts.

Mahuay

The next production zone, termed *mahuay*, is under irrigation and therefore permits a more intensive use of the land. In this zone a different kind of field is used, known as *potrero* ("paddock"). These fields are on the alluvial plains of the Laraos creek. They combine the construction techniques underlying slope terraces and proper terraces and utilize the natural slopes to form gently sloping paddocks interconnected with each other along S-shaped surfaces whose steep walls are often lined with stones to permit easy irrigation and cattle grazing. Each field has its own fence and its own free water source derived from the Laraos creek.

Land can be cultivated every year and all year round. The rotation decisions are no longer in community hands but in each farmer's. Those more interested in subsistence cultivate early-maturing potatoes in the first season; *ocas, mashuas,* and *ollucos* in the second season; and broad beans (*habas*) in the third. Then they can either repeat the cycle or plant alfalfa. Alfalfa, as fodder, remains for five to six years before the cycle is repeated, and its nitrogen-fixing properties allow for recuperation of fertility. Other *comuneros*, more interested in dairy production, plant more alfalfa at the expense of food crops. The whole upper Cañete Valley has seen an expansion of alfalfa production at the expense of maize and *mahuay* terraces—a phenomenon associated with the marketing of cheese to the Lima metropolitan market.[18]

In this production zone, communal decisions about land use are no longer operative. The community is not responsible for the maintenance of soil fertility, nor is it concerned about crop or animal theft. Each farmer has to validate his own rights to exclusive use, and that is why complex stone walls, fences, and other means of denying access (to other peoples' animals) are evident here. Since the community exercises little control, a greater diversity of crop assemblages, sequences, and forms of cultivation are evident as individual farmers make their own decisions. Inheritance is partible, and plots are bought and sold between community members; absentee ownership is not unknown, either.

Maizal

The next production zone is the *maizal,* which is located below the village and made up of irrigated terraces for the exclusive cultivation of maize. There are thousands of small terraces in this maize zone. The *moya* is like an enormous amphitheater, built in pre-Hispanic times but maintained and in production to this day. Though not so symmetrical or large as the famous terraces in Macchupicchu or Pisac, the *maizal* terraces are nevertheless impressive, exemplifying a majestic feat of engineering. When maize is growing on them, the view of the landscape is exceptionally beautiful. Terraces are built using unique construction techniques. First there is a back wall with deep stone foundations. Between this wall and the front wall (which is also the next terrace's foundation wall) different soil layers are placed. The lowest layer is gravel, which serves as a filter for water, followed by layers of clay. On top is the active productive soil, a mixture of humus, sands, and clays that is repeatedly and continuously worked and maintained. The top layer is carefully leveled in an effort to make the outer border a little bit higher to contain irrigation water. Each terrace has its own small canal that permits irrigation water to enter; it also has an exit to conduct the excess water to the next convenient terrace. The intricate network of tertiary canals is truly amazing, involving numerous underground conduits, bypasses, and small waterfalls. The terraces are generally quite small, never exceeding the maximum of 20 meters long by 4 meters wide (and only a few are that size). Certain retaining walls are 3 to 4 meters high, and in some places they curve outward in order to gain a few more centimeters of planting surface. Stirrup stepping stones allow farmers to climb from one terrace to the next. When a terrace wall collapses (a frequent occurrence), the owner has to reconstruct it, pressured by the lower

neighbor whose planting surface is covered with rubble. In order to reconstruct it, the owner uses a wire mesh to separate the stones from the soils
and then replaces the parts in the correct order. Larger stones are placed at
the bottom; smaller ones end up at the top. Note that the responsibility of
terrace maintenance is an individual matter, whereas canal, footpath, and
fence maintenance is a communal obligation. In this zone, maize has been
planted each year for hundreds of years.

Also note that maize has a high symbolic value in Laraos. Production is
purely for home use; the production cycle of maize marks the social and
ceremonial rhythms of the community. Maize is planted in conjunction
with family ceremonies; the canal-cleaning feast on May 15 emphasizes the
importance of maize; and great quantities of maize are consumed in festive
pachamancas ("earth ovens"). Echoing John Murra (1960), B. Varillas
Gallardo (1965: 98–103, 184–189), a local teacher and folklorist, notes
that, in Yauyos, maize was the most appreciated and prestigious product.
Maize production in Laraos is not considerable, in terms of either area
sown or yields, but enough is produced for home use and ceremonial purposes. My colleagues and I have found that, since 1900, the area under
maize cultivation has shrunk in the Cañete basin (Mayer and Fonseca
1979; Wiegers et. al 1990).

The *maizal* zone consists of the maize *moya* and its secure communal
fence; an irrigation system that includes a natural spring, the intake, the
main canal, and a reservoir; secondary and tertiary canals; and access and
exit ditches for each one of the thousands of tiny terraces (see Map 9.1 and
Photo 9.1). Today each terrace receives water in an equitable system of distribution, by which the terrace farthest from the reservoir receives water
first in compensation for its inherent disadvantage, proceeding from terrace to terrace in strict order to the closest one along the canal; then water
passes along the second canal and so on, until all the terraces have been irrigated and the cycle can start again. The community controls the distribution of water and, through these rules, also controls land use. It is nearly
impossible to grow any crop other than maize with the present system of
water allocation, and nearly impossible for any cultivator to alter the
planting or harvest dates since these depend on how and when he or she receives water. If anyone wanted to change the crops or the way they are
grown in the *maizal*, that person would have to change the rules that govern irrigation in this production zone. These rules are less strictly enforced
in areas close to the village, which forms the upper boundary of the maize
zone. Here surplus water sometimes runs along the canals and people plant
other crops, notably potatoes. On some of the terraces, owners have
planted eucalyptus trees (a forbidden practice, according to informants).
Fava beans are intercropped with maize on a regular basis, since these
comprise the most suitable cap (*tapa*) for filling out areas where maize
seeds have not sprouted properly. Parts of the maize zone are no longer

Photo 9.1 *Laraos maize terraces. (Photo taken by Enrique Mayer.)*

reached by irrigation water due to canal decay and the building of a road that destroyed the irrigation system. In 1974, Laraoinos were beginning to plant potatoes in *aisha* style in these areas on a limited basis.

Communal control over water conditions the land tenure in this zone. Just as there is a *mesero* for the *aisha* zone, the irrigation system has an institutionalized authority that enforces communal decisions, using as its most stringent punishment the threat to cut off an offender's access to water. In exchange for rights to water, the community requires work contributions to the maintenance or expansion of the irrigation system, participation in the administrative system of water distribution, involvement in the *fiesta* that affirms the bonds of community solidarity, and financing of the necessary ritual and social expenses. Today the authority system overseeing the hydraulic regime is the most hierarchical of all those associated with production zones. The obligation to pass through one of the *cargos* is a *sine qua non* requirement in exchange for access to water and community membership. Also, as in the *aisha* zone, the community delegates to the irrigation authorities the power to grant stubble grazing rights, which they sell to cattle owners for a fixed low fee of approximately US$.20 per animal (equivalent to 20 *soles* in 1974) when the maize harvest has concluded. The owner of the maize crop is allowed to pick only the cobs, since the stalks become a communal resource that benefit everybody's cattle as well as the community coffers. Because maize stalks become available when other grass is scarce at the onset of the dry season, communal authorities are under pressure to open up the *maizal* sooner rather than later; thus the community also has control over the agricultural calendar, since after the *maizal* has been officially declared open for grazing, the community is no longer responsible for crop damage incurred by farmers who were late in harvesting.

Huertas

The last zone is located in the *bajillo* and consists of orchards or *huertas*. These orchards have a mixed aspect and look to Western eyes like small farms. In the appropriate place a house is constructed with a corral for animals. Each adjoining field is carefully enclosed with adobe and stone walls. Overall, there are fields with annual crops, paddocks with alfalfa, and fruit orchards. Kitchen gardens are also cultivated with seedlings for fruit trees, little-known tubers such as *llacón* and *achira* (which regenerate annually), and many herbs. Some *huerats* are inhabited temporarily, but in the majority of cases a member of the family is there on a rotating or permanent basis. In communities lower down in the Cañete basin, these orchards have become the principal cash crop, with apples, citrus, and vineyards as the principal crops (Mayer and Fonseca 1979; Eresue 1988). The community of Laraos does not control the irrigation system; rather, each orchard holder digs his own ditches from the nearby rivers and creeks. Restrictive rules of use emerged only when the area became more densely populated and the local orchard owners along a shared canal had to reach mutually acceptable agreements over using resources in such a way as to avoid causing damage to their neighbors.

Today the property of orchards is completely private in every sense. They were acquired by individuals through formal written requests to the community authorities in which they claimed need for land and demonstrated the performance of invaluable services to the community. In 1900 these lands were called *camachicos* because the beneficiaries claimed to have performed the service of *camachico*.[19] Once the land had been assigned and the owner proceeded to clear it, he acquired all the rights over it as well as complete autonomy in decisions concerning what was to be planted. The only condition was to be a *comunero*. It is not surprising that the most permanent crops, such as alfalfa and fruit trees, are grown on these lands. The reason for the absence of communal controls in this zone is that it is a zone of recent colonization. Until the turn of the century, the area was of little interest to the *comuneros*. I found in this zone the greatest number of plots belonging to outsiders; they were bought from the original colonizers. In other communities of the Cañete Valley, the authorities frequently leased this zone to outsiders so that they could use the monetary rents for community purposes. In the context of the 1970s agrarian reform, such communities were trying to recover the lands by both legal and violent means.

Individual Rights

Regarding individual rights, which go beyond the particular use-rights in the four zones, each family can transmit its use-rights to other parties through inheritance or sale. Each family is also permitted to temporarily cede use-rights of plots of land to third parties through loans, rental agreements, sharecropping arrangements, or the newest form (a favorite among migrant *comuneros*), which involves leaving plots "under the care" of a relative. Emigration from Laraos is considerable. It has a significant impact on the social structure of the village, on the rights that migrants retain to land, and on the work obligations in communal *faenas* (Brougère 1992).

Rights to sell land, however, are restricted by the community. When family members decide to sell a plot, they first have to offer it to close relatives. If no interested buyers can be found, they can offer it to relatives by marriage or to any nonrelated Laraoino. I have seen deeds of sale involving potential heirs of the land—especially sons-in-law—who agree in writing to the act of alienation and renounce any future claim on the land. I quote from one in translation: "Present were for the party of the sellers, Doña X together with her sons in law, and for the part of the buyers, Don Y, ... I sell this land together with my sons-in-law and the executor of my will, and my descendants will not place any obstacle over this piece of land. ... " There is a certain amount of restriction against the sale of land to outsiders. What generally prevails (though more in spirit than in practice) is the notion that the outsider should be married to a community member, settle permanently in the village, and assume the responsibilities of being a community member before such a sale is approved. An intermediate category of *comunero* (a sort of second-class citizen) is the "son-in-law of the village"— an outsider who marries into the village, indicating that his access to land is more difficult and less automatic than that of a person born in the village.

Land is much more under communal control from the standpoint of rights and obligations concerning its use than from the standpoint of rights and obligations concerning transmission of these rights to third parties. And as I have shown (Mayer 1977a), the rules of use vary by production zones, restricting or giving greater individual freedom to make independent decisions zone by zone. A single land-tenure system does not exist for the whole community. Rather, community land tenure needs to be understood as a differentiated bundle of coordinated rights and obligations concerning the rules and regulations that are implemented in each production zone. It follows that domination over land tenure cannot be exercised solely by the individual who has more land than others or who attempts to monopolize it. Rather, control over land can be exercised only by the group that is capable of capturing the mechanisms of power in community organization and then, once in power, imposing modifications in the rules of land use in accordance with its interests. Hence the degree of communalization—or privatization—of land depends very much on who is in power in the community and on how centralized this power is. As Murra (1975: 59–116) has shown in his work on "verticality," the push toward control of a "maximum" number of ecological niches is in all senses a political control. "Vertical" organization should be understood as an attempt to centralize in the hands of a single political entity the control of the rules of use of as many diverse production zones as possible. In this analysis we can see that the community today effectively controls three of the five vertically located production zones, whereas two zones have become independent from community control. And as noted in Chapter 8, the limits of how many production zones can come under vertical control depend on the political limitations of the controlling group. The more the administrative capacities of the controlling group expand, the greater the number of zones that will be incorporated under this centralized control.

Diachronic Variation

The foregoing discussion indicates that land tenure varies spatially according to the uses to which land is put. Now I want to demonstrate that land-tenure rules also vary over time, depending on who is in power. I will illustrate this process with a historical reconstruction of land tenure from 1900 to the present, relating it to the power struggles in the community.

We can assume that, before 1900, each production zone had its own rules associated with the production practices of different crops and the authority system in charge of administering them. The introduction in the sixteenth century of European crops such as wheat and barley and their incorporation into the tuber sectorial fallow system must have altered pre-Hispanic rules and regulations, as did the need to coordinate stubble and fallow grazing rights of the newly introduced domesticated ruminants (Gade 1967). By 1900 the great majority of Laraos families had access to each agricultural production zone, although the grazing *estancias* were in the hands of a smaller number of privileged families. The unit by which these pastures was measured is the *mudadero* (although I am unable to say what area this covered). In 1901 there were seventeen named persons with two *mudaderos*, fifteen with three, three with four, and thirteen with only one. The political instability that resulted from the Chilean war[20] (1876–1879) and persisted until the 1890s helped to create an opportunity for rich Laraoinos to develop contacts with the world beyond the community. Immigrants who had lived in Lima and other regional centers began to come back to the villages.

In Laraos the process of capturing local power was intimately linked to the developments surrounding the creation of a school in the village, and this, in turn, was financed by the economic boom that took place in the *puna*. Around the year 1900, Juan Castillo, son of a Laraoino whose mother was from a neighboring village called Alis, returned to Laraos. Castillo attended school in Lima and became an accountant. He had traveled to Chile, Argentina, and Colombia acquiring important experiences that he now was determined to introduce to Laraos by becoming the village's schoolteacher. The school dates from the year 1828, judging from the first levy imposed to run it, but there is little evidence that it really began to operate until the turn of the century. The first teachers were brought in from Huancayo, and they received subsistence goods, firewood, housing, horses for transportation, and a small monetary salary. The second school teacher was Juan Castillo, and from 1915 on, the teachers were Laraoinos. Castillo trained a whole generation of children of the wealthier villagers, teaching them Spanish, reading, writing, and arithmetic. As important as his teaching was his ideological work. He founded a voluntary association called the *Unión Fraternal Progreso* ("Progressive Fraternal Brotherhood") which attracted a group of people who called themselves *Libre Pensadores* ("Free Thinkers"). The ideology of this movement was fiercely anticlerical, and its members led a fight against tithes, successfully expropriating lands allotted to religious sodalities known as *cofradías* and to the church.[21]

The members of this movement were against tradition in any of its forms, they opposed the use of Quechua, and they despised the *varayoq* system and the powers of the elders in the community. In 1901, in an act meant to humiliate, Juan Castillo broke the staff of authority of the *alcalde mayor* and banished the *fiestas* associated with it. In the municipal records, the latter are described as "antiquated customs with food gorging, drunkenness and repugnant dances." In their place, Juan Castillo and his group proposed that all power be concentrated in the district's municipality, organized democratically following the modern rules and regulations sanctioned by national laws, assemblies, written *actas*, memorandums, parliamentary rules of order, and so on. They also pushed for privatization of land, since property was considered a symbol of Peruvian citizenship; indeed, it was believed that private property would create the conditions of progress for every citizen and also for the development of the whole community.

This movement also pushed for education, and succeeded in establishing the best school in the region. By 1910 the school had a physics and chemistry laboratory and a school library that included English and German texts. The high quality of the education imparted by the Laraos school is well remembered today. It surpassed many schools in provincial towns and rivaled those of department capitals. When Laraos became district capital, it was *cabecera* of several surrounding villages. Laraos ruled those villages with an iron hand. From a *Libro de Actas* of a three-year period between 1891 and 1899, one can see that the Municipal Council frequently discussed educational matters such as salaries of teachers, financing of school expenses, and the prohibition of traditional fiestas.

The teachers formed an association for the development of the province and started their own magazine to which each contributed a monograph of their community. They sponsored literary events and invited Julio C. Tello, founder of Peruvian archaeology, leading *indigenista,* and a native Huarochiriano (from the neighboring province), to visit the ancient archaeological sites and lecture them on "progress." Several books written by local intellectuals such as Brígido Varillas, Nonato Beltrán, and Ezequiel Beltrán were published; these can still be found in the villages. Increased literacy also produced the wealth of documentation that has made this study possible. Laraoinos say that during this period their district was the Athens of Yauyos.

School expenses were financed by both regular and special levies exacted from the users of *puna estancias.* The legal basis of this "school tax" was the fact that the pasture lands were the property of the Municipal Council of Laraos; thus a rent could be extracted from its users. The decision taken on the first of January 1900 is a landmark one in the history of Laraos, since in that year all the users of pasture lands were registered, ensuring each user continued possession for five years as long as the regular levy was paid. In exchange, the agreement reads, the municipality would "rectify all the boundaries of each *estancia* to insure possession of the pastures to the interested parties, and to indicate rights of possession to each user in conformity with the written titles issued accordingly." (Source: *Acuerdo comunal,* registered in the *Libro de Ventas de enero* [1891–1910] in the Laraos communal archive.) These taxes soon became a community fund and a source of wealth for the original *estancieros.*[22] Juan Castillo's best students were also leading members of the *Libre Pensadores,* sons of the original *estancia* owners who continued their education in Lima and Huancayo and became leaders of the movement in all of Yauyos, where, as teachers in village schools, they carried through similar reforms in all the communities of the province. Juan Castillo retired to Lima. Later he moved to Buenos Aires and is said to have become a millionaire. From there he maintained occasional contact with his followers and advised them on political matters.

Liberal reforms continued to transform the region, but the original altruism began to dissipate. The Free Thinkers had defeated the traditional powers, destroyed the *varayoq* system, disapproved of the associated system of fiestas, and isolated the church hierarchy. They now controlled power through the municipality and the school. From these positions they proceeded to modify the rules in the production zones, giving individuals much more freedom about agricultural decisions (in line with the liberal notion of private property) and encouraging production for regional export. The strongest impact was felt in the modification of the rules governing access to the *puna* and the *mahuay* zone, in the modification of the rules governing water distribution, and in the colonization of the *bajillo*.

Once paper titles had been distributed to the users of the *puna estancias*, the possibility of buying and selling them arose for the first time. Over a period of thirty years, a number of *estancias* were consolidated in the hands of a few owners who began to form real *haciendas* within the confines of a still fiercely defended and respected community territory; yet these new "*hacendados*" never lost their status as community members. Quite the contrary, they were the staunchest leaders in the municipality and the school, and they preached progress and the values of individual improvement. A similar process has been documented by Carlos Samaniego (1978) in his study of the historical evolution of the communities in the Mantaro Valley. The *puna estancias* became independent private properties, often in the hands of *caciques*, who appropriated communal lands for themselves. Samaniego characterizes this period of the expansion of *puna* sheep grazing as one of "Kulak" differentiation. Some Laraos people also retrospectively refer to the *Libre Pensadores* as the "Laraos aristocracy," who intermarried in order to maintain the "purity of their blood." Visitors to Laraos in the early 1950s remarked on the refined habits and excellent hospitality with which they were received by these aristocrats (José Matos Mar: personal communication).

In the sectorial fallow system, the plots no longer reverted to community control once they entered the period of fallow, and the annual distribution of plots in each new sector was abolished. Today each family keeps residual rights over their plots during the fallow period, going back to their own when the new cropping cycle begins.

In the early maturing potato *mahuay* zone, natural conditions to expand alfalfa cultivation and increase dairy production were favorable. A revealing document, dated 1928, indicates that on the important first-of-January meeting of that year,

> [t]he mayor made a speech in which he stressed that as the economic aspects were most important in achieving pecuniary progress and with more reason for the improvement of collective life, it was important for younger villagers to acquire occupations or professions, and to foment with more effort what they have, and in general to launch themselves on any kind of enterprise where perhaps in the future they can count on a considerable capital; and with this purpose in mind, each citizen came up to voluntarily announce the major occupation in addition to the domestic tasks [subsistence agriculture]. Within these promises, the preparation of alfalfa fields for raising dairy cattle is included. Any citizen who fails to keep with his promise, will be sanctioned by a public vote of disapproval.

The citizens then signed statements outlining their intentions to incorporate themselves into the market economy. One example: "I promise to prepare a small alfalfa paddock in Lusama. . . . (signature)." Ten of the fourteen statements contained promises to plant alfalfa, and one stated the citizen's intention to improve the stock of his cattle. (Source: *Libro del Concejo de Laraos* [1908–1932], in the Laraos communal archive.)

In order for the expansion of alfala cultivation to take place, however, it was necessary to concentrate the many small plots throughout the zone into one larger field suitable for paddock-like grazing. When alfalfa cultivation was introduced in this zone, it suffered from dis-economies of scale when compared with the way potato cultivation used to be carried out in many dispersed little fields in this production zone. Accordingly, the village leaders organized a program of plot consolidation,[23] regrouping the plots into larger ones and compensating the losers with money. It seems that there were protests by people whose access rights to the production zone were being trampled. A communal assembly was necessary to quiet down opposition. The terms of the agreement, duly recorded in 1918, eloquently demonstrate how political power succeeds in changing the rules of use in a production zone:

> In the village of Laraos on the first day of January of 1918 with all the citizens assembled . . . and in consideration:
>
> 1. That the world conflagration has brought as a consequence the rise in prices of subsistence goods.
> 2. That one of the ways to counteract the effects of this rise in prices consists of increasing and improving our agriculture industry which, together with cattle raising, are the only ones that provide the inhabitants of this village with the means of livelihood. Because of this, it should merit the preferred attention of the authorities and citizens of this village.
> 3. That in order to achieve this purpose it is necessary to remove certain obstacles such as the lack of irrigation, the extreme subdivision of the properties; and
> 4. That this extreme subdivision of plots makes it difficult to obtain legal property titles which guarantee the individual right to cover a person from any emergency [i.e., to mortgage it].
>
> It is decided to:
>
> 1. Divide in proportional lots to the number of families the plots of Pirhuapaqui. . . . [There are 15 place names].
> 2. Each plot will be assessed for its monetary value by experts who will be named *ad-hoc* so that those who had plots of more or less value than the lot they will be receiving, will be compensated for the deficit, or pay for the difference.

3. That the existing properties of the citizens will be assessed by another commission in order to be able to carry out the previous agreement.

4. Within a month of this date, the heads of families, wards of minors, etc. will be registered in a special ledger and the results of this list shall be published so that those who have been omitted or believe themselves with rights can present their respective claims.

5. Each new plot will be assigned in the place where the candidate previously had the largest amount of land.

6. To arrive at the just price, the unit of measurement shall be the square meter, and the value assessment will take into account the quality of the soils and its location [slope].

7. In order to facilitate the division of the lands, all paths and irrigation canals will be laid out before the distribution.

The integration of plots did not take place in such a neat or honest way as the paper agreements may lead us to think. Rather, it resulted in a concentration of land among the wealthier families. But once the process of crop changes and modification of land tenure got under way, the opposing parties had no recourse other than to participate in the changes, since it would have been impossible to maintain the old agricultural regime in some plots surrounded by the new ones. Those who did not have enough land sold out to the richer ones, and resisters' fields were gradually surrounded by very hungry cows and "negligent" herders, until they had to give up.

Ten years earlier, the community had decided to expand the irrigation system of that zone by constructing a new irrigation canal that would enlarge the zone, increase the volume of water, and improve irrigation necessary for alfalfa cultivation (which, on average, requires water every two weeks). The project met with many difficulties: opposition and sabotage as well as technical problems, accidents, and general opposition by villagers who convinced themselves that the mountain gods had become angry and that, were they to persist, their anger would result in worse disasters. This irrigation canal was nevertheless part of a plan to enlarge the area of the production zone to its highest possible limits (Punto Molino Chico on Map 9.1). By 1974 the project was finished.

Even water was privatized by the Free Thinkers. In 1905 Pedro A. Tupiño, in charge of inspecting the municipalities and ensuring compliance with the new national law governing water distribution, protested energetically in his report:

In Laraos . . . the water is distributed according to the order of proprietors, and it is they who decide on its distribution under the presidency of the inspector or alderman of the irrigation system. Therefore, there is almost no order in its distribution. For the future, I have recommended a more ordered process and I have named water distributors.

The Free Thinkers also started the colonization of the *bajillo,* pushing for the creation of the annex hamlet of Tintín, which had previously been one of the sectors of the sectorial fallow system under *aisha.* They distributed among themselves the readily cultivable lands and assigned new plots to those who requested them.

The downfall of the *Libre Pensadores* in the late 1920s arose from internal dissension. The group split into two factions, the *Libre Pensadores* and the *Quinta Internacional* ("Fifth International"). The latter eventually took up the ideology of the *Indigenista* movement[24] and pushed for a return to communal land tenure—in other words, for a return to certain aspects of the rules of land use that the Free Thinkers had abolished. This group succeeded in having Laraos inscribed as a *Comunidad Indígena,* creating at least another legal barrier against the increasing trends of land privatization within its boundaries.

By this time, exploitation of the Yaurcocha mine (owned by an American company, the Cerro de Pasco Corporation) had begun. The best workers and employees, given their excellent education, were Laraoinos. An advantage was that the mine was only a three-hour walk from the village, literally on the other side of the mountain. Many Laraoinos worked in the mine and, from that perspective, began to view the agricultural fields and the pasture lands of their community in a way different from that of their liberal teachers. They became very critical of the process of land concentration that the Free Thinkers had been bringing about to their own personal benefit. By 1957 the opposition was ready to take action.

The miners captured power, this time utilizing the authority structure provided by the *Comunidad de Indígenas* as their base. A miner was elected to become *personero* of the community. He initiated a long, complex, and bitter lawsuit against some of the heirs of the Free Thinkers, who, in the most blatant way, had created *haciendas* within community territory. The leaders of the Fifth International wanted the sales of *estancias,* with which these large units had come into existence, to be declared void. They could not ask to have the lands expropriated, since it was impossible to argue that these people were not *comuneros.* Litigation reached Peru's Supreme Court, and the miner's group won the case, recovering some of the portions of the original *estancias* that were first privatized in 1900. In 1965 a communal cooperative with ninety members was created on two important *estancias.* By the time I was doing my fieldwork, other groups in Laraos had come to feel that only the miners were benefiting from this cooperative—not the whole community. The miners denied this charge, saying that anyone could have participated in the cooperative when inscriptions were opened by contributing a quota of sheep. In 1974 the cooperative was not a real money-making proposition. The community also achieved a partial victory in the sense that other sales between original *estancieros* were declared void, even though present owners were allowed to continue using them until they died.

The *estancieros* tried to defend themselves by showing the original titles of 1900 (although the community countered by insisting that legally they were rental agreements). The Free Thinkers also incited the two herder *anexos* of Lanca and Langayco to secede from Laraos to become two new autonomous communities; and then, the Free Thinkers made sure that their vast private holdings would be respected within the boundaries of the new communities.

The government recognized the community of Lanca but later reversed itself when the representative of Laraos protested, arguing that the government could recognize existing communities but not create them. The government's retraction was based on the view that "the recognition of the jural rights of a community is a function of the ethnic group that occupies a given territory which is the source of its livelihood and which they use in common. . . . " (Source: titles of Laraos in *Archivo Nacional.*) The conflict between Lanca and Langayco against Laraos is still unresolved, especially concerning the possession and use of these newly recovered tracts of pasture land. In 1984, one person died and six people were injured in a violent confrontation between Langayco and Laraos. At issue now are the rights of herding families (previously dispossessed and subservient to the large landowners) who want greater access to land, whereas Laraos wants to retain control over the *puna anexos*.

Once the Free Thinkers had been partially defeated, the miners who had not abandoned their interests in agriculture and sheep raising reinstituted some of the communal rules in the various production zones. The new leaders insisted, though not entirely consistently, that the pastures be given to individuals in usufruct and not in property.[25] The system of *moyas* in the *aisha* zone was restored, even though the annual distribution of land in them was not reinstituted. In addition, water distribution in the maize zone was recommunalized. Today the terraces are irrigated by turns; in the past, it was the owners who took turns. The *fiesta* of the canal cleaning is preferentially organized by the members of the *Centro Social Yauricocha*, an association of Laraos miners that levies one days' wages per month from each member and thus has become the community's most secure source of financial support. The Municipal Council has lost all control over land.

In 1975 the community was firmly in the hands of the miner group, whereas the Municipal Council still responded to the interests of the sons of *comuneros* who lived in Lima and were descended from the original Free Thinkers. Both absentee groups watched each other jealously and tried to keep their interests represented in both community and municipal organizations. In this way they attempted to control land tenure from a distance, utilizing the local population as their shock troops.

The agrarian reform of 1970 threatened both power groups without creating a local one to counter them. The Lima migrants were threatened with expropriation of their numerous sheep and vast pastures because they were absentees—a condition not allowed by the Agrarian Reform Law. The miners, meanwhile, were also threatened with expulsion from the community, since the application of the *Estatuto de Comunidades* meant that one could not be a *comunero* and a worker in the recently nationalized mine of the Cerro de Pasco at the same time. At the time of my fieldwork, the *comuneros* had successfully created a distinction between "full-time" *comunero* and "passive" *comunero* that allowed miner participation in community affairs; but this was a clear act of peasant resistance, which the government had to reluctantly accept. In any case it is ironic that those who had fought so hard to preserve the notion of community ended up, by 1974, under government threat of exclusion from participating in it. Note, as an aside, that none of these threats really worked out. By 1986 the government had backed down from excluding migrants in community participation. The big landlords were insisting that their heirs be recognized with rights to pasture and then were dying out one by one. The prospects of a future in mining, given that the state corporations were in crisis and being sold off to foreign investors, were no longer so golden for the Laraoinos. In a last visit to Laraos in 1984, I was given to understand that the *puna* areas of Yauyos were under threat by Shining Path—so much so that I was told very little about the situation. I did notice, however, that the community had organized *rondas* ("self-defense groups").

Old Liberalism

From independence to the 1900s, Laraos as a village—and with it quite a large segment of the region—took a historical course different from that of other parts of Peru. For example, in terms of the legislation affecting land tenure, instead of distributing land titles as Laraos leaders were supposed to do, they maintained the notion of *común* and registered their titles as a corporate property. And instead of assigning land to the government in support of schooling, they demanded "voluntary" contributions from renters of their communal property.

Liberal laws were enacted to liberate Indians from the fetters of communal property. As a sign of the citizenship to which they were elevated in the new nation, property holding was considered to be an emancipating act. The right to buy and sell land, to borrow against it, and to mortgage it went along with this legislation. The people of Laraos found a way around it by taking on the full rights of citizenship while at the same time maintaining the advantages of keeping their lands under the communal property regime.

An interesting question is why Laraoinos took so long to realize the advantages of the legal mechanisms established nearly sixty years before. The time-lag explanation is not very useful in this case. According to this explanation, it would take some time for the idea to filter down to the village level. However, Laraoinos actively participated in the independence movement and thus knew about and supported the policies of the new republic. The pro-independence guerrillas of Yauyos harassed Viceroy La Serna as he retreated from Lima into the sierra as early as 1821. On July 29, 1821, guerrilla leader José María Palomo had destroyed the bridge over the Cañete River and harassed royalist troops as they climbed the narrow mountain gorges to Laraos. In revenge the village was sacked. Patriotic *comuneros* from the region, as well as village priests, including Don Nicolás de la Piedra from Laraos, had already declared themselves for the republican cause on November 12, 1820, under the leadership of Juan Evangelista Vivas, an *estanciero* native of Laraos.[26] Bolivar's private property decree of 1824 and La Mar's of 1828 (see Note 13) were known to Laraoinos at the time they were issued and were carefully copied into their *Libros de Actas*. A conscious decision must have been made by the village leaders to preserve their communal integrity by assigning lands to the municipality and circumventing laws issued by generals whose cause they supported.

It is also evident that much litigation was pursued against other collectivities, and perhaps this is what kept the notion of community alive in Laraos.[27] Despite these protective measures, however, *hacienda* encroachment onto *puna* lands did take place in the region. Laraos's borders in the *puna* are shared with *haciendas* notorious for their expansionist tendencies, including the devious ways in which the landowners persuaded other communities in the region to sell them land as well as the legal tactics used by the landowners' lawyers to expand their dominions. Neighboring Huancachi, Tomas, Vilca, Huancaya, and Tanta all lost lands to *hacienda* expansion in the period from 1820 to 1940. However, these losses were more often than not "legal" sales by community authorities "legally" empowered to carry them out. Some sort of approval by the villagers must have been given. Current versions of this history have it that their leaders were corrupted and persuaded to sign away the land by agents of the *hacendados* in drunken orgies. Although the reason to maintain communal property may have been to protect themselves from *hacienda* encroachment, for many communities this strategy did not work, particularly when, after 1900, these *haciendas* became modern corporations such as the Sociedad Ganadera del Centro or the extensive División Ganadera of the Cerro de Pasco Corporation. In other cases, individual *estancieros*—empowered by their land titles—sold their property to these expanding corporations (Martinez Alier 1973, 1977; Mallon 1983; Smith 1989; Smith and Pedro Cano 1978).

In Laraos, however, the threat to community integrity came from inside the village itself, when liberal ideology in the hands of the Free Thinkers really took hold. If the spirit of the documents is true to what was going on, liberal notions of private property began to fire the imagination of leaders only when the possibility of selling mutton and wool became a real, lucrative option. We thus have to look at the expansion of the market and its timing in the region to find an explanation of the time lag.

Railroad construction in the Central Highlands began to pay off by the 1880s and 1890s when it reached La Oroya, a nodal point where, during the same decade, ore processing and smelting operations were built. The growth of an enclave urban meat market provided a stimulus to expand *puna* sheep herding operations, to provide llama trains for transportation, and to sell wool to an expanding export trade as well as a growing national textile industry.[28] It is not surprising to see the processes of privatization and land concentration, as well as the growth of expanded *hacienda*-like *estancias* within the *punas* of Laraos and neighboring communities, during this particular period and not before.

The liberal reforms did have an impact in the highland peasant communities once the growth of the market made them congruent with the expansion of economic possibilities. Contrary to the textbook argument that liberalism provoked the expropriation of Indians from their lands, in this case—and many others—the alienation took place within the community itself, enriching a group of privileged community members. However, in many other parts of the Peruvian highlands, particularly the southern regions, the liberal reforms heralded an unprecedented expansion of *hacienda* growth at the expense of Indian communities; it also led to a massive series of uprisings and rebellions that must have influenced the reversal of legislation concerning private Indian property (Jacobsen 1993).

There is also a time lag of sixteen years between the enactment of the laws reinstituting communal property for *comunidades indígenas* in 1920 and the moment that some Laraoinos felt it necessary to take advantage of these laws in 1936. Part of the answer is that the government department empowered to implement it, the *Sección de Asuntos Indígenas*, was slow to get organized. However, the internal conditions described above provide a sufficient explanation. A new generation with a new source of wealth from wages in mining overthrew the old power elite and used the legislation to legitimize itself and its actions.

What is more difficult to understand is why the arch-liberal government of Augusto B. Leguia would have been moved to enact such anti-liberal legislation. Historian Frederick B. Pike (1967: 221–222) notes that much of *indigenísmo* of that period was a modish pose to which Leguía himself was addicted. The *Sección de Asuntos Indígenas*, under the able leadership of Hildebrando Castro Pozo, was quickly dismantled and Castro Pozo sent into exile. I think that this legislation was , in part, a measure to sweeten the pill of the labor draft introduced in Peru as the *Ley de Conscripción Vial*,[29] which forced Indians to work on road construction while, ostensibly, the rest of the nation paid a small monetary fee. For the Indian communities this law was disastrous. That some communities did manage to benefit from the pro-Indian legislation and gain some protection from *ha-*

cienda encroachment is largely due to private groups such as the *Aso-ciación Pro Indígena* led by Pedro Zulén and Dora Mayer,[30] who provided legal aid to these groups. That these measures did not stop *hacienda* expansion is also well documented. They did, however, slow it down. They also provided communities with some paltry mechanisms to defend themselves and began to reverse the trend of *hacienda* expansion and community contraction. Capitalist economic expansion continued in the high *punas*, despite the reversal of liberal legislative measures and their application on the ground; but this is a matter far beyond the scope of the present chapter. (Nevertheless, it is well documented for the Central Andes by Kapsoli [1977], Caballero Martín [1979, 1981], and Mallon [1983].)

Other questions remain as well, such as why the liberal reforms did not succeed in destroying the communities, why their numbers grew, and why they emerged strengthened as soon as the national government began to enact protective legislation. These new laws recognized the inherent social cohesion of Indian villages and their struggles to maintain their resources. However, beyond the outer shell of protective legislation introduced in the colonial period, temporarily removed by liberalism, and reintroduced in the 1920s, we must look at internal social processes that create, maintain, and reproduce peasant communities. We can find answers in the role played by the community in productive activities. David Guillet (1978) and I have argued in this and the previous chapter that the community as a collective rule-making body intervenes in the productive process and thus affects land use and tenure. Legislative policies inspired by economic philosophies, and even new economic relationships ushered in by capitalism, had little influence in changing these relationships because the community was part of a complex productive apparatus that operated in difficult mountain environments such as the Andes, Alps, and Himalayas.

Communal control over productive activities is a matter of degree and, as I have shown above, varies not only across production zones but also over time. I end with a brief discussion of the factors that enter into the equations that make certain productive zones more communally controlled than others. As I hope to have demonstrated here, the conditions are not static, nor is any one factor the prime causal influence. Rather, it is the interaction of these factors over time and at a particular place that accounts for the specific configurations that I observed in 1974.

> The first factor is the open field system, which involves simultaneous use of land for agriculture and for raising animals. The need to simultaneously exploit the same space for both uses makes it necessary to coordinate agricultural and pastoral activities in the community territory, especially if cattle are not raised in stables.

The greater the degree of negative animal-plant interactions, the greater the need for communal zoning regulations.

The second factor is *ecological* in nature: The more specialized the ecological zone (in terms of altitude gradient, for example), the greater the level of communal controls. The more generalized the environment,[31] the lower the level of communal controls.

The third factor has to do with *agronomics:* The more intensively the land is worked (involving less fallow, more cropping per season, and more permanent plants), the greater the individual control over production decisions. The more generalized the environment, the greater the possibilities of intensifying land use. Note, too, that intensification is a historical process whereby human and material inputs substitute natural ones, increasing yields per hectare but diminishing labor productivity. As land use becomes intensified, communal controls diminish (as demonstrated by Boserup 1965).

Density, the fourth factor, translates into land pressure. The greater the subdivision of a production zone into parcels of land, the greater the need for farmers to coordinate their activities so as not to cause damage to their neighbors. The less densely a zone is worked, the greater is the freedom to make one's own decisions. Increased demographic pressure on land can also lead to intensification.

Fifth, if one of the resources is a *limiting factor*, greater communal control tends to result. This is the case with irrigation water.

The sixth factor concerns the *degree of commercialization of production*. Since many communal rules are subsistence oriented, the introduction of cash crops tends to bring about at least a modification in the rules—and often also a movement toward abolishing them. Individuals want to be free and unfettered to organize the productive cycle according to market advantages (e.g., by harvesting during periods of high prices) rather than by majority decisions of convenience. This pressure toward commercial cropping often translates into a secessionist move to free a production zone from overall communal organization.

The seventh factor concerns the *property regime imposed by the state*. As noted, the existence of different property regimes has given diverse interest groups within the village the legal justification to impose their will while other groups resist it.

Eight, and last, is the *social factor*. The characteristics of the kinds of communal controls that are imposed in a village depend on the group dynamics of the contending factions and classes in that village, as well as on the degree of resistance that the opposition can muster. Monopolizing land within one production zone is one just variable in this power equation.

Throughout this chapter I have come dangerously close to confusing the formal property regimes imposed by the state with different forms of production such as capitalist and noncapitalist enterprises. Lest there be some lingering doubt, let me clarify. In the Andes, vast stretches of homogeneous environments such as the *puna* and the coastal deltas were, until 1970, clearly capitalist forms of production from which peasant forms of production were displaced (i.e., by sheep ranches in the *puna* and by capitalist plantations on the coast). Peasants were driven off these lands as communities were expropriated and private *haciendas* replaced them, followed by the introduction of very different and clearly capitalist forms of production. Sheep breeds were improved, fencing introduced, and attempts at stabilizing a small wage-labor force were implemented in the *puna* (Mallon 1983; Caballero Martín 1981; Long and Roberts 1978, 1984). And on the coast, mechanization, large-scale irrigation, and a temporary migrant labor force to pick cotton or cut cane for export were introduced on huge corporate and private plantations. Liberal reforms backing private property certainly benefited plantation and ranch owners. But private property rights existed for non-Indians since colonial times anyway!

In areas where the environment is diverse and fractured, and where technological change is difficult to introduce because of variations in local soil, slope, and climatic conditions, peasant forms of production prevailed because capitalist plantation and ranch-style production was uninterested in such marginal lands. Despite improvements and a remarkable degree of commercial production, household-based, small-scale peasant agriculture is still the main form of production in diverse fractured environments (Netting 1993). It is within these parameters that land-use patterns differ, and under these conditions that the liberal reforms played out within the framework of communal control—sometimes weakening community rule-making powers, at other times strengthening them. The nature of production in peasant communities is such that the apparent paradox can be quite comfortably stated: Even if land in Laraos were to become completely private, agricultural production would continue to operate with strong communal controls over the use of this very private land.

Postscript

The Spanish version of this chapter initially appeared in 1977 in a special edition of a newly created state organ, the *Concejo Nacional de la Universidad Peruana*. The edition was meant to showcase the institution. However, as soon as it came off the presses, it was impounded due to internal disputes about another article in that issue, and it never circulated. I had to make a mimeographed version at the Catholic University. The second edition was the volume on the Cañete Valley edited by Mayer and Fonseca (1988). This work appears in English for the first time here, with considerable revisions and updating—especially in the section on old liberalism. Oral presentations and the second edition were well received in Peru and the United States.

When I first arrived in Laraos in 1974, I met Ezequiel Beltrán and his father Nonato, the latter a retired teacher who had been trained by Juan Castillo. After explaining my presence, I was asked to present my credentials and also to show them something I had written. During the next two days I was treated politely, but coldly. Yet, after the two of them read the article on Inca redistribution and trade, the whole village opened up, and I was given official blessing to proceed with my project. I never realized that I had been put through a tough exam. The whole village participated in this study—particularly Ezequiel, a trained historian, who showed me the village's documents and interpreted them. This chapter is essentially his version of the land-tenure history of Laraos. Historians may be amazed to learn that I never went to the archives but, instead, tramped through the maize terraces. I delighted in writing all the endnotes because such rich and unusual documentation tells such wonderful stories and illuminates the issues of tenure in such a vivid way. The Spanish text of this chapter now circulates in Laraos, and the original version of Don Daniel Huallullo's sketch map (Map 9.1) used to hang in the municipal office where council members enjoyed showing it to government officials but would not allow them to photocopy it.

In 1997 I was asked to give a speech to the Peruvian Congress, at a time when the Fujimori government had issued a new land law that intended to provide each individual owner with a brand-new neo-liberal property title. However, the regulations of this new law were stuck in committees. I presented the case of Laraos without giving away the dates until I had reached the middle of my speech. They were amazed when they realized that the issue of private property on communal lands had already been handled by the *comuneros* of Yauyos so early in the twentieth century. And riding on Laraos's laurels, I took the opportunity to suggest to lawmakers that the authority to provide legal title for landed property would best be transferred directly to the *comunidad campesina*. Legal title, I argued, is not a magic wand that converts something into something else, but a written document that witnesses a portion of reality. A land title is the guarantee by neighbors to respect boundaries and privileges of the owner. Better to put the supervision of these rights into the hands of community members and their elected authorities, who know every person and every square meter of their territory, than to entrust it to indifferent bureaucrats in distant provincial capitals. Whether I had any impact in my plea is not certain; but I do know that the regulations to implement Fujimori's land laws have not been made public, nor have they been implemented, to this date.

Notes

1. See Jimenez de la Espada (1965, Vol. I: 55). *Corregidor* Dávila Briceño reduced the Mancos and Laraos ethnic group to seven *pueblos* in the headwaters of the Cañete River before 1586.

2. The complete Laraos titles, containing all the litigation over land, were deposited in the *Archivo Nacional* by the *comuneros* in order to ensure that they would remain in impartial hands. The first title dates back to 1597.

3. In 1824 Simón Bolivar issued his famous decree abolishing communal property, as a way to sell state lands in order to obtain funds for his military campaign. However, *tierras de indios* received a different treatment: "Article 1. The State will sell all lands it owns for a third of its legitimate value. Article 2. Exempt from this article are lands that the so-called Indians possess; instead, they are declared their owners, so that they can sell or alienate them at any time. Article 3: Lands called *de comunidad* shall be distributed according to rules among all Indians who do not have any allotment and they shall become their owners as is declared in Article 2. Article 4: distribution of said lands shall consider the situation of each holder, giving more to one who is married than to one who is not, so that none may be left out without his respective piece of land" (translated by Mayer). By 1826 the Prefect of Yauyos consulted the government about how to proceed. The answer: "The Prefect consulted the government whether mixed Indians should be included in the distribution of lands; and his excellency has responded that this grace should be conceded to all those who were considered *contribuyentes* ("Indian tax payers") in the old regime, with the difference that in those places where there is not enough land for everyone, those with status of *originarios* should have preference" (Source: Juan M. de Pando, Archivo Comunal de Laraos, 1826; translated by Mayer). Early on, Laraos made its move to resist this measure. In 1867 all the lands were registered as municipal property of the Común de Laraos, which as a corporation could hold land.

4. Legislation reintroducing communal property dates back to 1919, when Article 209 of the Constitution was written.

5. Source: Plano Oficial del Conjunto de la Comunidad Indígena de Laraos.

6. Tosi's classifications are as follows: (a) subalpine humid *páramo*, associated with a rainy and very cold climate between 4,800 to 4,000 meters above sea level; (b) montane steppe, associated with a subhumid and cold climate between 4,000 and 3,000 meters above sea level; and (c) mountain brush desert, associated with a semiarid and temperate climate between 3,000 and 2,000 meters above sea level. In Laraos, this latter zone is actually a transitional zone with many of the characteristics of the higher montane steppe. (See ONERN [1970: 58–66] and the ecological map in the same report.)

7. *Ecological zones* are representations of natural zones with a specific configuration of the natural vegetation and fauna that form biotic communities. These biotic communities vary according to their degree of generalized or specialized populations of cohabiting species. Under extreme environmental conditions, biotic communities become specialized, with only a few dominant species adapted to the extreme conditions; under more favorable conditions, by contrast, the number of species in a biocommunity increases. Transitions between ecological zones are gradual, and many areas can be characterized as transitional in which the dominant vegetation of one zone gradually diminishes in favor of the other. On the other hand, *production zones*, being manmade, are characterized by the predominance of

one kind of crop or another and therefore are "artificially" more specialized than their natural environments. There can be several production zones in one ecological zone, or one production zone can extend beyond its base environmental area, or the two kinds of zones can overlap. Production zones have clearly defined boundaries either owing to the absolute environmental limitations of producing a crop or because diminishing marginal productivity reaches a point where a given form of cultivation is no longer worthwhile for the group using the zone. The distinction is one of classification of natural environments versus a cultural or social division superimposed over the same space. Another caution concerns the term *niche*, which is used in at least three different ways: It can mean (a) the particular physical space that the species occupies (though here the correct term is *habitat)*; (b) the particular function that the species performs within the ecosystem (and in this sense the term is correctly used by Odum [1971: 234]); and (c), from the human point of view, a particular place where exploitable resources are concentrated (Hardesty 1975). Murra (1972) uses *niche, tier,* and *ecological floor* interchangeably. Production zones are discussed in Chapter 8.

8. The original title of 1597 includes a beautiful sketch map with a long explicative text in Quechua in the center. Surrounding it, marked in rectangles, each *estancia* is named and sometimes described. Twenty-seven of the estancia place names can be found in current government topographical maps. In 1900 there were 240 *estancias* total.

9. This communal decision was recorded in the *Libro de Ventas de Enero* (1891–1910) in the Laraos communal archive. The *Libro de Matrícula de los Pastos*, which started in 1901, registered all decisions regarding pasture land assignation and its finances.

10. The term *wacchillero* refers to a dependent herder who takes care of the owner's sheep and alpacas, in return for the right to herd a specified number of his own animals on the same pastures. By the time of my fieldwork, remuneration of *wacchilleros* included a monthly supply of foodstuffs, such as sugar, noodles, and agricultural produce. The same relationship existed on *haciendas,* as perceptively described by Martinez Alier (1973) and G. Smith (1989).

11. Source: *Titulación de Laraos.*

12. In 1906 the community sold lands belonging to Patrón de Santo Domingo and the Virgin Santa Isabel to private individuals—namely, community members.

13. An extremely complex dispute arose between the community and the republican state over this issue. A decree of president La Mar in 1828 assigned surplus land not distributed to individuals under Bolivar's decree to fund schooling for Indian *pueblos.* Laraoinos interpreted the spirit of the law as assigning contributions from users of pastures to maintenance of the school; but they argued that these were voluntary contributions. The state, on the other hand, assumed these lands to be in the hands of the government, with rights to revenue from them, and also the right to rent it out to people it considered worthy. Laraos disputed this, and Laraos succeeded in having two *estancias* struck from the Ministry of Education's property register (*margesí escolar*).

14. The Laraos agricultural system has recently been restudied by Brunschwig (1986: 27–52), whose more carefully constructed maps demonstrate that each macro-sector described by me is actually composed of four to six smaller sectors. There are seventy-two smaller sectors, aggregated into larger units by communal

decision: Communal authorities decide on how many sectors are to be aggregated according to need. In addition, the community can decide to skip one set of sub-sectors in its rotations or (as in 1984) to prematurely set aside one macro-sector for fallow when conditions are not appropriate for barley cultivation. Brougère, a member of the research team in Laraos, notes, too, that in the intervening nine years between my study and hers, rules and regulations regarding production zones and, especially, irrigation have changed very little (Brougère 1986: 139 and n.5). For a summary and improved maps, see Morlon (1996: 89–93).

15. The community controls the agricultural calendar in this zone by fixing the dates between which certain agricultural tasks have to be initiated and finished. Generally, selected Catholic saints' days are used as a rough guide. (Nevertheless, the agricultural calendar must be coordinated with yearly variations in rainfall patterns, incidence of frosts, and determination of whether the crops have matured enough to be ready for harvest. Indeed, the dates can be changed at short notice in response to irregularities in climate.) In many communities, including Laraos, this agricultural activity is ceremonially initiated and closed off by the authorities, who also arrange to have communal lands worked that day. The desire by some individual farmers to start work on their own fields is counterbalanced by the authorities' prohibition, and this pressure ensures greater attendance in the communal work.

16. An analogous example should make this flexible restriction clear: In a university the dates for the initiation of classes, midterms, and finals are scheduled by the administration. The actual dates of the exams, however, may vary among departments, courses, and even individual students as they make private arrangements with their professors.

17. The intimate relationship between the *fiesta* and *cargo* system and the communal control of land is discussed in Chapter 4 of this book as well as in Fonseca (1972a: 322–327; 1972b: 99–104) and Isbell (1971). The various *cargo* ranks are based on different degrees of responsibility associated with the communal management of the various production zones. In the Cusco area the *arariwa* is responsible for warding off frost and hail as well as the more social tasks of controlling damage caused by humans and animals. As these "old-fashioned" *cargos* are being abolished (Mitchell 1991: ch. 7), important collective, agriculturally significant tasks are increasingly being abandoned, too.

18. Trawick (1994), in a study of the spread of the dairy/alfalfa complex on irrigated lands in Cotahuasi, shows how this system uses water inefficiently, creating scarcities that lead to conflicts over its distribution. See also Mayer (1994: 492), who notes that alfalfa expansion is an important trend on the Western slopes of the Andes.

19. Here is a petition for such an allocation from 1885, in free translation: "Honorable Justice of the Peace and honorable Mayor of the District of Laraos: Citizen T.J. native and resident of this village of Santo Domingo of Laraos in the Province of Yauyos, I appear before you and say: That having served in the service of *camachico,* such an onerous and bothersome *cargo,* and since the community has not responded with the kinds of rewards that once used to be customary, such as a bull, or pieces of land or house plots. For this reason, I demand that . . . some vacant and uncleared pieces of land in the area of Chochipe which is called Puca Caca . . . be given to me. Well, sirs, my petition is just, and I ask you to be considerate, because

last year I have passed through great torments [in the fulfillment of my duties] to the extent that my fellow citizens and neighbors must be angry with me since I have molested them with the daily demands of contributions. So, please, Sirs, you can adjudicate to me this piece of land that I am asking; and thus I may end up consoled, and in this way start to farm in order to pass more *cargos* and to sustain my family, and because, as you already know, I have no other lands." Cotler (1959) has noted a similar process in the neighboring communities of San Lorenzo de Quinti. Land grants were called *dádivas,* and they went to *comuneros* who had successfully financed religious *fiestas* in the *cargo* system. Moreover, in this community, land was actually subdivided and sold to *comuneros* for nominal prices at the turn of the twentieth century—the same period as in Laraos. Despite this privatization, communal controls remained strong enough for Cotler to insist that there was a "double status" in the property relationships: communal and private.

20. One local document pertaining to the Chilean war requests the discharge of a Laraoino soldier who fought in the battle of Tarapacá; it also mentions that the village was sacked. It is well known that many peasant communities in the neighboring Mantaro Valley participated actively against Chilean invading armies with General Andrés Avelino Cáceres in the *Campaña de la Breña.* Since Laraos was closely linked to these communities, it is likely that the communities in Yauyos did play a part. The local history of the Chilean war in Yauyos has yet to be written. Folk history has it that Chinese coolies escaped from the coastal *haciendas* and settled in the neighboring community of Carania, where they introduced the commercial cultivation of garlic in their *maizal.* Manrique (1981) and Mallon (1983) point out that in the aftermath of the war, peasant communities in the Central region gained an unprecedented degree of autonomy and independence, occupying *haciendas,* declaring themselves autonomous regions, and defying a weakened central government.

21. Tithes were discussed at a meeting of Municipal Council members in 1867. They decided to leave the decision of whether to abolish them to each village in the district. Here I translate one entry: "Discussion centered on tithes and first fruits, which at one time were laws of the state; these continued until yesterday in the villages only because the parish priests always exercised temporal power over these villagers—victims of their ignorance. It was decided that it would be very useful if the villages instead created a common fund to use the moneys for their own benefit, so that these villages should not depend on funds provided by this honorable municipality. It was mentioned that there would be opposition to such measures; it was therefore resolved that the district municipality nominate in each village two persons among the most capable, who would, in as short a time as possible, send to this municipality an *acta* signed by all citizens, indicating their desire, be it in favor, or against, the continuation of the custom of paying first fruits to the priests." (Source: *Libro de Actas del H. Concejo Distrital de Laraos.*) As late as 1897 the villagers were still fighting the priests. Ultimately, they wrote to the minister of education for support against the priests.

22. The *Libro de Ventas* also contains the annual accounts of the capital accumulated on account of this quota. In order to make the capital grow, forced loans were introduced. Interest payments were due from two treasurers on a rotational basis. They had the obligation to accept a forced loan of half the capital and to return it at the end of the year at a hefty 5 percent monthly interest rate. By 1906

there was enough capital in the account (1,956 *Libras Peruanas*) for there to be withdrawals, although the highest amount peaked in 1910. The treasurers regularly paid a *cantor* (to sing at religious services), covered expenses of the administration and costs associated with lawsuits, and paid for a bottle of champagne presented to the *Diputado* of the province. Contributions to school construction and equipment from 1908 to 1910 were the most regular expenses. In 1914 they also bought material for road construction. By this time, capital from the society was disappearing, since about one-third of the assets comprised promissory notes rather than real money. In 1916 someone dipped into the pot illegally. By 1918 debt notes accounted for two-thirds of the funds, and in 1926 total capital supposedly amounted to 282.17 *Libras Peruanas*, of which 244 were in difficult-to-collect notes and 33.96 were owed by the treasurers from the previous year. Only 3.80 were in cash. Because there was little money left to keep track of, annotations ended that year.

23. Plot consolidation was one of the most important themes that agronomists preached as a precondition for development in the Andean highlands. I remember hearing in the same breath, however, that this was one of the most difficult things to do, given peasant mentality about private property. That Laraos community leaders organized such a program long before the advent of development professionals is remarkable indeed.

24. *Indigenismo* was an intellectual movement in the 1920s and 1930s that fiercely debated the "role" of the Indian in national society. Among its many facets and developments, apart from a pseudoscientific assertion of Indian virtues against centuries of exploitation, were regional movements against Lima domination, the organization of associations that began defending Indian land and labor complaints, and the establishment of linkages with labor movements. *Indigenismo* is also closely associated with the establishment of socialist and communist parties in Peru, most notably José Carlos Mariátegui and the intellectual circle he formed in association with the Journal *Amauta,* which he edited. In this connection, see Kapsoli (1977, 1980), Tamayo Herrera (1980), Tord (1978), Degregori et al. (1978), and De la Cadena (2,000). *Indigenísmo* opposed liberal ideology from the left; hence the *Quinta Internacional* of Laraos, although I doubt that the latter actually had real links with the Fifth International.

25. All this infighting ultimately reduced the community's authority to settle disputes between *estancia* holders. One such dispute about co-inheritance rights dragged on for eight years. The contenders preferred to litigate in the national court system. They continued fighting, bribing, falsifying testimony, appealing, and spending money on lawyers all the way to the Supreme Court. The very same documents from 1900, which the community considered rental agreements in its suit against other *estancieros*, were used in this case as evidence for private property between the contending *estancieros*. The current owner says that the *estancia* is his, but also recognizes that it is the property of the community if there are no heirs after he dies.

26. Ezequiel Beltrán Gallardo (1977: 14, 38), a native Laraoino, economist, and historian, has meticulously researched the actions and activities of the independence republicans in Yauyos, tracing much of the crucial documentation to the Lilly Library in Bloomington, Indiana.

27. From 1702 to 1722 Laraos disputed with Chongos (in the Mantaro Valley) about their *puna* boundaries. In 1733 Laraos repelled the pretensions against *cacique* Blas Astocuri Apoalaya, who declared himself "owner" of the *hacienda* Laive. By 1769, Astocuri (who had alienated these communal lands for himself) sold them to the Condesa de Vista Florida, whose authorized horsemen (*caporales*) violently displaced the herders working for Laraoinos. It took thirty-eight years of litigation to successfully assert the rights of Laraos. From 1815 to 1851 Laraos disputed against the neighboring community of Huantán, winning that case as well. From 1865 to 1891 they were engaged in dispossessing a renter from Chongos who claimed to be renting it from another landlord *gamonal*, whose claims to the property were proven to be false. Finally, from 1917 to 1918 the neighboring community of Alis planted in agricultural lands belonging to Laraos and had to be dispossessed. Such continuous litigation and constant appeals to communal colonial titles must have patently demonstrated the advantages of collective action. (Source: Archivo de la Comunidad de Laraos.)

28. See Long and Roberts (1978, 1984: chs. 2 and 3) and Mallon (1983: Part II) for a detailed analysis of the expansion of capitalism in the Central Highlands. On the wool market in the Central Highlands, see Mallon and Rénique (1977).

29. Although it established age limits, time frames, and other safeguards, the *Ley de Conscripción Vial*—which was promulgated the same year as the Constitution of 1920—turned into an abusive manhunt, creating opportunities for graft for authorities and chain-gang labor supplied to construction companies. The law lasted throughout the eleven years of the Leguía government and was very unpopular. As his first measure, Coronel Sánchez Cerro, who overthrew Leguía, abolished it.

30. See Dora Mayer (1912, 1926, 1984) and Kapsoli (1980). This is a good opportunity to state that I am not related to Dora Mayer, the daughter of a German immigrant whose life among the founders of the socialist movement in Peru is an interesting episode.

31. Odum (1971) describes the characteristics of both generalized and specialized environments. Agriculture, of course, involves a manmade trend toward specialization and is not the variable considered here. Rather, the reference is to specialized natural environments, which are under stress and thus require more extensive agricultural strategies (see Netting 1965). In addition, specialized natural environments tend to be utilized by humans in communal arrangements to a greater extent than more productive generalized environmental zones.

10

Household Economies
Under Neo-Liberalism

This chapter takes a wider perspective in that it focuses on the worldwide negative impact of neo-liberal policies. First, it describes the 1990 structural readjustment in Peru and the way that privatization of land is being implemented. Next, it critiques the uses that neo-liberalism makes of poverty studies and poverty alleviation programs. The chapter ends with a proposal for environmental restoration of the fragile and degraded lands in Andean communities as one viable option for peasants, making the important point that better wages and prices for their products need to be addressed at the macro-economic level.

Structural Readjustment

The worldwide ideological shift to neo-liberalism in response to the collapse of socialist economies as well as the growing power of international financial institutions comprise the historical context that forced Third World governments to implement open-market policies. These governments quite literally went broke in the face of changing financial and commodity markets and shifts in power toward the interests of corporate expansion on a global scale. Neo-liberalism was a policy that the international financial institutions imposed on the Third World.

As a 1980s political movement, neo-liberalism reacted against too much state intervention and rejected over-regulation, protectionism, state-owned enterprises, and collective production systems. Between World War II and the 1990s, governments had implemented state intervention, regulation, protectionism, state-owned enterprises, and collective production systems in well-intentioned attempts to implement economies that served national interests and to foster greater internal coherence by incorporating different sectors through protection policies and special-interest programs. But these efforts were critiqued because they fostered systems that were inefficient because they were not competitive. Instead neo-liberalism placed its faith in the engines of growth that individual initiative acting in free and self-regulating markets could bring about. Neo-liberal governments deregulated markets, eliminated subsidies, dismantled development programs, and privatized state enterprises. Public services such as education and health, among many other programs, were cut back, canceled, or abandoned. In addition, because they were heavily in debt with international financial institutions, governments embarked on drastic structural readjustment programs to control inflation by cutting back on the supply of money and devaluating their currencies.

In the Andean countries, these programs came to be called "shock treatments," which Bolivia (NACLA 1991) and Peru, following an earlier Chilean example, implemented in the 1980s and 1990s. The dramatic Peruvian Fujishock of 1990 was regarded as drastic, cruel, and excessive (Figueroa 1995; Sheahan 1999). Yet it stopped inflation and introduced a degree of stability in the chaotic and violence-ridden society that President Alberto Fujimori had inherited from the Alan García administration. Latin American neo-liberal reforms have been criticized for increasing inequalities in Latin America, but according to John Sheahan (1999: 177), the drastic negative impact of Peru's shock treatment began to correct itself somewhat after two years with a remarkable recuperation of GNP growth and a return of the *status quo ante* in terms of lost income streams for many but not all social groups. Sheahan's history of the Peruvian economy over five decades is very instructive, for it tracks policy changes and their impact over time. Inequality, he says, grew after the shock treatment, but not as much as expected—because the Fujimori regime reconstructed deteriorated roads and infrastructure, which reopened markets; because firms with unused capacity cranked up their engines; and because the agrarian sector reacted with increased production. Foreign investment resumed after the civil war ended, finding opportunities for revamping collapsed urban services such as telephones and other state-owned industries that were rapidly and cheaply being privatized. The government also embarked on an effective short-term poverty alleviation program in the later years of its regime.

The agricultural sector in Peru responded positively to neo-liberal shock treatment (Sheahan 1999: 64–70). However, as small producers, responsible citizens, and market incentive–responsive businesses, the agricultural producers continued to have problems. Large demonstrations in all departments took place in October 2000 in Peru and Bolivia, demanding financial relief against falling prices of their products.

In the current era of neo-liberal hegemony, what do peasant households demand? The answer is realistic prices for their products. I am in support of this demand, and my argument is as follows: Realistic prices call for a reversal of cheap food policies and, possibly, for certain restrictions against competition of foreign imports in the national interest and in the defense of peasants' small farms. Advocates should refute the anti-subsidy argument and demand that subsidies go to the producer and not the consumers. Producer subsidies—which are currently being practiced in Europe, the United States, and Japan—have multiplier effects in the economy. Subsidies to consumers maintain income levels but do not generate employment, and they have long been practiced in Latin America to the detriment of the agricultural sector.

Small-scale producers should also defend their comparative advantage, given that they are in marginal lands and produce under constraints such as those against better lands. According to comparative advantage theory, countries need to look for their comparative advantage and not just seek to exploit absolute advantages, because there is greater benefit to all. Applying this theory to Andean conditions, we discover that a role for smallholders as food producers in the economy of the nation can still be found for them. Economists from the Andean Pact countries—which include Colombia and Venezuela as well as Ecuador, Peru, and Bolivia—estimate that peasant agriculture generates between 50 and 60 percent of the basic agricultural consumption commodities of these five countries (Ortega 1982). Producers on the Peruvian coast have the absolute advantage in relation to the highlands but only a comparative advantage in the export market. The coastal producers should therefore concentrate on export products, leaving space for highland peasant food production for the national market, where small holders do have the comparative advantage. Providing export incentives to coastal producers to wean them away from producing food for the national market not only benefits both coastal and highland farmers but also recuperates Peru's foreign exchange reserves. In the long run, Andean countries have to recuperate their capacity to produce enough food to feed their own populations, even if doing so results in higher prices for consumers. This outcome would also generate employment opportunities for a large number of people for whom there are fewer and fewer opportunities for effective economic participation.

Campesino households as sellers of labor also need to resume the fight for fair labor practices, to pressure for the reintroduction of basic rights that labor has lost, and to fight for higher minimum wages. The wage level has important effects on household income (Escobal et al. 1998); although the current stress on improving the quality of labor through education and job training is important as a way to raise wages in relation to productivity, the demand for more humane wages *now* is not incompatible with the long-term project of better qualifying the entire labor force over the medium term. In addition, a decent wage for parents may allow their children time to go to school rather than work. Under conditions of rising productivity, increasing income through wages stimulates the internal market and gets people out of poverty.

Neo-Liberalism

By going back to neo-classical economics as ideology, the neo-liberal movement has fundamentally shifted the perspective from which peasant household-based units are regarded. Classical economics stresses the separation of households from firms as a starting assumption. In this model, the household as owner of assets (capital, land, and labor) sells them to firms, which use the free market to produce goods and services that they sell back to the household, which buys them with the income that the sale of its assets has generated. (An additional function of the household is to save.) The separation of households from firms assigns different roles to each; firms are to efficiently produce goods and services driven by market forces; households are to consume them by optimizing choice through consumer preferences. With expanding markets the emphasis of late capitalism is on the households' capacity to consume more and more. Inasmuch as the household economies we have been studying do not separate into consuming households and producing firms, they create ideological problems for neo-liberals because they are messy. To the neo-liberals they are neither efficient producers nor expanded consumers. Returning to a simplified reading of European examples in which rural populations became an industrial labor force, neo-liberals have decided that the peasant households, in their role as producer firms, are largely inefficient and uneconomic and should disappear. According to the ideology of modernization, as Deborah Brycerson (2000: 6) characterizes this view, "peasants are technologically backward and doomed by the forces of modernization and industrialization." Policy shifts under neo-liberalism revert to these tendencies. The neo-liberals would like to see the household's production functions dissolved, at least among the most inefficient ones—which are the majority.

The new emphasis is on the household's role as asset holder and consumption unit. Policy shifts clearly support this role by assisting education and improvement in marketable labor skills. Appropriately, in neo-liberal jargon this upgrade of assets is called "human capital development," which could be more freely sold in the labor market at a better price (market conditions permitting). Revamping the household's assets is reflected in a renewed emphasis on property, especially on valuing and making land a marketable commodity; but it also includes the monetary valuation of houses in shantytowns through titling programs. Once it enters into an efficient factor market, land, so the theory goes, will be put to maximum productive uses; or, if not, it will be sold to more efficient units. Hence the modern emphasis on rural land registry and titling programs. Under these schemes, inefficient producers should sell their assets and move into other sectors of the economy rather than remain on the land (provided that alternative jobs become available). Those families that stay will embark on the road toward prosperity by establishing capitalized family farms as the rural version of businesses (provided that markets and prices are favorable). Those that sell out will earn their income from wages shifting between agricultural and urban jobs in response to demand and skill. The faith that neo-liberalism places in the self-regulating market—the belief that it will eventually bring favorable conditions to rural householders—is admirable, especially given that the opposite has for so long been the case in the Third World. Seasonal migrant labor does not give up land base because secure jobs and decent wages are hard to find, even if Andean migrants are now venturing as far as the United States and Europe (Altamirano 1990, 1992).

The real new focus of neo-liberals, however, is on the households' role as consumers. And in this respect they regard the peasant households as total failures. The households' incapacity to generate enough income to properly consume from market sources is their main gripe. A second theme is that they regard subsistence production with a jaundiced eye, because it does not pass the efficiency test of the market system. The argument is that the world market could feed these households with cheaper food. In the meantime, a large-scale shift in terminology has occurred. The peasants have become "the poor," a large new category of people. As Brycerson (2000: 1) aptly puts it, "peasants and hippies are relegated to the same dustbin of history." Simply put, the poor are regarded as beyond the reach of market-oriented policies; they are people who fall through the cracks of their systems. Moreover, there is not much one can do about the poor, although a few targeted social programs are implemented to reduce their suffering. In this view most peasants in the Andes have lost their role and have become social burdens. The newest trend could be characterized by the abbreviation *from p to p*, meaning "from peasants to poor"; but it could also stand for "from peasants to proletarians," given that the latter process is largely the cause of the former one (Goodman and Redclift 1981).

It is easy to parody neo-liberalism, especially to an audience already convinced of its errors. But it is difficult to critique its position, given neo-liberalism's theoretical foundation in the "laws" of positive economics (McCloskey 1985). Therefore, I think that a more constructive role for academics is to take up the challenge posed by neo-liberalism and put forward within the neo-liberal frame of reference (i.e., neo-classical economics and later developments) some very uncomfortable questions, while at the same time pointing to the ideological nature of its program. A critique must also recognize that not all practitioners of the discipline share the same ideology. Economist Amartya Sen (1981), speaking with a forceful moral voice, discusses the relationship between entitlements to poverty and starvation, and how both are affected by market relations. Arturo

Escobar's (1995) excellent deconstruction of the development discourse challenges the neo-liberals' positivistic self-assurance. In an interesting twist involving both rhetoric and action in Brazil, the *Movimento dos Sem Terra* (MST; Stedile 1999) and its urban associate the *Movimento dos Sem Teto* have assumed the stigma of World Bank categories of the poor as their own political platform in fighting for their entitlements.

In the following sections, I will deconstruct the new neo-liberal concept of "the poor" in Peru. As a discourse designed to pluck at the purse strings of reluctant donors, this concept needs to be challenged. Next, I will discuss the issue of property in relation to environmental issues. Finally, I will review environmental conservation, arguing for the alternative of making the human landscapes habitable and tolerable for the millions of people in the Andes whom neo-liberalism has written off. The improvement of the environmental basis of their livelihoods is a program that may permit rural households to weather the neo-liberal storm until it passes, at which time newer and more favorable economic winds may blow once again. Because I am mildly pessimistic, I think that one of the few options left for rural Andean households is to fortify their *regions of refuge* (Aguirre Beltran 1979) by reconstructing their decayed ecological systems. At the same time, however, they need to continue to fight for better conditions in the marketplace. Since the end of the twentieth century, peasants in Latin America and the Andes have made remarkable gains, so current conditions should be seen a temporary setback. Cristóbal Kay's (2000: 133) assessment is apposite here:

> For a peasant path to rural development to succeed would require a major shift away from the current emphasis on liberalization, a development which at present appears unlikely. This does not mean that the neo-liberal project has gone unchallenged by peasants. Indeed the peasant rebellion in Chiapas, Mexico at the beginning of 1994 has come to symbolize the new character of social movements in the countryside in Latin America.

The Poor Household

New conditions in the world have converted economics, in a cruel reversal of Adam Smith's title, into the study of the poverty of nations. In the last ten years there have been over three hundred publications on poverty in Peru alone (Trivelli 2000: 205), measuring, refining, mapping, questioning older studies, and improving estimation methodologies (Elías 1994). These publications confirm one depressingly persistent trend: growing poverty in Peru (Sheahan 1999). In 1996 there were 11 million poor people; of these, 3 million resided in the rural areas. According to studies by the Economic Commission for Latin America and the Caribbean (ECLAC), Peru's proportion of poor people increased from 50 percent of the nation's households in poverty in 1970 to 52 percent in 1986. (During the same period, the figures for Latin America as a whole, including the Caribbean, decreased from 40 to 37 percent.) In 1985, the monthly per capita income in Peru was $25; by 1989 it had shrunk to $15 for the poorest 40 percent of poor families (Elías 1994: 56). Table 10.1 tracks household expenditures from 1994 to 1996, comparing the poorest 40 percent to the national average.

Table 10.1 *Average Per Capita Monthly Income of Peruvian Households in US $*

	Income			Expenditure		
	1985	1991	1994	1985	1991	1994
National Average	98	85	90	126	69	89
Average for the poorest 40%	28	31	32	46	30	38

Source: Adapted from Saavedra and Díaz (1999: 80).

Poverty is found in the shantytowns of all cities and in the rural areas, but it is overwhelmingly concentrated in the rural highlands. In fact, the rural highlands have led the nation with a rising headcount of poor households from 49 percent of all households in the region in 1985 to 73 percent in 1991. Although this figure dropped to 68 percent in 1994, it remained steady through 1997 (Sheahan 1999: 112; Trivelli 2000: 215; Escobal et al. 1998).

According to these figures, the households that are the subject of this book are all (or nearly all) poor, and many are extremely poor. We can recognize them in the following description by Sheahan (1999: 112):

> The leading characteristics associated with poverty are closely related. Poverty is highest for people in rural areas, for those with low levels of education, and for those whose maternal language is Quechua or other Indigenous languages. In terms of economic activity it is highest for people in agriculture, for workers other than salaried employees, and for independent (self-employed) workers in both rural and urban areas.

By occupation, self-employed people (including those in agriculture) comprise 35 percent of the poor in Peru; unemployed family laborers add another 44 percent. Sixty-eight percent of all poor do agriculture; 13 percent are employed in trading, another common occupation among articulated households. Steady employment and manufacturing involve only 14 percent of the poor (Sheahan 1999: 113).

Using the Internet, I was able to download from Peru's *Mapa de la pobreza* (INEI: 2000) a spreadsheet with poverty measures for the communities

Table 10.2   Poverty Rankings of the Villages Studied (1999)

Field Site	District	Index of Income	% of Poor Households	% of Households with 1 NBI
Tangor	Paucar	162.8	84	99.7
Laraos	Laraos	258.4	28	86.3
Tulumayo	Cochas	275	39.4	94.2
Tulumayo	Comas	288.2	28.2	88
Paucartambo	Paucartambo	179.3	81.4	95.1
Paucartambo	Colquepata	204	78.1	83.8

100 = lowest, 1,006 = highest
NBI = unsatisfied basic necessity
Source: Perú, Instituto Nacional de Estadística e Informática

described in this book (see Table 10.2). Tangor is the poorest community on income measures; Laraos is the least poor, with good income from employment in mining; and the Tulumayo Valley is less poor than the Paucartambo Valley for reasons that are discussed in Chapter 7. (In all three districts, the houses lack running water and bathrooms, something I know from firsthand experience.) Such measurements are based on the NBI, which stands for *necesidad básica insatisfecha* ("unsatisfied basic necessity").

How does one react to such statistics? Vladimir Gil, a Peruvian anthropologist, tells me that when he arrived at Haquira, a village ranked among the poorest in the poverty map from the Department of Apurimac, he found that the authorities were delighted with this datum; they felt that they had won a lottery because their inclusion on the poverty map meant that they would be recipients of alleviation programs. Now that poverty is "official," there is competition among the poor to appear the poorest of the poorest. The government's poverty map serves as a ranking method to operate a perverse version of Karl Polanyi's redistribution systems. Carolina Trivelli (2000) and L. Elías (1994) show that there are now many categories of poor—the extremely poor, the merely poor, the chronically poor, the indigent, the temporary poor, the structurally poor, and so on. Being poor, then, becomes a role, not a condition—something that requires a performance in a collective soup kitchen, a mother's club, or a food-for-work program where people act out their assigned role as the deserving poor.

I follow economist Carolina Trivelli (2000: 200–255), whose insightful review of the rural poverty issue in Peru makes three very important comments. The first has to do with the magnitude of the problem. With half the country classed as poor, Trivelli says, further efforts at refining descriptors and measuring techniques become counterproductive and add little information to the basic disastrous fact. But what exactly does it mean when half the population of a country is defined as poor? How is one supposed to react to statistical measures that designate households as "1 NBI" if they lack running water, as "2 NBI" if they lack human waste disposal, and as "3 NBI" if they lack electricity? Interestingly, Trivelli cites a study indicating that 60 percent of the *not*-poor also have at least one unsatisfied basic necessity. In short, the poor and the not-poor lack the goods that we Westerners take for granted, and they take for granted the fact that they don't have them.

The NBI analysis reflects the vision of households' incapacity to consume in line with neo-liberalism. This failure to consume is so bad that they lack even basic necessities. But the means of satisfying them is defined by urban and middle-class standards. Although wonderful conveniences, running water and sewer systems are expensive ways to reduce contamination and hygiene problems in rural areas; so the comparison with urban standards proposes a rather difficult way to solve them. Also puzzling is the exclusion of phone connections (Manrique 2000) and television sets from the category of NBIs. Without falling into the trap of cultural relativism, which can easily be seen as an argument for disguising misery as if it were a separate culture that we must respect, we must challenge the unthinking ethnocentrism of modernization encapsulated in the NBIs. Nor need we assume that Andean people do not want the things that modernity has to offer, as Orin Starn (1992a) reminds us; but I suspect that the goods they would buy with increased income are different from those the Lima- and Washington-based economists have decided that they need most.[1] The country's real purpose behind measuring poverty is to negotiate soft loans from international financial institutions to obtain foreign exchange.

What is really meant when 80 to 90 percent of the households in the highlands villages are defined as poor? I recognize that *poverty* is a relative term; but even so, it is effective as a concept only if one segment of households in a given society is measured in relation to another segment and there is a dividing line between them that compares one against the other. But if the line stops dividing these segments, they are all infinitely rich and infinitely poor at the same time. In the 1950s such measures were collectively called the "standard of living." I consider this a better descriptor. Now, the dividing line is called the "poverty line," because the standard of living has dropped, remained steady against changed expectations, or been abruptly redefined as a standard of intolerable living. What is written in this book projects another image: that of people who are actively involved in running a complex household/interhousehold economy; they produce, build houses, save, trade, tax themselves, and redistribute income between themselves. They do not appear to be the hopeless apathetic beings that new technical measurings of poverty aim to convey.

Trivelli's second comment is that "most of the research in the 90's takes on the topic of poverty as a datum and not as a result" (2000: 203). In the 1960s, she says, economists wanted to understand the process of transformation of *indios* to *campesinos;* in the 1980s they sought to empower these *campesinos* by stressing their citizenship and participation in wider aspects of national society; and in the 1990s, they turned these very same people into a category: "the poor, understood as those who are 'lacking,' with analysts no longer paying attention to the processes that carried those people into the condition of poverty" (Trivelli 2000: 203–204).

Thus this is a debate about causes. Evading the issue, poverty studies run correlation programs to associate features with the condition of poverty and mistake these for its causes. Instead of being an effect, then, poverty is reduced to a set of attributes of the household that contains them or of the person who lives in it (Escobal et al. 1998). This kind of poverty research comes close to blaming the victim for his condition. And it pays scant attention to the external factors that cause income to fall. The explanation as to why self-employed households are poor is that they are unprofitable. Wages fall because deregulation of labor laws has broken unions and feminized and casualized labor (Kay 2000: 130–131). Wage rates have collapsed because of devaluation and then have been allowed to find their "true" market level. They have also fallen because of the intense competition represented by a growing labor force seeking work against a static or even diminishing demand for agricultural and urban labor (de Janvri, Sadulet, and Young 1989). None of these factors are attributable to individual poor persons or their household.

However, discrimination against Indigenous people is correctly identified as a cause in poverty studies by Sheahan (1999: 114): "Households headed by people speaking indigenous languages suffer an incidence of extreme poverty that is 89 percent higher than their share in the nation's households." The Indian groups of today continue in many ways to be second-class citizens—a fact reflected in the unequal infant mortality rates of Indian and non-Indian groups and their differential access to effective education. Departments with high levels of Indigenous populations have exhibited infant mortality rates ranging four to five times higher than those of Lima; and although the former rates have been falling since the 1980s, Sheahan (1999: 108) observes that "the rates of decrease for all five departments were much slower" than those in the rest of the country. The same can be said about the poor state of education, which produces high incidences of illiteracy in these same regions. Note that this illiteracy is in a foreign language.[2]

Trivelli's (2000: 222) third comment is that, in the rural areas, the poor and the not-poor are in almost the same situation: "The poor, as a group, are closer to being poor than being rich" (translation by Mayer). They share the same environmental constraints, lack the same basic necessities, face the same depressing macro-economic conditions, have the same diversified household strategies that combine subsistence agriculture with market activities and off-farm income, and, to a surprising degree, partake and benefit from the same government-targeted programs to alleviate poverty. The differences are only in degree, and the line that separates the two groups is so thin that even if households were to cross it, they would sink back at the fist sign of adversity. The poor and the non-poor in the Andes lead precarious lives.

Therefore, Trivelli questions the utility of targeted poverty alleviation programs, as prescribed by the World Bank. Although Sheahan (1999) credits the Fujimori government with fairly effective targeted rural social programs, he is critical of the regime for pursuing neo-liberal policies that hurt the poor and the not-poor alike. Trivelli and Sheahan agree that macro-economic policies and sustained rural development programs help all, whether poor or non-poor, and both therefore strongly recommend broader rather than targeted approaches. In Bolivia, President Guillermo Sánchez de Lozada's Popular Participation Law program (Albó 1996), though not without its own problems, has not only energized rural areas but also broadened the concept of citizenship. Indeed, this program expanded and recognized the legality of local groups to include traditional Indian forms of organization, created new municipalities to give them a power base, and awarded them grants in proportion to the population they contained. It thus provided a great deal of local autonomy to set priorities and select mechanisms of implementation that foster local participation for the same amount of government expenditure. By contrast, Fujimori's programs were extremely centralized and demobilizing; they were also clearly used for narrow political purposes. Ironically, Sánchez de Lozada lost his reelection bid in 1997, and Fujimori's vote-getting machinery malfunctioned in 2000.

Property

As a measure intended to upgrade the value of the household's assets, land registration and titling programs contain a hidden agenda that needs to be mentioned. Although these programs may provide the owner with security of tenure, they also provide the prospective buyer with a legally secure mechanism to alienate rural property, thus setting the stage for possible land concentration in the future—a situation that will need careful monitoring (Lastarria 1989). Note that Fujimori's 1996 legislation set no upper limits as to how much land can be held by a person or a corporation, thereby abolishing older restrictions.

Environmental economists who follow G. Hardin (1968) argue that one practical way to reduce externalities is to alter property regimes, because, with clear property rights, owners will take better care of their resources; they are the ones who will benefit from these resources in the long run, so they will tend to exploit them in sustainable ways. Open resources, by contrast, are exposed to depredation. Even though this school of thought may appear to be an apologia for neo-liberalism, it proposes the interesting hypothesis that there are causal relationships between the type of property and the form in which humans use or destroy natural resources.

My aim is not to discuss the theory here but, rather, to draw attention to how this argument is currently being played out in Peru. Rural areas are in the process of changing the land tenure and property regime as a consequence of a 180-degree turn that resulted from the agrarian reform of 1970; when this reform adjudicated land, it did so primarily in collective units as cooperatives. These units have since dissolved, and its members have parceled the land to themselves as *de facto* private property on the coast; meanwhile, they are slowly obtaining legal title from the state. In the highlands there are also many small private properties; but for the most part the expropriated *haciendas* have dissolved into *communidades campesinas* (Mayer 1988), which, as we have seen, manage their commons. Their land-tenure systems have aspects of collective property, which disturbs neo-liberals because, they say, it discourages private investment in land improvement.

Nonetheless, as I have shown in Chapters 8 and 9, where *comunidades* prevail, communal controls and regulation change according to environmental conditions and over time, and property relationships also vary from restricted access to community members to private property strictly defined. Future research will have to reveal the extent to which communal control can also be associated with sustainable land use, not only in agriculture but also in pastures (Pinedo 2000), access to firewood, irrigation systems, and symbiosis with semi-domesticates and non-cultivated species. Even more interesting would be a delimitation of those factors that make for effective communal control and a recipe for how they can be fostered in all the Andean countries.

Commons systems in Latin America are under attack by neo-liberalism. In 1991, Mexico changed one of the most fundamental articles of its constitution, permitting the dissolution of the *ejido* system by a vote of a majority of its members. Peruvian legislation has rapidly followed suit with Fujimori's 1991 and 1996 laws relating to agricultural property (del Castillo 1997). The rationale behind these laws was that privatization would allow investments in land improvements and thus push toward higher productivity levels; however, little was said in them about the dispossession that such a process might entail. Privatization is also thought to endow the user with assets that can be realized in the market; moreover, creation of a land market, so the argument goes, will efficiently adjust productive land to conditions of supply and demand. Whether fragile or poor-quality land cultivated by *campesino* methods will ever fetch a high monetary value is a question that has not been answered; but then, "buy cheap and upgrade" is a strategy well known to speculators in gentrifying neighborhoods. Interestingly, neither in Mexico nor in Peru was there a great rush to dissolve *ejidos* or *comunidades*.

Regarding Mexico, the *Ejido* Reform Research Project (Cornelius and Myre 1998) has analyzed the implications of the reform process after ten years of implementation. It has three components, the first of which involves the titling of the domain of the *ejidos* and providing the owners of the individual parcels with their certificates. By 1998 about 59 percent of the *ejidos* were participating in the program. As for the next step, W. Cornelius and D. Myre (1998: 12–13) report that "relatively few *ejidatarios* have rushed to sell their land," and "the market for [*ejido*] land is very limited." These authors also point out that in lands close to expanding cities, tourist areas, and heavily commercial agricultural areas, the third step— the formal dissolution of the *ejido*—has taken place; but elsewhere it is rare. Private businesses have found easier legal solutions to gain access to *ejido* resources—namely, through rentals, sharecropping, partnerships, and collective contracts with the *ejido* authorities than through outright ownership. As Cornelius and Myre note, however, this is an early monitoring, and a generation or two may have to pass before the policy has an impact. In Peru the first phase of legally recognizing the lands of *comunidades* is at an early stage. When the proposed law was in the news, an exploratory survey conducted by Carlos Monge and Jaime Urrutia (1999) reported that, for the most part, people were interested in receiving an individual title but not in dissolving their communities.

Despite the neo-liberal push, the Fujimori government has quietly been using foreign aid to legalize land titles for *comunidades* as a priority before proceeding with titling individual properties within them. There are political economies of scale at work here: Fujimori gets all the *comuneros'* votes for one legal title, whereas titling each little *chacra* is too costly and may lead to intense disputes within the communities. The task of mapping each one of the millions of little parcels dotted on the hills must be daunting.

Communities refuse to go away despite the inducements to privatize. It seems that the legal status of communities as communal land with individual usufruct is unsettling to neo-liberal minds. Yet neo-liberalism happily admits to condominium property regimes in urban areas, and there is no reason why Andean communities could not be under the same legal regime. It is not as if members of the *comunidades campesinas* haven't carefully pondered the advantages and disadvantages of private property. On the contrary, they have thought about it with greater care than the theorizers. Where clear advantages to privatization present themselves, land has been privatized. Monge and Urrutia (1999) note that a limited market for lands does exist in the communities. Given the tremendous ecological diversity of the Andes, it is unlikely that a vigorous land market is going to develop for second- or third-quality land, and therefore it is questionable to suppose that a privatized market for land is going to lead to its improvement.[3] Reconversion of grass-lands from large private estates to community access certainly has changed their ecology, but as far as I know, the latter has not been properly evaluated, although community leaders do recognize that overgrazing has become a problem. This matter needs urgent and careful future research.

The conclusion worth underlining is that members of the communities have already carried out a tenure reform more effective than that of theoretically oriented policy advisers. To reform that which has already reformed is going to produce nothing but administrative and political chaos. Rather, as I suggested in Chapter 9, land registry systems should be entrusted to the local community to bring legal requirements into line with actual practice.

In the tropical areas, Roxana Barrantes (1992) discovered, there's an entire range of property regimes. Indigenous groups would like to collectively claim whole territories as original possessors, but the government is adjudicating limited land to them under the system of *comunidades nativas,* which is similar to the highland model. With advice from NGOs and sometimes sympathetic officers in the ministry, several *comunidades nativas* have sought adjacent allotments in order to approximate a broader notion of a continuous Indigenous ethnic territory. In this respect, Peru is far behind Brazil and Colombia, which have recognized large territorial claims for tropical Indigenous groups.

Settlers (*colonos*) in the tropical areas have a wide array of individual property forms, ranging from the most precarious recent occupation to informal systems and the legalized properly titled system. Roxana Barrantes (1992: 145) tested whether security of tenure as per proper titling was associated with sounder land management near Pucalpa in the Department of Ucayali. Results were mixed because the tenure arrangements—informal versus formal—overlapped with and even contradicted each other. Peru's cadastral system is in total disarray; therefore, the security of tenure that the legal piece of paper is supposed to guarantee is not a given. The Fujimori regime has upgraded the system, but the question of how effective it is now is requires further study (Lastarria 1989).

On the coast, practically all land has been privatized. Coastal smallholders are rightfully demanding their legal titles from the state. Gols (1988), Carter (1985), and Alvarez and Carter (1989) have shown that, with privatization, productivity did increase over the cooperative form; but as far as I am aware, studies of environmental impact of the new forms of tenure in coastal agricultural ecosystems have not yet been done. Common problems in areas of intense commercial production are overuse of pesticides and insecticides, leading to silent-spring conditions, contamination of the humans applying them, and salinization common to aging irrigation systems.

Another dimension of the property issue that concerns Andean and tropical Indigenous groups is their ownership of plant genetic resources. In this case, the West is reluctant to recognize these property rights, and the discussion of whether genes should remain a commons with open access, because they are the world's patrimony, is a heated one. In a strange reversal, agricultural businesses and agronomy departments argue for open access to genes, but want to patent them after they have been manipulated in laboratories. Indigenous people in the Third World are experimenting with various legal stances to counter this trend, but they have made little headway (Mooney 1979; Fowler and Mooney 1990; Brush and Stabinski 1996; Kloppenburg and Kleinman 1998).

We have seen throughout this book that the house economy is the bulwark that maintains genetic diversity. Specific research in joint projects by Brush (1984–1986) and Zimmerer (1985–1986), in which I participated, corroborates that to a large degree it is consumer preferences and the persistence of a subsistence agriculture carried out at monetary loss (see Chapter 7), whereby products often are kept off the market, that maintains genetic diversity in potatoes and other crops. Local botanical knowledge (principally that of women [Franquemont 1988]), a rich local taxonomy, and local pride in producing these varieties are important factors in maintaining genetic diversity. In each region there are a few enthusiastic "green-thumb" farming families who maintain high-diversity plant collections, and they do this without any apparent profit motive. Their seeds spread across the region through the support of the local inter-household economy, involving special patterns of seed inheritance, payment in kind, barter networks that include seed exchanges, and an active regional seed market. All of the above features are described by the neo-liberal model as symptoms of underdevelopment; nonetheless, they represent convenient hunting grounds for gene collectors of the green revolution, which in its next phase is moving away from public institutions to private corporations that seek profit from selling genetically modified crops. Andean genetic diversity is a case where common access leads to an increase in biological diversity rather than to a reduction. Keeping the market and its copywriters at bay may be a crucial task for all of us in the very near future. The environmental justice movement, too, may want to charge a large bill to the West reflecting the important services that a household-based mode of livelihood performs for humanity in gene storage and supply.

Neo-Liberal Approaches to Environmental Conservation

Neo-liberal environmental views of Andean landscapes would also stress that despite Andean people's admirable technology, survival skills, and environmental management, they are nonetheless a cause of environmental degradation through overpopulation, inadequate technology, poverty, and ignorance. Their proposals to mitigate such problems revolve around four solutions. One is to clear up property rights. The second is to impose environmental values through education and to induce self-regulation as a personal habit. The third solution, to evict the local population to create ecological reserves, has been implemented to some extent; but it also has been so severely criticized that nowadays environmental activists seek to find economically viable but environmentally friendly activities for the local populations, among which ecotourism is a popular but heatedly debated alternative of limited applicability.

The fourth solution, in opposition to neo-liberalism, but also a powerful movement from the developed First World, is to pressure the state and international donors to invest in environmental restoration and implement sustainable land uses in degraded and fragile lands, thereby improving the livelihood of the people and protecting the environment at the same time. I strongly support this last measure, although I would recommend that the investment be financed nationally so as to free the country from dependence on international donors. The economics of environmental restoration are complex. They are summed up in an apt term—*fragile lands*—coined by a Washington NGO called Development Alternatives Inc. (1984). Its main points are summarized in the next paragraph. (See also Mayer 1989b.)

Fragile lands are highly susceptible to ecological deterioration under current exploitation systems. Degradation manifests as secular declines in production, loss of productive potential over time, negative impacts that this land deterioration can have on other areas, and very slow and difficult regeneration of ecosystems once they have been degraded. In the Andes the important land formations that are subject to degradation are the slope lands in the mountains, which are extremely vulnerable to erosion; areas susceptible to desertification; and cleared land in the subtropical and tropical regions in the Amazon basin, which is deforested and exposed to inadequate agricultural and cattle-raising systems. Fragile lands are settled by poor peasant households and the negative impact of environmental degradation falls largely on them, but it also affects other regions downstream.

The secular trend, after an initial bounty, is toward falling incomes for those who settle in fragile lands; families sink into poverty before they abandon the land. Several economic-political factors cause degradation. Occupation of these lands is the result of long-term social processes that have pushed and keep pushing marginal populations onto ever more marginal lands. In the highlands, population increase on a limited land base is also a cause, although demographic growth is offset by high rates of emigration. Inadequate agricultural practices on fragile areas—such as slope agriculture, diminishing fallow, and overgrazing—are among the direct causes of soil erosion. But José María Caballero (1981) also points to social and economic determinants for the serious erosion problems in the highlands: the decadence of the *hacienda* system and the disintegration of the community as institutions. Both the *hacienda* system and the community used to play a role in regulating land use. Other causes are the increase in livestock and the intensification of agriculture due to the expansion of cash cropping.

In the tropical areas, inadequate colonization policies, pursued by international and national interests to construct roads for the extraction of non-renewable resources, have left numerous poor settlers in their wake (Hecht 1983). Government policies that promote colonization to offer escape valves to a growing unemployable population are also to blame. The cycle of establishing illegal cocaine fields, eradicating them, and subsequently relocating them to more inaccessible areas is clearly another cause. And coca growers, whose livelihood involves the most insecure cash crop of all, have no options but to apply a short-term extractive economic calculus that forces them to use land in unsuitable ways (Dourojeanni 1990).

Fragile lands are subject to the most complex *crematistic* economic calculus. They are marginal in every sense of the word. In comparison to good land, fragile lands yield less. And because they are less productive, they incur higher production costs than better lands. The investment required to improve and adequately maintain fragile lands is higher and yields lower profits than an equivalent investment in good land, at least in the short run. Finally, improving fragile lands is problematic because the benefits of doing so tend to take a long time to materialize and will benefit only future generations. Indeed, improving such lands is a long-term strategy difficult to impose on poor people whose capacity to save is very low. In the short run, the additional investment to improve fragile lands raises production costs, so the products from these lands cannot compete in the market with those from better lands. Recuperating fragile lands therefore has characteristics that recall the tragedy of the commons, as well as its benefits.

Should the improvement of marginal land be subsidized? For the poor Andean republics this is a crucial question, and the answer is yes. But who pays the bill? Impoverished national governments prefer to pass the hat to the international financial institutions, which in turn pass it on to private donors; and private donors' impatience for quick results, and the dynamics of their own changing intervention agendas, militates against long-term sustained environmental investments and their management. As many critics also note, donations come attached with too many strings to be effective. In any case, the amount donated relative to the quantity needed is so pitiful that results are bound to be disappointing. Seeking funds in this way is also demeaning, as it reeks of charity and carries the stigma of poverty. No wonder PRATEC and similar organizations react so negatively.

However, given a chance, along with a stable market, a better cash flow, and initial outside expenditure in land recuperation in public goods or as a commons, these activities could generate long-term and steady growth. The rural peasant household's proverbial capacity to self-finance long-term investments through its own labor process lies at the heart of the project. This capacity is sustained by subsistence production that feeds the household while the project matures. A lot of faith is required to accomplish such activities. Nonetheless, they are better options than poverty alleviation because they build on both a collective and an individual goal, rather than temporarily mitigating the worst symptoms of the stigma of poverty.

I think that the organizations best able to carry out these activities are the organized peasant communities in the Andes and the new Indigenous communities in the tropics. In the highlands, peasant communities control more than 30 percent of the fragile lands. They have experience that goes back for many centuries. And as an organization, they have the capacity to mobilize the local population in matters of collective interest. They are also more or less legitimate institutions recognized by the state, which may be persuaded to maintain special legislation in their favor. Environmental programs always have to work at the supra-household level, thus requiring interventions that are collectively organized and implemented. Locally elected authorities may be the best vehicle to implement new environmental policies at the local level. The autonomy and self-government capacity of the *comunidades,* which have a long tradition in their assemblies of creating, enforcing, and changing internal use regulations, should be seen as one of the most promising factors. *Comunidades* have the necessary judiciary mechanisms, allowing them to determine the best way to punish infractions. They can also tax the local population in labor, in goods, and sometimes in money to finance the long-term project of recuperating their environment. Indeed, today's communities manage complex grazing systems, regulate the consumption of forestry resources, administer the common infrastructure to control sanitary problems of their cattle, and sign contracts with firms, NGOs, and the state to carry out development, limited environmental recuperation,[4] and local irrigation projects. They have also organized vigilante groups to defend themselves from cattle thieves, boundary disputes, and, most recently, guerrillas.

Revitalizing the Andean community as an environmental recuperation project is a better idea than spending the same resources on targeted poverty alleviation for the same people. Hopefully more funds can flow in their direction. Andean villagers and Indigenous populations in the tropics, given the bleak outlook these days for neo-liberal hegemony, may find that in undertaking projects of cultural revitalization and ethnic reaffirmation, and in challenging the stigma of being "the underdeveloped" or "the poor," they can actually reaffirm their cultures through efforts at regenerating their own natural resources.

Notes

1. The way the *Mapa de la pobreza* has been constructed is critiqued by Trivelli (2000: 218), who points to various technical problems such as failure to find the right indicator for distinguishing between the poor and the not-poor, and between the chronically poor and those suffering a temporary loss of income; and underestimation of the contribution of subsistence production to income. On the other hand, two surprises emerged from the data: (a) the fact that women-headed households in Peru maintain viability (although rates of death during childbirth, infant mortality, and child malnutrition in rural Peru, are some of the worst in the continent) and (b) the positive correlation between number of children per household and its poverty level, contrary to Chayanovian expectations. Escobal et al. (1998) have also stated that access to land does not predict higher or lower poverty levels in rural areas—a finding that can likely be explained in terms of communal and kinship access to land; in other words, a little land produces subsistence but poverty is caused by difficulties in realizing monetary incomes.

2. Another cultural term for these pockets of poverty—*Perú profundo* (coined for different purposes by historian Jorge Basadre)—was used by the famous Peruvian writer Mario Vargas Llosa in reference to chronic structural poverty. My critique of Vargas Llosa's use of this term (Mayer 1992) is summarized at the end of this note because it expresses my concern with stigmatizing people. The context in question is Vargas Llosa's participation in an official investigation of an incident in January 1983, when the *comuneros* of Uchuraccay mistakenly killed eight journalists whom they believed to be Shining Path guerrillas. The deaths caused an uproar, and Vargas Llosa tried to mitigate the guilt of the *comuneros* by arguing that they should be forgiven because they were part of *Perú profundo*, which I have translated as "deep Peru." In the following critique (Mayer 1992: 193), page numbers in parentheses refer to the official report on this incident, which can be found in Vargas Llosa et al. (1983). "For Vargas Llosa deep Peru is 'archaic,' 'primitive.' It is economically depressed, with poor resources. The communities of the highlands 'represent perhaps the most miserable, needy human conglomerate' (p. 36). Deep Peru is defined by negatives and wants: 'Without water (i.e., faucets), without light (i.e., that kind of light which can be turned on and off), without medical attention, without roads that link them to the rest of the world' (p. 36). The people who live in deep Peru are isolated, malnourished ('condemned to survive on a meager diet of potatoes and lima beans') and cannot read and write (in Spanish, a language they do not speak). The 'struggle for existence is very hard, where death through starvation, sickness, or natural catastrophe threatens at every step' (p. 36). Deep Peru has only experienced official Peru through the ugliest expressions: 'Since republican times Iquichanos of Uchuraccay have known only landlord exploitation, the cheating exactions of the tax collector and the backlashes of mutinies and civil wars by military authorities' (p. 36). Deep Peru has not known progress. . . . '[T]he very notion of progress must be difficult to conceive by the communities whose members never remember having experienced any improvement in the conditions of their lives, but rather, prolonged stasis with periods of regression' (p. 36).

Identity defined by wants is a serious problem once poverty enters into the discourse; and when this problem gets refined into statistics, it grates even more. But then, poverty is an ugly thing and most of us would rather look away than have to stare at it. Rarefied numbers may stop us from averting our eyes. Readers may be pleased to know that my article (Mayer 1992), which ended by describing Uchuraccay as a deserted place, requires updating because the Fujimori government has provided nice-looking brick and tile roofed housing with running water and electricity to the fugitives who returned from the violence that wracked the region in the 1980s. Another sign that the people of Uchuraccay have abandoned the darkness of "deep Peru" is that most are now converts to evangelical sects (Del Pino 2000; Theidon 2000).

3. Privatization of land through the market has occurred as an unintended consequence of the agrarian reform. This consequence is well documented for the Cajamarca region (Deere 1990). Landowners kept the best land and sold the poorer slope lands to their peasants. In Ecuador good valley land is private and communal lands are on the slopes, although Otavaleño Indian entrepreneurs are slowly buying back valley lands piece by piece (Leonard Field 1995: personal communication).

4. The Peruvian government has been running anti-erosion and land-recuperation projects through a program known as Programa Nacional de Manejo de Cuencas Hidrográficas y Conservación de Suelos (PRONAMACHCS), which is independent of poverty alleviation financing and thus has a longer-lasting financial horizon. But it is directly related to poverty alleviation itself, because it provides employment at the local level. It also generates a degree of local participation since the ministry is mandated to create inter-community committees to plan and implement programs in a watershed. Trivelli (2000: 241) evaluates PRONAMACHCS positively, although she points out that it suffers from the general malaise of government-administered bureaucratic programs. Another program—Fondo Nacional Comunal de Desarrollo (FONCODES), which provides poverty alleviation funding and is run in a fairly decentralized fashion—has had similarly positive effects. FONCODES's main goal is to fund small projects in response to requests from local groups; thus it is driven by demand rather than by an imposition from above. It also fosters local organizations by allowing them to design and implement projects themselves. Although Palmer (n.d.) is enthusiastic about FONCODES's role in helping to pacify the Ayacucho region after the Shining Path movement, the program has been criticized for becoming bureaucratized and for allowing itself to be blatantly linked with the Fujimori electoral machinery (Trivelli 2000: 239).

Glossary

Note: (A.) = Aymara, (E.) = English, (Q.) = Quechua, and (Sp.) = Spanish.

aculli (Sp.): To chew coca the proper way.

actas (Sp.): Minutes of a meeting.

aguardiente (Sp.): Strong cane alcohol.

aisha (Q.): Rainfed agricultural system in Laraos.

ají (Sp.): Hot pepper capsicum. (Q.): *uchu.*

alcalde (Sp.): Highest position in the civil religious hierarchy. Translates as "mayor."

alcaldeza (Sp.): Highest position in the women's *cargo* system in Tangor.

alguito para ganar (Sp.): Common phrase meaning "a little something to earn."

allapakur (Q.): Payment in kind for help in the harvest.

altiplano (Sp.): High plateau in Puno and Bolivia.

amancebado (Sp.): To live in concubinage.

anaco (Q.): A woman's woven garment made from a single piece of cloth.

anexo (Sp.): A small dependent village that is part of a larger community or district.

apu (Q.): Literally, "lord"; a male deity who resides inside a mountain. Termed *wamani, jirka,* or *cabildo* in other regions.

arroba (Sp.): A weight measurement approximately equivalent to 25 pounds.

ayllu (Q.): A kinship and social unit.

ayni (Q.): Symmetrical reciprocal exchange. See also *waje-waje.*

aynoqa (Q. & A.): A sectorial fallow system of communal nonirrigated crop rotation.

ayuda (Sp.): Help. The term used in Tangor to mean "reciprocal exchange." Also, (Q.): *yanapa.*

bajillo (Sp.): A descriptive geographical term for "lower-lying lands suitable for orchards" in Laraos.

barrio (Sp.): A community subdivision in Tangor.

base (Sp.): A term used by Gudeman (1990) to describe the natural resource base of a house economy.

cacique (Sp.): A recognized Indian chief in the Spanish colonies. (The word is derived from the Caribbean languages.)

camachico (Q.): A local or minor authority. Also, land given to a person who has fulfilled his role as *cargo* holder in Laraos.

camarico (Q.) "Something done in favor of he who is absent in *mit'a* obligation, contribution of food for those who could not cultivate, gifts" (Murra and Adorno 1980: 1083).

cambio (Sp.): Change; exchange; rate of exchange. ("Change" as when one pays in a higher denomination and gets change back.) Also, rotation of crops; rotation of authorities; exchange; equivalence.

campesino (Sp.): Peasant. Also, a politically charged word describing a rural dweller. (In 1969 the government of Peru officialized this word as a substitute for the derogatory *indio*.)

cancha (Q.): Enclosed space. In Laraos it means "an extension of pasture land allotted to a family." Also refers to toasted whole kernels of maize.

cargo (Sp.): A position in the civil religious hierarchy. Literally, "burden."

ccatu (Q.): Market.

chacchay (Q.): To chew coca the proper way; *chacchapakuy* refers to the ceremonial chewing of coca.

centavo (Sp.): 1 cent in the *sol* coinage system of Peru; now termed a *céntimo*.

cereta (Sp.): A basket that measures volume used for barter.

chala (Q.): The tedious piling together of handfuls of staples as a form of laborious bulking by market women in Puno. (See Appelby 1976.)

ch'alla (A.): Libation.

chacchapakuy (Q.): A ceremonial session of coca consumption.

chacha (A.): Man. (Q.): *Qari*.

chachawarmi (A.): Husband-wife team. (Q.): *Qari-warmi*. See also *trukay wawa*.

chacmeo (Q.): First plowing with a *chaquitaclla* ("footplow").

chacra jitay (Q.): A ceremony to open a new sector of land in Tangor.

chacra (Q.): Field. (Termed *chacara* in old documents.).

chala (Q. & Sp.): Stalks of the maize plant used as fodder.

chalo (Q.): An assortment of native potato varieties. Also, any assortment.

chaupi (Q.): The midpoint or line dividing something in two halves, usually in dual asymmetry. Used in reference to fields, weavings, paintings, rows, groups, and regions.

chicha (Q.): Maize beer. Also, a new musical style in urban Lima involving Andean melodies and electronic instruments.

choclo (Q. & Sp.): Fresh corn on the cob.

chola, cholo (Sp.): Depending on context and tone of voice, a derogatory or admiring term for women and men in the marketplace. (See Seligmann 1989.)

chuño (Q.): Freeze-dried potato.

cocaquintu (Q.): Three leaves of coca held in the hand and used as an offering. Probably derives from *quinto* in colonial Spanish, referring to the royal fifth tax that had to be paid on gold and silver captured from Indians or mined.

cofradía (Sp.): A religious sodality in honor of a saint.

compadre (Sp.): Ritual kinsman.

común (Sp.): Commons; community of people.

comunero (Sp.): Member of a community.

comunidad de indígenas (Sp.): Indigenous peasant community; known after 1970 as *comunidades campesinas*.

comunidad madre (Sp.): Mother community; the larger village that rules over an *anexo*.

conversions (E.): A term used by Bohannan (1959) to mean "exchange between spheres."

conveyance (E.): A term used by Bohannan (1959) to mean "exchange within a sphere."

corregidor (Sp.): Spanish colonial official in charge of a rural area.

corvée (French): Obligatory labor draft.

costumbre (Sp.): Custom.

crematistic (Greek): A term used by Martínez Alier (1987) to refer to profit-seeking calculations that employ monetary measures of value.

cumbi (Q.): Textile cloth of high prestige value. Also termed *kumpi*.

cumplimiento (Sp.): To fulfill a promise. In Tangor the term refers to a meal and a gift that acknowledge, respectively, a service rendered and a debt that is still outstanding.

curaca (Q.): A chief or authority in the Andean region. Literally, "senior in birth order." Spaniards used the term interchangeably with *cacique*.

curacazgo (Sp.): Chieftainship.

derechos (Sp.): Rights. In Tangor the term refers to expected customary payments.

despacho (Q.): A religious ritual involving burnt offerings. Derived from the Spanish term meaning "sending away."

dyadic (E.): A relationship between two people at the expense of others. (See Note 21 in Chapter 4.)

edaphic (E.): A term used in ecology to refer to a configuration of plant organisms that establish themselves in a particular area due to conditions of soil and climate.

ejido (Sp.): Mexican communities with collective ownership and individual usufruct institutionalized by the Mexican agrarian reform.

ekeko (A.): A good-luck figurine depicting a smiling, smoking trader.

encargo (Sp.): To entrust; to send something to another person via a trusted person.

en vano (Sp.): In vain; for nothing.

encomendero (Sp.): The owner of an *encomienda*.

encomienda (Sp.): A group of Indians given by royal grant to a Spaniard.

estancia (Sp.): In the Andes, a pasture with a small house away from the main house.

estar en la chacra nomás (Sp.): An expression meaning "to be on the farm only" (hence a category of self-perceived unemployment and unworthiness).

faena (Sp.): Obligatory work for a community or a section of a community.

falderón (Sp.): Hillside. In Laraos, the term refers to a sloping land terrace (technically, a lynchette).

faltones (Sp.): Remiss; a person who regularly misses obligatory *faena* work.

fanega (Sp.): In Spain, a measure of land; in the Andes, a measure of seed and also of the land that absorbs a *fanega* of maize seed.

fiesta (Sp.): Feast. In the context of the Andes, a feast for the whole village sponsored by a person, often as part of a *cargo*.

forastero (Sp.): Foreigner. In the Andes, the term refers to a resident of a community who is not recognized as a full member. In colonial times, *forasteros* received tribute relief.

ganancias (Sp.): Earnings; profits.

ganar (Sp.): To win; to make profits.

ganarse la vida (Sp.): To make a living.

gasto (Sp.): Expenditures. In the house economy, *gasto* is an accounting category.

hacendado (Sp.): Landlord.

hacienda (Sp.): Landed estate in Latin America. Also, wealth or treasury.

hallmay (Q.): To chew coca the proper way.

hanegas (Sp.): Old Spanish for *fanega*. In the *visita* it refers to a measure of weight and a measure of land.

hilacata (Q): A traditional authority figure not necessarily associated with the *vara* system in Bolivia.

huayunca (Q.): A pair of ears of maize tied together by the pulled-back husks and hung on the rafters of a house to dry and to prevent it from being eaten by mice.

huerta (Sp.): Orchard.

huidos (Sp.): From the verb "to flee"; refers to runaway Indians fleeing from obligatory work services, especially the *mita*.

Indigenista (Sp.): A twentieth-century intellectual and social movement in Mexico and the Andean countries that proposed policies intended to integrate the Indigenous populations into the national mainstream.

indio coquero (Sp.): A derogatory term meaning "coca-chewing Indian."

indio (Sp.): Indian. A loaded word that, in current usage, refers to Indians as an insult. The polite term is *indígena*.

inti (Q.): A now-defunct Peruvian currency, in use from 1984 to 1989. Also, (Q.): sun; sun divinity.

jalka (Q.): An environmental descriptive term meaning "high *puna* lands"; but also a relative term referring to higher-lying land zones when compared to lower ones (used in the Huánuco region).

jornal (Sp.): Wage; day wage.

kichwa (Q.): An environmental descriptive term meaning "mid-level valley potato and maize lands"; but also a relative term referring to lower-lying land zones when compared to higher lying ones (used in the Huánuco region).

kuyaq (Q.): A phrase describing relatives who love the sponsor of a *fiesta*. (See Note 22 in Chapter 4.)

lata (Sp.): A measure of the volume of a tin can.

laymi (A.): A sector in a sectorial fallow system.

Libras Peruanas (Sp.): Coinage equivalent to one pound sterling, valid from 1860 to 1940.

llano (Sp.): Plain, not just in the geographical sense but also in terms of a person's character as straightforward, accessible, and honest.

llanta takay (Q.): Cutting and storing firewood. The term refers to ceremonial family work in Tangor.

llapa (Q.): Literally, "a little bit more"; the extra amount a vendor adds to a purchase after the bargained price has been agreed upon.

llaqtaruna (Q.): Members of a town; members of a community. The term is often used to distinguish members from outsiders.

lo andino (Sp.): An intellectual term used in Andean countries to refer to the specificity of Andean culture.

máchica (Q.): Toasted barley meal.

mahuay (Q.): Early-maturing potatoes; zones where early maturing crops can be grown; early-maturing agricultural cycle.

maizal (Sp.): The production zone where maize is grown.

manay (Q.): A request for a right or a claim; an obligation that is met only when called for.

manceba (Sp.): A female concubine.

marca del ganado (Sp.): Rituals celebrating the fertility of animals and marking them with tassels, firebrands, or other means of identification.

marka masha (Q.): Literally, "a son-in-law of the village." An outsider with diminished rights in a community.

mashua (Q): Andean tuber (*Traepoleum tuberosum*).

mayordomo (Sp.): Steward; employee of an *hacendado*. Also, *fiesta* sponsor.

medio (Sp.): Half. When referring to Peruvian money, it means 5 cents (half of 10 cents) in the *sol* coinage system.

menudencias (Sp.): Merchandise in very small quantities.

menudeo (Sp.): Retail; to trade in very small quantities.

mesa (Sp.): Table; a ritual table with an array of objects and coca used in divination and *despachos*. (Q.): *misa*.

mesero (Sp.): Waiter. In Laraos the term refers to a *cargo* for a year to guard crops in the sectorial fallow system. In Cusco, the *cargo* is called *arariwa*; the job includes warning farmers of the danger of impending frost.

mestizos (Sp.): A hierarchical "ethnic" and class term in rural areas that distinguishes them from *indios* or *campesinos*.

mindalaes (Q.): Full-time traders in pre-Hispanic chiefdoms of Quito, Ecuador. (See Salomon 1986.)

minka (Q.): Reciprocal exchange in which a quantity of goods and a meal compensates for work or a service performed. It can be reversible or irreversible; the latter is also known as "asymmetrical reciprocity."

minkado (Q.& Sp.): A person recruited to do a *minka*.

minkador (Q.& Sp.): A person who recruits another to do a *minka*.

misti (Q.): A Quechuaized and derogatory term for *mestizo*.

mita (Q.): Turn; obligatory work by turns; colonial labor draft to work in mines.

mit'a (Q.): Same as *mita*. Following Murra, some authors spell the term this way to distinguish the pre-Hispanic and village forms from the colonial labor draft.

mitas de agua (Sp. & Q.): Water distribution by turns for irrigation.

mitimaes, mitimaqkuna (Q.): Groups of people transplanted from their homelands under Inca rule, supposedly to help pacify a newly incorporated region.

montaña (Sp.): Literally, "mountain." An area of intense colonization. In the Andes it refers to the tropical mountain lowlands where coffee, coca, and other such crops can be grown.

morocho (Sp.): Strong, robust, dark. In Tangor the term refers to a ceremony of counting community members who had passed a *cargo*.

moya (Q.): In Laraos, a fenced communal area that is closed off to grazing during a cropping season.

mudaderos (Sp.): Rotational pastures; allotments of pasture land to permit rotational pasturing within it. The term is used in documents in Laraos.

mujeres de servicio (Sp.): Servant women.

mullu (Q.): A *spondylus* shell used for offerings and jewelry. Also, a trade item in pre-Hispanic Andes.

oca (Q): An Andean tuber (*Oxalis tuberosa*).

olluco (Q): An Andean tuber (*Ullucus tuberosus*). Also called *lisa* in the Southern Andes.

pachaca (Q.): An Incas census unit referring to approximately one hundred families.

pachamama (Q.): A female earth divinity.

pachamanca (Q.): A way of cooking a large festive meal, involving hot stones in a hole in the earth.

padrón (Sp.): A list or register.

para el gasto (Sp.): For home expenditure.

para plata (Sp.): For money. The term also refers to a field in which to plant a commercial crop.

parcela (Sp.): A small field; a small allotment.

parcialidad (Sp.): A section of a village; a territory (in the political sense); a kinship group (in colonial times).

patrón (Sp.): Boss; owner of an enterprise.

peón (Sp.): A worker. The term can have derogatory implications.

pérdida (Sp.): Loss.

personero (Sp.): Legal representative. The term used to refer to the highest-ranking representative who dealt with government, judiciary, and the legal profession in the name of the community. This office is now known as the *presidente* of the community.

peseta (Sp.): A now-defunct coin in Peru equal to 20 cents of the *sol*.

phaxsima (A.): Libation for money and metals. (See Harris 1987.)

pichicata (Sp.): Slang for "unrefined cocaine paste."

pichicatero (Sp.): A person who consumes cocaine paste; a person who works in the cocaine trade.

piso ecológico (Sp.): Ecotype; ecological zone.

plata (Sp.): Silver; money.

potreros (Sp.): A paddock or field with alfalfa.

principales (Sp.): Chiefs; authorities. In colonial documents, the word refers to native authorities.

pueblo (Sp.): Village; settlement.

puna (Sp. & Q.): High, cold, treeless areas in the Andes.

punaruna (Q.): People who live in the *puna*.

qollqa (Q.): A round storage structure in Inca administrative centers.

quebrada (Sp.): Ravine; deep narrow valley. In Laraos it refers to the lowest-lying lands within the community territory.

quintal (Sp.): A measure of weight equivalent to 46 kilos.

quipu (Q.): An Inca counting and information-storage device that uses knotted strings.

quipucamayoc (Q.): The person who knows how to use a *quipu*.

reál (Sp.): Ten cents in the *sol* coinage system.

reducción (Sp.): The colonial reform that congregated dispersed populations into nucleated villages.

regalo (Sp.): Gift. In the Tulumayo Valley the term refers to an assortment of non-commercial native varieties of potatoes, reserved for home consumption or as gifts.

rentable (Sp.): Profitable.

rescate (Sp.): Ransom; rescue. In colonial documents, it probably referred to barter and buying ore.

respeto (Sp.): Respect; dignity. The term is used in response to a racial slur or derogatory remark. *Faltar el respeto* means "to commit an offense that violates social hierarchies."

romanilla (Sp.): A weighing device that uses a spring.

rondas (Sp.): To do rounds. Also, a communally organized self-defense group guarding against cattle rustling. In recent times, the term has come to mean the self-defense organization that the peasants built up, with some coordination by the military, to protect the village from guerrillas.

secano (Sp.): Nonirrigated farming land.

señorío (Sp.): Pre-Hispanic political groups. John Murra and his followers use the term *ethnic groups* when translating *señorío* into English. It refers to a type of ethnicity different from the contemporary *indio-mestizo-blanco* racial-ethnic continuum.

Shining Path or *Sendero Luminoso.* (Sp.): Nickname for the Partido Comunista Peruano SL (Sendero Luminoso), a revolutionary guerrilla group. Members were locally referred to as *cumpas*, a term that derives from *compañero* ("comrade").

sierra (Sp.): Highland region, as opposed to the *costa* ("coast") or *montaña*.

sobra (Sp.): Remainder. Used by Gudeman (1990) as a concept in the house economy.

sol, soles (Sp.): Peruvian currency valid until 1982.

soltera (Sp.): Unmarried woman.

tambo (Q.): A way station on the Inca road system.

tasa (Sp.): Rate; tax rate.

taypi (A.): Middle. (Q.): *chaupi.*

tercio (Sp.): A measure of weight to be loaded onto burros or mules.

tiangues (Sp.): Market. This term is derived from Mesoamerican languages.

toma libre (Sp.): Free water.

tomin (Sp.): A coin of small denomination in early colonial times (8 *tomines* = 1 peso).

trago (Sp.): Cane alcohol distributed in shot glasses. From *tragar, meaning* "to swallow."

trato (Sp.): How one treats a person. See also *indio, cholo, mestizo, respeto.*

tributario (Sp.): A person obligated to pay Indian tribute in colonial times.

trocar (Sp.): To barter.

trukay wawa (Q.): Baked bread shaped like a human couple to indicate a change of sponsors in the *fiesta* system of Tangor. See also *chachawarmi.*

turnos (Sp.): Literally, "turns." The term refers to sectors in rainfed sectorial fallow systems.

uchu (Q.): Peppers of the genus capsicum. (Sp.): *ají.*

unay precio (Q. & Sp.): Old prices. The term is used in Tangor as a standard of value in barter.

vara (Sp.): Literally, "staff." The term is used to refer to the traditional authorities in communities, who use the staff as a symbol of their authority.

varayoq (Q.): The traditional authorities in communities who use the *vara.*

vecino (Sp.): Nonindigenous resident of a village or town. Translatable as "notable," the term avoids the use of *mestizo*.

verticality (E.): A term used by Murra and his students to refer to multiple use of Andean ecotypes.

visita (Sp.): Literally, "visit." The term refers to sixteenth-century inspection documents in *encomienda* tribute systems.

viuda (Sp.): Widow.

voluntad (Sp.): A term referring to symmetrical reciprocal exchange in which no accounts should be kept.

wacchillero (Q. & Sp.): A dependent herder in a *hacienda* who works for pastoralists.

waje-waje (Q.): A term referring to symmetrical reciprocal exchange in Tangor.

warmi (Q.): Woman; wife

yana (Q.): A servant of *curacas* in pre-Hispanic times. Also, the color black.

yanacona (Q.): The plural of *yana*. In modern times it refers to serfs on a *hacienda*.

yanaconaje (Sp.): The institution of serfdom and sharecropping in Peru.

yanantin (Q.): A pair of unequal elements. (See Platt 1986.)

yanapa (Q.): Help. The term refers to reciprocal exchange. See also *ayuda*.

yawasinakuy (Q.): Customary hospitality in Tangor.

yerba mate (Sp.): The leaf of the *mate* plant, used in Argentina and Paraguay.

yugada (Sp.): Day of plowing with a team of oxen. Also, a measure of land.

yunga (Q.): Hot lowlands, especially the zone between coastal valleys and the highlands where fruit and coca grow on the eastern slopes of the Andes.

References Cited

Abercrombie, T. (1998). *Pathways of Memory and Power: Ethnography and History Among Andean People*. Madison, University of Wisconsin Press.

Aguirre Beltrán, G. (1979). *Regions of Refuge*. Washington, D.C., Society for Applied Anthropology.

Alberti, G. (1970). Los movimientos campesinos. *La hacienda, la comunidad y el campesino en el Perú*. J. M. Mar (ed.). Lima, Instituto de Estudios Peruanos: 164–215.

Alberti, G., and F. Fuenzalida (1969). Pluralismo, dominación y personalidad. *Dominación y cambios en el Perú rural*. J. M. Mar (ed.). Lima, Instituto de Estuidos Peruanos.

Alberti, G., and E. Mayer (1974a). *Reciprocidad e intercambio en los Andes peruanos*. Lima, Instituto de Estudios Peruanos.

_____ (1974b). Reciprocidad andina: ayer y hoy. *Reciprocidad e intercambio en los Andes*. E. Mayer and G. Alberti (eds.). Lima, Instituto de Estudios Peruanos: 13–36.

Alberti, G., and R. Sánchez (1974). *Poder y conflicto social en el valle del Mantaro (1900–1974)*. Lima, Instituto de Estudios Peruanos.

Albó, X. (1996). "Making the Leap: From Local Mobilization to National Politics." *NACLA Report on the Americas* 29(5): 1522.

Allen, C. J. (1981). "To Be Quechua: The Symbolism of Coca Chewing in Highland Peru." *American Ethnologist* 8(1): 157–171.

_____ (1988). *The Hold Life Has: Coca and Cultural Identity in an Andean Community*. Washington, D.C., Smithsonian Press.

Allpanchis (1971). "Ritos agrícolas y ganaderos del sur andino." *Revista del Instituto de Pastoral Andina* 3.

Altamirano, T. (1990). *Los que se fueron: Peruanos en Estados Unidos*. Lima, Pontificia Universidad Católica del Perú.

_____ (1992). *Exodo: Peruanos en el Exterior*. Lima, Pontificia Universidad Católica del Perú.

Alvarez, E. (1998). The Economic Effects of the Illicit Drug Sector in Peru. *Fujimori's Peru: The Political Economy*. J. Crabtree and J. Thomas (eds.). London, Institute of Latin American Studies, Brookings Institution: 106–124.

Alvarez, E., and C. M. Carter (1989). Changing Paths: The Decollectivization of Agrarian Reform Agriculture in Coastal Peru. *Agrarian Structure and Reform in Latin America*. W. Thiesenhusen (ed.). Boston, Allen & Unwin: 156–187.

Anderlini, L., and H. Sabourian (1992). Some Notes on the Economics of Barter, Money and Credit. *Barter, Exchange and Value*. C. Humphrey and S. H. Jones (eds.). Cambridge, Cambridge University Press: 75–107.

Anders, M. B. (1990). *Historia y etnografía: Los mitmaq de Huánuco en las visitas de 1549, 1557 y 1562*. Lima, Instituto de Estudios Peruanos.

Annis, S. (1987). *God and Production in a Guatemalan Town*. Austin, University of Texas Press.

Apffel-Marglin, F., and PRATEC. (eds.) (1988). *The Spirit of Regeneration: Andean Culture Confronting Western Notions of Development*. London, Zed Books.

Appadurai, A. (1986). *The Social Life of Things*. Cambridge, Cambridge University Press.

Appelby, G. (1976a). The Role of Urban Food Needs in Regional Development, Puno, Peru. *Regional Analysis: Economic Systems*, Vol. 1. C. A. Smith (ed.). New York, Academic Press: 147–178.

_____ (1976b). Export Monoculture and Regional Social Structure in Puno, Peru. *Regional Analysis Economic Systems*, Vol. 2. C. A. Smith (ed.). New York, Academic Press: 291–307.

Arnillas Laffert, F. (1996). "Ekeko, alacitas y calvarios: La fiesta de Stanta Cruz en Juliaca." *Allpanchis* 47: 119–135.

Arnold Y., D. (1997). Introducción. *Parentesco y género en los Andes: Mas allá del silencio: Las fronteras del género en los Andes*, Vol. 1. D. Arnold Y. (ed.). La Paz, Biblioteca de Estudios Andinos: 13–52.

_____ (1998). De "castas" a "kastas" enfoques hacia el parentesco andino. *Parentesco y género en los Andes: Gente de carne y hueso: Las tramas del parentesco en los Andes*, Vol. 2. D. Arnold Y. La Paz (ed.), Biblioteca de Estudios Andinos: 15–66.

Arnold Y., D. (ed.) (1997/1998). *Parentesco y género en los Andes*. La Paz, Biblioteca de Estudios Andinos.

Assadourian, C. S. (1995). Exchange in the Ethnic Territories Between 1530 and 1567: The Visitas of Huánuco and Chucuito. *Ethnicity, Markets, and Migration in the Andes: At the Crossroads of History and Anthropology*. B. Larson and O. Harris (eds.). Durham, Duke University Press: 101–134.

Babb, F. E. (1998). *Between Field and Cooking Pot: The Political Economy of Marketwomen in Peru*. Austin, University of Texas Press.

Bachelard, G. (1964). *The Poetics of Space*. Translated by Maria Jolas. New York: Orion Press.

Baker, P. T., and M. A. Little (eds.) (1976). *Man in the Andes: A Multidisciplinary Study of High-Altitude Quechua*. Stroudsburg, Pa., Dowden, Hutchinson & Ross.

Banfield, E. (1958). *The Moral Basis of a Backward Society*. New York, Free Press.

Barlett, P. F. (1980). Cost-Benefit Analysis: A Test of Alternative Methodologies. *Agricultural Decision Making: Anthropological Contributions to Rural Development*. P. F. Barlett (ed.). New York, Academic Press: 137–160.

_____ (1989). Introduction: Dimensions and Dilemmas of Householding. *The Household Economy: Reconsidering the Domestic Mode of Production*. R. R. Wilk (ed.). Boulder, Colo., Westview Press: 3–10.

Barnett, C. (1960). *An Analysis of Social Movements on a Peruvian Highland Hacienda*. Ann Arbor, Dissertation Abstracts.

Barrantes, R. (1992). Land Tenure Security and Resource Use in the Peruvian Amazon: A Case Study of the Ucayali Region. Ph.D. thesis, University of Illinois at Urbana, Champaign.

Barrig, M. (1993). *Seis familias en la crisis*. Lima, Asociación Laboral para el Desarrollo.

Barth, F. (1956). "Ecologic Relationships of Ethnic Groups in Swat, North Pakistan." *American Anthropologist* 58: 1079–1089.

_____ (1967). Economic Spheres in Dafur. *Themes in economic anthropology*. R. Firth (ed.). London, Tavistock Publications. A.S.A. Monograph Series No 8: 149–174.

_____ (1969). *Ethnic Groups and Boundaries*. London, Allen and Unwin.

Basadre, J. (1947). *La multitúd, la ciudad y el campo en la historia del Perú*. Lima, Editorial Huascarán.

Baudin, L. (1961). *A Socialist Empire: The Incas of Peru*. Princeton, N.J., Van Nostrand.

Bayliss-Smith, T. P. (1982). *The Ecology of Agricultural Systems*. Cambridge, Cambridge University Press.

Becker, G. (1981). *A Treatise on the Family*. Cambridge, Harvard University Press.

Beltrán Gallardo, E. (1977). *Las guerrillas de Yauyos en la emancipación del Perú 1820–1824*. Lima, Editories Técnicos Associados.

Bernard, C. (1998). ¿Poliginia cacical o poliginia generalizada? El caso de Huánuco, Perú (1562). *Parentesco y género en los Andes: Gente de carne y hueso: Las tramas del parentesco en los Andes*, Vol. 2. D. Arnold Y. La Paz (ed.), Biblioteca de Estudios Andinos: 341–362.

Bernstein, H. (1994). Agrarian Classes in Capitalist Development. *Capitalism and Development*. L. Sklair (ed.). London, Routledge: 40–71.

Bigenho, M. (1998). "Coca as a Musical Trope of Bolivian Nation-ness." *Political and Legal Anthropology Review* 12: 114–122.

Blau, P. (1967). *Exchange and Power in Social Life*. New York, Wiley.

Blondet, C., and C. Montero (1995). *Hoy: Menú poular, comedores en Lima*. Lima, Instituto de Estudios Peruanos.

Blum, V. (1995). *Campesinos y teóricos agrarios: Pequeña agricultura en los Andes del sur del Perú*. Lima, Instituto de Estudios Peruanos.

Bohannan, P. (1959). "The Impact of Money in an African Subsistence Economy." *Journal of Economic History* 19(4): 491–503.

_____ (1963). *Social Anthropology*. New York, Holt, Reinhart and Winston.

Bohannan, P., and G. Dalton (1965). Introduction. *Markets in Africa*. A. M. o. N. History. Garden City, N.J., Doubleday & Anchor.

Boldó y Clement, J. (1986). *La coca andina: Visión de una planta satanizada*. Mexico, Boldó y Clement, Juan (editore) & Instituto Indigenista Interamericano.

Boletín IFEA (1975). "Número especial dedicado a San Juan de Huascoy." *Boletín del Instituto Francés de Estudios Andinos* 4(1–2, 3–4).

Bolton, R. (1974). "To Kill a Thief: A Kallawalla Sorcery Session in the Lake Titicaca Region of Peru." *Anthropos* 69: 191–215.

_____ (1977). The Qolla Marriage Process. *Andean Kinship and Marriage*. R. Bolton and E. Mayer (eds.). Washington, D.C., American Anthropological Association.

Bolton, R., and C. Bolton (1975). *Conflictos en la familia andina*. Cusco, Centro de Estudios Andinos.

Bolton, R., and E. Mayer (eds.) (1977). *Andean Kinship and Marriage*. Washington, D.C., American Anthropological Association.

Boserup, E. (1965). *The Conditions of Agricultural Growth*. Chicago, Aldine.

Bourdieu, P. (1977). *Outline of a Theory of Practice*. Cambridge, Cambridge University Press.

Bourque, S. C., and K. Warren (1981). *Women of the Andes: Patriarchy and Social Change in Two Peruvian Towns*. Ann Arbor, University of Michigan Press.

Boza Barducci, T. (1972). Ecological Consequences of Pesticides Used for the Control of Cotton Insects in Cañete Valley, Peru. *The Careless Technology: Ecology and International Development*. M. T. Farvar and J. P. Milton (eds.). Garden City, N.Y., Natural History Press: 423–438.

Brack, A. (2000). Biodiversidad y mercado. *Peru: El problema agrario en debate SEPIA VIII*. I. Hurtado, C. Trivelli, and A. Brack (eds.). Lima, Seminario Permanente de Investigacion Agraria: 443–501.

Bradby, B. (1975). "The Destruction of the Natural Economy." *Economy and Society* 4: 127–161.

_____ (1982). "Resistance to capitalism" in the Peruvian Andes. *Ecology and Exchange in the Andes*. D. Lehmann (ed.). Cambridge, Cambridge University Press: 97–123.

Brougère, A. M. (1986). "Transformaciones sociales y movilidad de las poblaciones en una comunidad del Nor-Yauyos." *Edición Especial Políticas Agrarias y Estrategias Campesinas, Boletín del Instituto Francés de Estudios Andinos* 15(2).

_____ (1992). *¿Y por qué no quedarse en Laraos? Migración y retorno en una comunidad altoandina*. Lima, Instituto Francés de Estudios Andinos (IFEA) & Instituto Andino de Estudios de Población y Desarrollo (INANDEP).

Browman, D. (1974). "Pastoral Nomadism in the Andes." *Current Anthropology* 15(2): 188–196.

Brunel, G. R. (1975). Variation in Quechua Folk Biology. Ph.D. thesis, University of California at Berkeley.

Brunschwig, G. (1986). "Sistemas de producción de laderas de altura." *Edición Especial Politicas Agrarias y Estrategias Campesinas, Boletín del Instituto Francés de Estudios Andinos* 15(2).

_____ (1996). El alto valle de Cañete: El matorral y la puna. *Comprender la agricultura campesina en los Andes Centrales Perú-Bolivia*. P. Morlon (ed.). Lima/Cusco, Instituto Francés de Estudios Andinos Centro de Estudios Regionales Andinos, Bartolomé de las Casas: 374–398.

Brush, S. B. (1976a). "Man's Use of an Andean Ecosystem." *Human Ecology* 4(2): 147–166.

_____ (1976b). "Introduction to Cultural Adaptations to Mountain Ecosystems." *Human Ecology* 4(2): 125–134.

_____ (1977a). Mountain, Field, and Family: The Economy and Human Ecology of an Andean Village. Philadelphia, University of Pennsylvania Press.

_____ (1977b). The Myth of the Idle Peasant: Employment in a Subsistence Economy. Peasant Livelihood. *Studies in Economic Anthropology and Cultural Ecology*. R. Halperin (ed.). New York, St. Martin's Press: 60–78.

_____ (1986). "Genetic Diversity and Conservation in Traditional Farming Systems." *Journal of Ethnobiology* 6: 151–167.

_____ (1989). Crop Development in Centers of Domestication: A Case Study of Andean Potato Agriculture. *Agroecology and Small Farm Development in the Third World*. M. Altieri and S. Hecht (eds.). Boca Raton, CRC Press: 161–170.

_____ (2000). The issues of in situ conservation of crop genetic resources. *Genes in the Field.* S. B. Brush (ed.). Boca Raton, Lewis Publishers: 3–26.

Brush, S. B., H. J. Carney, et al. (1981). "Dynamics of Andean Potato Agriculture." *Economic Botany* 35(1): 70–85.

Brush, S. B., and D. Stabinsky (eds.) (1996). *Valuing Local Knowledge: Indigenous People and Intellectual Property Rights.* Washington, D.C., Island Press.

Brush, S. B., and J. E. Taylor (1992). Diversidad biológica en el cultivo de papa. *La chacra de papa: economía y ecología.* E. Mayer, M. Glave, S. B. Brush, and J. E. Taylor (eds.). Lima, Centro Peruano de Investigación Social: 217–256.

Brush, S. B., J. E. Taylor, et al. (1992). "Biological Diversity and Technology Adoption in Andean Potato Agriculture." *Journal of Development Economics* 39: 365–387.

Brycerson, D. (2000). Peasant Theories and Smallholder Policies: Past and Present. *Disappearing peasantries? Rural Labor in Africa, Asia and Latin America.* D. Brycerson, C. Kay, and J. Mooij (eds.). London, Intermediate Technology Publications: 1–36.

Brycerson, D., C. Kay, et al. (eds.) (2000). *Disappearing peasantries? Rural Labor in Africa, Asia and Latin America.* London, Intermediate Technology Publications.

Buechler, H. C., and J. M. Buechler (1996). *The World of Sofía Velazquez: The Autobiography of a Bolivian Market Vendor.* New York, Columbia University Press.

Buechler, J. M. (1997). The Visible and Vocal Politics of Female Traders and Small Scale Producers in La Paz. *Women and Economic Change: Andean Perspectives.* A. Miles and H. Buechler (eds.). Washington, D.C., Society for Latin American Anthropology Publication Series, American Anthropology Association: 75–88.

Burchard, R. E. (1974). La coca y trueque de alimentos. *Reciprocidad e intercambio en los Andes.* G. Alberti and E. Mayer (eds.). Lima, Instituto de Estudios Peruanos: 209–251.

_____ (1978). "Una nueva perspectiva sobre la masticación de la coca." *América Indígena* 38(4): 809–835.

Burga, M., and W. Reátegui (1981). *Lanas y capital mercantil en el sur del Perú: La casa Ricketts, 1895–1935.* Lima, Instituto de Estudios Peruanos.

Bustamante, A., E. Chávez, et al. (1990). *De Marginales a Informales.* Lima, Desco.

Caballero, J. M. (1981). *Economía Agraria de la sierra peruana antes de la reforma agraria de 1969.* Lima, Instituto de Estudios Peruanos.

_____ (1984). "Agricultura peruana y campesinado: Balance de la investigación reciente y patrón de evolución." *Apuntes* 14: 3–38.

Caballero Martín, V. (1979). Historia de las haciendas de la División Ganadera de la Cerro de Pasco. *Campesinado y capitalismo: Ponencias en el primer seminario sobre campesinado y proceso regional en la sierra central:* 101–118.

_____ (1981). *Imperialismo y campesinado en la sierra central.* Huancayo, Instituto de Estudios Andinos.

Cabieses, F. (1980). Aspectos etnológicos de la coca y de la cocaína. *Cocaína.* R. Jerí (ed.). Lima, Pacific Press.

Cáceres, B. (1978). "La Coca, el mundo andino y los extirpadores de idolatrías del siglo xx." *América Indígena* 37(4): 849–866.

_____ (1990). "Historia, prejuicios y versión psiquiátrica del coqueo andino." *Perú Indígena* 12(28): 31–72.

Camino, A. (1981). Tiempo y espacio en la estrategia de subsistencia andina: Un caso de las vertientes orientales sud-Peruanas. *El Hombre y su ambiente en los Andes centrales.* Osaka, National Museum of Ethnology: 11–38.

Camino, A., J. Recharte, et al. (1981). Flexibilidad calendárica en la agricultura tradicional de las vertientes orientales de los Andes. *La Tecnología en el mundo andino: runakunap kawsayninkupaq rurasqan kunanqa.* H. Lechtman and A. M. Soldi (eds.). Mexico City, Universidad Nacional Autónoma de México.

Campbell, B., and R. Godoy (1986). *Commonfield Agriculture: The Andes and Medieval England Compared.* Proceedings of the Conference on Common Property Resource Management. Washington, D.C., National Academy Press.

Canelas Orellana, A., and J. C. Canelas Zannier (1983). *Bolivia—Coca cocaina: Subdesarrollo y poder político.* Cochabamba, Los Amigos del Libro.

Caro, D. A. (1978). "Review of Alpacas, Sheep and Men." *Annales: Economies, Sociétés, Civilizations* 33e Année (5–6): 1214–1217.

Carter, M. R. (1985). Parcelación y productividad del sector reformado: cuestiones teoricas y una eficiente alternativa institucional mixta. *Las parcelaciones de las cooperativas agrarias del Perú.* A. González Zúñiga and G. Torre (eds.). Chiclayo, Centro de Estudios Sociales Solidaridad: 311.

Carter, W. (1973a). *Comunidades Aymaras y reforma agraria en Bolivia.* México, Instituto Indigenista Interaméricano.

_____ (1973b). *Land in a Traditional Aymara Community.* Symposium on the Community and the Hacienda Reconsidered, Mexico City, American Anthropological Association.

_____ (1977). Trial Marriage in the Andes. *Andean Kinship and Marriage.* R. Bolton and E. Mayer (eds.). Washington, D.C., American Anthropological Association: 177–216.

_____ (1989). Uso tradicional de la hoja de coca y narcotráfico. *La coca, tradición, rito, identidad.* Mexico, Instituto Indigenista Interamericano: 17–29.

Carter, W., and M. Mamani (1978). "Patrones de uso de coca en Bolivia." *América Indígena* 38(4): 905–937.

Casaverde, J. (1977). El trueque en la economía pastoril. *Pastores de puna: uywamichiq punarunakuna.* J. A. Flores Ochoa (ed.). Lima, Instituto de Estudios Peruanos: 171–191.

Castelli, A., M. Koth de Paredes, and M. Mould de Pease (eds.) (1981). *Etnohistoria y Antropología andina: Ayllu, parcialidad y etnía.* Segunda jornada del Museo Nacional de Historia. Lima, Museo Nacional de Historia.

Castro Pozo, H. (1924). *Nuestra comunidad indígena.* Lima. Editorial "El Lucero" Del Ayllu al cooperativismo socialista. P. Barrantes Castro

_____ (1936). "Del Ayllu al cooperativismo socialista." Lima. "El Lucero" Del Ayllu al cooperativismo socialista. P. Barrantes Castro

Castro, V. (2000). *Nispa Ninchis/Decimos Diciendo: Conversaciones con John Murra.* Lima, Instituto de Estudios Peruanos.

Chambers, R. (1983). *Rural Development: Putting the Last First.* London, Longman.

Chapman, A. (1980). "Barter as a universal mode of exchange." *L'Homme* 20(3): 33–88.

Chávez, E., and J. Chacaltana (1994). *Cómo se financian las microempresas y el agro*. Lima, Stilo Novo.

Chayanov, A. V. (1966). *The Theory of Peasant Economy*. Homewood, Ill., American Economic Association.

Cheal, D. (1989). Strategies of Resource Management in Household Economies: Moral Economy or Political Economy? *The Household Economy: Reconsidering the Domestic Mode of Production*. R. R. Wilk (ed.). Boulder, Colo., Westview Press: 11–22.

Chibnik, M. (1978). "The Value of Subsistence Production." *Journal of Anthropological Research* 34(4): 551–576.

Choque Canqui, R. (1987). Los caciques aymaras y el comercio en el Alto Perú. *La participación indígena en los mercados surandinos*. O. Harris, B. Larson, and E. Tandeter (eds.). La Paz, Centro de Estudios de la Realidad Económica y Social: 357–377.

Cieza de León, P. (1947). *Primera parte de la crónica del Perú*. Madrid, Biblioteca de Autores Españoles.

Clark, G. (1994). *Onions Are My Husband: Survival and Accumulation by West African Market Women*. Chicago, University of Chicago Press.

Claverías, R. (1978). "El mercado interno y la espontaneidad de los movimientos campesinos: Puno 1950–1968." *Allpanchis* 11/12: 151–173.

Cobo, B. (1979). *History of the Inca Empire*. Austin, University of Texas Press.

Collins, J. L. (1986). "The Household and Relations of Production in Southern Peru." *Comparative Studies in Society and History* 28(4): 651–671.

——— (1988). *Unseasonal Migrations: Rural Labor Scarcity in Peru*. Princeton, Princeton University Press.

Comisión Andina de Juristas (ed.) (1994). *Drogas y control penal en los andes: Deseos, utopias y efectos perversos*. Lima, Comisión Andina de Juristas.

Concha Contreras, J. (1975). "Relacion entre pastores y agricultores." *Allpanchis* 8: 67–102.

Cornelius, W., and D. Myre (eds.) (1998). *The Transformation of Rural Mexico: Reforming the Ejido Sector*. San Diego, University of California, San Diego.

Cornick, T., and R. A. Kirby (1981). *Interactions of Crops and Livestock Production in the Generation of Technology in Sloped Areas*. Ithaca, Cornell University.

Cotlear, D. (1989). *Desarrollo campesino en los Andes: Cambio tecnológico y transformación social en las comunidades de la sierra del Perú*. Lima, Instituto de Estudios Peruanos.

Cotler, J. (1959). *Los Cambios en la propiedad, la comunidad y la familia en San Lorenzo de Quinti*. Lima, Instituto de Etnología y Arqueología, Universidad Nacional Mayor de San Marcos.

——— (1968). La Mecánica de Dominación Interna y el cambio social en la Sociedad Rural. *Perú Problema: 5 Ensayos*. Lima, Instituto de Estudios Peruanos.

——— (1999). *Drogas y política en el Perú: La conexión norteamericana*. Lima, Instituto de Estudios Peruanos.

Craig, A. K. (1985). Cis-Andean Environmental Transects: Late Quaternary Ecology of Northern and Southern Peru. *Andean Ecology and Civilization: An Interdisciplinary Perspective on Andean Ecological Complementarity*. S. Masuda, I. Shimada, and C. Morris (eds.). Tokyo, University of Tokyo Press: 23–44.

Custred, G. (1974). Llameros y el trueque interzonal. *Reciprocidad e intercambio en los Andes peruanos*. G. Alberti and E. Mayer (eds.). Lima, Instituto de Estudios Peruanos: 252–289.

———— (1977). Las punas de los Andes centrales. *Pastores de Puna*. J. Flores Ochoa (ed.). Lima, Instituto de Estudios Peruanos.

———— (1980). Parentesco, subsistencia y economía en zonas de puna. *Parentesco y matrimonio en los Andes*. E. Mayer and R. Bolton (eds.). Lima, Pontificia Universidad Católica: 539–568.

Dalton, G. (1960). "A Note on the Clarification on Economic Surplus." *American Anthropologist* 64(2): 483–490.

Dalton, G. (ed.) (1981). *Symposium: Economic Anthropology and History: The Work of Karl Polanyi*. Research in Economic Anthropology. Greenwich, Conn., JAI Press.

de Janvry, A. (1981). *The Agrarian Question and Reformism in Latin America*. Baltimore, Johns Hopkins University Press.

de Janvri, A., E. Sadulet, et al. (1989). "Land and Labor in Latin American Agriculture from the 1950s to the 1980s." *Journal of Peasant Studies* 16(3): 396–424.

De la Cadena, M. (1977). *Hombres y Tierras: Población y Estructura Agraria en la Cuenca del Río Cañete. Departamento de Ciencias Sociales*. Lima, Pontificia Universidad Católica.

———— (1980). *Economía campesina: Familia y comunidad en Yauyos. Departamento de Ciencias Sociales*. Lima, Pontificia Universidad Católica.

———— (1989). Cooperación y conflicto. *Cooperación y conflicto en la comunidad andina: Zonas de producción y organización social*. E. Mayer and M. De la Cadena (eds.). Lima, Instituto de Estudios Peruanos: 77–112.

———— (1997). Matrimonio y etnicidad en las comunidades andinas (Chitapampa, Cusco). *Parentesco y género en los Andes: Mas allá del silencio: Las fronteras del género en los Andes*, Vol. 1. D. Arnold Y (ed.). La Paz, Biblioteca de Estudios Andinos: 123–149.

———— (2000). *Indigenous Mestizos: The Politics of Race and Culture in Cuzco, Peru, 1919–1991*. Durham, Duke University Press.

De la Torre, C., and M. Burga (1987). *Andenes y Camellones en el Peru andino*. Lima, CONCYTEC.

Deere, C. D. (1990). *Household and Class Relations: Peasants and Landlords in Northern Peru*. Berkeley, University of California Press.

Deere, C. D., and A. de Janvry (1981). "Demographic and Social Differentiation Among Northern Peruvian Peasants." *Journal of Peasant Studies* 8(3): 335–366.

Deere, C. D., and M. León de Leal (1982). *Women in Andean Agriculture: Peasant Production and Rural Wage Employment in Colombia and Peru*. Rome, International Labour Office.

Degegori, C., and M. Valderrama, et al. (1978). *Indigenismo, Clases Sociales y Problema Nacional*. Lima, Ediciones CELTAS (Centro Latinoamericano de Trabajo Social).

Del Castillo, L. (1997). "Propiedad rural, titulación de tierras y propiedad comunal." *Debate Agrario* 26: 59–80.

Del Pino, P. (2000). "Uchuraccay: memoria y representación de la violencia política en los Andes." Paper presented at the seminar "Memoria colectiva y violencia política en América del Sur." Social Science Research Council, Montevideo, Uruguay, November 26–December 2, 2000.

Denevan, W. M. (1987). Abandono de terrazas en el Perú andino: Extensión, causas y propuestas de restauración. *Andenes y Camellones en el Peru andino.* C. De la Torre and M. Burga (eds.). Lima, CONCYTEC: 255–259.

Development Alternatives Inc. (1984). *Fragile Lands: A Theme Paper on Problems, Issues, and Approaches for Development of Humid Tropical Lowlands and Steep Slopes in the Latin American Region.* Washington, D.C., Development Alternatives Inc.: 98.

Díaz Martínez, A. (1969). *Ayacucho, hambre y esperanza.* Ayacucho, Ediciones Waman Puma.

Dirección de Comunidades Campesinas (1980). *Comunidades campesinas del Perú, información básica.* Lima, Ministerio de Agricultura, Dirección de Comunidades Campesinas y Nativas.

Dobbyns, H., P. Doughty, et al. (1971). *Peasants, Power, and Applied Social Change: Vicos as a Model.* Beverly Hills, Sage Publications.

Dollfus, O. (1981). *El reto del espacio andino.* Lima, Instituto de Estudios Peruanos.

Donkin, R. A. (1979). *Agricultural Terracing in the Aboriginal New World.* Tucson, University of Arizona Press.

Dourojeanni, M. J. (1990). *Amazonía: ¿Qué hacer?* Iquitos, Centro de Estudios Amazónicos.

Duviols, P. (1973). "Huari y Llacuaz, Agricultores y pastores: Un dualismo prehispánico de oposición y complementaridad." *Revista del Museo Nacional* 39: 153–192.

Earle, T. (1985). Commodity Exchange and Markets in the Inca State: Recent Archaeological Evidence. *Markets and Marketing, Monographs in Economic Anthropology*, Vol. 4. S. Plattner (ed.). Lanham, Md., University Press of America and Society for Economic Anthropology: 399–416.

Earls, J. (1992). Viabilidad productiva de la comunidad andina. *Futuro de la comunidad campesina.* CIPCA. La Paz, CIPCA: 155–172.

Eigner, U. (1997). "Alimentación y nutrición infantil en los Andes: Nuevos enfoques en la medición e interpretación del estado nutricional de la niñez." *Revista Andina* 30(2): 283–324.

Elías, L. (1994). Estudios sobre la pobreza en el Perú: Bibliografía comentada. *Pobreza y políticas sociales en el Perú.* J. Anderson, J. Chacaltana, L. Elías et al. (eds.). Lima, Universidad del Pacífico.

Ellen, R. (1982). *Environment, Subsistence and System: The Ecology of Small-Scale Social Formations.* Cambridge, Cambridge University Press.

Ellenberg, H. (1955). "Vegetationsstufen in den Prehumiden bis Preariden Bereichen der Tropischen Anden." *Phytoconologia* 2: 368–387.

Ellis, F. (1988). *Peasant Economics: Farm Households and Agrarian Development.* Cambridge, Cambridge University Press.

Eresue, M., and A. M. Brougère (eds.) (1988). *Politicas agrarias y estrategias campesinas en la cuenca del Cañete.* Lima, Universidad Nacional Agraria and Instituto Francés de Estudios Andinos.

Erickson, C. (1987). Agricultura en camellones en la cuenca del Lago Titicaca: Aspectos técnicos y su futuro. *Andenes y camellones en el Perú andino*. C. De la Torre and M. Burga (eds.). Lima, CONCYTEC. 331–351.

Escobal, J. (1991). La Agricultura peruana en el contexto internacional. *Perú: el problema agrario en debate SEPIA IV*. C. I. Degregori, J. Escobal, and B. Marticorena (eds.). Lima, Seminario Permanente de Investigación Agraria: 19–54.

_____ (1994). "Impacto de las políticas de ajuste sobre la pequeña agricultura." *Debate Agrario* 20: 51–76.

Escobal, J., J. Saavedra, et al. (1998). *Los activos de los pobres en el Perú*. Lima, GRADE: 64.

Escobar, A. (1995). *Encountering Development: The Making and Unmaking of the Third World*. Princeton, Princeton University Press.

Favre, H. (1976). Evolución y situación de la hacienda tradicional de la región de Huancavelica. *La hacienda, la comunidad y el campesino en el Perú*. J. M. Mar (ed.). Lima, Instituto de Estudios Peruanos: 105–139.

Ferroni, M. (1980). The Urban Food Bias of Peruvian Food Policy: Consequences and Alternatives. Ph.D. thesis, Ithaca, Cornell University.

Figueroa, A. (1984). *Capitalist Development and the Peasant Economy in Peru*. Cambridge, Cambridge University Press.

_____ (1995). Peru: Social Policies and Economic Adjustment in the 1980's. *Coping with Austerity: Poverty and Inequality in Latin America*. N. Lustig (ed.). Washington, D.C., Brookings Institution.

Fioravanti Molinié, A. (1978). "La Communauté aujourd'hui." *Annales: Economies, Societés, Civilizations* 33e Année(5–6): 1182–1196.

_____ (1982). Multi-levelled Andean Society and Market Exchange: The case of Yucay (Peru). *Ecology and Exchange in the Andes*. D. Lehmann (ed.). Cambridge, Cambridge University Press: 211–230.

Firth, R. (1966). *Housekeeping Among Malay Peasants*. New York, Althone Press.

Flannery, K., J. Marcus, et al. (1989). *The Flocks of the Wamani: A Study of Llama Herders on the Punas of Ayacucho, Peru*. San Diego, Academic Press.

Flores Galindo, A. (1977). *Arequipa y el sur andino, Siglo XVIII a XX*. Lima, Editorial Horizonte.

Flores Ochoa, J. (1968). *Pastores de Paratía*. México, Instituto Indigenista Interamericano.

Flores Ochoa, J. (ed.) (1977). *Pastores de puna*. Lima, Instituto de Estudios Peruanos.

Fonseca Martel, C. (1972a). *Sistemas económicos en las comunidades campesinas del Perú. Departamento de Antropología*. Lima, Universidad Nacional Mayor de San Marcos.

_____ (1972b). La economía vertical y la economía de mercado en las comunidades alteñas del Perú. *Visita de la provincia de León de Huánuco en 1562 (Iñigo Ortiz de Zúñiga, visitador)*, Vol. 2. J. V. Murra (ed.). Huánuco, Perú, Universidad Nacional Hermilio Valdizán: 315–338.

_____ (1974). Modalidades de la Minka. *Reciprocidad e intercambio en los Andes peruanos*. G. Alberti and E. Mayer (eds.). Lima, Instituto de Estudios Peruanos: 86–109.

_____ (1978). "Proceso de cambio de cultivos en una comunidad campesina de los Andes." *Discusión Antropológica*.

_____ (1981). Los Ayllus las Marcas de Chaupiwaranga. Etnohistoria y antropología andina. A. Castelli, M. Koth de Paredes, and M. Mould de Pease (eds.). Lima, Museo Nacional de Historia: 167–188.

_____ (1983). "El control comunal del agua en la cuenca del río Cañete." *Allpanchis* 22(19): 61–74.

_____ (1986). "Comentario a 'Dos vías de desarrollo capitalista en la agricultura, o crítica de la razón Chayanov-Marxisante.'" *Revista Andina Cusco* 3: 379–380.

_____ (1988). Diferenciación campesina en los Andes peruanos. *Comunidad y producción en la agricultura andina*. C. Fonseca Martel and E. Mayer (eds.). Lima, FOMCIENCIAS: 165–196.

Fonseca Martel, C., and E. Mayer (1978). "Sistemas agrarios y ecología en la cuenca del Río Cañete." *Debates en Antropología* 2: 25–51.

Fonseca Martel, C., and E. Mayer (eds.) (1988). *Comunidad y producción en la agricultura andina*. Lima, FOMCIENCIAS.

Foster, G. (1967). The Dyadic Contract: A Model for the Social Structure of a Mexican Peasant Village. *Peasant Society: A Reader*. J. Potter, M. Diaz, and G. Foster (eds.). Boston, Little, Brown & Co: 213–230.

Fowler, C., and P. Mooney (1990). *Shattering: Food, Politics, and the Loss of Genetic Diversity*. Tucson, University of Arizona Press.

Franco, E. (1974). *Estudio de diagnóstico socio-económico del área de influencia del Proyecto Piloto Cajamarca—La Libertad*. Cajamarca, Ministerio de Agricultura—CRIAN (Centro Regional de Investigación Agropecuaria del Norte) Programa de Estudios Socio-Económicos. Proyecto Piloto Cajamarca—La Libertad.

Franquemont, C. R. (1988). Chinchero Plant Categories: An Andean Logic of Observation. Ph.D. thesis, Ithaca, Cornell University.

Fuenzalida, F. (1971). "La matríz colonial de la comunidad de Indígenas peruana: Una hipótesis de trabajo." *Revista del Museo Nacional* 35: 92–122.

Fuenzalida, F., E. Mayer, et al. (1970). Poder, raza y etnia en el Perú contemporáneo. *El Indio y el Poder*. Lima, Instituto de Estudios Peruanos.

Fuenzalida, F., T. Valiente, et al. (1982). *El desafío de Huayopampa: Comuneros y empresarios*. Lima, Instituto de Estudios Peruanos.

Fuenzalida, F., J. Villarán, et al. (1968). *Estructuras tradicionales y economía de mercado: La Comunidad de indígenas de Huayopampa*. Lima, Instituto de Estudios Peruanos.

Fujii, T., and H. Tomoeda (1981). Chacra, layme y auquénidos: Explotación ambiental en una comunidad andina. *Estudios etnográficos del Perú meridional*. S. Masuda (ed.). Tokyo, University of Tokyo.

Gade, D. (1967). Plant Use and Folk Agriculture in the Vilcanota Valley of Peru: A Cultural-Historical Geography of Plant Resources. Ph.D. thesis, Madison, University of Wisconsin.

_____ (1970). "Ecología del robo agrícola en las tierras alstas de los andes centrales." *América Indígena* 30(1): 3–14.

_____ (1991). Reflecciones sobre el asentamiento andino de la época Toledana hasta el presente. *Reproducción y transformación de las sociedades andinas*. F. Salomon and S. Moreno (eds.). Quito, Ediciones Abya-Yala.

Gade, D., and R. Ríos (1972). "Chaquitaclla: The Native Footplow and Its Persistence in Central Andean Agriculture." *Tools and Tillage* 2(1): 3–15.

_____ (1976). "La Chaquitaclla: Herramienta indígena sudamericana." *América Indígena* 36(2): 359–374.

Gagliano, Joseph (1978). "La Medicina popular y la coca en el Peru: Un análisis histórico de actitudes." *América Indígena* 38(4): 789–805.

_____ (1994). Coca Prohibition in Peru: The Historical Debates. Tucson, University of Arizona Press.

Ganzer, J., H. Kasischke, et al. (1977). *Der Cocagebrauch bei den Andenindianern in Peru*. Berlin, Freie Universität Berlin: 1–89.

García Márquez, G. (1997). *News of a Kidnapping*. New York, Knopf.

García Sayan, D. (ed.) (1989). *Coca, cocaina y narcotrafico: Laberinto en los Andes*. Lima, Lima Comisión Andina de Juristas.

Garcilaso de la Vega, E. I. (1966). *Royal Commentaries of the Incas*, Parts I and II. Austin, University of Texas.

Gelles, P. H. (1984). "Agua, faenas y organización comunal: San Pedro de Casta, Huarochirí." *Antropológica* 2(2): 305–334.

_____ (1995). "Equilibrium and Extraction: Dual Organization in the Andes." *American Ethnologist* 22(4): 710–742.

_____ (1999). *Water and Power in Highland Peru*. New Brunswick, Rutgers University Press.

Gladwin, C. H. (1989). *Ethnographic Decision Tree Modeling*. Newbury Park, Sage Publications.

Glave, M. (1992). Economic Analysis of Peasant Family Farms: Agricultural Intensification, Cost-Accounting, and Sharecropping in Andean Peasant Communities. Ph.D. thesis, University of Illinois at Urbana-Champaign.

_____ (1992). La aparcería en comunidades campesinas. *La chacra de papa: economía y ecología*. E. Mayer, M. Glave, S. B. Brush, and J. E. Taylor (eds.). Lima, Centro Peruano de Investigación Social: 191–214.

Godelier, M. (1977). The Concept of "Social and Economic Formation": The Inca Example. *Perspectives in Marxist Anthropology*. Cambridge, Cambridge University Press: 63–69.

Goffman, E. (1965). *Stigma*. Englewood Cliffs, N.J., Prentice-Hall.

Goland, C. (1992). Cultivating Diversity: Field Scattering as Agricultural Risk Management in Cuyo Cuyo, Department of Puno, Peru. Ph.D. thesis, Chapel Hill, University of North Carolina.

Gols, J. (1988). La parcelación de las empresas asociativas en la costa peruana: El caso del Valle del Cañete. *Peru: El problema agrario en debate SEPIA II*. F. Eguren, R. Hopkins, and B. Kervyn (eds.). Lima, Seminario Permanente de Investigación Agraria: 241–259.

Golte, J. (1980). *La racionalidad de la organización andina*. Lima, Instituto de Estudios Peruanos.

Golte, J., and N. Adams (1987). *Los caballos de troya de los invasores: Estrategias campesinas en la conquista de la gran Lima*. Lima, Instituto de Estudios Peruanos.

Golte, J., and M. De la Cadena (1983). "La codeterminación de la organización social andina." *Alpanchis* 19(22): 7–34.

Gómez, V. (1986). *Economía campesina: Balance y perspectivas. Perú: el problema agrario en debate SEPIA I.* V. Gómez, B. Revesz, E. Grillo, and R. Montoya (eds.). Lima, Seminario Permanente de Investigación Agraria: 23–51.

Gonzales de Olarte, E. (1987). *Inflación y campesinado: comunidades y microrregiones frente a la crisis.* Lima, Instituto de Estudios Peruanos.

_____ (1994). *En las fronteras del mercado: Economía política del campesinado en el Perú.* Lima, Instituto de Estudios Peruanos.

_____ (1997). *Mercados en el ámbito rural peruano. Peru: El problema agrario en debate SEPIA VIII.* E.G.D. Olarte, B. Revesz, and M. Tapia (eds.). Lima, Seminario Permanente de Investigación Agraria. 6: 19–68.

Gonzales Manrique, J. E. (1989). Sendero Luminoso en el valle de la coca. *Coca, Cocaina y narcotráfico: Laberinto en los Andes.* D. Garcia Sayan (ed.). Lima, Comisión Andina de Juristas: 207–222.

Goodman, D., and M. Redclift (1981). *From Peasant to Proletarian: Capitalist Development and Agrarian Transformations.* Oxford, Blackwell.

Goody, J. (1966). *The Developmental Cycle in Domestic Groups.* Cambridge, Cambridge University Press.

Gootenberg, P. (ed.) (1999). *Cocaine: Global Histories.* London, Routledge.

Gose, P. (1991). "House Rethatching in an Andean Annual Cycle: Practice, Meaning, and Contradiction." *American Ethnologist* 18(1): 39–66.

_____ (1994). *Deathly Waters and Hungry Mountains: Agrarian Ritual and Class Formation in an Andean Town.* Toronto, University of Toronto Press.

Gow, R. (1981). Yawar Mayu: Revolution in the Southern Andes 1860–1980. Ph.D. thesis, Madison, University of Wisconsin.

Grinspoon, L., and J. A. Bakalar (1976). *Cocaine: A Drug and Its Social Evolution.* New York, Basic Books.

Guaman Poma de Ayala, F. (1980). *El primer nueva corónica y buen gobierno por Felipe Guaman Poma de Ayala.* Critical edition (J. V. Murra and R. Adorno, eds.). Mexico City, Editorial Siglo XXI.

Gudeman, S. (1978). *The Demise of a Rural Economy: From Subsistence to Rural Capitalism in a Latin American Village.* London, Routledge & Kegan Paul.

_____ (1986). *Economics As Culture: Models and Metaphors of Livelihood.* Cambridge, Cambridge University Press.

Gudeman, S., and A. Rivera (1990). *Conversations in Colombia: The Domestic Economy in Life and Text.* Cambridge, Cambridge University Press.

Guillet, D. (1978). *The Supra-Household Sphere of Production in the Andean Peasant Economy.* XLII Congrès International des Américanistes, Paris.

_____ (1979). *Agrarian Reform and Peasant Economy in Southern Peru.* Columbia, University of Missouri Press.

_____ (1981). "Land Tenure, Ecological Zone, and Agricultural Regime in the Andes." *American Ethnologist* 8(1): 139–156.

_____ (1983). "Toward a Cultural Ecology of Mountains: The Andes and the Himalayas Compared." *Current Anthropology* 24(5): 561–74.

_____ (1992). *Covering Ground: Communal Water Management and the State in the Peruvian Highlands.* Ann Arbor, University of Michigan Press.

Gutierrez Noriega, C. (1948). "El cocaismo y la alimentación en el Perú." *Anales de la Facultad de Medicina* 31.

Gutierrez Noriega, C., and V. Zapata Ortiz (1950). "La inteligencia y la personalidad en los habituados a la coca." *Revista Peruana de Neuropsiquiatría* 13: 22–60.

Hadden, G. (1967). Un ensayo de demografía histórica y etnológica en Huánuco. *Visita de la provincia de León de Huánuco en 1562 (Iñigo Ortiz de Zúñiga, visitador)*, Vol. 1. J. V. Murra (Ed.). Huánuco, Perú, Universidad Nacional Hermilio Valdizán: 369–380.

Halperin, R. H. (1994). *Cultural Economies Past and Present*. Austin, University of Texas Press.

Handelman, H. (1975). *Struggle in the Andes: Peasant Political Mobilization in Peru*. Austin, University of Texas Press.

Hanna, J. (1974). "Coca Leaf Use in Southern Peru: Some Biological Aspects." *American Anthropologist* 76(2): 281–296.

Hanna, J., and C. Hornick (1977). "Use of Coca Leaf in Southern Peru: Adaptation or Addiction." *Bulletin on Narcotics* 29(1): 63—74.

Hardesty, D. L. (1975). "The Niche Concept: Suggestions for Its Use in the Studies of Human Ecology." *Human Ecology* (3): 71–85.

Hardin, G. (1968). "The Tragedy of the Commons." *Science* 162: 1243–48.

Harlan, J. R. (1975). "Our Vanishing Genetic Resources." *Science* 188: 618–621.

Harris, O. (1978). Complementarity and Conflict: An Andean View of Men and Women. *Sex and Age as Principles of Social Differentiation*. J.S.L. Fontaine (ed.). London, Academic Press: 21–40.

———— (1978). "El parentesco y la economía vertical del Ayllu Laymi (Norte de Potosí)." *Avances* 1: 51–64.

———— (1981). Households as Natural Units. *Of Marriage and the Market: Women's Subordination in International Perspective*. K. Young, C. Wolkowitz, and R. McCullogh (eds.). London, Committee of Socialist Economists Books.

———— (1982). Labour and Produce in an Ethnic Economy, Northern Potosí, Bolivia. *Ecology and Exchange in the Andes*. D. Lehmann (ed.). Cambridge, Cambridge University Press: 70–97.

———— (1985). Ecological Duality and the Role of the Center: Northern Potosí. *Andean Ecology and Civilization: An Interdisciplinary Perspective on Andean Ecological Complementarity*. S. Masuda, I. Shimada, and C. Morris (eds.). Tokyo, University of Tokyo Press: 311–335.

———— (1986). From Asymmetry to Triangle. Symbolic Transformations in Northern Potosí. *Anthropological History of Andean Polities*. J. V. Murra, N. Watchel, and J. Revel (eds.). Cambridge, Cambridge University Press: 260–279.

———— (1987). Phaxsima y qullqui: los poderes y significados del dinero en el Norte de Potosí. *La participación indígena en los mercados surandinos*. O. Harris, B. Larson, and E. Tandeter (eds.). La Paz, Centro de Estudios de la Realidad Económica y Social: 235–280.

———— (1995a). Sources and Meanings of Money: Beyond the Market Paradigm in an Ayllu of Northern Potosí. *Ethnicity, Markets, and Migration in the Andes*. B. Larson, O. Harris, and E. Tandeter (eds.). Durham, NC, Duke University Press: 297–328.

———— (1995b). Ethnic Identity and Market Relations. *Ethnicity, Markets, and Migration in the Andes: At the Crossroads of History and Anthropology*. B. Larson and O. Harris (eds.). Durham, Duke University Press: 351–390.

Hart, R. D. (1980). "Una Finca en Honduras como un sistema." *CATIE* 8(1).

Hartmann, R. (1971). "Mercados y ferias prehispánicos en el area andina." *Boletín de la Academia Nacional de Historia* (Quito) 54(118): 214–235.

Hawkes, J. B., and J. P. Hjerting (1989). *The Potatoes of Bolivia: Their Breeding Value and Evolutionary Relationships*. Oxford, Clarendon Press.

Healy, K. (1986). The Boom Within the Crisis: Some Recent Effects of Foreign Cocaine Markets on Bolivian Rural Society and Economy. *Coca and Cocaine: Effects on People and Policy in Latin America*. D. Pacini and C. Franquemont (eds.). Cambridge, Cultural Survival: 101–143.

Hecht, S. (1983). Cattle Ranching in the Eastern Amazon: Environmental and Social Implications. *The Dilemma of Amazonian Development*. E. Moran (ed.). Boulder, Colo., Westview Press.

Henderson, J. S., and P. J. Netherly (eds.) (1993). *Configurations of Power: Holistic Anthropology in Theory and Practice*. Ithaca, Cornell University Press.

Hendriks, J. (1988). Promoción rural y proyectos de riego. *La experiencia del proyecto "Rehabilitación del antiguo canal La Estrella-Mollepata."* Cusco, Centro Andino de Educación y Promoción José María Arguedas.

Henman, A. (1978). *Mamacoca*. Aldringham, Suffolk, Practical Paradise Publications.

Hervé, D. (1987). Zonas de producción y sistemas de cultivo en la cuenca alta del Cañete (Algunas reflecciones). *Sistemas agrarios en el Perú*. E. Malpartida and H. Poupon (eds.). Lima, Universidad Nacional Agraria La Molina & Instituto Francés de Estudios Andinos: 329–347.

Hervé, D., D. Genin, et al. (eds.) (1994). *Dinamicas de descanso de la tierra en los Andes*. La Paz, ORSTOM, IBTA.

Hobsbawm, E., and T. Ranger (eds.) (1984). *The Invention of Tradition*. Cambridge/New York, Cambridge University Press.

Hocquenghem, A. M. (1988). *Para vencer la muerte*. Lima, Instituto Francés de Estudios Andinos.

Holdridge, L. R. (1967). *Life Zone Ecology*. San José, Costa Rica, Tropical Science Center.

Horton, D. (1987). *Potatoes: Production, Marketing and Programs for Developing Countries*. Boulder, Colo., Westview Press.

Hulshof, J. (1978). "La coca en la medicina tradicional andina." *América Indígena* 37(4): 837–846.

Humphrey, C., and S. Hugh-Jones (1992). Introduction: Barter, Exchange and Value. *Barter, Exchange and Value*. C. Humphrey and S. H. Jones (eds.). Cambridge, Cambridge University Press: 1–20.

Husson, P. (1992). *De la guerra a la rebelión (Huanta, siglo XIX)*. Cusco: Centro de Estudios Regionales Andinos "Bartolomé de Las Casas." Lima, Instituto Francés de Estudios Andinos.

Huxley, A. (1946). *Brave New World*. New York, Harper & Row.

ICRISAT (1979). *Socioeconomic Constraints to Development of Semi-tropical Agriculture*. Hyderabad, India, International Crop Research Institute for the Semi-Arid Tropics.

Inamura, T. (1981). Adaptación ambiental de los pastores altoandinos del sur del Perú: Simbiosis económico-social con los agricultores. *Estudios etnográficos del Perú meridional*. S. Masuda (ed.). Tokyo, University of Tokyo.

Instituto Indigenista Interamericano. (1989). *La coca, tradición, rito, identidad.* Mexico, Instituto Indigenista Interamericano.

INEI (2000). *Peru, Mapa de la Pobreza.* Instituto Nacional de Estadística e Informática.

Isbell, B. J. (1971). "No servimos más: un estudio de la efectos de disipar un sistema de autoridad tradicional en un pueblo ayacuchano." *Revista del Muséo Nacional* 37: 285–98.

────── (1976). "La otra mitad esencial: un estudio de complementaridad sexual andina." *Estudios Andinos* 5(12): 37–56.

────── (1977). Kuyaq: Those Who Love Me: An Analysis of Andean Kinship and Reciprocity in a Ritual Context. *Andean Kinship and Marriage.* R. Bolton and E. Mayer (eds.). Washington, D.C., American Anthropological Association: 81–105.

────── (1978). *To Defend Ourselves: Ecology and Ritual in an Andean Village.* Austin, University of Texas Press.

────── (1997). De inmaduro a duro: lo simbólico femenino y los esquemas andinos de género. *Parentesco y género en los Andes: Mas allá del silencio: Las fronteras del género en los Andes,* Vol. 1. D. Y. Arnold (ed.). La Paz, Biblioteca de Estudios Andinos: 253–302.

Jacobsen, N. (1993). *Mirages of Transition: The Peruvian Altiplano, 1780–1930.* Berkeley, University of California Press.

Jerí, F. R. (1980). *Cocaína 1980: Actas del seminario interamericano sobre aspectos médicos y sociológicos de la coca y de la cocaina.* Lima, Oficina Sanitaria Panamericana/Organización Mundial de la Salud.

Jimenez de la Espada, M. (ed.) (1965). *Relaciones geográficas de Indias.* Madrid, Biblioteca de Autores Españoles.

Johnson, A. W. (1972). "Individuality and Experimentation in Traditional Agriculture." *Human Ecology* 1(2): 149–60.

Jordán Pando, R., J. Ortiz Mercado, et al. (1989). Coca, cocaísmo y cocaínismo en Bolivia. *La Coca: tradicon rito e identidad.* Mexico, Insituto Indigenista Interamericano: 79–107.

Kahn, J. (1980). *Minankabau Social Formations.* Cambridge, Cambridge University Press.

Kaplan, D. (1960). The Mexican Marketplace in Historical Perspective. Ph.D. thesis, Ann Arbor, University of Michigan.

────── (1965). *The Mexican Marketplace, Then and Now.* Proceedings of the 1965 Annual Spring Meetings of the American Ethnological Society, Seatle, University of Washington.

Kapsoli, W. (1975). *Movimientos campesinos en Cerro de Pasco: 1880–1913.* Huancayo, Instituto de Estudios Andinos.

────── (1977). *Los movimientos campesinos en el Perú: 1879–1965.* Lima, Delva Editores.

────── (1980). "El pensamiento de la Asociación Pro-Indígena." *Debates Rurales* 3 (Centro de Estudios Rurales Bartolomé de las Casas, Cusco).

Kawell, J. A. (1989). "Coca, the Real Green Revolution." *NACLA Report on the Americas* 17(6).

Kay, C. (2000). Latin American Transformation: Proletarianization and Peasantization. *Disappearing peasantries? Rural Labor in Africa, Asia and Latin Amer-*

ica. D. Brycerson, C. Kay, and J. Mooij (eds.). London, Intermediate Technology Publications.

Kervyn, B. (1989). "Campesinos y acción colectiva: La utilización del espacio en comunidades de la sierra Sur del Peru." *Revista Andina* 7(1): 7–83.

Kloppenburg, J. J., and D. L. Kleinman (1998). Seeds of Controversy: National Property Versus Common Heritage. *The Use and Control of Plant Genetic Resources.* J. J. Kloppenburg (ed.). Durham, Duke University Press: 173–203.

Kraft, K. (1994). La intensificacion agraria bajo el manejo comunal. Modificaciones del descanso rotativo en los Andes. *Dinamicas de descanso de la tierra en los Andes.* D. Hervé, D. Genin, and G. Riviere (eds.). La Paz, ORSTOM, IBTA: 305–320.

———— (1995). Andean Fields and Fallow pasture: Communal Land Use Management Under Pressures for Intensification. Ph.D. thesis, Gainesville, University of Florida.

Kula, W. (1976). *An Economic Theory of the Feudal System: Towards a Model of the Polish Economy, 1500–1800.* London, N.L.B.

Laite, J. (1981). *Industrial Development and Migrant Labour in Latin America.* Austin, University of Texas Press.

La Lone, D. (ed.) (1982). The Inca as a Nonmarket Economy: Supply on Command Versus Supply and Demand. Contexts for Prehistoric Exchange. New York, Academic Press.

Lambert, B. (1977). Bilaterality in the Andes. R. Bolton and E. Mayer (eds.). Washington, D.C., American Anthropological Association: 1–27.

Lanning, E. (1967). *Peru Before the Incas.* Englewood Cliffs, N.J., Prentice-Hall.

Larson, B. (1995). Andean Communities, Political Cultures, and Markets: The Changing Contours of a Field. *Ethnicity, Markets, and Migration in the Andes: At the Crossroads of History and Anthropology.* B. Larson and O. Harris (eds.). Durham, Duke University Press: 5–53.

Las Casas, B. (1967). *Apologética Historia Sumaria.* Mexico, Universidad Nacional Autónoma de Mexico (Instituto de Investigaciones Históricas).

Lastarria-Cornhiel, S. (1989). Agrarian Reforms of the 1960s and 1970s in Peru. *Agrarian Structure and Reform in Latin America.* W. Thiesenhusen (ed.). Boston, Allen & Unwin: 127–155.

Lastarria-Cornhiel, S., and G. Barnes (1999). *Formalizing Informality: The Praedial Registration System in Peru.* Madison, Land Tenure Center, University of Wisconsin.

Lauer, M. (1989). *La producción artesanal en América Latina.* Lima, Mosca Azul.

Lechtman, H. (1977). Style and Technology—Some Early Thoughts. *Material Culture: Styles, Organization, and Dynamics of Technology.* H. Lecthman and R. S. Merril (eds.). St. Paul, West Publishing Co.

Lehmann, D. (1982). "After Chayanov and Lenin: New Paths of Agrarian Capitalism." *Journal of Development Economics* 11: 133–161.

Lehmann, D. (ed.) (1982). *Ecology and Exchange in the Andes.* Cambridge, Cambridge University Press.

Lenin, V. I. (1974). *The Development of Capitalism in Russia.* Moscow, Progress Publishers.

León, R. F., and R. Castro de la Mata (eds.) (1989). *Pasta básica de cocaína: Un estudio multidisciplinario*. Lima, Centro de Información y Educación Para la Prevención y el Abuso de Drogas (CEDRO).

Levi-Strauss, C. (1969). *The Elementary Structures of Kinship*. Boston, Beacon Press.

Lipton, M. (1968). "The Theory of the Optimizing Peasant." *Journal of Developing Areas* 4: 327–351.

Lobo, S. (1982). *A House of My Own: Social Organization in the Squatter Settlements of Lima, Peru*. Tucson, University of Arizona Press.

Long, N., and B. Roberts (1978). *Peasant Cooperation and Capitalist Expansion in Central Peru*. Austin, University of Texas Press.

_____ (1984). *Miners, Peasants and Entrepeneurs: Regional Development in the Central Highlands of Peru*. Cambridge, Cambridge University Press.

Love, T. (1988). "Andean Interzonal Bartering: Why Does It Persist in a Cash-Market Economy?" *Michigan Discussions in Anthropology* 8(Fall): 87–101.

Lund Skar, S. (1994). *Lives Together-Worlds Apart: Quechua Colonization in Jungle and City*. Oslo, Scandinavian University Press.

Luxemburg, R. (1968). *The Accumulation of Capital*. New York, Monthly Review Press.

MacLaine, S. (1983). Out on a Limb. Toronto/New York, Bantam Books.

Malinowski, B. (1932). *Argonauts of the Western Pacific*. London, George Routledge & Sons, Ltd.

Mallon, F. (1983). *The Defense of Community in Peru's Central Highlands: Peasant Struggle and Capitalist Transition, 1840–1940*. Palo Alto, Stanford University Press.

Mallon, F., G. Renique, et al. (1977). *Lanas y capitalismo en los Andes centrales*. Lima, Taller de Estudios Rurales.

Malpartida, E., and H. Poupon (eds.) (1987). *Sistemas agrarios en el Perú*. Lima, Universidad Nacional Agraria La Molina & Instituto Francés de Estudios Andinos.

Mancall, P. C. (1995). *Deadly Medicine: Indians and Alcohol in Early America*. Ithaca, Cornell University Press.

Manrique, N. (1981). *Las guerrillas indígenas en la guerra con Chile*. Lima, Editora Ital Perú S.A.

_____ (1987). *Mercado Interno y Región: La Sierra Central 1820–1930*. Lima, DESCO.

_____ (2000). Agro y regiones en la sociedad de información: La revolución de las tecnologías y el nuevo escenario mundial. *Peru: El problema agrario en debate SEPIA VIII*, Vol. 8. I. Hurtado, C. Trivelli, and A. Brack (eds.). Lima, Seminario Permanente de Investigación Agraria: 395–425.

Martínez Alier, J. (1973). *Los huachilleros del Perú: dos estudios de formaciones sociales agrarias*. Lima, Instituto de Estudios Peruanos, Ruedo Ibérico.

_____ (1977). *Haciendas, Plantations and Communities*. London, Frank Cass.

_____ (1987). "Economía y ecología: Cuestiones fundamentales." *Pensamiento Iberoamericano*(12): 41–60.

Martínez Arellano, H. (1962). "La hacienda capana." *Perú Indígena* 10(24): 37–74.

Matos Mar, J. (1964). La propiedad en la isla de Taquile. *Estudios sobre la cultura actual en el Perú*. J. Matos Mar (ed.). Lima, Universidad Nacional San Marcos.

———— (1987). *Desborde popular y crisis del estado: el nuevo rostro del Perú en la década de 1980*. Lima, Instituto de Estudios Peruanos.

Matos Mendieta, R. (1972). Wakan y Wamalli: Estudio arqueológico de dos aldeas rurales. *Visita de la Provincia de León de Huánuco en 1562 (Iñigo Ortiz de Zúñiga, visitador)*, Vol. 2. J. V. Murra (ed.). Huánuco, Perú, Universidad Nacional Hermilio Valdizán: 367–382.

Mauss, M. (1954). *The Gift: Forms and Functions of Exchange in Archaic Societies*. London, Cohen and West.

Mayer, D. (1912). "El estado de la causa." *El Deber Pro-Indígena* 1(1).

———— (1926). "Lo que ha significado la Pro-Indígena." *Amauta* 1(1).

———— (1984). *La conducta de la compañia minera del Cerro de Pasco*. Lima, Fondo Editorial Labor. (Original in English, 1913).

Mayer, E. (1971). *Un carnero por un saco de papas: Aspectos del trueque en la zona de Chaupiwaranga (Pasco)*. XXXIX Congreso Internacional de Americanistas, Lima.

———— (1972). Censos insensatos: Evaluación de los censos campesinos en la historia de Tangor. *Visita de la Provincia de León de Huánuco en 1562 (Iñigo Ortiz de Zúñiga, visitador)*, Vol. 2. J. V. Murra (Ed.). Huánuco, Perú, Universidad Nacional Hermilio Valdizán: 339–366.

———— (1974a). Reciprocity, Self-Sufficiency and Market Relations in a Contemporary Community in the Central Andes of Peru. Ithaca, Cornell University.

———— (1974b). Las reglas del juego en la reciprocidad andina. *Reciprocidad e intercambio en los Andes Peruanos*. G. Alberti and E. Mayer (eds.). Lima, Instituto de Estudios Peruanos: 37–65.

———— (1974c). El trueque y los mercados en el imperio Incaico. *Los campesinos y el mercado*. E. Mayer, S. Mintz, and G. W. Skinner (eds.). Lima, Pontificia Universidad Catolica: 13–50.

———— (1977a). "Tenencia y control comunal de la tierra: El caso de Laraos (Yauyos)." *Cuadernos del Consejo Nacional de la Universidad Peruana* 24–25: 59–72.

———— (1977b). Beyond the Nuclear Family. *Andean Kinship and Marriage*. R. Bolton and E. Mayer (eds.). Washington, D.C., American Anthropological Association: 60–80.

———— (1978a). "El uso social de la coca en el mundo andino: Contribución a un debate y toma de posición." *América Indígena* 37(4): 849–865.

———— (1978b). *Aspectos colectivos en la agricultura andina*. Primer Congreso Internacional de Cultivos Andinos, Ayacucho, Instituto Interamericano de Ciencias Agrícolas.

———— (1979). *Land Use in the Andes: Ecology and Agriculture in Mantaro Valley of Peru with Special Reference to Potatoes*. Lima, International Potato Center.

———— (1984). A Tribute to the Household: Domestic Economy and the Encomienda in Colonial Peru. *Kinship Ideology and Practice in Latin America*. R. T. Smith (ed.). Chapel Hill, University of North Carolina Press.

———— (1985). Production Zones. *Andean Ecology and Civilization: An Interdisciplinary Perspective on Andean Ecological Complementarity*. S. Masuda, I. Shimada, and C. Morris (eds.). Tokyo, University of Tokyo Press: 45–84.

———— (1987). "Macro-Ethno-Economics." *Reviews in Anthropology* 14(3): 250–255.

———— (1988). De hacienda a comunidad: El impacto de la reforma agraria en la provincia de Paucartambo, Cusco. *Sociedad andina, pasado y presente: Contribuciones en homenaje a la memoria de César Fonseca Martel*. R. Matos Mendieta (ed.). Lima, FOMCIENCIAS: 59–100.

———— (1989a). "Coca Use in the Andes." *Drugs in Latin America, Studies in Third World Societies* 37: 1–25.

———— (1989b). *Steps Towards a Coherent Policy for Andean Agriculture*. Washington, D.C., DESFIL (Development Strategies for Fragile Lands): 35.

———— (1992). Peru in Deep Trouble: Mario Vargas Llosa's "Inquest in the Andes" Reexamined. *Rereading Cultural Anthropology*. G. E. Marcus (ed.). Durham, Duke University Press: 181–219.

———— (1993). "Factores sociales en la revaloración de la coca." *Debate Agrario* 17: 131–143.

———— (1994). Recursos naturales, medio ambiente, tecnología y desarrollo. *Perú: El problema agrario en debate: SEPIA V*. O. Dancourt, E. Mayer, and C. Monge (eds.). Lima, Seminario Permanente de Investigación Agraria: 479–533.

Mayer, E., and M. De la Cadena (1989). *Cooperación y conflicto en la comunidad andina: Zonas de producción y organización social*. Lima, Instituto de Estudios Peruanos.

Mayer, E., and C. Fonseca (1979). *Sistemas agrarios en la cuenca del Río Cañete*. Lima, Oficina Nacional de Evaluación de Recursos Naturales (ONERN).

Mayer, E., and M. Glave (1990). Papas regaladas y papas regalo: rentabilidad, costos e inversión. *Perú: El problema agrario en debate: SEPIA III*. A. Chirif, N. Manrique, and B. Quijandría (eds.). Lima, Seminario Permanente de Investigación Agraria: 87–120.

———— (1999). "Alguito para ganar (A Little Something to Earn): Profits and Losses in Peasant Economies." *American Ethnologist* 26(2): 344–369.

Mayer, E., M. Glave, et al. (1992). *La chacra de papa: Economía y ecología*. Lima, Centro Peruano de Investigación Social.

Mayer, E., and C. Zamalloa (1974). Reciprocidad en las relaciones de producción. *Reciprocidad e intercambio en los Andes Peruanos*. E. Mayer and G. Alberti (eds.). Lima, Instituto de Estudios Peruanos: 77–85.

McCay, B., and J. M. Acheson (eds.) (1987). *The Question of the Commons: The Culture and Ecology of Community Resources*. Tucson, University of Arizona Press.

McCloskey, D. (1985). *The Rhetoric of Economics*. Madison, University of Wisconsin Press.

McKee, L. (1992). Men's Rights/Women's Wrongs: Domestic Violence in Ecuador. *Sanctions and Sanctuary: Cultural Perspectives on the Beating of Wives*. D. Counts, J. K. Brown, and J. Campbell (eds.). Boulder, Colo., Westview Press: 139–104.

———— (1997). Women's Work in Rural Ecuador: Multiple Resource Strategies and the Gendered Division of Labor. *Women and Economic Change: Andean Perspectives*. A. Miles and H. Buechler (eds.). Washington, DC, Society for Latin American Anthropology Publication Series, American Anthropology Association. 14.

Mead, M. (1972). *Blackberry Winter: My Earlier Years*. New York, Morrow.

Mellafe, R. (1967). Consideraciones históricas sobre la Visita. *Visita de la Provincia de León de Huánuco en 1562 (Iñigo Ortiz de Zúñiga, visitador)*, Vol. 1. J. V. Murra (ed.). Huánuco, Perú, Universidad Nacional Hermilio Valdizán: 323–344.

Méndez, C. (1991). Los campesinos, la independencia y la iniciación de la república: el caso de los Iquichanos realistas. *Poder y violencia en los Andes, Cusco*. H. Urbano and M. Lauer (eds.). Cusco, Centro de Estudios Regionales Andinos Bartolomé de las Casas: 165–188.

Miles, A., and H. Buechler (eds.) (1997). *Women and Economic Change: Andean Perspectives*. Washington, D.C., Society for Latin American Anthropology Publication Series, American Anthropology Association.

Mintz, S. (1959). *Internal Marketing Systems as Mechanisms of Social Articulation*. Proceedings of the Annual Spring Meetings of the American Ethnological Society, Seattle, University of Washington Press.

——— (1961). *"Pratik": Haitian Personal Economic Relationships*. Proceedings of the 1961 Annual Spring Meetings of the American Ethnological Society, Seattle, University of Washington.

Mintz, S., and E. Wolf (1967). An Analysis of Ritual Coparenthood (Compadrasgo). *Peasant Society: A Reader*. J. Potter, M. Diaz, and G. Foster (eds.). Boston, Little, Brown & Co: 174–199.

Mishkin, B. (1946). The Contemporary Quechua. *Handbook of South American Indians*, Vol. 4. J. Steward (eds.). Washington, D.C., Bureau of American Ethnology Bulletin 143: 411–470.

Mitchell, W. P. (1976a). Social Adaptation to the Mountain Environment of an Andean Village. *Hill Lands: Proceedings of an International Symposium*. J. Luchop et al. (eds.). Morgantown, University of West Virginia Press.

——— (1976b). "Irrigation and Community in the Central Peruvian Highlands." *American Anthropologist* 78(1): 25–44.

——— (1980). Local Ecology and the State: Implications of Contemporary Quechua Land Use for the Inca Sequence of Agricultural Work. *Beyond the Myths of Culture*. E. B. Ross (ed.). New York, Academic Press: 139–154.

——— (1991). *Peasants on the Edge: Crop, Cult and Crisis in the Andes*. Austin, University of Texas Press.

Mitchell, W. P., and D. W. Guillet (eds.) (1993). *Irrigation at High Altitudes: The Social Organization of Water Control Systems in the Andes*. Washington, D.C., Society for Latin American Anthropology and the American Anthropological Association.

Monge, C., and J. Urrutia (1999). El debate sobre la titulación en las comunidades del sur Andino. *Perú problema agrario en debate: SEPIA VII*. V. Agreda, A. Diez, and M. Glave (eds.). Lima, Seminario Permanente de Investigación Agraria: 393–408.

Monge M., C. (1946). "El problema de la coca en el Perú." *Anales de la Facultad de Medicina* 29: 311–15.

Montoya, B., P. Morlon, et al. (1996). Vender para vivir. *Comprender la agricultura campesina en los Andes Centrales Perú-Bolivia*. P. Morlon (ed.). Lima/Cusco, Instituto Francés de Estudios Andinos Centro de Estudios Regionales Andinos, Bartolomé de las Casas: 357–360.

Montoya, R. (1970). *A propósito del carácter predominantemente capitalista de la economía peruana actual.* Lima, Ediciones Tierra y Realidad.

_____ (1980). *Capitalismo y no capitalismo en el Perú: Un estudio histórico de su articulación en un eje regional.* Lima, Mosca Azul.

Mooney, P. (1979). Seeds of the Earth: A Private or Public Resource? London, Inter Pares.

Morales, E. (1989). *Cocaine: White Gold Rush in Peru.* Tucson, University of Arizona Press.

Morlon, P. (ed.) (1996). *Comprender la agricultura campesina en los Andes Centrales Perú-Bolivia.* Lima/Cusco, Instituto Francés de Estudios Andinos Centro de Estudios Regionales Andinos, Bartolomé de las Casas.

Mörner, M. (1985). *The Andean Past.* New York, Columbia University Press.

Morris, C. (1967). Storage in Tawantinsuyu. Ph.D. thesis, Chicago, University of Chicago.

_____ (1972). El almacenaje en dos aldeas de los Chupaychu. *Visita de la Provincia de León de Huánuco en 1562 (Iñigo Ortiz de Zúñiga, visitador),* Vol. 2. J. V. Murra (Ed.). Huánuco, Perú, Universidad Nacional Hermilio Valdizán.

Morris, C., and D. E. Thompson (1985). *Huánuco Pampa: An Inca City and Its Hinterland.* New York, Thames and Hudson.

Mossbrucker, H. (1990). *La economía campesina y el concepto "comunidad" un enfoque crítico.* Lima, Instituto de Estudios Peruanos.

Murra, J. V. (1956). *The Economic Organization of the Inca State.* Anthropology. Chicago, University of Chicago.

_____ (1958). On Inca Political Structure. *Proceedings of the Annual Spring Meetings of the American Ethnological Society.* Seattle, University.

_____ (1960). Rite and Crop in the Inca State. *Culture in History: Essays in Honor of Paul Radin.* S. Diamond (ed.). New York, published for Brandeis University by Columbia University Press.

_____ (1961). "Economic and Social Structural Themes in Andean Ethnohistory." *Anthropological Quarterly* 34(2).

_____ (1962). "Cloth and Its Functions in the Inca State." *American Anthropologist* 64(4).

_____ (1964). Una apreciación etnológica de la visita. *Visita hecha a la provincia de Chucuito por Garci Diez de San Miguel en el año 1567.* J. V. Murra (ed.). Lima, Casa de la Cultura del Peru: 419–442.

_____ (1967). La Visita de los Chupachu como fuente etnológica. *Visita de la Provincia de León de Huánuco en 1562 (Iñigo Ortíz de Zúñiga, visitador),* Vol. 1. J. V. Murra (Ed.). Huánuco, Perú, Universidad Nacional Hermilio Valdizán: 427–476.

_____ (1968). "An Aymara Kingdom in 1567." *Ethnohistory* 6(2): 115–51.

_____ (1972). El "control vertical" de un máximo de pisos ecológicos en la economía de las sociedades andinas. *Visita de la Provincia de León de Huánuco en 1562 (Iñigo Ortíz de Zúñiga, visitador),* Vol. 2. J. V. Murra (ed.). Huánuco, Perú, Universidad Nacional Hermilio Valdizán: 427–476.

_____ (1975). *Formaciones económicas y políticas del mundo andino.* Lima, Instituto de Estudios Peruanos.

_____ (1978). *La organización económica y política del estado Inca.* Mexico, Siglo XXI.

_____ (1981). *Socio-Political and Demographic Aspects of Multi-Altitude Land Use in the Andes*. L'Homme Et son environnement à haute altitude, Paris, Séminaire CNRS NSF.

_____ (1982). The *Mita* Obligations of Ethnic Groups to the Inca State. *The Inca and Aztec States, 1400–1800*. G. Collier et al. (eds.). New York, Academic Press.

_____ (1984). Andean Societies Before 1532. *The Cambridge History of Latin America (Colonial Latin America)*, Vol. 1. L. Bethel (ed.). Cambridge, Cambridge University Press: Ch. 3.

_____ (1985). "El Archipiélago Vertical" Revisited. *Andean Ecology and Civilization: An Interdisciplinary Perspective on Ecological Complementarity*. S. Masuda, I. Shimada, and C. Morris (eds.). Tokyo, Tokyo University Press.

_____ (1986a). Notes on Pre-Columbian cultivation of coca leaf. *Coca and Cocaine: Effects on People and Policy in Latin America*. D. Pacini and C. Frankemont (eds.). Boston, Cultural Survival: 49–52.

_____ (1986b). The Expansion of the Inca State: Armies, War and Rebellions. *Anthropological History of Andean Polities*. J. Murra, N. Wachtel, and J. Revel (eds.). Cambridge, Cambridge University Press: 49–58.

_____ (1995). Did Tribute and Markets Prevail in the Andes Before the European Invasion? *Ethnicity, Markets, and Migration in the Andes: At the Crossroads of History and Anthropology*. B. Larson and O. Harris (eds.). Durham, Duke University Press: 57–72.

Murra, J. V., and M. Lopez Barralt (eds.) (1996). *Las cartas de Arguedas*. Lima, Pontificia Universidad del Peru.

Murra, J. V. (ed.) (1964). *Visita hecha a la provincia de Chucuito por Garci Diez de San Miguel en el año 1567*. Lima, Casa de la Cultura del Peru.

Murra, J. V. (ed.) (1967). *Visita de la Provincia de León de Huánuco en 1562 (Iñigo Ortiz de Zúñiga, visitador)*, Vol. 1. Huánuco, Perú, Universidad Nacional Hermilio Valdizán.

Murra, J. V. (ed.) (1972). *Visita de la Provincia de León de Huánuco en 1562 (Iñigo Ortiz de Zúñiga, visitador)*, Vol. 2. Huánuco, Universidad Nacional Hermilio Valdizán.

Murra, J. V. (ed.) (1991). *Visita de los valles de Sonqo en los yunka de coca de La Paz [1568–1570]*. Madrid, Monografías Quinto Centenario.

NACLA (1991). *Report on the Americas Bolivia: The Poverty of Progress*. New York, North American Congress on Latin America: 36.

Narotzky, S. (1997). *New Directions in Economic Anthropology*. London, Pluto Press.

Nash, J. (ed.) (1993). *Crafts in the World Market: The Impact of Global Exchange on Middle American Artisans*. Albany, State University of New York Press.

National Research Council (1989). *Lost Crops of the Incas: Little Known Plants of the Andes with Promise for World Wide Cultivation*. Washington, D.C., National Academy Press.

Netting, R. M. (1976). "What Alpine Peasants Have in Common: Observations on Communal Tenure in a Swiss Village." *Human Ecology* 4(2).

_____ (1981). *Balancing on an Alp: Ecological Change and Continuity in a Swiss Mountain Community*. Cambridge, Cambridge University Press.

_____ (1993). *Smallholders, Householders: Farm Families and the Ecology of Intensive, Sustainable Agriculture*. Palo Alto, Stanford University Press.

Netting, R. M., R. R. Wilk, and E. J. Arnould, (eds.) (1984). *Households: Comparative and Historical Studies of the Domestic Group*. Berkeley, University of California Press.

Núñez del Prado Béjar, D. (1975). "El poder de decisión de la mujer quechua andina." *América Indígena* 35: 609–622.

Núñez del Prado, O. (1965). Aspects of Andean Life. *Contemporary Cultures and Societies of Latin America*. D. B. Heath and R. N. Adams (eds.). New York, Random House: 102–123.

Ochoa, C. (1975). "Las papas cultivadas triploides de *Solanum x chaucha* y su distribución geográfica en el Perú." *Anales Científicos de la Universidad Agraria* 13: 31–44.

Odum, E. (1971). *Fundamentals of Ecology*. Philadelphia, W. B. Saunders Co.

ONERN (Ofinina Nacional de Evaluacion de Recursas Naturales) (1970). *Inventario, evaluación y uso racional de los recursos naturales de la costa: La cuenca del Río Cañete*. Lima, Oficina Nacional de Evaluación de Recursos Naturales.

———— (1978). *Mapa ecológico del Perú Lima*, Oficina Nacional de Evaluación de Recursos Naturales.

Orlove, B. S. (1977a). *Alpacas, Sheep and Men: The Wool Export Economy and Regional Society in Southern Peru*. New York, Academic Press.

———— (1977b). Inequalities Among Peasants: The Forms and Uses of Reciprocal Exchange in Andean Peru. *Peasant Livelihood: Studies in Economic and Cultural Ecology*. R. Halperin (ed.). New York, St. Martins Press: 201–214.

———— (1986). "Barter and Cash Sale on Lake Titicaca: A Test of Competing Approaches." *Current Anthropology* 27(2): 85–106.

———— (1987). Stability and Change in Highland Andean Dietary Patterns. *Food and Evolution*. M. Harris and E. Ross (eds.). Philadelphia, Temple University Press: 481–515.

———— (1991). "Mapping Reeds and Reading Maps: The Politics of Representation in Lake Titicaca." *American Ethnologist* 18(1): 3–38.

Orlove, B. S., and R. Godoy (1986). "Sectorial Fallow System in the Central Andes." *Journal of Ethnobiology* 6(1): 169–204.

Orlove, B. S., and D. Guillet (1982). "Theoretical and Methodological Considerations of the Study of Mountain Peoples: Reflections on the Idea of Subsistence Type and the Role of History in Human Ecology." *Mountain Research and Development* 5(1): 3–18.

Ortega, E. (1982). "La agricultura campesina en América Latina: Situaciones y tendencias." *Revista de la CEPAL* 16: 77–114.

Ortiz de Zevallos, P., and L. del Río de Calmell (1978). Las lagunas como fuentes de recursos naturales en el siglo XVI. *Etnohistoria y Antropología andina*. M. Koth de Paredes and A. Castelli (eds.). Lima, Museo Nacional De Historia: 57–62.

Ortiz, S. (1973). *Uncertainties in Peasant Farming: A Colombian Case*. London, Althone Press.

———— (1979). "Expectations and Forecasts in the Face of Uncertainty." *Man* 14(1): 64–80.

Ossio, J. (1984). Cultural Continuity, Structure, and Context: Some Peculiarities of Andean Compadrazgo. *Kinship Ideology and Practice in Latin America*. R. T. Smith (ed.). Chapel Hill, University of North Carolina Press: 118–146.

———— (1988). Obligaciones rituales prescritas en el parentesco andino por afinidad. Parentesco y género en los Andes. *Gentes de carne y hueso: Las tramas de parentesco en los andes*, Vol. 2. D. Arnold Y. La Paz, Biblioteca de Estudios Andinos: 265–290.

_____ (1992). *Parentesco, reciprocidad y jerarquía en los Andes*. Lima, Pontificia Universidad Católica del Perú.

Ostrom, E. (1990). *Governing the Commons: The Evolution of Institutions for Collective Action*. Cambridge, Cambridge University Press.

Pacini, D., and C. Franquemont (1986). *Coca and Cocaine: Effects of People and Policy in Latin America*. Cambridge, Cultural Survival.

Paerregaard, K. (1997). *Linking Separate Worlds: Urban Migrants and Rural Lives in Peru*. Oxford, Berg.

Painter, M. (1986). "The Value of Peasant Labor Power in a Prolonged Transition to Capitalism." *Journal of Peasant Studies* 13(4): 221–239.

_____ (1987). "Spatial Analysis and Regional Inequality: Some Suggestions for Development Planning." *Human Organization* 46: 318–329.

Palacios Ríos, F. (1977). Pastizales de regadío para alpacas. *Pastores de puna*. J. Flores Ochoa (ed.). Lima, Instituto de Estudios Peruanos: 155–170.

Palmer, D. S. (n.d.). "FONCODES y su impacto en la pacificación en el Perú: Observaciones generales y el caso de Ayacucho." Unpublished manuscript.

Palomino, S. (1971). "Duality in the Sociocultural Organization of Several Andean Populations." *Folk* 13: 65–68.

Parkerson, P. T. (1989). Neither "Green Gold" nor "The Devil's Leaf": Coca Farming in Bolivia. *State, Capital and Rural Society: Anthropological Perspectives on Political Economy in Mexico and the Andes*. B. S. Orlove, M. W. Foley, and T. F. Love (eds.). Boulder, Colo., Westview Press: 267–297.

Paz Flores, P. (1989). Cosmovisión andina y uso de la coca. *La Coca: tradición, rito, identidad*. Mexico, Instituto Indigenista Interamericano: 232–381.

Pease, F. (1978). Las Visitas como testimonio andino. *Historia, problema y promesa: Homenaje a Jorge Basadre*. F. Pease and D. Sobrevilla (eds.). Lima, Pontificia Universidad Católica del Perú: 437–453.

Picón Reátegui, E. (1976). Nutrition. *Man in the Andes: A Multidisciplinary Study of High-Altitude Quechua*. P. T. Baker and M. Little (eds.). Stroudsburg, Pa., Dowden, Hutchinson & Ross: 208–236.

Pike, F. (1967). *The Modern History of Peru*. New York, Frederick Praeger.

Pimentel, D., and M. Pimentel (1987). *Food, Energy and Society*. London, Edward Arnold.

Pinedo, D. (2000). Manejo comunal de pastos: equidad y sostenibilidad en una comunidad de la Cordillera de Huayhuash. *Peru: El problema agrario en debate SEPIA VIII*. I. Hurtado, C. Trivelli, and A. Brack (eds.). Lima, Seminario Permanente de Investigacion Agraria: 277–326.

Platt, T. (1982). *El estado Boliviano y el ayllu andino*. Lima, Instituto de Estudios Peruanos.

_____ (1986). Mirrors and Maize: The Concept of Yanantin Among the Macha of Bolivia. *Anthropological History of Andean Polities*. J. V. Murra, N. Wachtel, and J. Revel (eds.). Cambridge, Cambridge University Press: 228–259.

Plattner, S. (ed.) (1998). *Economic Anthropology*. Stanford, Stanford University Press.

Plowman, T. (1984). "The Ethnobotany of Coca (*Erythroxylum SPP., Erythroxylacae*)." *Advances in Economic Botany* 1: 62–111.

_____ (1986). Coca Chewing and the Botanical Origins of Coca (*Erythroxylum SPP.*) in South America. Coca and Cocaine: Effects on People and Policy in Latin

America. D. Pacini and Christine Franquemont (eds.). Cambridge, Cultural Survival.

Polanyi, K. (1997). *The Livelihood of Man*. New York, Academic Press.

Polanyi, K., K. M. Arensberg, et al. (eds.) (1957). *Trade and Market in the Early Empires*. New York, Free Press.

Polo de Ondegardo, J. (1916). Relación de los fundamentos acerca del notable daño que resulta de guardar a los indios sus fueros. *Colección de libros y documentos referentes a la historia del Perú*, Vol. 3. Lima: 45–188.

Polo de Ondegardo, J. (1940). "Informe al Licenciado Briviesca de Muñatones." *Revista Historica* 13: 125–196.

Poole, D. A. (1997). *Vision, Race and Modernity: A Visual Economy of the Andean Image World*. Princeton, N.J., Princeton University Press.

_____ (1982). Ritual and Economic Calendars in Paruro. Ph.D. thesis, University of Illinois at Urbana-Champaign, Department of Anthropology.

Popkin, S. (1979). *The Rational Peasant: The Political Economy of Rural Society in Vietnam*. Berkeley, University of California Press.

Portocarrero M., F. (1999). *Microfinanzas en el Perú: experiencias y perspectivas*. Lima, Universidad del Pacifico.

PRODERM-MAG (Projeto de Desarrollo Rural en Micro-regiones—Ministerio de Agricultura) (1985). *Flujo de productos agrícolas, Boletín Anual*. Lima, Ministry of Agriculture Annual Publications.

Pulgar Vidal, J. (n.d.). *Las ocho regiones naturales del Perú*. Lima, Editorial Universo.

Quijada Jara, S. (1957). *Canciones del ganado y pastores*. Huancayo, La Muestra del Libro Selecto Huancayo.

_____ (1977). "Cantos a la coca." *Runa* 4: 7.

Quijano, A. (1967). Contemporary Peasant Movements. *Elites in Latin America*. S. M. Lipsett (ed.). Oxford, Oxford University Press: 301–343.

Ramirez, S. E. (1982). "Retainers of the Lords or Merchants: A Case of Mistaken Identity?" *Senri Ethnological Studies* 10: 123–136.

_____ (1985). Social Frontiers and the Territorial Base of Curacazgos. *Andean Ecology and Civilization: An Interdisciplinary Perspective on Andean Ecological Complementarity*. S. Masuda, I. Shimada, and C. Morris (eds.). Tokyo, University of Tokyo Press: 423–442.

_____ (1995a). "An Oral History of the Valley of Chicama circa 1524–1565." *Journal of the Steward Anthropological Society* 23(1 & 2): 299–342.

(1995b). Exchange and Markets in the Sixteenth Century: A View from the North. *Ethnicity, Markets, and Migration in the Andes: At the Crossroads of History and Anthropology*. B. Larson and O. Harris (eds.). Durham, Duke University Press: 135–164.

_____ (1996). *The World Upside Down: Cross-Cultural Contact and Conflict in Sixteenth-Century Peru*. Stanford, Stanford University Press.

Rasnake, R. N. (1988). *Domination and Cultural Resistance: Authority and Power Among an Andean People*. Durham, Duke University Press.

Reinhardt, N. (1988). *Our Daily Bread: The Peasant Question and Family Farming in the Columbian Andes*. Berkeley, University of California Press.

Rengifo, G. (1991). La chacra en la cultura andina. *Vigorización de la chacra*. PRATEC. Lima.

Rénique, G. (n.d.). *Comunidades campesinas y 'recuperaciones' de tierras en el Valle del Mantaro.* Lima, Taller de Estudios Andinos, Universidad Nacional Agraria, La Molina, Lima.

Rhoades, R., and S. I. Thompson (1975). "Adaptive Strategies in Alpine Environments: Beyond Ecological Particularism." *American Ethnologist* 2(3): 535–51.

Ricketts, C. (1952). "El cocaísmo en el Perú." *América Indígena* 12(4): 310–322.

_____ (1954). "La masticación de las hojas de coca en el Perú." *América Indígena* 16(2): 113–126.

Romano, R. (1986). ¿Coca buena, coca mala? *La coca andina: Visión de una planta satanizada.* Mexico, Boldó y Clement, Juan (editore) & Instituto Indigenista Interamericano.

Roseberry, W. (1994). *Anthropologies and Histories: Essays in Culture, History and Political Economy.* New Brunswick, Rutgers University Press.

_____ (1995). "Latin American Studies in a 'Post-Colonial' Era." *Journal of Latin American Anthropology* 1(1): 150–177.

Rostworowski de Diez Canseco, M. (1977). *Etnía y Sociedad: Costa peruana prehispánica.* Lima, Instituto de Estudios Peruanos.

_____ (1985). Patronyms with the consonant F in the Guarangas of Cajamarca. *Andean Ecology and Civilization: An Interdisciplinary Perspective on Ecological Complementarity.* S. Masuda, I. Shimada, and C. Morris (eds.). Tokyo, Tokyo University Press.

_____ (1988). *Conflicts over Coca Fields in XVIth Century Peru.* Ann Arbor, University of Michigan Press.

Roth, E., and R. Bohrt P. (1989). Actitudes de la población de La Paz ante la hoja de coca. *La coca: tradición, rito, identidad.* Mexico, Insituto Indigenista Interamericano: 171–230.

Rowe, J. H. (1946). Inca Culture at the Time of the Spanish Conquest. *Handbook of South American Indians.* Washington, D.C., Bureau of American Ethnology. Bulletin 143, No 2: 183–330.

_____ (1958). *The Age Grades of the Inca Census.* 31 Congreso Internacional de Americanistas, Mexico City, Universidad Nacional Autónoma de México.

_____ (1984). "An Interview with John V. Murra." *Hispanic American Historical Review* 64(4): 633–653.

Royal Anthropological Institute (1954). *Notes and Queries in Anthropology.* London, Routledge, Kegan Paul.

Saavedra Chanduví, J., and J. J. Díaz (1999). Desigualdad del ingreso y del gasto en el Perú antes y después de las reformas estructurales Santiago, Serie Reformas Económicas 34 Comisión Económica para América Latina (CEPAL).

Sahlins, M. D. (1958). *Social Stratification in Polynesia.* Seattle, University of Washington Press.

_____ (1972). *Stone-Age Economics.* New York, Aldine Publishing Company.

Saignes, T. (1978). "De La filiation a la residénce: les ethnies dans les vallées de Larecaja." *Annales: Economies, Sociétés, Civilizations* 33e Année (5–6): 1160–1181.

Salisbury, R. F. (1962). *From Stone to Steel: Economic Eonsequences of Technological Change in New Guinea.* Melbourne, Melbourne University Press.

Salomon, F. (1985). The Dynamic Potential of the Complementarity Concept. *Andean Ecology and Civilization: An Interdisciplinary Perspective on Andean Ecological Complementarity*. S. Masuda, I. Shimada, and C. Morris (eds.). Tokyo, University of Tokyo Press: 511–533.

———— (1986). *Native Lords of Quito in the Age of the Incas*. Cambridge, Cambridge University Press.

———— (1992). Image and Legend in the Croquises of Tupicocha, Peru. Paper presented at a Symposium on "Visual and Verbal Literacy," American Anthropological Association, Annual Meeting.

Salomon, F., and G. L. Urioste (1991). *The Huarochirí Manuscript: A Testament of Ancient and Colonial Andean Religion*. Austin, University of Texas Press.

Samaniego, C. (1978). Peasant Movements at the Turn of the Century and the Rise of the Independent Farmer. *Peasant Cooperation and Capitalist Expansion in Central Peru*. N. Long and B. Roberts (eds.). Austin, University of Texas Press.

Sánchez, R. (1982). "La teoría de 'lo andino' y el campesinado de hoy." *Alpanchis* 17(20): 255–284.

Santillán, F. d. (ed.). (1927). Historia de los Incas y relación de su gobierno. *(Crónicas del siglo XVI)*. Lima, San Martí.

Schejtman, A. (1988). The Peasant Economy: Internal Logic. Articulation, and Persistence. *The Political Economy of Development and Underdevelopment*. C. K. Wilbur (ed.). New York, Random House: 364–392.

Schultz, T. W. (1964). *Transforming Traditional Agriculture*. New Haven, Yale University Press.

Schwartz, B. (1967). "The Social Psychology of the Gift." *American Journal of Sociology* 73(1).

Scott, C. D. (1974). Asignacion de recursos y formas de intercambio. *Reciprocidad e Intercambio en los Andes peruanos*. G. Alberti and E. Mayer (eds.). Lima, Instituto de Estudios Peruanos.

Scott, G. J. (1985). *Markets, Myths and Middlemen: A Study of Potato Marketing in Central Peru*. Lima, Centro Internacional de la Papa.

Scott, J. C. (1976). *The Moral Economy of the Peasant: Rebellion and Subsistence in Southeast Asia*. New Haven, Yale University Press.

———— (1985). *Weapons of the Weak: Everyday Forms of Peasant Resistance*. New Haven, Yale University Press.

Seligmann, L. (1989). "To Be in Between: The Cholas as Market Women." *Comparative Studies in Society and History* 31(4): 694–721.

Seligmann, L. J., and S. G. Bunker (1993). An Andean Irrigation System: Ecological Visions and Social Organization. *Irrigation at High Altitudes: The Social Organization of Water Control Systems in the Andes*. W. P. Mitchell and D. W. Guillet (eds.). Washington, D.C., Society for Latin American Anthropology and the American Anthropological Association: 203–232.

Sen, A. K. (1966). "Peasants and Dualism With and Without Surplus Labor." *Journal of Political Economy* 74: 425–450.

———— (1981). *Poverty and Famines: An Essay on Entitlement and Deprivation*. Oxford, Oxford University Press.

SEPAR Servicios Educativos Promoción y Apoyo Rural (1992). *Cifras y cronología de la violencia política en la región central del Perú (1980–1991)*. Huancayo, Servicios Educativos Promoción y Apoyo Rural.

Shaner, W. W., P. F. Philipp, et al. (1981). *Farming Systems Research and Development: Guidelines for Developing Countries*. Boulder, Colo., Westview Press.

Sharon, D. (1978). *Wizard of the Four Winds: A Shaman's Story*. New York, Free Press.

Sheahan, J. (1999). *Searching for a Better Society: The Peruvian Economy from 1950*. University Park, Pennsylvania State University Press.

Shimada, I. (1985). Perception, Procurement, and Management of Resources: Archeological Perspective. *Andean Ecology and Civilization: An Interdisciplinary Perspective on Andean Ecological Complementarity*. S. Masuda, I. Shimada, and C. Morris (eds.). Tokyo, University of Tokyo Press: 357–399.

Shoemaker, R. (1981). *The Peasants of El Dorado: Conflict and Contradiction in a Peruvian Frontier Settlement*. Ithaca, Cornell University Press.

Skinner, W. G. (1964). "Marketing and Social Structure in Rural China Part I." *Journal of Asian Studies* 34(1).

_____ (1968). Chinese Peasants and the Closed Corporate Community: An Open and Shut Case. *Peasants in a Changing World*. Berkeley, University of California Press.

Smith, C., W. M. Denevan, and P. Hamilton (1981). Antiguos campos de camellones en la región del Lago Titicaca. *La tecnología del mundo andino: Runakunap Kawsaninkupaq Rurasqankunaqa*. H. Lechtman and A. M. Soldi (eds.). México, Universidad Nacional Autónoma de México: 25–50.

Smith, C. A. (1976). Regional economic systems: Linking geographical models and socioeconomic problems. *Regional Analysis: Economic Systems*, Vol. 1. C. A. Smith (ed.). New York, Academic Press: 3–63.

Smith, G. (1985). "Reflections on the Social Relations of Simple Commodity Production." *Journal of Peasant Studies* 13(1): 99–108.

_____ (1989). *Livelihood and Resistance: Peasants and the Politics of Land in Peru*. Berkeley, University of California Press.

Smith, G. A., and P. Cano (1978). Some Factors Contributing to Peasant Land Occupations in Peru: The Example of Huasicancha. *Peasant Cooperation and Capitalist Expansion in Central Peru*. N. Long and B. Roberts (eds.). Austin, University of Texas Press.

Soldi, A. M. (1982). *La agricultura tradicional en hoyas*. Lima, Pontificia Universidad Católica.

Soto de, H. (1989). *The Other Path: The Invisible Revolution in the Third World*. New York, Harper & Row.

Spalding, K. (1970). "Social Climbers: Changing Patterns of Mobility among the Indians in Peru." *Hispanic American Historical Review* 50: 645–664.

_____ (1973). "Kurakas and Commerce: A Chapter in the Evolution of Andean Society." *Hispanic American Historical Review* 53: 581–599.

_____ (1974). *De indio a campesino: Cambios en la estructura social del Perú colonial*. Lima, Instituto de Estudios Peruanos.

_____ (1984). *Huarochorí: An Andean Society Under Inca and Spanish Rule*. Stanford, Stanford University Press.

Spedding, A. P. (1997a). Investigaciones sobre género en Bolivia: Un comentario crítico. *Parentesco y género en los Andes: Mas allá del silencio: Las fronteras del género en los Andes*. D. Arnold Y. La Paz, Biblioteca de Estudios Andinos. I: 53–74.

_____ (1997b). Esa mujer no necesita hombre: en contra de la dualidad andina—
imágenes de género en los yungas de La Paz. *Parentesco y género en los Andes:
Mas allá del silencio: Las fronteras del género en los Andes*, Vol. 1. D. Arnold Y
(ed.). La Paz, Biblioteca de Estudios Andinos: 325–343.

Starn, O. (1991). "Sendero, soldados y ronderos en el Mantaro." *Quehacer* 74:
60–68.

_____ (1992a). Missing the Revolution: Anthropologists and the War in Peru.
Rereading Cultural Anthropology. G. E. Marcus (ed.). Durham, Duke University
Press: 152–180.

_____ (1992b). "Antropología andina, 'Andinismo' y Sendero Luminoso." *Allpanchis* 39: 15–129.

_____ (1994). "Rethinking the Politics of Anthropology: The Case of the Andes."
Current Anthropology 35(1): 13–28.

_____ (1999). *Nightwatch: The Politics of Protest in the Andes.* Durham, Duke
University Press.

Stedile, J. P. (1999). *Brava gente: a trajetória do MST e a luta pela terra no Brasil.*
São Paulo, Fundaçao Perseu Abramo.

Stein, W. (1961). *Hualcan: Life in the Highlands of Peru.* Ithaca, Cornell University Press.

Stern, S. J. (ed.) (1987). *Resistance, Rebellion and Consciousness in the Andean
Peasant World: 18th to 20th Centuries.* Madison, University of Wisconsin Press.

Strug, D. L. (1986). The Foreign Politics of Cocaine: Comments on a Plan to Eradicate the Coca Leaf in Peru. *Coca and Cocaine: Effects of People and Policy in
Latin America.* D. Pacini and C. Franquemont (eds.). Cambridge, Cultural Survival.

Super, J. C. (1988). *Food, Conquest, and Colonization in Sixteenth-Century Spanish America.* Lincoln, University of Nebraska Press.

Tamayo Herrera, J. (1980). *Historia del indigenismo cuzqueño siglos XVI-XX.*
Lima, Instituto Nacional de Cultura.

Tantahuilca, C. (1990). *Economía cocalera y violencia social. Perú: El Problema
Agrario en Debate: SEPIA III.* A. Chirif, N. Manrique, and B. Quijandría (eds.).
Lima, Seminario Permanente de Investigación Agraria: 435–450.

Tapia, M. E. (1996). *Ecodesarrollo en los Andes altos.* Lima, Fundación Friederich
Ebert.

Tarazona-Sevillano, G. (1990). *Sendero Luminoso and the Threat of Narcoterror-
ism.* New York, Praeger.

Tax, S. (1963). *Penny Capitalism: A Guatemalan Indian Economy.* Chicago, University of Chicago Press.

Theidon, K. (2000). "How We Learned to Kill Our Brother: Memory, Morality,
and Reconciliation in Peru." Paper presented at the 99th Annual Meeting of the
American Anthropological Association, San Francisco, November 15–19, 2000.

Thomas, R. B. (1976). Energy Flow in High Altitude. *Man in the Andes.* P. T. Baker
and M. Little (eds.). Stroudsburg, Pa., Dowden, Hutchinson & Ross: 379–404.

Thünen, J. H. von. (1826). *Der Isolierte Staat.* C. M. Wartenberg (ed.). Hamburg,
Friederich Perthes.

Tomoeda, H. (1985). The Llama Is My Chacra: Metaphor of Andean Pastoralists.
Andean Ecology and Civilization: An Interdisciplinary Perspective on Andean

Ecological Complementarity. S. Masuda, I. Shimada, and C. Morris (eds.). Tokyo, University of Tokyo Press: 277–299.

Tord, L. E. (1978). *El indio en los ensayistas peruanos: 1848–1948*. Lima, Editoriales Unidas.

Tosi, J. J. (1960). *Zonas de vida natural en el Perú Lima*. Instituto Inter-Americano de Ciencias Agrícolas de la OEA, Zona Andina. (Reprinted in ONERN in 1978.)

Trawick, P. B. (1994). The Struggle for Water in the Andes: A Study of Technological Change and Social Decline in the Cotahuasi Valley of Peru. Ph.D. thesis, New Haven, Yale University.

Treacy, J. M. (1994). *Las chacras de Coporaque: Andenería y riego en el valle del Colca*. Lima, Instituto de Estudios Peruanos.

Trivelli, C. (1992). "Reconocimiento legal de comunidades campesinas: Una revisión estadística." *Debate Agrario* 14: 23–39.

_____ (2000). Pobreza rural: Investigaciones, mediciones y políticas públicas. *Peru: El problema agrario en debate SEPIA VIII*. I. Hurtado, C. Trivelli and A. Brack (eds.). Lima, Seminario Permanente de Investigacion Agraria: 200–255.

Troll, C. (1968). "Geo-Ecology of the Mountainous Regions of the Tropical Americas." *Colloquium Geographicum 9*.

Turino, T. (1993). *Moving Away from Silence: Music of the Peruvian Altiplano and the Experience of Urban Migration*. Chicago, University of Chicago Press.

Urton, G. (1981). *At the Crossroads of the Earth and the Sky: An Andean Cosmology*. Austin, University of Texas Press.

_____ (1997). *The Social Life of Numbers: A Quechua Ontology of Numbers and Philosophy of Arithmetic*. Austin, University of Texas Press.

Valderrama Fernandez, R., C. Escalante Gutierrez, et al. (1996). *Gregorio Condori Mamani and Asunta Quispe Huamán*. Austin, University of Texas Press.

Valée, L. (1971). "La ecología subjectiva como elemento esencial de la verticalidad." *Revista del Museo Nacional* 37: 167–175.

Valencia, A. (1982). *Pesas y medidas Inkas: continuidad en los mercados de Canas*. Cusco, Centro de Estudios Andinos.

Valera Moreno, G. (1998). *Las comunidades en el Peru: Una visión nacional desde las series departamentales*. Lima, Instituto Rural del Perú.

Valladolid Rivera, J. (1998). Andean Peasant Agriculture: Nurturing a Diversity of Life in the Chacra. *The Spirit of Regeneration: Andean Culture Confronting Western Notions of Development*. F. Apffel-Marglin and PRATEC (eds.). London, Zed Books: 51–88.

Van Buren, M. (1996). "Rethinking the Vertical Archipelago: Ethnicity, Exchange, and History in the South Central Andes." *American Anthropologist* 98(2): 338–351.

Varallanos, J. (1959). *Historia de Huánuco*. Buenos Aires, Imprenta López.

Vargas Llosa, M., A. Guzman Figueroa, et al. (1983). *Informe de la Comisión Investigadora de los Sucesos de Uchuraccay*. Lima, Editora Peru.

Varillas Gallardo, B. (1965). *Apuntes para el folklore de Yauyos*. Lima, Litografía Huascarán.

Vásquez, M. (1961). *Hacienda, peonaje y servidumbre en los Andes*. Lima, Editorial Estudios Andinos.

Viola Recasens, A. (1995). "'La coca es oro verde' el fracaso del desarrollo alternativo en Bolivia." *Ecología Política* 40: 73–84.

_____ (1996). *Causachun Coca: Wañuchun Gringos*. Etnicidad e invención de tradiciones en el Chapare (Bolivia) VII Congreso de antropología social, Zaragosa, Spain.

Wagner, C. J. (C. J. Allen) (1978). "Coca y estructura social en los Andes." *América Indígena* 38(4): 877–902.

Wallerstein, I. (1974). *The Modern World System: Capitalist Agriculture and the Origins of the European World-Economy in the Sixteenth Century*. New York, Academic Press.

Webster, S. (1980). Parentesco y afinidad en una comunidad indígena quechua. *Parentesco y matrimonio en los Andes*. E. Mayer and R. Bolton (eds.). Lima, Pontificia Universidad Católica.

Weil, A. (1995). The New Politics of Coca. *New Yorker* 71: 70–80.

Weismantel, M. J. (1988). *Food, Gender and Poverty in the Ecuadorian Andes*. Philadelphia, University of Pennsylvania Press.

_____ (1989). Making Breakfast and Raising Babies: The Zumbagua Household as a Constituted Process. *The Household Economy: Reconsidering the Domestic Mode of Production*. R. R. Wilk (ed.). Boulder, Colo., Westview Press: 55–72.

West, T. L. (1981). "Llama Caravans in the Andes." *Natural History* 90(12): 62–73.

Wiegers Esther, S., R. H. Dominique Hervé, and L. O. Fresco (1999). "Land Use Intensification and Disintensification in the Upper Cañete Valley, Peru." *Human Ecology* 27(2): 319–339.

Wightman, A. M. (1990). *Indigenous Migration and Social Change: The Forasteros of Cuzco, 152–1720*. Durham, Duke University Press.

Wilk, R. R. (1989a). Decision Making and Resource Flows within the Household: Beyond the Black Box. *The Household Economy: Reconsidering the Domestic Mode of Production*. R. R. Wilk (ed.). Boulder, Colo., Westview Press: 23–52.

_____ (ed.). (1989b). *The Household Economy: Reconsidering the Domestic Mode of Production*. Boulder, Colo., Westview Press.

Winterhalder, B., R. Larsen, et al. (1974). "Dung as an Essential Resource in a Highland Peruvian Community." *Human Ecology* 2(2): 89–104.

Winterhalder, B. R., and R. B. Thomas (1978). *Geoecology in the Southern Highlands of Peru: A Human Adaptation Perspective*. Boulder, Institute of Arctic and Alpine Research, University of Colorado: 27.

Wolf, E. R. (1955). "Types of Latin American Peasantry: A Preliminary Discussion." *American Anthropologist* 57: 452–471.

_____ (1966). *Peasants*. Englewood Cliffs, N.J., Prentice-Hall.

Wolf, M. (1968). *The House of Lim: A Study of a Chinese Farm Family*. Englewood Cliffs, Prentice-Hall.

Wright-St. Clair, R. E. (1970). "Poison or Medicine?" *New Zealand Medical Journal* 71: 224.

Yamamoto, N. (1981). Investigación preliminar sobre las actividades agro-pastoriles en el distrito de Marcapata, Departamento de Cuzco. *Estudios etnográficos del Perú meridional*. S. Masuda (ed.). Tokyo, University of Tokyo: 85–137.

Yambert, K. (1989). The Peasant Community of Catacaos and the Peruvian Agrarian Reform. *State, Capital and Rural Society: Anthropological Perspectives on*

Political Economy in Mexico and the Andes. B. S. Orlove, M. W. Foley, and T. F. Love (eds.). Boulder, Colo., Westview Press: 181–209.

Yanagisako, S. J. (1979). "Family and Household: The Analysis of Domestic Groups." *Annual Review of Anthropology* 8: 161–205.

Zavala, S. (1978). *El servicio personal de los indios en el Perú.* Mexico, El Colegio de Mexico.

Zimmerer, K. S. (1988a). "The Ecogeography of Andean Potatoes." *BioScience* 84(6): 445–454.

_____ (1988b). Seeds of Peasant Subsistence: Agrarian Structure, Crop Ecology and Quechua Agriculture in Reference to Loss of Biological Diversity in the Southern Peruvian Andes. Ph.D. thesis, University of California at Berkeley.

_____ (1991). "Managing Diversity in Potato and Maize Fields of the Peruvian Andes." *Journal of Ethnobiology* 11: 33–49.

_____ (1996). *Changing Fortunes: Biodiversity and Peasant Livelihood in the Peruvian Andes.* Berkeley, University of California Press.

_____ (1999). "Overlapping Patchworks of Mountain Agriculture in Peru and Bolivia: Toward a Regional-Global Landscape Model." *Human Ecology* 27(1): 135–165.

Zimmerer, K. S., and D. S. Douches (1990). "Geographical Approaches to Native Crop Research and Conservation: The Partitioning of Allelic Diversity in Andean Potatoes." *Economic Botany* 45: 176–189.

Zorilla Eguren, J. (1978). "El hombre Andino y su relación mágico-religiosa con la coca." *América Indígena* 37(4): 867–874.

Zuidema, R. T. (1977). The Inca Kinship System: A New Theoretical View. *Andean Kinship and Marriage.* R. Bolton and E. Mayer (eds.). Washington, D.C., American Anthropological Association: 240–281.

Zuidema, R. T. (1990). *Inca Civilization in Cuzco.* Austin, University of Texas Press.

Credits and Acknowledgments

Several chapters in this book are revised versions of articles previously published in the following sources, to whom grateful acknowledgment is made:

Chapter 3:

"A Tribute to the Household: Domestic Economy and the Encomienda in Colonial Peru," by Enrique Mayer. *From Kinship Ideology and Practice in Latin America* [pages 85-117] by Raymond T. Smith. Copyright © 1984 by the University of North Carolina Press. Used by permission of the publisher.

Chapter 4:

"Las reglas del juego en la reciprocidad Andina" [pages 37-65] by Giorgia Alberti and Enrique Mayer; "Reciprocidad Andina: ayer y hoy" [pages 13-36] by Enrique Mayer; and "Reciprocidad en las relaciones de producción [pages 77-85] by Enrique Mayer and César Zamalloa. From *Reciprocidad e intercambio en los Andes,* edited by Giorgio Alberti and Enrique Mayer. Copyright © 1974 by the Instituto de Estudios Peruanos, Lima.

Chapter 6:

"Factores sociales en la revaloración de la coca," by Enrique Mayer. *Debate Agrario* No. 17 (1993), pages 131-143, CEPES, Lima.
"Coca Use in the Andes," by Enrique Mayer. *Studies in Third World Societies, Publication Number 37, September 1986.*

Chapter 8:

"Production Zones" by Enrique Mayer. From *An Interdisciplinary Perspective on Andean Ecological Complementarity,* pages 45-84, edited by Craig Morris and Shozo Masuda. Copyright © 1984 by the University of Tokyo Press.

Index

systems, 9, 131
See also Negotiation

Labor
 and Chayanovís theory 25, 27–28,
  207–208
 as human capital, 316
 between households, 100, 131–32, 135,
  257, 285
 casual, 322
 community labor, 7, 40, 123–125, 128,
  251, 258, 260, 261, 282
 concentrated/dispersed, 17, 262
 division of labor within households, 9,
  11–14, 31, 131–2
 extra-household labor, 149
 household labor, 6, 14–15, 32, 114, 131,
  149, 245, 251, 257, 330
 in environmental improvement, 26, 260
 inputs in production 17, 206, 231
 intensive, 16, 25, 26, 100, 231, 262
 returns to labor, 25, 26, 149, 236n11
 sale of, 24, 26, 15, 161, 163, 262, 316
 seasonal 317,
 servile and slave, 69, 76, 116, 263
 tribute labor, 27, 36, 81–89, 265
 value of household labor, 25, 229,
  231–32, 235n7
 wage level, 210, 232, 315, 322
 wages 112, 114, 132, 162: in kind 149,
  177, 181
Land
 access to, 248
 allotment, 251, 256
 as marketable commodity, 290, 294,
  299, 316, 324, 325
 concentration of, 323
 expropriation of, 160, 174, 252, 300,
  301, 323
 for tribute, 53, 82
 fragile lands, 233, 304, 315, 324, 325,
  328–329
 in pre-Hispanic societies, 54
 insufficiency, 27–28, 88–89, 208, 303
 intensive use of, 41, 248, 257
 rent, 297–208, 290
 sustainable use, 324
 See also Land tenure; Property, property
  regime, titles
Land tenure, 32, 254–257, 279–311, 323,
  326
 collectively owned, 36, 248

defined, 279–280, 290
diachronic variation, 291–299
parallel land ownership, 254–257
privatization, 254, 265, 292, 324, 326,
 332n3
rights, 15, 100, 251. *See also*
 Community, membership
spatial variation, 282–291
See also Laraos; Production zone; Property,
 property regime, titles; Rights
Laraos, 250, 255, 256, 267, 281
 absentee members, 298–299
 aisha, 283–285, 294, 298. *See also*
  Sectorial fallow/rotation systems
 and agrarian reform, 298–299
 and *haciendas* 294, 297, 300
 aristocracy, 291, 293, 294, 296
 as *comunidad de indÍgenas*, 281, 297,
  298, 301
 church lands, 266
 disputes within, 282
 emigration, 290
 estancias, 282–283, 291, 293, 294, 297,
  298
 field work in, 305, 320
 fiesta, 298
 history, 281, 291–292, 297, 299–300,
  310n26
 huertas, 289–290, 297. *See also* Fruit
  production
 intellectuals in, 287, 293
 land litigation, 281, 297–298, 300
 Libre pensadores 255, 265, 266, 292,
  293, 294, 300
 mahuay, 285–286, 294–296. *See also*
  Alfalfa
 maizal, 286–289, 298. *See also* Maize
 miners, 297, 298, 299, 300
 municipality, 267, 281, 292, 294, 298
 Quinta internacional, 255, 297, 310n24
 school, 283, 292, 293, 299
 threat of expulsion from the community,
  299
Liberalism, 292–293
 and capitalism, 302
 and the expropriation of Indian lands,
  301, 302
 ideology, 300
See also Neo-liberalism
Life zones. *See* Ecotypes; Environment;
 Production zones
Livelihood, 21, 39, 168, 207, 327

Losses
  in small scale agriculture, 206, 208, 209,
    213–220, 233
  in developed countries, 209
See also Profits

Maize, 240, 250, 251, 256, 257, 258, 262,
    286
Mapa de la pobreza, 319, 320
Market
  as a form of exchange, 107, 169
  beyond the, 317, 327
  competition in the, 35, 232–233
  distortions, 224
  domination, 137, 158, 163, 208, 308,
    313, 314
  extractive, 24, 158, 165, 167
  free, 32, 158, 233, 234
  impersonal character of, 137, 162, 168
  integration, 165, 168, 22, 300
  monetary market, 136, 145, 158
  nexus, 161, 303
  participation, 206
  regulation, 314: self-regulating, 317
  retreat from, 217, 220, 234, 237, 327
  share, 35, 232
  subordinate to colonial economy, 69, 77
  unfavorable, 25, 155, 163–164, 167,
    167, 208, 210
Marketplaces
  abuses in, 163–164, 165, 185, 188
  and barter, 145, 151–153
  bulking and bulk breaking, 151–153,
    158, 167
  in colonial times, 59, 68–69
  in contemporary times, 3, 70, 151, 167
  in pre-Hispanic times, 55, 59, 62
  regional market expansion, 300
Marriage
  and transmission of resources, 290
  and tribute, 90–91
  conjugal relations, 10, 11–14, 131
  polygamy, 92–93
  process, 10, 91–93
Marxism, 137, 142n27, 168, 208, 280,
    310n27. *See also* Natural Economy;
    Petty commodity production
Material flows, 15, 16–18, 24, 131. *See also*
    Energy
Measurements
  budgets, 24
  in house economies, 206, 225, 230

inaccuracy of, 19, 85
incommensurable, 20
kinds of measures, 19–20, 140n11,
    153–157, 206
  of costs in production, 211–212. *See also*
    Accounting; Potato
  of equivalencies in barter, 129, 144, 149,
    153–157
  of labor inputs in environmental
    restoration, 27
  of non-market inputs (imputation), 213,
    235n11
  of poverty, 318, 319, 320–21
  of profits and losses, 213, 220, 230
  of value, 137, 143, 144, 149, 155, 168,
    176, 225, 226, 231
  of yields in agriculture, 19–20
  undervaluation, 24, 232, 233
See also Boundaries; Spheres
Men
  and the control of money, 12, 225, 226,
    227–228
  as heads of household, 11, 24, 90–91
  as producers, 11
  as semi-proletarians, 27
Mestizo
  and ethnic divisions in the market 69–70,
    171n12
  and market abuse, 163, 164
  and reciprocity, 117
  exploitation of Indians, 160
  indio/mestizo prestige scale, 13, 39, 110,
    133, 182, 183
  stereotypes held about *indios* 179, 183
See also Race
Micro-enterprises, *See* Firms; Informal
    Sector
Migration, 33, 36, 90
  emigration, 28, 209, 290
  for money, 4. *See also* Labor, sale of
    labor
  relationships among villagers and
    migrants, 133–135
Mines, 267. *See also* Laraos
Models
  as culture, 5
  black box model, 5–8, 16, 30, 42n1
  house model, 5, 14–23, 19–23, 31, 131,
    207
  kinship model, 5, 8–14
  of pre-Hispanic economies, 49–54, 257
  of the household as a unit, 4

LaVergne, TN USA
15 February 2010
173164LV00001B/97/A